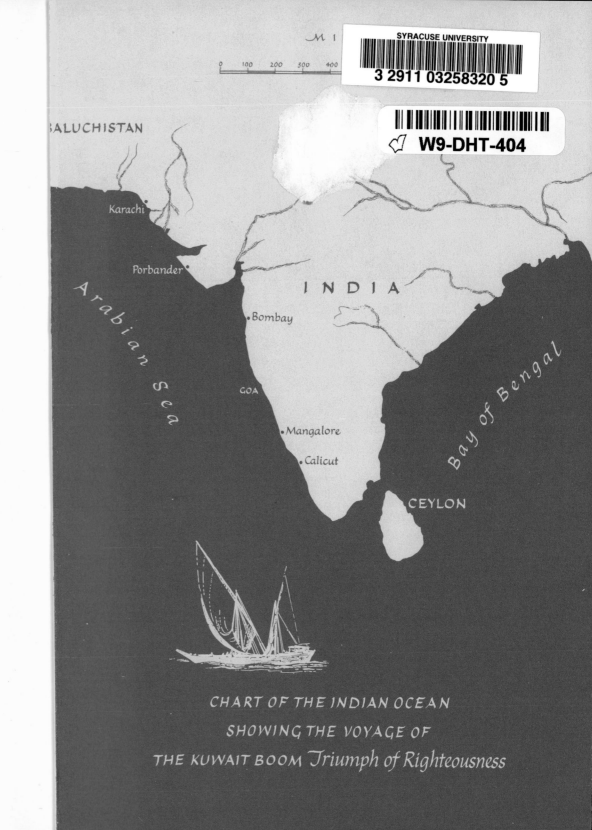

M I

0   100   200   300   400

BALUCHISTAN

Karachi

Porbander

I N D I A

Arabian Sea

Bombay

GOA

Mangalore

Calicut

CEYLON

Bay of Bengal

CHART OF THE INDIAN OCEAN
SHOWING THE VOYAGE OF
THE KUWAIT BOOM *Triumph of Righteousness*

Sons of Sinbad

ALAN VILLIERS

Sons of Sinbad

AN ACCOUNT OF SAILING WITH THE ARABS
IN THEIR DHOWS, IN THE RED SEA, AROUND
THE COASTS OF ARABIA, AND TO ZANZIBAR
AND TANGANYIKA: PEARLING IN THE PERSIAN
GULF: AND THE LIFE OF THE SHIPMASTERS,
THE MARINERS AND MERCHANTS OF KUWAIT

Illustrated with photographs by the author

CHARLES SCRIBNER'S SONS · NEW YORK

To my friends

the Al-Hamads of Kuwait

Preface

IN THE LATE 1930's, having been compelled to sell that perfect sailing school-ship, the full-rigged *Joseph Conrad,* because of the lack of national interest in her or any other such ship in Britain, U.S.A., and my own Australia, I decided to go to the Indian Ocean and sail with the Arabs in their dhows. It bothered me to give up my ship, for it seemed obvious that the need for such vessels was bound to increase. It did, indeed, but I was before my time; I had kept the ship as long as I could and sailed her a voyage round the world.

Well, there were still the Arabs, and some Indians, Malays, and Chinese sailing. I knew that the Arabs maintained some remnant of their former maritime supremacy in the tropics of the Indian Ocean, relatively unchanged probably for two thousand years, come down in straight line of descent from Phoenician days despite Vasco da Gama and the Suez Canal, and Iranian and Iraqi oil and all else. How fascinating to step back into this world! I knew that the Arabs' remarkable maritime enterprise touched the very dawn of our recorded history. Those able seamen had known at least two great periods, that of Arab astronomy and mathematics out of which the whole idea of celestial navigation grew; and that of their own dominance, before the Portuguese at last blazed the European way to Asian waters around the Cape they called Good Hope. The Arabs dominated at sea no longer, but they were still there.

Because these great Semitic seamen were still with us, nobody paid much attention to them. Well, now I had something of the background, the time, the inclination, just about all the experience that could then be gained of our European sailing ships; and the stamina too, I hoped. Not that I worried much about this, for I was rash enough to think that having survived—among other trials—a few Horn winter roundings and the pioneer whaling voyage into the Ross Sea in the Antarctic, I was fit for anything the sea had to offer. (This proved to be optimism, for with the Arabs I was badly lamed for about three months once and temporarily blind as well for one of those months.)

I planned a five-year program to be devoted to the sailing mariners of Eastern waters—first with the Arabs, then with the Indians, and the Pakistanis of Chittagong and the Brahmaputra River. After that, I would move on to Makassar in the Celebes, Singapore, and Indonesian waters generally: I would finish with the Chinese and the Japanese. All this was worth doing and, I thought, needed to be done, for no one else seemed to have any such plans. It was fashionable for European and American seamen and most maritime scholars almost totally to disregard the achievements and knowledge of all others.

A five-year plan, did I say? All this could well have taken ten. As things turned out, in 1938 there were about two fully productive years left in this general field, in which—except for another decade or so on the Brahmaputra and for a while in the Maldive Islands—such changes were imminent as to bring it to a rapid end.

My plan was to sail in all the seagoing Asian ship-types I could find, and not just for a dog-watch. I wanted to see how they were officered and manned, and navigated and handled, and how exactly they went about their ancient commerce and voyages—how they were maintained and financed, and managed to keep with them an adequate group of ancillary services essential to their seafaring, and a reserve of skilled and satisfied officers and mariners to man them. Unduly academic questions of evolution of ship-types, the painstaking taking off of lines and so forth were not for me and were mainly beyond me anyway. Lines can be taken off dead ships on beaches.

First, I tried to find out how much was known of Semitic seafaring, what records already existed. At the time there were almost none. I was informed that there was nothing in Arabic and nothing later than a few references in the Old Testament in Hebrew either. The Semitic mariners had been a close-lipped lot, for good reasons: they kept the trade secrets they had painfully learned to themselves, and not as much as an unquestioned representation of a Phoenician ship remained in existence. The Arab traveller Ibn Batuta (fourteenth century) was more interested in people and geography than in shipping, and did most of his travelling ashore. The same applied to the few other great Muslim travellers.

As far as I could discover, the most recent European chronicler of some shipping in Asian waters was Marco Polo, who took passage in several large ships there. Whatever else he may have been, Signor Polo was no sailor. The handful of great European travellers in Arabia—Doughty, Lawrence, Stark, Niebuhr, Bertram Thomas, Bell—kept inland, which was fascinating enough. Burton was a passenger at times in some sort of short-passage dhows, and so were Ingrams and a few others. But they were landsmen necessarily accommodated for brief periods in such vessels because this was the only way to reach someplace they wished to visit. They had little real opportunity for studying such seafaring even if they wished: as far as they were concerned, the life was temporarily altered for them, as Europeans. The good manners of the Arab made him do his best for them, and this meant upset to his ordinary routine.

Some dhows were captured when operating in the forbidden slave trade but, if the report left by Captain Colomb, R.N., of H.M.S. *Dryad* is any guide, little was learned of them except that they were fast.

"If a pear be sharpened at the thin end and then cut in halves longitudinally, two models will have been made resembling in all essential respects the ordinary slave dhow," the captain is quoted by Sir Arnold Wilson as reporting in 1873.[*]

"From their form," he continues, "it is evident the bow must sink deeply in the water whilst the stern floats lightly upon it. In this they differ from the universal practice of European shipbuilding. . . . These vessels are enormously swift: the most speedy man-of-war, under steam and sail, has her hands full when she gives chase to them in a breeze. . . . The dhow is generally leaky. . . . If a very large proportion do not sink, their general proximity to the shore and not the tightness of the hull must save them. To tow them at any speed would generally pull them to pieces. . . ."

Indeed! An execrable sketch of a "baghallah" in the Shatt-al-Arab accompanies this, showing a vessel with a hull like an outsize barrel and the grace of a fat elephant.

I had seen baggalas and sambuks in Djibouti and Aden, and knew better than this. Small or large, their lines were invariably excellent and their hull shapes beautiful. They had the grace almost of the natural thing, as

---

[*] *The Persian Gulf*, Sir Arnold T. Wilson, K.C.I.E., etc., Oxford University Press, 1928. The excellent "Arab Seafaring in the Indian Ocean," a study by George Fadlo Hourani (Princeton University Press) was not published until 1951.

if those who had built them had long ago learned to produce the perfect form of the sea-swift ship and, having learned, preserved the knowledge. These vessels "down by the head," with sterns like haystacks?
Such reports must be the result of poor observation, for the sweep of
their lovely sheer was towards the cutwater, and (in the baggala type)
there was a stern-castle built up ornately, copied from the galleons of
the Portuguese pioneers. The big Portuguese ships greatly impressed the
Arabs, for they made long and difficult voyages and were obviously more
stable gun-platforms than their own. The after-castle, too, was a good
fighting place.

The idea that the Arab ships were dependent on a handy beach to
land survivors when they sank was even odder. The shapely dhows I
saw had made long sea voyages, some in the East African trade, others to
the west coast of India. They had to go about their sea ways far from
convenient beaches.

Captain Colomb and his brother officers did a splendid job of driving
at least some of the slavers from the sea, but it seemed to me that they
had learned remarkably little about their ships. It struck me as odd, too,
that in all the writings about clipper-ships real and alleged, I found not the
slightest reference from any European or American "expert" to the fact
that the Semitic seamen had known how to build and sail fast ships for
centuries if not for thousands of years before the age of the "clipper."
Perhaps it was not appreciated that the so-called dhows *were* seagoing,
deep-draft ships: or possibly the fact that they were not in competition
with the later-day ships of the Western Hemisphere caused their study
to be neglected. At any rate, no one had bothered to learn much about
them.

The Arabs shouted of no "record" passages or fantastic day's runs
and so forth, and no one shouted for them. When all ships were swift, what
was there to shout about? The competitive packet and tea-clipper pub-
licity was for the furtherance of trade. There was more than a touch of
Madison Avenue-type promotion behind it. On the Arabian peninsula
there was no Madison Avenue.

The Arabs had gone quietly and effectively about their voyages. So
had the Indians, the Malays, the Chinese. When upset political conditions
and lack of commercial stability in further Asian waters made voyages to
China too difficult to be worth while, the Malay had his own archipelago
and the Arab (and Indian) their own coasts and the whole monsoonal
range of the Indian Ocean still left to them.

The coming of the Portuguese, their pioneering Vasco da Gama piloted to the rich ports of India by the veteran Arab navigator Ibn Majid—and after them the Dutch, the French, the British—affected European trade, particularly Mediterranean monopolies. But the Eastern fleets still flourished in their own well-established way, above all the Arab in the Western Indian Ocean, sailing down the east coast of Africa and to the great ports of India. The European, indeed, helped for he provided more ports and some increase of trade. He siphoned off his own trade, it is true, in spices and silks and the treasures of the East. Such things, though valuable, never had provided bulk cargoes. It was necessities which did that. They remained.

In time, he obligingly marked headlands and harbor entrances, and provided charts and services—political stability, too, now and again. This last was a blessing: but the Arab did not really need his aids to navigation. His own seafaring was based on personal knowledge handed on to him by practical experience when young and fostered for a lifetime. His sailing was seasonal, in the good monsoon not the bad.

These things I had to find out, of course, for there were no textbooks —not since *The Periplus of the Erythræan Sea*,* produced by the Greeks at the beginning of the Christian era, after an enterprising countryman of theirs named Hippalus had "discovered" what the Eastern mariners had known and used for untold years—the monsoonal system of the northern waters of the Indian Ocean. There the alternating northeast and southwest monsoons or seasons could be put to valuable use in the circulatory movements of able sailing-ships. Seasons, one says, and not winds. A monsoon is not a wind. It is a season, during which a considerable proportion of the oceanic winds may be expected to blow from a more or less constant direction. The ships of the tropic waters of the Indian Ocean, said the followers of Hippalus, sailed south with the NE monsoon and, when that blew out, back they came north again before the SW. The same thing applied to voyages across the Arabian Sea, between Arabia or East Africa and India.

Even the land-bound did not imagine, surely, that the Eastern ships required winds from *right* behind them to make their voyages. Indeed they did not, for they were most weatherly vessels, able to sail closer to the eye of the wind than Europeans. The lateen-rigged Arab, I thought, had no need of strictly favorable winds. It was the good-weather *season*

* *The Periplus of the Erythræan Sea, Travel and Trade in the Indian Ocean,* by a Merchant of the First Century. London, Longmans, Green & Co., 1912.

of the NE monsoon he did his sailing in, I was sure, and not the SW at all, if he could help it. The SW was a season of bad weather and worse visibility: the dhows I'd seen were not rigged or built to stand too many storms. Nor was there need, for they could do their year's trading *both* ways while the good weather lasted.

I studied that *Periplus,* of course. I knew the theory about monsoonal sailing. But to a sailing-ship seaman that statement was lubberly nonsense as a practical proposition, and in no sense a necessity for Arab dhows.

This was not just theory on my part. I had sailed a little in the Indian Ocean, and well-known sailors such as Joseph Conrad had sailed a great deal more. One of the routes for big square-riggers bound from South Australian wheat ports to Europe, in the summer months, was to round Cape Leeuwin at Western Australia's SW tip, then stand up into the tropic area of the Indian Ocean's SE Trades and make westing in good weather there. I'd gone that way in 1921 in the big English four-masted barque *Bellands,* and we'd taken an awful dusting from a hurricane somewhere near Mauritius. Conrad had the barque *Otago* in the Mauritius trade: once he'd sailed north-about around Australia, I knew, on a ballast passage from Sydney to the sugar island. He did not try it twice. In the pre-Suez Canal era, big European sailing-ships shifted much of the Indian jute and Burmese rice: they'd had a small share of both trades right up to 1914.

A copy of that sailing-ship man's sea-bible, Findlay's Indian Ocean Directory* was aboard the *Parma,* ex-*Arrow,* when we bought her in 1931, and this matter-of-fact tome was very much to the point on the subject of the SW monsoon.

"One of the most formidable manifestations of the power of the wind that can be adduced in any part of the globe," says Findlay, going on to warn of "great fury and violent storms," and "abundant and frequently terrific displays of electric phenomena."

Arabs sailing *regularly* in that kind of thing? In wooden ships small and sometimes weakly built by European standards, spreading huge, unwieldy lateen sails which I knew were fitted with no gear at all for ease in handling them? (As European sails invariably were.) I did not believe it. This was just one aspect of Arab seafaring I planned to look into: the sooner I went to Arabia the better.

* *A Directory for the Navigation of the Indian Ocean, etc.,* fourth edition, by Alexander George Findlay, F.R.G.S., London, Richard Holmes Laurie, 156 Minories, E. 1897. The *Arrow,* as an Anglo-American Oil Company ship, was originally in the case-oil trade to the East.

But one cannot just go to Arabia and expect to find out about Arab sailing commerce, or anything else. It was of not the slightest use to go in steamships, to sit in ports however interesting and talk with Europeans or a few selected Asians whose English, perhaps, was better than their seafaring knowledge. No, I had to *sail in Arab ships* and stay with them, for years if necessary—learn the seamen's language, gain their confidence. Well, sailing-ship seamen of Europe and the Americas were a thoroughly international lot who knew how to get along together. I had found no trouble getting along with Finns, Norwegians, Portuguese, Germans, Peruvians in their own sailing-ships. Seamen's work was obvious: so was ship-handling. You knew it or you didn't: if you did, you fitted well enough with brother-seamen of all nationalities. There was a *lingua franca* of the sailing sea, based on English. I expected there would be something of the sort in the Indian Ocean, too. (There were several —Swahili on the African side, Hindustani round Indian waters, Malay in the Archipelago and—among Muslims at least—Arabic all over. But I could use none of these then, and they took time to master.)

There were pessimists who said that Arabia was a dangerous country where, in many parts, life was cheap. I was advised to set off with the right backing, to become at least known about by the right people. Much of Arabia was then loosely "covered" by British political agents of one sort or another—a governor and staff in Aden, a resident adviser to the Sultan in the Hadhramaut, former Indian Army officers at Muscat and Kuwait, a senior political agent at Bahrein and so on. Through these, there was some sort of loose contact at least with the coastal Sheikhs and Emirs, except in remoter areas of the Yemen and Saudi Arabia.

I had heard, too, from Dwight Long that he had found himself in serious trouble once or twice when going ashore in the Red Sea from his ketch *Idle Hour*, and thought that it might be as well if these officials knew about me. Reports of my presence on their doorsteps were bound to trickle through to them. There was an odd Frenchman allegedly gun-running to the Yemen with a dhow at the time, and I did not want to be confused with him.

My friend, Admiral Sir William Goodenough, retired from the Royal Navy and then President of the Royal Geographical Society (of which I was a Fellow), looked after the officials for me. Distinguished for his handling of the light cruisers at the Battle of Jutland, he had been one of the handful of my supporters in the *Joseph Conrad* venture. He was a quiet man who got things done. Before long, I had met the British resident adviser to the Sultan of the Hadhramaut in Mukalla—a considerable port in South Arabia—had letters in English to His Brittanic Majesty's governor at Aden and his residents at Muscat and elsewhere, in Arabic to various Emirs, Sultans and Sheikhs of coastal districts bordering the Red Sea and the Arabian Gulf, and King Ibn Saud's ambassador in London, the Sheikh Hafiz Wahba, scribbled a paragraph or two in my passport in Arabic.

All this was essential documentation and these were to prove invaluable contacts. Even so, chancing to arrive at Gizan once when the Emir was asleep and no one would dare waken him, I landed temporarily in jail; and the Sultan of Shihir was so concerned for my well-being and personal safety while in his territory that he kept me in a state of incarceration in his very large and well-guarded palace, during the time my boom was anchored in his waters. He was a nice man with red whiskers who took no chances. As for the Gizan jail, the governor entertained me pleasantly to coffee and sweetmeats, but it was a long wait. Some of the malefactors were shackled: a few had amputated hands—the serious thieves, the governor said—and all seemed dependent upon the benevolence of relatives or passers-by to hand them a little food through the communal bars.

The Admiral's ground-work led me, at the Crater in Aden, to the al-Hamad family of Kuwait where two younger brothers, Ali and Abdulla Abdul-Latif al-Hamad, were looking after the family business over an area from Jidda, the port of Mecca, to Berbera in what was then British Somaliland, and from Adis Ababa in the interior of Ethiopia to Mukalla and al-Shihr in the Hadhramaut. It appeared that their influence reached into every port small and large on both sides of the Red Sea and down the coast of Africa as far as Arab ships could sail (which was as far as the NE monsoon blew) and, with other brothers and close relations, they looked after Arab trading points in India, Iraq, Iran, Asir, the Hedjaz, and much of Saudi Arabia. They had interests in Kuwait's famous booms, the packet-ships of the Indian Ocean trade, and they chartered Red Sea sambuks and the like for the distributive trade out of Aden to Djibouti and to Berbera, to Eritrea, to Asir, and with the faithful to Jidda.

He had a first-class sambuk, the *Sheikh Mansur*, loading off Ma'alla for Gizan in the Red Sea at the moment, said Ali, over the coffee cups in his Crater office. She should sail in a day or two. Would I care to go with her?

Would I care to go? Of course! Though I thought I saw a merry twinkle in Ali's dark eyes, as if he were amused at something. I thought I understood that twinkle when I joined the *Sheikh Mansur* the next evening. (It was November 8, 1938.) She seemed to be the grimmest vessel of the hundred or so jostling off Ma'alla, though from outboard she was a fleet and graceful little thing, sleek, double-ended, with a handsome seat upon the water and the swift look of easy speed. She was fifty-five-feet long on deck by fourteen-feet beam, with a six-and-a-half-feet depth of hold. The hull was undecked except for small working platforms for'-ard and aft, and the sea was kept out—I hoped—by date-matting above each side, stitched to the upper planking and stretched optimistically along light wooden poles on uprights formed by forked pieces of small trees, about three feet high. She had two masts and one sail, made of light cotton strengthened at the lower corners by bits of sacking. She had no boat but a dugout canoe, and no shelter anywhere. Instead of a pump to dry her out, some boys were hauling up water from the bilge by means of an old kerosene can, and that bilgewater stank abominably. The air around it shimmered with its noxious fumes, and even the surface waters of Ma'alla Bay seemed to smart as each odious canful assaulted them.

An obvious product of well-nourished optimism and a belief—apparently justified, for she was old—in continuous good weather, she was quite the worst-outfitted vessel I had ever been aboard. Her crew seemed to consist of four or five rather ragged urchins, a grizzled old Turk left over from the First World War, a fierce-looking Mate, and her Nakhoda. The Nakhoda was a Yemenite from Loheiya, about thirty-five years old, slight though well built, with a gentle face and the hands of a musician. He welcomed me aboard pleasantly though with obvious astonishment, and he seemed well content with his deeply laden and—to me—sadly inadequate little vessel.

I sailed with the *Sheikh Mansur* for the following two weeks, round the southwestern corner of Arabia, through the Straits of Babel-Mandeb and up the Red Sea, the inner way, inside the reefs. I learned that the smelly little vessel going her accustomed way about the coasting trade that she was built for was not inadequate at all. We anchored by night in the shelter of sand-cays or reefs, and sailed by day, guided by the gentle Nakhoda's personal knowledge. This and his religion, being all he had, were well developed and adequate. Much of the Red Sea leaked through the vessel and all was baled out again. The weather was good, the wind favorable, the sea slight. Our food was fish caught in the sea, a little rice, some unleavened bread baked in a few ashes—the fuel brushwood from the cays, dried seaweed, old camel-dung, anything.

We washed in sea-water but all hands were scrupulously clean, for the laws of Islam saw to that. The toilet was a box with two planks missing in the bottom, lashed outboard at deck level. In this was a small and much-battered tin for hauling up sea-water to throw at one's own bottom as necessary, and some dexterity was required at this. European clothes were most unsuitable. The box was bathroom, too. There was no other. If needed, another box could be lashed on the other side, and the simple toilet arrangements worked very well. There was no plumbing to go wrong. All hands performed their ablutions and offered their prayers, cleaned and facing Mecca, at the appointed five times daily, cleaning their teeth scrupulously, though for utensils they had only a teased-out end of cane or a piece of cuttlefish. It was the fasting month of Ramadhan: neither drink nor food could pass one's lips from dawn to sunset. This was little real loss for there were no sea stores.

I was sometimes hungry. I suffered from dysentery. The nights were cold, the days long and hot. But I learned to respect the Nakhoda and his crew, and the shapely, smelly, sea-thirsty *Sheikh Mansur*.

A little emaciated perhaps and sunburnt and tired, I got back to Aden some weeks later by way of a small motor-ship from Jidda. I thought Ali al-Hamad seemed a little surprised to see me.

"Like it?" he asked.

"It was fascinating," I said.

He gave me a long, searching look. I had the impression that I had passed some trial—perhaps a lot of trials.

"Well, now the Kuwaiti are ready," he said. "I will arrange for you to make the African voyage with Nejdi, the best Nakhoda from Kuwait, with the best boom. No more short passages—you can be six months with Nejdi, sail back to Kuwait, and make an Indian voyage later if you want."

I had seen some fine booms flying the red flag of Kuwait in the harbor, big fellows, sleek and handsome and oiled, with great high masts, and their crews, in immaculate head-cloths and gowns, rowing their long-boats with style, like the old East Indiamen. Imperious figures of nakhodas and sailing mates trod their poops, and the sound of drums and song rose from their waists.

Here were the liners of Araby the Blest, the great ships of the Indian

Ocean! They were as like the lowly little *Sheikh Mansur* as the clipper-ship *Thermopylae* resembled an old Irish collier-schooner.

Now I could get on with stepping back in seafaring history, in a stately ship of the Arab deep-sea fleet directly in descent from the argosies of the incense trade of long ago.

And so it proved. Nejdi's boom was good and her long voyage memorable, though the premature arrival of the Second World War put an end to my hopes of making the Indian voyage. Before the end of that war, the new, fabulously oil-rich Sheikhdom of Kuwait was already taking shape, putting an end to the great Arab sailing traditions and trade which had lasted so long. In the new economy, the deep-sea boom had no place.

I was only just in time. At the end of 1939, as I found from the Sheikh's registrar *at Kuwait*, there were 106 ocean-going dhows sailing out of the port of Kuwait, three of them baggalas and the others all booms. Their average tonnage was about one hundred, the largest being 300-odd and the smallest about seventy. They were not measured for tonnage, but by their capacity for stowing standard packages of Iraqi dates. They were all built in Kuwait, and their average value was ten to twelve thousand Indian rupees, which were then the local currency. This was the approximate equivalent of U.S. $3,250 to $3,750. They laid up in their home port during the months of the SW monsoon in the Indian Ocean. At the beginning of the NE, they began trading voyages by loading full cargoes of the new season's dates in the Basra River. These were carried in standard packages, flatly cylindrical in shape, so heavy that one was about as much as the most stalwart porter could possibly stagger under. These dates were for the Asian trade: many came from riverside plantations owned by Kuwaiti merchant families like the al-Hamads. The dhows carried dates as freight, either to Indian ports or round the coasts of Arabia, peddling them to merchants' account, not their own.

I did not see or hear of any Kuwait vessel which took dates to East African ports, for this trade had apparently passed to European hands. Those which carried cargoes for South Arabia made Aden their turn-round port, warehousing unsold dates there and continuing to Africa with other cargo, and passengers. These made only the one African voyage annually: I was told that those in the Indian trade, which was shorter and perhaps then better organized, tried to make two. From India the dhows brought back shipbuilding materials, coir for cordage and teak:

from East Africa they brought mainly mangrove poles from the Rufiji
Delta in what was then Tanganyika, or from Lamu in Kenya Colony.

There were also hailing from Kuwait at that time, between one hundred and 150 pearlers, some up to seventy feet long but many of them
small, all propelled by sweeps as well as sails. These worked the nearer
banks in the northern end of the Gulf, during the hot season, when there
were plenty of divers and their tenders back from the long-voyage vessels. There were also fifty or sixty small dhows, many of them single-
masted but the majority of the boom hull-shape, in local trades such as
bringing fresh water from the Basra River. New vessels were being built
on the beach at the rate of two or three a month, large, for deep-sea, and
at least that many for coastal trade. But pearling was depressed because,
I gathered, of the success of the Japanese cultured-pearl industry.

Old and smaller booms were sold down-gulf to ports in Qatar and Trucial Oman, which used them mainly in their own African trade.

Outside the Gulf, the port of Sur, near Ras-al-Hadd on the Gulf of
Oman, was the only rival to Kuwait. It built large sambuks and baggalas—
no booms. The Kuwaiti did not call at Sur and I did not go there, nor
could any statistics be obtained. We saw many fine new Suri vessels up to
150 tons or so. Nejdi estimated the Suri Indian Ocean fleet at probably
about a hundred dhows. He did not appear to think highly of them. From
Trucial Oman I saw no large ships at all, but a few outsize booms showed
Iranian colors from the ancient ports of Quishm and Lingeh.

Other ports in Arabia where I saw considerable fleets of dhows were
Mukalla in the Hadhramaut, Ma'alla at Aden, Hodeida, Mocha and
Luhaiya in the Yemen, and Gizan (or Qizan) in Asir, on the Red Sea.
These all built dhows, mostly coasters. Nejdi and other nakhodas calculated that, in 1939-40, the total fleet of seagoing Arab craft was something
between two and two-and-a-half thousand, employing directly at least
thirty thousand or forty thousand men. There was not an engine in any
of them, nor were such things wanted.*

"Allah is great and merciful and His winds are free. Therefore His
faithful use them," said Nejdi, who was a seaman well content with the
career to which he had been born and raised.

Yet within a decade not a single deep-sea boom was building in Kuwait,
a non-auxiliary large Arab sailing craft had become a rarity (except from
Sur), and the 106 so distinctive great Kuwaiti booms and baggalas had

* M. Besse operated one or two auxiliary sambuks from Ma'alla in the nearer Red
Sea trade: M. Besse was not an Arab.

disappeared from the face of the sea. For the Sheikhdom floated upon another "sea," rich and removable crude oil, and the fantastic wealth accruing from this, though kept under wise control, quite finished the older ways of life not only among the nakhodas, the mariners, and the pearling crews.

In a little while as the Arab measures time, the old walled city-port was smothered under a vast new monstrous place—characterless and car-filled, but full of good schools, hospitals, housing estates, with a great new port where the cargo-liners of the world jostled and queued to discharge a million things my old Kuwaiti had never missed. From a tremendous tank-farm outside the city, oil gushed in endless, unseen streams to fill the maws of the hundred enormous tankers lying silent and unhuman in the Gulf's adjacent waters. As one bloated steel box sank to her sea-marks, slipped and staggered off towards the refineries of the world, another took its place—another and another and another endlessly, as if they would never be satisfied until they had sucked away everything from beneath the Sheikhdom and the city, down to hell's fires. They paid and paid and paid. Except for one pair of the old city gates allowed to survive incongruously in the shadow of a huge hotel, all that was old was destroyed—the gracious old homes, the shady courtyards, the fine old palaces, the fascinating waterfront.

And the Arab sea trade, of course: for that was old, too.

I flew out by jet Comet of Kuwait Airlines in early 1967 from London via Rome and Beirut, to the enormous airfield in what was so recently desert outside the city of Kuwait. (The head-clothed nakhoda of the Comet knew his business.) Some shadowy figures in long robes and stately cloaks, black-roped white headcloths shining in the night, rose to greet me. I saw the hawk nose of Nakhoda Nejdi and, with him, some of his sons and the young sons of the al-Hamad family I'd kept in touch with through the years, and Nejdi's faithful serang, Hamid. Nejdi was a rich man now, I gathered, long a business tycoon ashore, with a large home beside a wide motorway and—more or less—everything that he could wish.

The night wind stirred his headcloth.

"Allah is great," I said. "His winds are free."

"Allah is great," he replied. After a while, he added as if to himself, "And sometimes I wish that I could use His winds again. For it was a good life that my sons can never know—no Kuwait sons shall know.

"We cannot bring those ways back again."

On the waterfront was one last boom, hauled ashore on the sand, not working but put there as a memorial to the great sailing days of the Sheikhdom's city-port, now gone forever.

I am glad I was in time to learn something at first-hand of it all and to do what I could to record it. The great Nakhoda Isa Kitami, who lay dying in his new home as I greeted Nejdi, has left a fine textbook, a new *Periplus* of the old Erythræan Sea, in Arabic.

His book, and this of mine, are all that now remain.

By the 1960's the old Arab Indian Ocean trade was done for anyway. The "emergent nations" of East Africa had managed what the Europeans had never tried to do, to bring Arab influence and trade to a halt. The ago-old migrant traffic was virtually at an end. In several of the new countries, the Arab and the Indian were no longer welcome. Restrictions were placed on them. They were, after all, such obviously successful businessmen and traders. Now it was felt that it was the African's turn. One hopes it is.

Even in some Arab countries, the shapely boom, the imposing baggala, the swift sambuk did not fit the new "image." In India and Pakistan, it was much the same story.

In 1956 I managed a voyage in an Indian-built baggala between Ceylon and Malé in the Maldive Islands, and noted her soundness and her strength. She was an Asian ship fit to run before the SW monsoon. Built in a land with plenty of good teak and—until then—plenty of experience and building skills, she was stronger than the average Arab vessel I had known. Her main-mast was stepped in a steel sleeve, her sails and gear were strong and good, her nakhoda was a skilful navigator. But one of the European powers thought it needed an atoll in the Maldives for a staging airfield in the Indian Ocean: the price the Sultan (prodded by his Majlis) demanded was a full-powered motor ship to replace his fleet of dhows. I was just in time in the Maldives, too.

In 1960 I was on the Brahmaputra where then a wonderful fleet of wind-driven craft still survived, some of types which dated back to the ships of ancient Egypt. But already the shipyards were building ugly big motor-launches, and the government was laying down a system of expensive roads for trucks to use. (The Brahmaputra-Meghna-Ganges river system was unkind to the idea of roads.) The great rivers flowed too frequently through Indian territory serving the Sundarbans and Assam as well as East Pakistan: at times of friction there could be intolerable delays at the too-numerous frontier posts.

In the Second World War, I saw the rice barques of Burma rotting on the beaches of Palk Strait and, afterwards, the great fleet of Malay and local sailing craft at anchor uselessly crowded into Singapore Roads when the ruler of the new Indonesia preferred "confrontation" to trade. I noted, too, this same Indonesia, home of the Makassar schooner and the graceful proa, had built a modern steel barquentine, with engines, to be a training-ship for the naval school. The proa did not fit the new "image" of the proud old land: I wonder if I was alone in hoping that the barquentine fitted even less.

So it went. By the time that ruler was at last deposed, half the laid-up fleet off Singapore was rotten. For idleness too long continued ruins ships, too.

At Hongkong, the junks are mechanized. Even in the remotest island groups of the far South Seas, the only engineless craft that one may see today is the occasional world-wandering sailing yacht, and along the coasts of Peru and of Brazil, on both sides of South America, the sailing balsa-raft fisherman is marked for the scrap-heap. Too old, too "inefficient." But the balsa-raft was a local product, cheaply financed, easily made, providing local livings. It caught fish and left stocks. It was silent, simple, and pleasant to look upon.

In their own ways, much the same could be said of the Islands sailing canoe, the Singalese fisherman, the junk, the proa, the schooner, the Brahmaputra boat, the baggala, the sambuk, and the boom. They did their local share of the world's work well for quite some time, often over a considerable range. They found a place in the lives of men, and sometimes also in their hearts.

I am glad that I have known them, and the world they served, and suited. Not only that world is, I think, the poorer for their passing, for much more than the lovely ships is lost when they are thrown away.

ALAN VILLIERS

Oxford
1968

Contents

Illustrations

Sons of Sinbad

Chapter 1

MA'ALLA BEACH

THE STERILE, pock-marked mountains of Aden stood hot and grim round Ma'alla Bay, as if designed and placed there deliberately to hem in the water from the ocean's cooling winds. Across the shallow bay the sand, curiously miraged, appeared to wash against the mountains of the coastal range, as if the sea had flung it there, and then gone, abandoning for ever the fruitless task of trying to moisten or to cool the parched hard rock of that barren land. The sky was blue and hard, and the hot sun burned. The sand underfoot was dark and foul, and the beach stank. Pariah dogs ran out from the poor huts and rapidly barked themselves into a state of exhaustion. Goats bleated, their heavy udders secured in dirty calico bags against their hungry kids. Children ran crying for bakhshish, seeming to know no other word. Along the roadway towards the Crater dun-colored camels plodded by, supercilious and deliberate, drawing little carts, or strode in empty caravan with ragged Beduin beside them dressed in indigo and rags, outward bound towards Lahej and the further Yemen valleys. By the side of the roadway, in monotonous stone lines, stood the houses of the Somali, migrants from near-by Berbera, who now were more numerous in Steamer Point than the Arabs themselves. The year was 1938, and overhead the drone of a bombing squadron, twelve ancient biplanes in ragged formation, reminded one that Aden would soon celebrate its centenary of British rule. Once meeting-place of East and West and still an important world and Arab port, Aden was now an outpost of the British Empire, an important refueling point for the Far Eastern and Australian trades. Yet it was once Eudæmon Arabia, known for its convenient anchorage and sweet water to the anonymous sea captain who compiled the *Periplus of the Erythræan Sea* in the first century of our era, and known probably to the Arab and Indian mariners of the

eastern seas for countless centuries before that. It was still an Arab port, as well as a post of importance for the policing of Europe's (and America's) trade routes.

I walked along Ma'alla beach, where in the eighth century a merchant had drawn an accurate map of the Indian Ocean in the sand and marked in its ports and routes and trade which were to remain unknown to us for almost a thousand years, and I thought of the ancient glories of this great port in the great days of eastern navigation. It was because I knew that something of those times still survived that I was there at all, for Aden is not ordinarily the kind of place in which one dallies. I knew that the Arab dhows of today were in the direct line of descent from the ancient vessels of eastern waters in which men probably first sailed; and I would have gone to hell to see them. I had to come no nearer to hell than Aden, which was close enough: but here at Ma'alla beach were the dhows, and here were the Arabs who still sailed them.

Along the beach where the hard brown earth merged into brackish, smelling mud, a dozen small dhows stood propped on stilts or leaned crazily towards the sea, while their skirted sailors carried out repairs, or, with endless chant and song, applied hot paying-stuff to their ships' undersides, using their bare hands. Here and there the shapely hulls of partly finished dhows rose from surrounding piles of twisted wood from the Yemen and logs from the Malabar coast, from which skilful carpenters, working only with adze and Indian drill, had hewn them. The sweetly curved bows of the new sambuks seemed to look in amazement over the odds and ends of wood which had given them birth. A gang of sail-makers, more Negro than Arab, squatted on the sand stitching the round seams of a lateen sail. Other sailors close by were laying up coir cable made of coconut fiber from India, or carrying out a rusted grapnel into the tidal water, to which to haul off a small dhow when next the tide served. In the bay twoscore small dhows swung to their moorings, or moved with jostling and chants towards the end of the stone jetty to take their turns at loading or discharging. The stench of putrid shark and fish oil which rose from them was a deterrent against close examination. These were the small fry from the nearer coastal ports of the Yemen and southern Arabia, come to Ma'alla to load cargoes for distribution to the ports of the Hadhramaut and the Red Sea. Beyond them lay the deep-sea dhows, the big booms from Kuwait and the baggalas and ocean-going sambuks from Sur, which had brought dates from the Basra River in Iraq and were loading for their annual voyage down to Africa.

Bow of a sambuk

If Steamer Point is given up to liners now, and bombing aircraft drone above the Crater, Ma'alla Bay between the two is still a great port for dhows both small and large, the small dhows bringing and distributing goods for the nearer ports and the deep-sea dhows carrying such cargoes as the competition of European steam still leaves to them. They can freight dates from Basra for the local market more cheaply than any steamer can bring them: they can load bulk salt for Mombasa and deliver it there more cheaply than powered vessels. And they still can carry on their age-old trading voyages, buying and selling their own merchandise as they go—dates, salt, dried shark, cotton stuffs brought from Japan instead of rare silks from China and dress goods from India, sesame seeds, ghee, Arab cooking oils, some frankincense and myrrh.

The songs of the sailors as they pulled the longboats to Ma'alla jetty were music in my ears as I walked along the hot beach, and the long-voyage dhows were a delight to see. Those big dhows were a heartening sight that hot, harsh morning, and I meant to find a berth in one of them before the day was ended. Ma'alla beach might smell, but to me it was a romantic, intensely interesting place, with its jetty facing Mecca where the faithful prayed, and its picturesque fleet of dhows. For these Arab dhows were almost the last unspoiled fleet of pure sailing vessels left in the world. The last of European sail were the square-riggers of Marie-hamn in the grain trade from Australia, but of these only a handful remain. These, a few brigantines in the Mediterranean, a Portuguese Banks fisherman or two, three barques in the Peruvian guano trade, one or two Germans carrying Chilean nitrate—these were about all the engineless, unsubsidized commercial sail left in our world. The white schooners of the South Seas have long been engined and the reek of Diesel oil now pollutes many an island lagoon. The junks of China are busy avoiding Japanese bombs: the deep-sea praus of the East Indies cannot compete with the K. P. M.: the coastal craft of India voyage under British regulation, and the steamers have taken most of their overseas trade. Gloucester fishermen, Balinese schooners, Tasmanian timber ketches, Baltic galeasses and barquentines—all these are engined.

It seemed to me, having looked far and wide over twenty years of a seafaring lifetime, that as pure sailing craft carrying on their unspoiled ways, only the Arab remained. Only the Arab remained making his voyages as he always had, in a wind-driven vessel sailing without benefit of engines. Only the Arab still sailed his wind ships over the free sea, keeping steadfastly to the ways of the past. Just as the grain ships of Fin-

Under way

land and the German nitrate ships were the last of European sail, the Arab
dhow was the last of the romantic East. I had sailed in most other kinds
of sailing ships, from a Trobriand canoe to a four-masted barque,
a Tasmanian ketch to a full-rigged ship. I had not hitherto had a chance
to sail in Arab dhows. With all else gone, I was glad to turn to them, glad
that they still survived. I had always been interested in Arab dhows, and
always admired the Arab for the fine independence and the quiet good
manners of his well-adjusted life. The Arabs had been sailing, and sailing
very well, for countless centuries before we even knew the ocean existed:
that they still sailed very much the same trade routes in much the same
way I thought remarkable evidence both of their ability and spirit. If I
could sail with them on an African voyage, to learn of their seafaring at
first hand, I should be pleased indeed.

I had already been sailing in coastal dhows in the Red Sea, in Ahmed
the Yemenite's small zarook, as a kind of trial voyage. As I stopped to look
over the animated waterfront I saw her swinging to her anchors out in
the bay, back empty from her voyage to Gizan. The passage in her had

been a good beginning; but it was the big deep-sea dhows which really attracted me, the big fellows from Kuwait and Sur and the Iranian ports. These were almost pure survival from Phœnician times, from the most ancient sailing of which we know. There they were, swinging in the sun of Ma'alla Bay, with their singing sailors rowing in longboats full of Basra dates. There they were, lying at noisy anchor off Ma'alla beach, making ready, perhaps for the thousandth or five-thousandth time, for the annual trading voyage down to Africa, as far as the monsoon blows. They were a handsome fleet of imposing vessels, with their oiled hulls shining over the blue waters of the bay, and their simple rig of two bare masts. They were a stirring fleet, as I thought of the great history and the tremendous traditions behind them. Yet now the airplanes roared overhead and tourists hurried, bound in their impatient motorcars to the Tanks and Sheikh Othman, while their liners filled their tanks with oil, and no one save Arabs spared as much as a glance towards the dhows. Here at Ma'alla the deep-sea dhows were in, and from no one in the European world could I learn about them.

Well, I was about, I hoped, to learn for myself, and the prospect pleased me. I continued along the beach, slowly, for there was much to see. My destination was the office of the Kuwait dhow-owners, Khalid Abdul-latif al-Hamad and Brothers, importers of dates and owners of date plantations in Iraq, charterers and owners of dhows trading to Africa, the Yemen, Eritrea, Saudi-Arabia, Somaliland, and India. I knew that I should find there the assembled nakhodas of the Kuwait and Suri fleets, for it was their custom to call on the merchants in the mornings. I liked to walk, though it was so hot. The scene was too interesting to hurry by heedlessly in a car: the zigzagging road to Aden's Crater gave delightful views over harbor and sea. I did not see the macadam road or the vehicles from Detroit and Dagenham which speeded on it. I looked back over Ma'alla Bay where the dhows lay, and thought of all the great centuries of their unhurried voyaging. The idea of going out with a dhow to join in this was indeed a pleasing prospect.

Yet I knew well that the voyage itself might not be wholly pleasing, for I had come but recently from Ahmed the Yemenite's small zarook, a mean, flea-bitten little thing that traded in the hot Red Sea. Ahmed's zarook was tough, hungry, and exceedingly primitive. In a brief month there I had lost twenty pounds weight and had picked up a little dysentery and some malaria. Yet I had thought it worth while. The name of

Ahmed's little ship was *Sheikh Mansur,* but there was nothing sheikhlike about her. She had a water-line length of less than fifty feet, two small masts raking forward, and a great thirst for the sea. She leaked as if she loved it, and only the delight of soaking more and more of the sea through her kept her afloat. She was built of odds and ends of indifferent wood scraped up on some Yemenite beach and nailed together with old iron, but her ribs and her knees were good. I had found her at Ma'alla, whence the al-Hamads were sending her with a cargo of Rangoon rice, Javanese sugar, and bales of Japanese cottons and printed stuffs for the harems, all destined for the bazaar at Gizan, by the southern borders of Asir in the Red Sea. The good *Sheikh* was nothing but an open boat with a lateen sail. Except for a small poop and a tiny working platform in the bows, she was undecked.

When I first boarded her they were hauling up clean water in goat-skins from her well, bailing her constantly, though she lay then in the quiet waters of Ma'alla Bay, and they bailed almost the whole way to Gizan. Of all the dhows in port she was undoubtedly the meanest, though none of her people thought so. She was dreadfully small, horribly over-loaded, and she stank frightfully. She had no accommodation of any kind, and there was never much to eat. A matting of loosely woven palm leaves, lashed above her bulwarks along both sides, served to keep out most of the sea when she rolled, but one angry sea breaking on board would have been the death of her. She was a low, rakish little thing, green-painted with a white limed mouth where her sweet cutwater bit the sea, and a pattern of triangles in reds and blues round the railing at her sharp stern. She sat prettily in the water, and her lines were excellent. She had a graceful and fleet little hull, and her high raking mainmast grew from her gracefully. Her lateen yard was constructed from the branches of two trees, lashed together end for end, and her one sail was a loosely seamed piece of cheap Japanese cotton, roped with coir made from Indian coconut fiber. Her rudder seemed balanced precariously on one pintle, from which it threatened every moment to break adrift, and even in the quiet waters of the harbor she seemed in imminent danger of foundering.

I voyaged in that little ship 600 miles, and I enjoyed every mile of it and was sorry when the time came to leave her. Mean and incredibly poor as she was, she was a ship, and there was a spirit aboard her rare in these days and never found in liners. We sailed from Ma'alla along the coast of Southern Arabia towards the westward, and through Bab-el-Mandeb and along the Yemen coast past Mocha, Hodeida, and Kamaran, and then

along the inside way, within the reefs, towards Gizan. We sailed by day
and anchored at night, for the way was dangerous. It was the fasting
month of Ramadhan, which is an unfortunate time to be with the Arabs
in their dhows, for during Ramadhan the faithful may neither eat nor
drink from before dawn until after sunset. If you are with the faithful, it
is mannerly to behave as they do. Our crew of eight Arabs under Ahmed
the Yemenite went hungry while we sailed, and in the evenings, when
the sun had set and they had said their prayers, we dined on a mess of rice
and fish, if there was any rice and we had caught a fish. We ate with our
right hands, in the Arab manner. Life was hard but also simple. If no one
had any possessions, no one was envious. If there were no bunks, the air was
warm, and there were the stars for company. The weather was good. The
little ship knew no routine, and kept no schedule. No one knew or cared
what day it was, for to them days were not uniform periods to be named
and numbered and regretted as they rushed by. We had a mild interest in
the progress of the Ramadhan moon, for its final setting would mean
the end of the long fast. I was surprised how easily I slipped into this timeless state, how pleasant it was when attained. Who cared what day it was?
The sun always rose again, and set, as Allah willed, and the days were

Grounded large sambuk

good for their own sake. It was a primitive and, at the same time, a surprisingly satisfactory existence.

Ahmed did his best with the ship and the winds Allah gave him, and did not fret when the conditions were adverse. There was a fine spirit in that happy little vessel where all men were so poor, and the master was the father of his sailors. He was in his early thirties, and most of them were grown men, but he acted as a father to them, and his leadership was benevolently patriarchal.

I was interested to see how Ahmed managed his vessel, for he knew no methods of navigation as we know them, and those seas are dangerous. He had no need of ordinary methods of navigation. The *Sheikh Mansur* was run very simply .Without any kind of windlass, and no anchor save a grapnel and a piece of stone in which a spike had been imbedded; with no boat other than one small dugout canoe; with no instruments or aids to navigation beyond one decrepit, hopeless, and largely invisible boat compass dating back at least a century; without even a leadline to sound, she somehow wandered along cheerfully and she had been sailing like that for at least thirty years in one of the most dangerous seas in the world. She had no shelter, no decks, no charts, no bell, no barometer, no clock. What need was there for shelter, when it never rained? Why have decks, when no sea broke on board? Who needed charts, when Ahmed knew every reef and every headland, every strip of beach and every rock by eye, from long and close personal association? What need was there of bells and clocks, when time was not a passing torrent to be vainly measured? Or of barometers, when the weather in the winter season was always fair? There was not even a tarpaulin to cover the cargo, which lay in the hold open to the sea: but if the sea ever came there not only the cargo would be finished. She had not even a simple pump. There was nothing to cook in save a box of sand with three stones, on which a boy kindled a brushwood fire in the evenings. The sea stores coming aboard at Aden consisted of some old palm leaves from which fibers were extracted as necessary, to be used as ropeyarns or sail yarn or gaskets, or whatever else might be needed. The food for twelve people (for she also carried passengers) was kept in half a small chest on the tiny poop, from which it soon disappeared. Then there were fish. The drinking water was kept in a rusted drum exposed daylong to the intense heat of the overhead sun, and in this small squirming things flourished. There was not so much as an old hurricane lamp on board. There was no light at all. When the sun set, we lived in unrelieved blackness, though the nights were soft and the stars were clear, while the moon of Ramadhan was light enough in the evenings.

The little ship rolled and pitched abominably in anything of a sea, with a short, sharp, jerky motion. She was infested with cockroaches and all kinds of insects, and there were rats. By night hungry mosquitoes came from the little cays off which we anchored, and dined on my too well-nourished blood. Food became scarce when a shark carried away our only fishing line, and we lived three days on a handful of old dates. We washed in the sea, ate with our hands, slept on the cargo, only a foot or so above the level of the outside water. We were sunburned, hungry, tired (for the constant motion of a little ship in a short sea is very tiring). I knew little Arabic, and understood almost nothing of the gibberish those Yemenite sailors spoke.

It was a tough life, but this was a reflection which occurred to no one else on board, and I was glad enough to be there. The sailors were all good friends. Their simplicity and their direct free honesty, their utter lack of hypocrisy and all shams, the calm unworried philosophy of their simple lives, were very appealing. They fasted, prayed, washed in the sea water, did such work as was necessary, and cheerfully ate their frugal meals. It seemed to me that the very simplicity of their hard lives gave them a quality most enviable, and missing too often from our own. Their satisfactions were their own, and their delights lay in a real world round them. They were free men, though one of them was a slave. They were freer men than we are.

Day after day we wandered leisurely to the northwards, inside the reefs of the eastern side of the Red Sea. The wind blew and the ship sailed. The crew prayed, and observed the fast, and Ahmed the Yemenite knew where he was going. He knew those waters and he knew his ship; he was a good sailor. His little ship was in many ways the quietest and most peaceful in which I had ever sailed. I learned to admire Ahmed and his crew, and to like them all. Such as their little ship was, they loved her. To them she had no imperfections. In a little while, living so closely with that spirit on board, I began almost to be ashamed that I had first thought her so lowly. She was a workable little craft, fit enough for the voyages she was called upon to make, though her main halliards might have been made from plaited straw. She ran well and sailed well, and she never behaved badly in the sea, though we were in a race once or twice, off Mocha and in the straits of Bab-el-Mandeb. Nothing of her cargo was ever touched, though some of it was food and we were hungry. Nothing was broached, though the crew was poor and anything from those bales would have meant wealth to them. When one day we sighted another dhow in distress, with her rudder gone, Ahmed put the helm up and ran at once to her assistance, though the wind was hard that day and we were in dangerous waters. When we spoke to small fishermen, they gave us fish and we gave them rice, if we had any.

So day followed day: beards grew, belts tightened, and the insects in the water-drum multiplied. On the evening of the eighth day we reached Gizan, coming in through the kelp and anchoring beside a pilgrim dhow bound for Jiddah.

That had been some weeks earlier: now I looked back from the Crater Road, and the *Sheikh Mansur*, come again to Aden, was a green-painted speck far below on the busy bay. It had been a tough life, perhaps, looked at by any of our standards. I had no great desire to spend more time voyaging in the small fry of the Red Sea, for one passage in them must be very like another. I liked the Arabs, and looked forward to shipping out with the big dhows bound on a long voyage, for deepseamen are always more interesting than coastwise craft. I continued slowly toiling up the incline of the Crater Road, and wished the day were not quite so insufferably hot.

In the cool of the al-Hamad office, a large stone building in the streets of Aden Camp, I found half a dozen nakhodas from the big dhows in the harbor. With them, seated writing at a desk with a modern filing cabinet beside it and a telephone on the table, was Ali Abdul-latif al-Hamid, second youngest of the al-Hamad brothers of Kuwait, who was at that time in charge of the Aden office. He was a tall, slightly built young man dressed in a well-made linen suit, and on his head was a sheepskin cap. The office was a plain room open to the street, with three of its sides lined with wooden benches on which carpets and cushions had been placed. The nakhodas, a bearded, silent lot, sat on the carpets. One of them had a fringe of hennaed beard that hung on his square jaw like seaweed, and a twig of the Hamdh bush was stuck in his turban to be used, I supposed, for cleaning his teeth. That this was indeed its use he proved then and there by quietly taking it out and nonchalantly scrubbing his teeth with its teased end. The other shipmasters were moustachioed men dressed in long white gowns. With the exception of one who was very Negroid, they were light-complexioned Arabs and, dressed in European clothes, would have passed as swarthy Greeks or Portuguese. They were a striking assembly, as they sat swinging their amber beads and waiting to give replies to such speech as might be addressed to them.

I thanked Ali Abdul-latif for the voyage to Gizan, for it was he who had arranged it, and I asked him if I could go out with one of the big deepwatermen on a voyage down to Zanzibar. Ali smiled, showing a large mouth of perfect teeth beneath his close-clipped black moustache. So I wanted to go to Africa in a big dhow, did I? I had not had enough in the *Sheikh Mansur?* Well, he went on, if I really did wish to sail in a dhow to Zanzibar I was in luck, for the best young nakhoda from Kuwait was then on the premises, having his lunch somewhere in the mysterious chambers upstairs. Would I care to meet him? Indeed I would: and so it came about that I first met Nejdi, that hawk-nosed, keen-eyed son of the Eastern seas—Nejdi, youthful master of one of Kuwait's fastest and largest booms, pilot of great dhows down to Zanzibar and the Malabar coast, pearl-master of the Persian Gulf.

When I first saw him he was eating a sheep. Ramadhan was past, and it was again lawful to eat by day. He appeared to be making up for lost time. He was squatting on a carpet in the shade of the parapet of the al-Hamad roof where the cooling air could blow upon him, and he was nonchalantly chewing large pieces of a well-done sheep, and shovelling down handfuls of rice as fast as he could. He stopped and stood up as we came. He was a small, slight man, with a very strong face which the ravages of smallpox had not spoiled. He was handsome, in his own way, with an oval face, a close-clipped black moustache, a hawk nose and well-defined, determined chin. He was wiry and lean, and he looked very strong. He was swarthy, darker than the other Kuwait shipmasters downstairs. He was strikingly dressed in a long flowing gown of white silk, which was gathered closely at the throat by two gold studs. On his head was a white headcloth, embroidered with needlework of pale gold, and kept in position by a black lamb's-wool aghal, the halolike headrope of the desert Arab. His cloak of camel's hair and wire of gold was thrown on the carpet beside him, and a set of amber prayer-beads peeped from one pocket. Leather sandals, embellished in red and green and looking very new, stood neatly on the roof by the edge of the carpet where he had discarded them, and a Malabar cane lay beside them. He had small, shapely hands, with long, delicate fingers. His features were strong and very good. There was about his face and all of him an air of alert ability which augured well for any ship he might command, and of complete self-assurance which boded ill for any who tried to thwart him. He had the stance of a master-mariner, of a seaman more used to the rolling poop than the dull roof of a city house. He stood there as if he half expected the roof to roll beneath him at any moment, and as if, too, he were ready for it, if it did.

Ali introduced us, and we joined him at the sheep, not speaking again until the meal was ended. This was about five minutes later, by which time most of the sheep was ended, too. After that we washed our hands with water brought in a jar by a servant, drank three thimblefuls of very strong unsweetened coffee, wafted some incense into our noses from a burner brought by another servant, and sat silently for some time. I began to think this was all we were going to do, when Ali began at last to speak with this strange young man who had, I gathered, already been in command of deep-sea dhows trading to Africa and India for more than ten years. What they said I did not know, for they spoke in Arabic and I did not then know much of that language. But Ali had good English, and afterwards he told me that it would be all right. I could go with Nejdi in his boom. Nejdi's name was Ali bin Nasir el-Nejdi, and he was a Kuwaiti of desert Arab descent. His dhow had a name which was translated as the *Triumph of Righteousness*. This seemed a very satisfactory name for any vessel which sailed so much under the guidance of Allah as the ordinary Arab dhow, but I wondered for a moment whether the name might not be the best thing about her. I remembered the poor *Sheikh Mansur*, which also had been proudly named but turned out to be the meanest little vessel in Ma'alla Bay. I was uncertain whether, after all, Ali had not meant that Red Sea passage as a test of my caliber and the depth of my real interest in the Arabs and their dhows, and I wondered whether the highfalutin *Triumph of Righteousness* might not turn out to be the smallest, meanest, oldest Kuwait boom in the harbor. But I kept these fears to myself, for I felt Nejdi's eyes on me: and whatever she was, I would go in her.

Nejdi had little to say throughout this interview, though I gathered he did not think much of the European business of writing books. In his view, there was only one book. The Quran was enough for him. But he knew I was a sailor and had sailed big ships on long voyages myself: perhaps I might be useful to him. As for books, he left no doubt (Ali said) that in his view there were more than enough European books about the Arabs already. Some of them were good—he mentioned Yawrens, and Stark*—but in many of the others the Arabs could recognize neither

* Colonel Lawrence (known to the Arabs as "Yawrens") and Miss Freya Stark.

themselves nor their country. Ali told him that I would write only about ships and the sea—ships, and sailors, but he still looked dubious. Apparently he held the firm opinion that the sea was no fit subject for books, and he thought that the Arabs having made their voyages unchronicled over so many centuries might be left in enjoyment of that privilege. Nobody wanted to read about sailors, he seemed to think, and the sailors certainly did not want to read about themselves. They would all live ashore, if they could. As for books, a list of distances and landfalls and descriptions of desirable ports would be more in their line. However, an extra navigator would be welcome in the vessel, if I would take her as I found her. I could come, if I wished. I could have six feet of the mates' bench aft, and join in the quarterdeck mess. But had I not better first see the ship?

This I thought an excellent idea, remembering the *Sheikh Mansur*. I was aboard on the Sunday. After one brief glance, I knew I need have no worries about Nejdi's boom. An upstanding, handsome thoroughbred of a ship, beside the *Sheikh Mansur* she was like a Cape Horner beside an old Thames barge. She was massive, without being heavy; strong, with no hint of sluggishness; stout, though sweetly lined. She sat the blue water of Ma'alla Bay like a handsome sea bird, and her beaklike bow added to the illusion. She was low in the bow and high aft, in the manner of deep-sea Arab dhows, though, as in all Kuwait booms, her cutwater was straight and carried up into a straight sort of built-up bowsprit, which reached out twenty feet before her, more as a symbol than for use. From the low bow the lines of her hull ran in a lovely sweep to her poop, which was roomy and high. She was a vessel, I judged, of about 150 tons, though none of the Arabs I asked knew her tonnage. They did not measure their ships by tons, but by their stowage capacities for packages of Basra dates. The *Triumph of Righteousness*, they said, could stow two and a half thousand packages of dates. She was light then, for the dates had been discharged, and she towered over all the sambuks and zarooks in the bay. Her teak mainmast stood ninety feet above the sea, and her tremendous lateen yard was made of the trunks of three trees, lashed stoutly end for end with many seizings of canvas-bound rope. She stank abominably of fish-oil, as do all dhows, but I was used to that by then. In spite of the fish-oil and the other queer odors which rose from her main hatch as we climbed on board, I knew this was the kind of vessel in which I wished to sail. The atmosphere of true adventure seemed to lie heavy on her graceful hull, and the very timbers of her worn decks were impregnated with the spirit of colorful wandering. What a grand ship she was! After twenty years, one learns to sense the atmosphere of ships when first putting a foot over their rails: one glance, and I knew this was a happy, well-run ship, though she reeked of fish-oil and no one on board knew where she was bound. It seemed to me that these Arabs and their ships, outmoded as they are and hopeless by every standard of our frantic world, have a delight in living we do not even know we lack. I came aboard with pleasure and looked about me with pride, for this was a ship beyond a doubt, and I was glad that I should be privileged to sail with her. My six feet of the navigators' bench aft looked very good to me, under a double awning of Indian duck (which never again was bent), and the stalwart crew went about their duties alert and cheery.

As for where exactly the *Triumph of Righteousness* might be going, I must confess that I did not quite know: but that could wait. It did not matter. She was off on the old round of the argosies of Araby, and it was enough for me that such a trade and such voyaging should still survive, and I should have the chance to see it.

Nejdi, dressed in a loose linen gown and headcloth of white and gold, with a white abba thrown carelessly over his shoulders, met us at the gang-way. His cloak was a handsome garment of white camel hair, with cloth of gold and gold-wire embellishments at lapels and cuffs, and along both arms. It was gathered across his chest by two golden tassels, loosely knot-ted, and his prayer-beads swung in his right hand. Beside him stood his younger brother Abdulla, petty officer in the boom. Abdulla was a pleas-ant-faced young man whose countenance also showed the ravages of smallpox, which must be common in Kuwait. Behind these stood the muallim, or mate, who was introduced as Hamed bin Salim. Hamed was taller than the others, and had a very black chin-point beard, so per-fectly geometrical that it looked as if it had been cut out and pasted on.

There was to be a dance in our honor, and the ship was spick and span. Both the poop and maindeck were shaded by large awnings, and Persian carpets in flowery reds and blues were spread about. The naviga-tors' bench aft was especially ornate, with heavy carpets and large num-bers of reclining cushions and leaning pillows, and a Beduin camel sad-dle or two which Nejdi was taking for sale to a curio dealer whose busi-ness was with tourists in Zanzibar. Here we reclined in easy state, the Arab guests barefoot and sucking at large hookahs made from Basra earth-enware, while refreshments of bitter coffee and too sweet tea were passed round endlessly, and the drums were warming for the dance. Sailors brought us trays of sherbet and sweetmeats, and figs and dates, all of which were very good. Nejdi, looking very dignified and very much the master of all in sight, smoked endlessly from a long hookah, while he listened courteously to the discourse of the merchant Ali and now and again softly murmured *Taiyib*, which means *good*, and signified his complete approval. These soft murmurings were interspersed by loud shouts for Yusuf, an ancient sailor in a long white gown with his face half hidden underneath a large, fierce moustache, and a fold of his headcloth over his left eye, like a visor. Yusuf seemed to act like the nakhoda's slave. Actually he was not a slave, and there were no slaves on board. His work appeared to be to replenish both the embers and the tobacco in Nejdi's hookah at frequent intervals, and to superintend the bringing of refreshments. I liked the look of Yusuf. He looked a good sailor, and a good sort.

We sat on the carpeted bench a long time, for the Arabs are never in a hurry. I looked at the animated, stirring scene all round me, with the fleet of big dhows at the crowded anchorage, among which were vessels from Kuwait, Sur, Muscat, the Trucial Coast, and the smaller ports of Persia. Nearest to us was a beautiful baggala from Kung, a port in southern Persia. The baggala was a stately galleon of a ship with a carved and quarter-galleried stern, and for the moment I regretted that I was not going out with her. Her sweet low bow sat in the water as smoothly and with as much effortless perfection as the head of a dolphin, and her windowed and galleried stern shimmered at her from its reflection in the clear waters of the bay. Several Suri sambuks, also very graceful, were moored right next to the baggala, and from them came an endless chanting and stamping of bare feet while their sailors took cargo on board. I looked with pleased interest at all this and the host of lesser ships, while I examined the swarthy skirted mariners who were to be my shipmates for perhaps the next half-year. They sat in dignified, stately line along the bulwarks on the starboard side, like a group of courtiers at a sheikh's council. Behind me the long yoke of the high rudder swung quietly on its chains, and the wheel kicked very softly, just enough to add animation to the general peace of the anchored ship. Overhead, the big oiled masts leaned into the blue sky: ashore the pock-marked mountains of Aden looked better, seen from the sea, and Ma'alla Bay took on more of its proper aspect of Eudæmon Arabia, that "village by the shore," market place for frankincense from the Hadhramaut, and all the spices and cloths of India. No odor of incense arose from it now, and the only cloths I saw had been mass-manufactured in Japan. But the same old water lapped quietly at the teak planks of much the same type of ship; the same swarthy mariners strode her decks and squatted on her poop, with very much the same methods and the same ideas as all their seagoing ancestors for so long before them.

The music began as I mused, and its discord brought me back to the present with a jar. We rose, and climbed down to the maindeck by way of the carved companion on the port side. The maindeck was also spread with carpets, and Yusuf fussed about to see that all were straight and everything was in order. The narrow, wedge-shaped main hatch, from the fore part of which the great mainmast rose, had been transformed into another reclining bench, with carpets and cushions. Here we sat while the sailors danced. The musician was a large Arab with fierce eyes and a big black moustache, who played a guitar which looked as if it might have come from Europe. (I learned later that it had been bought in Basra.) He probably played very well, according to Arab ideas of music, but unfortunately those ideas were not mine, and he made matters worse by singing endlessly in an unnatural, rasping voice. Whatever it was he sang, it seemed excellent to his listeners, but I could have done without it. Ali whispered to me that he was a famous singer from Kuwait, but even this advertisement of his fame did not make his singing any more bearable. I hoped he was not part of the permanent equipment of the vessel. They said his name was Ismael. I was glad to see the sailors and a little man who looked like a cook come along with tiny drums, which were made from cylindrical pieces of Basra pottery, across one end of which had been stretched warmed kid's skin. There were about six of these drums, and also some large tambourines. The sailors took turns at beating them, with their thumbs and forefingers, which they used with an excellent sense of rhythm. I liked the drums, for they had a pleasing low note, and they helped to subdue Ismael's music.

Now and again, sailors rose to their feet and danced in couples, shuffling along the carpet side by side. It was not very interesting dancing and I am afraid its meaning, if it had any, was lost on me. But to them it was great fun, and they all enjoyed it. They appeared to take more pleasure in it than I had ever seen at any formal European dancing, but I was unable to make head or tail out of it. I confess that as a rule ballet is lost on me; but I was able to understand much of the Balinese dancing, and a Fourteenth of July celebration at Tahiti, with its wonderful dance competitions, had been a treat. Even the Solomon Islanders had been able to express something reasonably intelligible in their dancing, but this Arab shuffling seemed quite meaningless. However, this it could not have been. Perhaps the boom's sailors were performing very badly. If they were, I never saw better.

Nejdi himself danced later, and the antics he performed were to me equally unintelligible. He danced with Abdulla Kitami, youthful nakhoda of another Kuwait boom moored close by. They, too, shuffled barefoot over the carpet, ranging fore and aft, keeping time with the moustachioed ruffian's music. Though a little more graceful, their dancing differed little from the sailors'. They kept the most solemn countenances, and their silken skirts swished as they shuffled to and fro. An important part of the performance seemed to consist of cracking their fingers, which they did with a very loud noise, in time with the music. They walked backwards and forwards hand in hand along the carpet, while Ismael's black fingers tortured the strings and his cracked voice wailed. Each time as they approached the musician they stopped a second or so before him, and cracked their fingers. Sometimes they agitated their bellies and their whole bodies up to the shoulders somewhat in the manner of a Moroccan dancing girl. Then again they would shuffle off along the carpet, eyes down and brown feet slithering, their swarthy faces dull masks covering whatever emotion they might have been expressing. As the music quickened and the performance dragged on I found myself looking out over the masts of vessels at the anchorage—they sometimes stopped and violently agitated their whole bodies. Then they would leap suddenly in the air, turn about, and walk away again. It was a curious business, and I wondered why they did it: but perhaps any other form of dancing would be unsuitable in that climate.

Sometimes the singing sailors, unable to contain themselves at some particularly moving stanza from the moaning singer, would leap up and form in formation behind the two nakhodas, while they cracked their fingers and trembled violently. With a final whoop of joy they would leap high, turn about in the air, and then go off to their places by the bulwarks again, laughing heartily. They were like a lot of merry boys. There was indeed a grand spirit of jollity about the affair which could not but be infectious, and when they all sang sea songs together, it was quite pleasant. But I felt that I should enjoy the coming voyage without either the music or the dancing.

All this time the ship's carpenter, a young man with a close-clipped black moustache, had been banging and hammering at the ribs of a new dhow in course of construction over the whole of the port side of the main deck. It was a large dhow, at least thirty-five feet long, and as beamy as half the deck would allow. Ali whispered that it was being built for sale in Africa. He whispered other things to me, in the brief intervals of quiet, for Ali was in a communicative mood that day. Knowing the rareness of communicative moods in Arabs, I listened carefully, but all I learned was the regrettable fact that Ismael was part of the permanent crew of the vessel. At that my heart sank: but perhaps he would put his guitar away when the ship was at sea, or I could buy a large drum.

In many ways the *Triumph of Righteousness* was an improvement on the *Sheikh Mansur*. There was a deck to walk on, which was a blessing. It was crowded with all sorts of things, from the ribs of the building dhow to the cook's firebox and the wooden water-tanks, but it was roomy enough. The poop, too, was crowded, for all the sailors' chests were there—rows and rows of them, ranged round both sides, with the head of an iron capstan peering out in some bewilderment on the port side. The *Triumph* boasted a real ship's wheel, of brassbound teak, a stylish brass binnacle, and a pair of quarter-davits for the cutter. In all else she was just a big dhow with sharp ends. She also had a great cabin, as became a deepwaterman. It occupied most of the poop, but any romantic notions I may have had concerning this traditional sanctum of ancient ships were quickly dispelled by one whiff from it. It was nothing but a dark, cavernous, and cockroach-filled storeroom, in which the reek of old dried fish fought a losing battle with the general stench of fish-oil and foul bilgewater. There was not even head room, and only a child could stand beneath its beams. Off the after end of this alleged "cabin," right in the stern of the ship, were two very small enclosed rooms which were more hutches than cabins. These palatial quarters, said Ali airily, could be mine, but I doubted it. In the first place the statement was open to doubt on general principles, for I had early discovered that the Arabs are sometimes given to extravagant statements and promises more indicative of temporary good feeling than of any actual intention. In the second place, they were foul places, and I preferred the open air. They were jammed to the deckhead with malodorous stores in which the predominant note seemed to be old fish. No, I thought, I shall not be down here, even when Nejdi pointed out how excellent these spots would be for the working of navigation problems and the storage of navigational instruments, for he was eager that I should bring along my chronometer and sextant. I thought differently about that, too, for it was obvious that whatever I brought in that ship would not be worth taking away again, and chronometers are sensitive and expensive instruments. Besides, if he could navigate without them, I wanted to learn how he did it. As for navigation, it did not seem to be an important matter. Nejdi said he didn't need it really, for he was only going to Zanzibar and he knew the way.

Altogether I liked the *Triumph* very much, and arranged at once to ship with Nejdi in his boom. There were few formalities: I had only to be checked out through the local police station, at Ma'alla. There were no articles to sign, nor anything like that. If you wished to ship with the Arabs, apparently, you just brought your sleeping carpet on board, and your chest, and moved in, after the necessary preliminary arrangement with the nakhoda. That is, you did these things if you were an Arab your-self: without Ali Abdul-latif's help, I don't think I should have found it so easy to ship with Nejdi in his boom, for many of the older-fashioned Arabs are still suspicious of the Christian from a Europe which has never treated them very well. However, there it was: my passage was arranged, and the ship had only to sail.

We were rowed ashore in the longboat with the traditional Kuwait style, the twenty stalwart men at the long oars dressed in their best robes, and all chanting lustily. They rowed very well and their chants were better than their songs. When they were not chanting they made a queer kind of low throaty growling sound like the distant rumbling of a squadron of bombing airplanes. They rowed with ceremony, and the stern of the long-boat was gay with carpets. It was a dashing scene, as we came slowly through the fleet of anchored dhows bound toward Ma'alla pier: I liked the ceremony and the style about it. There was obviously a dash to life in these deep-sea dhows that was missing from the *Sheikh Mansur*, and from the little I had then seen of life in the *Triumph of Righteousness*, I looked forward to the coming voyage, wherever it might take her.

She had, I gathered, completed the discharge of Basra dates at Ber-bera and was now on the loading berth for trade for Africa, loading goods to offer for sale at ports along the Benadir, Swahili, and Zanzibar coasts —in other words, along the coasts of Italian Somaliland, Kenya, Tangan-yika, and Zanzibar. Nejdi recited a list of ports to which he vaguely an-nounced his intention of going if the conditions were good and Allah willed—places with mellifluous and romantic names like Haifun, Obbia, Athelet, Merka, Mogadishu, Kisimayu, Malindi, Mikindani, Kilwa Ki-sinje, and many others of which I had never heard. How many of these places she might actually visit, if indeed she went to any of them at all, no one seemed to know, for the *Triumph*, like all her kind, was bound on a trading voyage on her own account, and not on a scheduled passage with goods for a merchant. What she carried was for sale, to be got rid of in the best markets. She was loading salt, rice, sugar, canned milk, some coarse Indian corn, and other foodstuffs, and they expected to be ready for sea in a few days. Then she would sail along the coast of the Hadhramaut to complete her cargo with tobacco, ghee, honey, and dried shark, and per-haps—they said—also to take aboard a few passengers for Mogadishu and Mombasa. She would certainly call at Mukalla and Shihr; and per-haps also at Hami and Seihut, farther to the eastwards. It would be as Al-lah willed, and Allah indeed seemed to know as much about the coming voyage as Nejdi, or any one else on board. At any rate, she would finally arrive—Allah willing—at Zanzibar, and from there she would make her way back somehow to the Persian Gulf. Perhaps she would go on to some-where in Madagascar or the Seychelles Islands: perhaps she would run up to Malabar and load teak for Bahrein and Basra. Her future was pleas-ingly indefinite: she would go where there seemed most chance of earning profits. Somehow or other, she would probably eventually arrive back at her home port of Kuwait, in six months—perhaps more. It did not seem to matter.

If it did not matter to the Arabs, neither did it matter to me. I liked that kind of voyage. I had never been down the east coast of Africa, and this seemed a good way of seeing it. I was still a little weak from dys-entery in the Red Sea, but after the *Sheikh Mansur* the big *Triumph* seemed almost to promise comfort. The wooden tanks for fresh water were at least an improvement on Ahmed's rusty drum, and though cock-roaches scampered in the great cabin, there did not appear to be any plague of insects on deck. The *Triumph* would do.

At last the day came when she was to sail. Her sailing had been an-nounced three times before, now at last it was definite. My metal chest was on the poop among the teak chests of the sailors, and I was ready to go aboard. I joined the boom after nightfall on the eve of her sailing, going out in her cutter from the jetty at Steamer Point. In the boat were Nejdi and his fellow nakhoda and boon companion, Abdulla Kitami, who had been his partner at the dance on the Sunday. Halfway across the harbor, the pair announced that they were not going to take their ships to sea. Nejdi said quite casually, as if it were the ordinary conduct of an Arab shipmaster, that he was going with Abdulla Kitami to Mukalla in one of Mr. Besse's small motorships, and the muallim would sail the dhow. I thought at first that this was strange procedure, but I learned later that it was normal. Several Kuwait and Suri dhows had already sailed for Mukalla, and the only way that Nejdi and Abdulla Kitami could steal a march on them was by this unorthodox means of going there by steam. Apparently competition for cargoes and passengers from the Hadhramaut ports was keen. A nakhoda in addition to sailing his ship had to be her agent, and collect her cargo and passengers besides. Indeed, the sailing of the ship on a comparatively simple passage such as the beat from Aden towards Mukalla was a minor matter which could safely be left to the mate. Mates, I gathered, were carried for that purpose. Hamed bin Salim in the *Triumph* was well able to take that noble vessel as far as Mukalla (or anywhere else), and an ex-slave of the Kitami family would have charge of Abdulla's boom.

With Nejdi and Abdulla Kitami safe aboard their steamer, whose comforts I did not envy them, the cutter pulled over to the place where the *Triumph* lay, a picture of sail-born majesty beneath the stars. She looked picturesque and almost incredibly romantic, fleet and deep and heavy-laden, with the tracery of her darkened masts high against the stars. The beating of drums and tomtoms and the stamp of dancing feet added a note of wild rhythm. There were lights aboard, as I came over the side, and I heard the sailors softly singing as they hurried at their work of bending the huge mainsail and getting ready for sea. Barefoot, their long shirts tucked about their waists and headcloths turned back, the big crew were working methodically, rapidly, going about the multifarious tasks of getting the ship ready for sea. This was different from the *Sheikh Mansur*, which was never readier for sea than Allah found her. Her preparations for departure usually took about five minutes. In this big ship there was much to do—gear to be rove off properly and set up in its place, the cutter to be hoisted to the quarter-davits, and the heavy longboat to be stowed on the starboard side of the maindeck, one of the anchors to be taken up and the other hove short, the huge mainsail to be bent along the whole length of the enormous lateen yard, and then, when all else was done, the yard itself to be mastheaded with the sail secured to it lightly by stops. This job alone took an hour, despite the fact that a longboat full of sailors from the Kitami boom came to help, and there were forty men sweating at those halliards. It was heavy, brutal work. They stopped frequently to dance and sing, stamping the deck rhythmically with their great bare feet and clapping their tremendous hands so that the handclaps rang through the harbor, and the serang banged an Indian drum. This dancing was good, far better than the formless shuffling of the Sunday's performance, and it seemed to act as a tonic for them, reviving the sailors for their heavy tasks. They did nothing without a preliminary dance, and they kept up a melodic chanting all the while they worked.

On the poop stood Hamed the muallim, an upright and very dignified figure in cloak and gown, with his large head bound in the folds of his headcloth so that only the eyes and the great nose showed. I had scarcely met Hamed before this, for he was a quiet man who said nothing when Nejdi was on board: now he gave orders, very quietly, from time to time, and the work proceeded. He was a picturesque figure standing on the poop barefoot in his gold-flecked robes, much, one supposes, as ten thousand Arab shipmasters might have stood upon the poops of their baggalas and booms in Eudæmon Arabia from time immemorial, setting out on voyages towards Sofala, Ophir, or Zanzibar. Hamed greeted me quietly, motioned me to a place on the bench aft, and sent Yusuf Shirazi to help me stow my gear. But I was in no mood to stow gear and Yusuf Shirazi had other employments. I wanted to watch that scene. The night had a bright moon, and the other laden booms at anchor beating their drums and playing their string instruments made the scene a stirring one. Even the harsh outlines of Aden's burned hills were softened beneath the moon so that all the background of bay and mountain seemed perfect setting for this departure of the deep-sea dhows for Zanzibar. The boom's high masts and great lateen yard, when it had been hoisted, seemed to reach to the lower stars. The rudder kicked softly on its pintles, and from the binnacle came the low glow of a colza-oil lamp, ready for use when the tide turned.

We came out from Ma'alla Bay with a breath of land air before three in the morning, and at daybreak were outside Aden. Behind us was the Kitami boom, and ahead a Persian baggala. The quartermaster seated cross-legged at his seat by the wheel was holding her with a spoke this way and a spoke that, and Hamed bin Salim watched alert and tireless squatting on the bench behind him.

Chapter 2

IN THE "TRIUMPH OF
RIGHTEOUSNESS"

IT WAS the first week in December when we sailed from Aden, and the northeast monsoon was blowing very quietly. This was the wind which was to take us down to Africa. It would blow until the end of March or early April, by which time we should be down at Zanzibar or along the Tanganyika or Portuguese East African coasts, wherever we were bound. From there, the beginning of the southwest monsoon would bring us home again. We must not wait for the change of monsoon to set in, but begin the passage north in the transition period. For the time being, the northeast wind was ahead, and we had to fight for the first five hundred miles. After that it would be all plain sailing. I did not mind the head wind or the length of the passage to our first port, for life in the big dhow soon proved most interesting and I had much to learn. I established myself on my six feet of the bench aft, on the starboard side, and proceeded to learn as much as possible.

My place on the bench was a good one, at the feet of the nakhoda. The bench there was about two and a half feet wide, which was room enough, and I had a carpet to sleep on. There was only the smallest protective railing to keep us aboard as the vessel rolled, but she did not roll much. At any rate at that stage of the voyage I never fell overboard, and I slept there at night for six months. The helmsman sat cross-legged on his stool beside me and steered sitting down. I had only to look across to peer into the binnacle and see he kept a good course, and a glance aloft showed me how things were with the sails. From my vantage post I could watch all that went on on board, except beneath the poop. I could watch the cook at his firebox forward, and the carpenter on his dhow; I could see the fresh water-tanks, the longboat, stowed on the starboard side, the main hatch. The reclining bench was protected by an awning which gave it shade enough, though Hamed had a rooted objection to spreading the awning any more than was strictly necessary. He preferred to be in the open, for he felt the wind better that way. Unfortunately we also felt the sun.

It was not unpleasantly hot, out in the open sea. After Aden it was quite mild. I gave up those early days to learning as much as I could, for, even after a month in the Red Sea, this was a strange kind of seafaring. Life went on smoothly in the big dhow, and we beat slowly to windward day after day. Hamed bin Salim, Abdulla Nejdi, and the rest seemed to accept me very well, and I settled into the ship's life easily. I had little to do. There was no navigation. There was almost as complete an absence of ordinary routine as there had been in the *Sheikh Mansur*. We trailed no patent log, kept no journal, struck no bells, had no musters, did no boat drills. There were no formal reliefs of the watch on deck. There was no formal going below. How could there be, when there was no "below" to go to? All hands lived on deck, and so they were always available. Time was of even less consequence than it had been in the Red Sea, for after all the little *Sheikh Mansur* had to make many voyages in a year. The big *Triumph*, I gathered, was satisfied with one. When a whole year did not matter, days were of no consequence whatever. I found this timeless, untroubled state very pleasant to live in, and soon I did not care what day it was, either. I kept myself busy looking after the health of the crew, and learning. I had a few medicines and some simple dressings with me, and some of the sailors had badly ulcerated legs.

In addition to this medical work, I learned all I could of the Arabic names of the sails and the gear, and the orders in the various maneuvers. Trying to learn Arabic in this way was not easy. I had a few books with me but these were in Syrian and Egyptian Arabic, which did not always agree with the language used by the sailors. I had crammed all the lessons I could from a spectacled sheikh in Aden, but the most helpful expression I had learned from him was the Arabic manner of saying "What do you call that?" I followed Hamed bin Salim, Abdulla Nejdi, Yusuf Shirazi, and the quartermasters declaiming this useful phrase until they were heartily sick of both it and me, but they always gave me some answer. Unfortunately the answers often did not tally and were sometimes incorrect. Learning Arabic was hard, and the Arabs made it no easier. But I soon reached the stage where I could communicate with the sailors and at least learn something from them, for, fortunately for me, the maritime idiom, as in most other languages, seems more simple than the speech of the land. As for the Yemenite Arabic I had acquired in Ahmed's little zarook, this was worse than useless, for I found after six months in the *Triumph* that some of the Yemenite words I had been using all that time were mistaken by the Kuwaiti for English. Expressions I had thought Arabic, they had acquired from me and used as English!

The sailors used many Swahili, Hindustani, and Persian words, all of which are more simple than Arabic, and their daily language also included some curious distortions of English. If for instance they wished to indicate that they were in a great hurry, they used to shout loudly "Fullspit, fullspit!" which I suppose meant full speed ahead, and they referred to their boom, which was alleged to be very fast, as "fes'mail," after the fast mail liners of the Persian Gulf. Abdulla Nejdi wished to learn English, and I exchanged lessons with him twice daily. I taught him English and he taught me Arabic, but both the teaching and the learning were far from easy. After a week I decided it was even more difficult to teach him English than for me to learn Arabic from him, for if I asked him, in my version of maritime Arabic, what he called this thing or that, he would give me the answer in his version of non-maritime English, and it was often several days before I realized that he had imagined he was using an English word. It was better to learn the language as a child does, in the language itself and not by translation. Nobody spoke any English. Abdulla might have had twenty words by the time I left, and he could count up to seven. Old Yusuf Shirazi could say "dammit bloodie buggah!" which he did frequently, with gusto. He said he had been called that in India.

If learning Arabic was a slow process it certainly gave me a full-time occupation. I was soon on terms of friendship with Abdulla, the carpenter, and old Yusuf Shirazi, but it was some time before I knew the names of all the sailors, or could tell them apart. In those early days, at least half of them seemed to be called Mohamed and the other half Abdulla, though I learned later that really there were only five Mohameds among the twenty-seven of them, and three Abdullas. The trouble was there were so many names that sounded to my untrained ears like Mohamed—Hamed, for instance, and Ahmed, and even Hamoud and Mahmoud. Yelled along the decks the way the Arabs yelled them, these names sounded much alike. It seemed to me that when they said Mohamed they barely

Nejdi

breathed the M, so that I thought they were saying Hamed. It was very confusing. If I wanted any one and old Yusuf was not about, I just shouted *"Mohamed,"* and let it go at that. Somebody always came. Indeed, generally half a dozen did. They usually included all the Abdullas.

Life was primitive enough and very much in the raw, but after the *Sheikh Mansur* the *Triumph* was like a palace. The possibility of taking exercise by walking on her decks was a great advantage, though the Arabs never did that and looked curiously at me when I paced up and down.

"You do not like our ship, O Nazarene?" old Hamed asked the third time he saw me doing this.

"Indeed I do like her, O Hamed muallim," I replied (or in words as near to that as I could manage): "Why do you think I should be unhappy here?"

"You pace like the lion. Your tread is of the caged beast," he answered. "If you were happy, O Nazarene, you would be still."

It was useless to argue that I walked only for exercise. Exercise? They had never heard of the word. None of my books gave any Arabic equivalent for that: I gave up the attempt to explain, and sat down. Sometimes I helped the sailors at the heavy work of shifting over the yard and the mainsail, or hoisting the yard when it had been lowered for some reason, but this was exercise too much in that hot sea, and their pace was killing. Sometimes there was sailmaking to do, and I helped with that, though they said I sewed the seams too well and made them too strong. They sewed them badly themselves, deliberately, with long, rambling stitches. At other times we made rope, using Indian coconut fiber.

We beat along, bound towards Mukalla. At first the ship made long tacks, over towards the coast of British Somaliland, and one day Hamed pointed me out the landmarks of Berbera. Later, as we made easting, we kept the Arab shore and ghosted along by the land. It was better that way, according to Hamed, who should have known, for this was his twenty-fifth time round those parts. Outside in the Gulf of Aden, he explained, there was still a heavy set towards the west. By keeping close inshore, he could avoid the worst of it and sometimes, if we were very lucky, pick up the advantage of a counter-set towards the east. Hamed knew all the tricks of the sailing trade. It was safe enough, close inshore, for that coast is comparatively free of dangers. We wandered along very pleasantly in the days of azure sun and gentle breezes, and if our progress was not all it might have been, nobody minded. I am sure I did not, for it was a peaceful life. One of the most striking things about that big Arab ship was the sense of peace and well-being which pervaded her.

We wore ship twice a day, usually, ate three meals, prayed the stipulated five times (at least the Arabs did), and minded our own business. We always wore round when going on the other tack, instead of tacking, for the lateen sail is dangerous if taken aback. The huge mainmast was supported largely by its own strength. As in all Arab ships, there was no standing rigging. Its only supports were some movable tackles, always set up to windward and let go when the ship was being put about. The main halliards, which led aft, acted as a backstay. So we always wore her round, running off with the wind behind the sail, and swinging the huge yard when she was dead before the wind. Whenever the sailors did this I watched most carefully, for it was a complicated and difficult process. The whole sail was thrown over, the sheet and the tack changing end for end, and the maneuver had to be done carefully when there was anything of a wind lest the sail take charge. But she was a handy ship and a very responsive one, for all the unwieldiness of the huge mainsail, and her crew certainly knew their business.

I soon discovered that I was not the only extraneous person on board, for when we were well out at sea two mysterious Arabs turned up from somewhere. Where they had been hidden I do not know and did not ask, for questions were not encouraged. To me, they were very odd Arabs, of a tribe obviously different from the Kuwaiti. One looked like a Suri, but the other I could not place. With them was a small boy, who appeared to be the servant of one of them. They were a strange pair, but I was the only person who seemed surprised by their sudden arrival. All the rest took it as a matter of course, and I resolved early that whatever happened on board that boom, I should never show surprise. I wondered who might appear next when this bearded gowned pair suddenly came up on the poop on the second day at sea: but no one else did. One of them was a wizened little man with a sly face and a chinstrap beard. He was a wily little devil with a shrewd, calculating expression in his slits of eyes. He carried a silver box of mascara which he applied to his eyelids twice daily, and in the folds of his pink turban was a tooth-stick with which he scrubbed his mouth every time he prayed. His beard was dyed with henna, in spots, and I saw him also applying henna to his toenails, fingernails, and the soles of his calloused feet. He was probably about fifty years old, and all I could find out about him then was that he was a merchant. What he dealt in I did not then know, but I was to find out later. He was a dealer in

Bow of a boom

hashish and haberdashery, a venturer ready for whatever turned up, a veritable modern Sinbad setting off with his pack. His name was Said— Said the Suri, though he said he came from farther up the coast of Oman and not from Sur.

The other was a very much younger man. He came marching up on the poop with imperious tread and had the look of a desert warrior in his fine eyes. He greeted Hamed, paid no attention to me, and proceeded to stow a large sword, a leather shield, and an elaborate dagger in the space behind my chest. This martial equipment intrigued me and I should have liked to ask him something about it, but I held my peace. What it was for, if anything, I should discover in due course. I was beginning to think that if I stayed in that ship long enough I might find out lots of things. He was dressed in a yellow gown, shorter than those the Kuwaiti wore, collarless, and gathered at the neck with a touch of red embroidery. He wore a silver dagger, lashed about his waist on a gold-embellished belt which also bore a silver purse. On his head was a cream turban, very large, wrapped loosely and held in position by a light headrope of black silk.

On the end of this headrope dangled his tooth-stick, and this, with his arms, seemed to comprise the whole of his luggage.

The pair settled down at once as if they had been living in the ship all their lives, and from that time onwards they were as much her fixtures as the mizzenmast. They joined in the officers' mess on the poop, and when there were all-hands jobs such as going about, they helped with the lighter labor. They were a queer pair. The small boy with them, too, interested me. He was more communicative than they were. His name was Mohamed, and he was a cheerful youth aged perhaps eight. He was dressed always in the same ragged shirt and even more ragged turban. He had no other clothes and no belongings, not even a tooth-stick. He worked for Said, he told me—it took about a week to get the information —for the passage to Africa, and his food. The ship gave him his food, and in return he worked for the officers and the sailors.

In the ports he worked for Said. On board he worked for the ship, as nakhoda's and sailors' servant. He did not know his father's name or where he was born, but it was somewhere on the Gulf of Oman. He had been wandering in ships since he was three, for boys begin their sea ca-

The Triumph of Righteousness

reers from Sur and Oman and the Trucial Coast incredibly young. Before he was three—as far as he remembered—he had been a beachcomber. This may seem almost unbelievable, but I was assured that it was probably so. Mohamed must have been tough. He was a wiry little fellow with a huge mouth and merry big eyes, and a very cheerful disposition. He had come to Aden as one of the crew of a Suri baggala. Meeting Said there (and Said being on the lookout for just such a youth), he left the baggala without the formality of asking for permission, and here he was going to Africa as if he were out for an afternoon's sailing. He had been to Zanzibar before, he said: this time he hoped to stay there, for he thought it a better place than Arabia.

Mohamed had no schooling and could neither read nor write. On board, he tended Said's hookah, and ran errands fore and aft, bringing the sailors things from their chests, and holding the water-jar for the hand-washing and mouth-rinsing at the daily meals. He slept coiled up behind a bag of rice underneath the poop, and he seemed extremely happy. What he did to help Said ashore I was to learn later.

The *Triumph of Righteousness* was altogether an extraordinary ship. The old interesting cargoes of former days in this trade have now long departed, and we carried no romantic frankincense and myrrh. Instead, we had salt, rice, sugar, coffee, cotton stuffs, and some old dates. In the smaller ports of the Hadhramaut we would complete our cargo with some ghee and dried fish, and perhaps some cooking-stones to sell in Kenya. In addition to the ship's goods, the nakhoda, Hamed, Abdulla the nakhoda's younger brother, the serang, the quartermasters, the cook, and all the crew had goods of their own. Each member of the crew, apparently, was allowed to bring one chest of goods, and the nakhoda had to advance them sufficient rupees—ten or twenty or so—to buy their stocks at Aden. They kept their chests on the poop, ranged in two rows along both sides, and one of their principal occupations, when there was no work afoot, was to come up on the poop and admire the haberdashery in each other's chests. Some of them had clubbed together to buy large bottles of French perfumes of the less expensive kinds, and they spent many hours painstakingly blending these and pouring the blend into tiny bottles. All sorts of queer things happened there on the *Triumph*'s poop, which sometimes looked more like a store. They had turbans of all kinds and gay rags galore, and some of them had gone in for fancy things like cheap Japanese thermos flasks, flashlamps, and safety razors. Anything they could sell to the Somalis of the Benadir coast or the Swahili down Zanzibar way they had brought along; I suspected that they proposed to pay duty on none of it. Well, I wished them luck: the crew were nearly all married men, back in Kuwait, and their share in the boom's earnings would never amount to much. There cannot be any fortune in selling salt.

In addition to the ship's own goods and the crew's ventures, and the two Sinbads we had along, I gathered that we should soon have a number of passengers. How many? I asked, not expecting to be told but hoping to be able at least to form some rough idea. Very many, said Hamed; the number would depend upon the degree of success met with by Nejdi. Nejdi had been in Mukalla a week already by that time; perhaps, Hamed said, he had already rounded up a hundred or so. A hundred or so! I exclaimed: where on earth could they be stowed? But Hamed said he hoped to embark a whole tribe. I looked about the ship in astonishment and for the life of me could see no place where we could stow a tribe. There was no accommodation anywhere. The poop was full of chests, the maindeck filled with boats, the hold full of cargo. It was a fact that the sailors seemed to be able to sleep in surprisingly little space, the whole lot coiling themselves down somewhere round the cook's firebox and round the bole of the mainmast in space that might with difficulty have accommodated six sheep. But a whole tribe! Hamed offered no further explanation and seemed indeed to regard any discussion of the subject as quite out of place and even foolish, for the Arabs always believed in allowing the future to take care of itself. He added only that Allah was invariably merciful, leaving me to place my own interpretation on this cryptic statement. Whether he meant that Allah in His mercy would provide the tribe, or that the tribe having been provided would need all Allah's mercy to survive, I did not know. After a few days, the subject not having been raised again, I put these rumors about a tribe down to Arab exaggeration. But in that I was wrong.

All this time our carpenter had continued banging away at his new dhow. A skilful and energetic young man, he seemed to be carried only as boatbuilder. He did little or no carpentry about the ship, which was left largely to look after herself. (Being comparatively new, she was sound and her woodwork was in order.) She was massively built and she had ribs enough—all of them the bent limbs of great trees in their natural state— almost to keep out the sea without any planking on them. This I know to be exaggeration, but the Arab gives his ships plenty of good ribs and puts them together solidly. It is in the fastenings that he falls short, for these are nothing but soft iron spikes. From before sunrise until after sunset every day, the carpenter banged away at his dhow. He had a large supply of natural ribs for her, some trunks of indifferent teak which he sawed lengthwise for planking, a furious energy, and very few tools. He built the dhow purely from his head. If you wanted him to build you a ship, apparently, you just told him to build you one with a capacity for so-and-so many packages of dates. He knew no other measurements. You told him the number of packages of dates, and the type of ship you preferred—sambuk, belem, jalboot, shewee*—and he went ahead. All were much the same: minor hull differences marked the type. The rigging was the same. The four types differed about as much, say, as four cutters of roughly the same size, from four different builders' yards. They all had much the same sailing qualities. Jalboots had straight cutwaters, belems were double-enders, small sambuks and shewees were graceful little things, very similar except that the stempost of a sambuk differed slightly from that of a shewee. He could make any of them. He could also turn out a small boom, if you wished, though booms were rarely made of less capacity than four or five hundred packages of dates. The dhow he was building at that time—she was a jalboot, with a straight stem—could stow perhaps 150 packages.

The tool he used most was the adze. His big bare feet were his only vice, and the adze and the Indian drill his customary tools. If he had been put in shoes he would have had to give up shipbuilding. He had also some small saws, and a kind of rough plane. He had built our cutter earlier on the voyage, on the way from Basra to Mukalla via Muscat. This also was for sale. Indeed, I gathered that all our boats were for sale. There was nothing the Arabs would not sell, if opportunity offered. Hamed said they would be glad to dispose of the *Triumph* herself at Zanzibar or anywhere else she might bring a profit, for they could then all come home in other Kuwait ships, and there would be no question of expensive repatriation. Any Kuwait ship, apparently, would always carry any sailors or even whole crews from other Kuwait ships which had been sold, or lost. It was obvious to me even in those early days, that the Kuwaiti were spared a great many of the problems which bother European masters and shipowners. But, to offset this, they had their own.

We had four boats at that stage of the voyage. According to Hamed, we should be fortunate if we returned with one.

On several days when the wind was light, we drifted close to other

* For descriptions of these types, see Appendix.

African-bound dhows which had sailed from Ma'alla the same day as ourselves. The Arabs, if they can manage it, like to sail in twos and threes, particularly along their own coasts. They do this partly for company, and partly for protection. We were often in company with Abdulla Kitami's small boom and a Persian baggala. When it was calm, we could hear clearly the sound of their carpenters banging away, too, busily building small dhows for sale in Africa. The business of building small dhows in big dhows, I gathered, is a very ancient one. The Kuwaiti have the name of being particularly good builders, and they are able to bring new craft to places like Lamu and sell them there more cheaply than the local Arabs, Swahili, and Bajun can construct them. The price to be asked for our new dhow was a thousand shillings. The cutter might go for three hundred.

The carpenter was the only man on board who worked consistently through the day, but the cook also worked hard. Hamed, our acting-master, spent much of his time reclining on the bench aft, though he rarely lay on it. Most of the day he sat hunched up there, watching or reading the Quran, and at night he squatted in his cloak with his great nose sniffing the wind. He was very good with the ship, and an excellent judge of wind. I thought I had known something about ghosting vessels along in catspaws and doldrums conditions, after all those grain-ship voyages and coaxing the *Joesph Conrad* through the Sulu Sea, but Hamed seemed to begin where I left off. In conditions under which I could neither be sure that there was a breath of air stirring nor predict whence the next air might come, Hamed would get some progress out of the vessel. He was a pastmaster at this sort of sailing, and he had no mercy on himself or the crew. For the slightest change or the most fleeting breath of air, he trimmed that huge lateen sail. Hamed showed himself a splendid sailorman, and though at that early stage I could not appreciate all the moves he made (and indeed wondered about some of them) later I learned to appreciate him as a very fine sailorman indeed.

So we ghosted on, sometimes with a breeze, sometimes without, treated to grand views of the South Arabian shore line and always able to watch the Kitami boom and the baggala with which we sailed in company. Life on board them went on very much as it did aboard ourselves: at least once a day we somehow managed to be close enough to one of them for a yarn, during which the masters, mates, and crews of the vessels conversed quietly across the few yards of intervening sea and now and again borrowed things from one another. We heard their muezzins, morning after morning, give the call to prayer: there used to be a kind of race between the three announcers. Ours was a sailor named Sultan, whose father had been a slave in Kuwait: every morning at the first graying of the eastern sky Sultan would mount to a high place in the vessel and, clapping his right hand to his right ear and his left forefinger to his left cheekbone (what effect this had I never discovered, but he always did exactly the same things) he would begin loudly with the call to prayer. To this pre-dawn cry he always added something about prayer being better than sleep, which I thought the sailors might question, for they frequently had a poor night's rest. They had no proper place to sleep and no bedding: they coiled up on deck, and seemed able to drop off to sleep at will. Whenever there was nothing else to do they slept, but they followed a regular routine of work. They had none too much rest. They slept in their clothes with their headcloths round them: but at the slightest call they were up like runners at the starting gun.

They began the day with prayer. First ablutions, then prayer. The dawn prayer was not communal: each man prayed as best pleased him, having first washed hands and face and feet in water hauled up from the sea. They always stood facing the direction of Mecca, threw down their sarongs or headcloths on the deck before them—they were too poor to own praying-mats—stood silent a moment or two in meditation, putting from their minds all worldly thoughts, and then fell easily and rhythmically into the exercise and words of the set prayers. It was interesting to watch the changes which came over some of their faces. The lines would soften, the flash fade from imperious eyes, and whatever there might have been of arrogance, pride, vanity, would quite disappear. There was no hypocrisy in these strong faces which looked towards Mecca. It was obvious that their religion was a real and living thing. Their prayers were not simply a formula to be mouthed, but a form of real communion with a very real God. None of them prayed hurriedly: they always spent a few moments first in silent meditation, in this discard of their worldly thoughts. I watched them with some envious interest, for I did not find my own worldly thoughts so easy to dismiss. Some stood on the water tanks, some on the hatches, some even in the cutter which was carried outboard at the davits.

Jassim, the morose little cook, always prayed on the forecastle head, standing there a tiny worried figure in his sackcloth clothes, and praying hurriedly lest the unleavened bread should burn. For if the bread burned Jassim was in trouble. Jassim was often in trouble. Hamed bin

Salim always led the quartermasters and Abdulla, the nakhoda's brother, in prayer on the poop; Said and Abdulla, the passengers, usually joined them. Hamed was the most devout man on board and was known to be the best Muslim, a distinction which I gathered was not without importance, for it is good that a ship should have at least one devout worshipper of the first rank on board, better still that he should be in command. Not that Hamed was really in command: he was too quiet, too gentle-natured. He was only a stopgap for the turbulent Nejdi.

Prayers over, the morning meal was eaten. This was always the same —a piece of unleavened bread. On great occasions and feast days it might be flavored with a little sesame—which if it were fresh from the firebox was not bad but, if it were from the previous day, was generally soggy. This bread was called *khubz*. We washed it down with very sweet tea, served in tiny glasses. There was never anything else. All hands ate the same food, fore and aft, but there was no special service and the mats were not brought out. A little sailor, named Kederfi, brought up the tea in a tin kettle and poured it without ceremony into the tiny glasses, which were kept in a rough box beneath the helmsman's seat: Yusuf Shirazi handed round the unleavened bread. In a minute or two it was all over. The youngest sailors poured the tea for their elders. There were two young sailors about 18 years old: the average age of the crew I would judge to be about 23, but it was difficult to say, for many of them looked older than they were. Breakfast over, they did whatever work was necessary. There was always a working period of four or five hours for all hands in the early mornings. They dried the well first, if this was necessary. She leaked very little and the well required drying only once in three days. The bilgewater that came up from there was horribly foul, reeking dreadfully of bad dates and worse fish oil and all sorts of nameless malodorous things which were most repugnant. The men stood in two lines from the well to the bulwarks, one line handing out the filled buckets and the other handing back the empty ones.

The bailing done, the sailors went on to other work. There was never any cleaning. Sometimes one or two of the younger ones helped Jassim saw firewood or pound corn for the next day's bread. Others twisted strands of coir rope from Indian roping stuff, or sewed sail. Ropemaking was their most regular employment. They sat in large groups in the shadow of the sail, yarning quietly and twisting rope. They worked so pleasantly together and always seemed to get along so well that for some months I was never able to discover who was the serang, and at first won-

dered whether any one was in charge at all. There was no yelling, no bullying, no slave-driving. Those Arab sailors had long ago learned how to
work together in peace for the common good, and all necessary employment went on so calmly and smoothly in that vessel that I was three
months aboard before I was quite sure who was the serang. Then I found
that there were two serangs, one for each watch. I had never previously
been sure that there were watches, for how could I tell there was a watch
below when there was no "below" to go to, when all hands turned out,
apparently, for every job? There was no timekeeping, and no set routine. No one in the *Triumph* ever knew what day it was, and quite a few
of them did not even know what year. But they all knew very well that
Ramadhan was over—a fact for which I felt no little gratitude to Allah
myself, for Ramadhan in a devout Muslim community is a trial.

From the post-breakfast hour until the midday meal, all hands worked,
stopping only if it became necessary to trim the sail. Usually we sailed
only with the lateen main, but sometimes on a decent breeze Hamed also
set the mizzen. This was much smaller than the mainsail, and it possessed
so many disadvantages that I could scarcely see that it was useful at all. In
really light winds, Hamed said we could set two more sails, by rigging
out a light boom along the stemhead and hoisting a jib, and by rigging
the longboat's mast in front of the wheel and setting the longboat main
there as a sort of spanker. One day we saw that the Persian baggala had
done this, and she was going along very well. Later I noticed that the
Arabs and Persians could spread even a fifth sail in this lateen rig, by
sending up a kind of a gossamer ringtail topsail above the main. We never
did this ourselves.

Sometime between 10:30 and 11 o'clock we had our morning meal.
The time was never definite: it depended upon the nakhoda's whim. There
was a timepiece aboard, but it was only a very old Swiss watch of the
cheapest kind, large and decrepit, which was kept in a drawer in the helmsman's seat. From time to time—usually once a day—whoever was at the
wheel would take out this watch, which was invariably stopped, shake it
disgustedly, peer at it a long while, and announce the time. If shaken vigor-
ously, it would sometimes go for two or three minutes, and it had a tick
like an infernal machine. Our morning meal, which was always rice
boiled with some flavoring and spread with ghee, and a little fresh or dried
fish boiled in some outlandish curry, was set out on the mat on the poop
and eaten with proper decorum. We sat round the mat and ate with our
fingers, but there was a proper style to this. It was proper only to use the

tips of the fingers of the right hand, and they must not be permitted to touch the lips. One first picked up a morsel of fish, or whatever it was, and then, carefully using the finger-tips, gathered as much rice as one could manage—at least, that was what the Arabs did; I always went carefully on the rice—and then, making a neat ball of the whole, using mainly the fingers and thumb, deftly propelled the food into the mouth by a flick of the thumb. The Arabs could eat in this way without spilling any rice, without leaving any on their fingers, and without touching their lips with their hands. It took me some time to reach this stage of perfection, and I was never expert at it. But I did my best, for their mat-manners were very good and I had no wish to appear a boor. They did not make fun of me when I did badly. We each ate carefully from our places on the tray. It was, when one became accustomed to it, quite a dignified way of eating, and there was a great deal to be said for the absence of talk. It was considered most unseemly to chatter at a meal. You ate until you had done, and then rose quietly and left. Nobody spoke.

There were three messes, but all had exactly the same food and the same quantities of it. There were two messes on the maindeck, consisting of the sailors and the two serangs, and Hamed, the nakhoda's brother (who sometimes worked as a quartermaster but often did nothing at all), the quartermasters, Kaleel the carpenter, and our two Sinbad passengers ate on the poop. The boy Mohamed held the water with which we washed our hands and rinsed our mouths. Eating was always in silence, fore and aft, as became so solemn and important an occasion, and it never wasted time. The whole meal, from the spreading of the mats until their removal, rarely took more than five minutes, and there were no dishes to clean. Our mat was spread on the poop abaft the mizzenmast, in the space between the rows of chests. The sailors' mats were spread wherever they wished to place them. If one did not have his fill, he could go from mess to mess cleaning up. There was always plenty. The only nourishment in these mounds of rice, it seemed to me, was in the ghee spread over them. This ghee was clarified goats' butter from the Hadhramaut, and though rank it probably helped to keep away the scurvy. There was very little fish.

The meal over, all hands sat about awhile. Those addicted to them puffed at their hookahs, which were made simply from Basra earthenware pots pierced with a hole for the hollow smoking reed, and the tobacco was placed on a little tin of embers from Jassim's fire. The sailors seemed to draw a great deal of enjoyment from these water-pipes, but the tobacco was very coarse and the taste of the burned cane reeds was enough to put me off, if not to make me ill. Most of the sailors used these pipes but very few owned them. They were always passed round while an ember glowed, the same drawing-reed doing service for as many men as could use it. This seemed unhygienic, but it did not bother them.

With the hookahs put away, and no catspaws coming, the men would drop off to sleep on deck in the shadow of the sail. Hamed slept, if he slept at all, always with one eye open, hunched up on the bench abaft the helmsman: near him was a tell-tale, a windvane in the form of a carved wooden bird with a feathered tail. These feathers quivered in anything of an air, and moved the bird. At the slightest movement of those feathers Hamed was up. The Arabs seemed to be able to sleep soundly and lightly at the same time, and in this I envied them. They never slept for more than an hour after the morning meal. When they woke, it was time for the midday prayer—more ablutions, always thoroughly performed in water drawn up from the sea, more bending towards Mecca, more mellifluous intonations of the formal prayers which no matter how often I heard them always sounded well. Prayers over—and they did not take long—it was usual for the sailors to work again, though they did not work so hard in the afternoons as they did in the mornings, and if there was no work requiring urgent attention, they did not look for any. Sometimes, if it was really hot or if they had to put the ship round now and again, they did not work again in the afternoon until about four o'clock, when they would work for an hour or so. Sometimes if the big sail were damaged and had to be lowered, repaired, and set again, they worked hard all day. The carpenter worked hard all day, always, in port and at sea. The Muslim sabbath, Friday, was never observed at sea: there was no weekly day of rest.

Prayers came again in midafternoon, announced as always by Sultan the muezzin. These prayers were individual and never led. At sunset, with the dipping of the last of the sun in the sea, there was a fourth call to prayer. This and the dawn prayers were really the main prayers of the day. The fourth prayer took about ten minutes, sometimes more: sometimes Hamed would offer up extra prayers. When this was over, we ate our evening meal, often just rice and ghee, and less often rice with dhall, a kind of fine Indian corn which was boiled with peppers or chilis. The sailors always enjoyed chilis, which were boiled, so long as we had them, with everything. The evening meal was over very quickly, before the last of the brief twilight had gone: this was the end of the day. Each sailor then came on the poop in his turn and greeted Hamed and all the others there, wishing them good evening, by name. Hamed replied to each by name, and they went down again to the maindeck. Later those of the first two night watches might gather round the bole of the mizzen-mast on the poop, and yarn there very quietly, passing the hookah round from mouth to mouth.

So the night would find us, drifting quietly under the moon, the ship a silent ghost of peace mirrored in the silvered darkness of the placid sea while the cloaked and hooded mariners puffed at their hookahs on the poop, and the quartermaster, the folds of his headcloth wrapped about him and his bare feet tucked in beneath his cloak, sat like a sphinx at the wheel keeping the big boom to something like her course. Behind him was Hamed, silent and watchful. We showed no lights. He never had any lights, except the weak light in the binnacle. There were lights on board but they were not trimmed, and in the six months I was on board they were never shown. I wondered why this was, for sometimes laden oil-tankers coming around from Bahrein and Abadan passed very closely to us. On such occasions Hamed always waited for them to change course and never, apparently, thought of showing his own lights. The steamers, he said, always kept good lookout, and Allah was kind. Visibility was always good. Hamed seemed to think that Allah would look after Arab dhows and the steamers could take care of themselves, and really it did seem to work that way.

The days in the big boom during the beat to Mukalla passed pleas-antly. I found the timelessness of things and the utter dismissal of the modern world very easy to become accustomed to. The only book on board was a copy of the Quran, in which Hamed, Abdulla the nak-hoda's brother, and the passengers often read. When he came to a good part Hamed would sometimes call a small group together and read aloud in a very pleasant and well-modulated voice, and they would discuss whatever they read for hours. They seemed to find perfect content in this book, and never tired of reading it. Sometimes one or other of them would chant chapters from the Quran, from memory. They were mostly a silent lot and were always quiet except when there was work afoot, when always a continuous chanting would go on. Sometimes there would not be a voice raised on those decks for hours. It was a new kind of sea-faring to me, and I was most astonished at the effortless smoothness of the ship's routine, the harmony of the big crew, and the pleasant agree-ment with which they worked together. They were all poor. They had

few clothes. Their chests held only the goods with which they were going to trade and they had no other possessions. They had nothing. After
a while I began to wonder whether it was not a very good idea to have
nothing.

This pleasant and most interesting life came to a sudden stop one day,
when we had been about a week at sea and I had well settled down. There
was an accident. What the details were I did not know then, and I do not
know now. At any rate, I was in it. Something, I believe, carried away
from aloft, and it must have struck me. How or why or where it carried
away I have no idea and questioning later did not clear up the mystery.
Questioning was not encouraged in the *Triumph of Righteousness* and
cleared up no mysteries. I asked only once. Allah is generous, Hamed
said. I hoped this meaning was that the accident might have been worse,
and that he did not intend to convey indirect gratitude to the All-Highest
for having struck down the infidel as a lesson to the Faithful in their
dhow. I am sure the first interpretation is the correct one, for Hamed was
not a narrow-minded man nor a fanatic. In any case, the accident happened. I don't remember anything about it, but it deprived me of my sight
for a week and gave me a bad limp for some months. The first thing I knew
was that I had bad pains in the head, and I was blind. I could not see anything, I did not know day from night. What kind of accidents have this
effect I did not know, for this was my first experience of the kind: it
was very unpleasant. I was lying somewhere in the interior of the ship, on
some sacking with a bag for a pillow. At first, I remember, I had some difficulty in believing that I could be blind, and thought it must be the darkness of the hold. My head ached and my eyes throbbed. Over me I could
hear and feel the fat rats run and cockroaches scamper, and the queer
creaking noises of the rolling ship sounded almost thunderous there. But
what worried me most was that the blindness might be permanent, for I
knew the danger of eye infections in Arab life. Blindness and semi-blind-
ness are common among the Arabs, and not thought of as serious disabili-
ties, but to me either would be disability enough. If I were blind, there
would be no use staying in the dhow. I could not observe what I could not
see.

The pain was so great that there must have been periods of delirium
and even unconsciousness: I can remember now only long periods of
ceaseless pain, followed by the most worrying nightmarish dreams. But in
my more conscious moments I was more troubled by the thought that I

might have to give up the voyage, than by any fear of permanent blindness. That would have been too sorry a blow from fate. Yet I wondered also whether, after all, it was reasonable to stay so long in a life where the risks one was compelled to run might be so great. I had thought myself inured to maritime hardship, merely because I had been a whaler in the Antarctic, and had been round Cape Horn once or twice. I learned better than that.

I found that I was in the great cabin—loathsome, frightful place. The stench was abominable, even after many days. There was no air. Rats scampered, and now and again I heard their noisy fighting among themselves. Fat, greasy cockroaches dropped from the deckhead, ran on my face, made a playground of my body. It was hot, foul and dreadful. The reek of nameless frightful things filled that fetid air, with behind all the putrid horror of decayed fish and the powerful tang of strong fish oil, and rotten bilgewater. I lay on sacking on top of some bales, with mysterious packages all round, which chafed me as the ship slowly labored. Now occasionally I tried to move, and pain racked me. I was not used to pain and did not take kindly to an experience so unintelligible and unintelligent. There was no getting rid of that burning in my eyes. My head felt as if it had been ploughed: sometimes I wished that was all that had been done to it. My eyes felt as if they had been taken out, rolled in cinders, and then put back again. My body felt as if I had some malignant fever. Days passed. The rancid reek of the frightful place was with me endlessly. My eyes could still not see. There was no air. The heat was worse than ever.

How long I was down there I did not know: it was at least a week. I knew the date of the last entry in my journal, but I did not know the date when I recovered. No one else knew what day it was, for no one on that ship at sea named days: they merely let them pass. Hamed guessed, but his guess was wrong. I never did discover the date till I reached Mukalla. Day followed day and night followed night, and I did not know one from the other. Sometimes the sound of the crew at work as they put the ship about came to me there; distantly in seeming dreams I heard the scamper of hurrying feet close overhead, the thrash of canvas, the cries of the sailors as they worked. Once I heard deep-throated chanting which went on an hour. Sometimes the sea water washed swiftly by and I could feel the ship's labor. At other times she stood upright, for there was then no movement in my couch, and beyond the hull the stilled sea gurgled. It was all quiet then, as if the crew had gone and I was left alone on board —alone with the rats and the frightful smells, the cockroaches and the other wretched things that scampered there. Sometimes it was rather bad.

But the days passed. Gradually the pain went down, even in my eyes. It was a heavenly relief at last slowly to feel my eyes trying to open, and to be able to look about the stinking loathsome den where I had lain, God knows how many days, and though I could not see properly or in true focus, I looked about me even at the smellsome casks and foul dried fish almost with affection, and wondered where it was the rats always ran. I saw the most enormous cockroaches scampering—well, not exactly scampering, for they were too sleek and fat and undisturbed to move with any such unleisurely speed. Rather they were scurvily ambling about the place, as if they owned it.

And there was old Yusuf—Yusuf Shirazi, Yusuf the old ruffian who had looked after me, Yusuf the grayhaired, tired old reprobate who seemed to combine the functions of leading hand, storekeeper, steward, and nakhoda's personal servant. If ever by any chance I needed him, Yusuf was not there, and if I did not need him he was never absent; if I ever slept he was sure to come and yell in my ear. There he was, the well-meaning blundering old ass, in sight again at last, squatting back on his horny heels, tired, and yet alert, and plaintive. Yusuf was there, with his horny feet planted across my pillow, such as it was, looking down at me out of his own tired eyes. Yusuf had looked after me well those days, and I regarded him now with some degree of affection. I had taken a liking to the gentle-faced old man from the start, though he did nothing to curry favor. He was a quiet old man born of a lowly Shiraz family in Kuwait, a Persian, reared in Arabia whither his parents had fled, indignant at some kingly decree against the faithful. Yusuf had obviously been bewildered when he was given the task of looking after an injured European, but he did his best. Three times a day he came down offering me delicacies I did not want, things such as pieces of the fatty tails of long dead Berbera sheep, and dishes of soggy dhall full of chilis and pickled lemons, and mounds of boiled rice smothered with Kuwait ghee. I wished the old chap would keep some of these things for himself, but that he would not. I talked with him sometimes, though this was difficult for we could converse only in broken Arabic. My Arabic was very broken and far from Arabic, and Yusuf's Persian, Swahili, and Hindustani were not much help. But he was a good old chap, and it was grand to be able to see him.

"Yusuf," I murmured, "get me out of here. Get me up on deck where there's some fresh air."

"But it's good down here," said Yusuf. (I understood that all right.

Taiyib hinna, taiyib hinna!—good here, good here! were his words.)

It did not seem so good to me and, after a while, with the help of Yusuf, a sailor named Zaid, who was a powerful Negro with shoulders three feet across and a figure any young athlete would have envied, Hamed bin Salim, and Said the mascaraed old Sinbad merchant, I struggled up the vertical ladder to the sweet fresh air on deck. How sweet that first breath was. My eyes were still misty and my head swam, but the air was heavenly. Dimly above me I could sense the shape of the swelling sail, for there was some wind, and the noises of the ship on her way through the sea had in them the ecstasy of music. I could see again: I was all right. I could stay in the dhow. The littered decks looked clear and clean and beautiful, in the shadow of the sail, and the brown crew looked like gowned young gods.

It was a long time before I could walk again properly, and in those awful days, cooped up in the great cabin, I had lost thirty pounds in weight. But now it was over, and I reflected that, if in the first week on board so serious an accident had overtaken me, by the law of averages that would probably be my share of mishaps for the voyage. So it proved. After that, I did not get much malaria even in the delta of the Rufiji, and my constitution thrived on water from Kenya's stagnant swamps. All hands, from Hamed bin Salim down, were very good to me while I was ill. It was embarrassing to be so lamed and to have such difficulty in getting about, even after the blindness had gone: but the mariners did not seem to mind having a cripple foisted on them. They helped me always, any who were near: old Yusuf always was ready. I lay on a carpet on my place on the transom bench, and night and morning as the sailors came aft with their greetings each of them would gently add something about the mercy of Allah on my ills. These were sincere and well-meant condolences, and I felt better for them. In the sun and the air, I soon picked up again, though it was long before I had back much weight. It was a very interesting experience, when it was over, but I should hate to have to go through it again.

When I was on deck again the ship was somewhere near Ras el Kelb, close in by the Hadhramaut shore. We were drifting near some precipitous islands, one of which was topped with a deposit of guano. We were very close in, so close, indeed, that when the tide turned Hamed had to anchor, and we lay there in quiet throughout the rest of the day. No breath stirred and there was no motion: away astern of us the Kitami boom lay also with an anchor down and her big sail gathered to the yard, which like ours rested vertically against the mainmast. But the Persian baggala was out of sight. Where was she? I asked Hamed: but he said only that Allah was compassionate. I looked astern. He looked ahead. I knew where the baggala was, then. She was much more lightly loaded than we were.

Next morning with a breath of air we ghosted on, and we made the rest of the passage to Mukalla almost within stone's throw of the Hadhramaut beach. Though burned and sterile it was not an unattractive coast, and in the dawns and sunsets sometimes it was wildly grand. Sometimes, when there was a better working breeze we would make a short tack off the land, but we always came back in alongshore again. Sometimes, when it was calm with an unfavorable tide, we anchored for a few hours, always leaving the sail aloft. The conditions were very good, apart from the lamentable persistence of the head wind. Hamed was ghosting to wind'ard by using the favorable sets along the land. In this he was wise, for if he had made long tacks out into the Gulf of Aden we should have lost more than we gained. Out there the set was always to the west'ard with the northeast monsoon. Hamed knew the local waters, and he knew what he was doing.

Once we tacked. It was the only time I saw the big boom put about head to wind in all the time I was on board. Hamed would not have done it then had the tide not suddenly turned on him as he was standing very close to weather a low spit of land, jutting out from a place where once a river might have flowed. We were too close; and the ship was being set ashore. There was neither room nor time to wear, for if we had fallen from the wind we should certainly have gone ashore. I was glad I had back something of my sight to see Hamed tack her round. He did not get excited (though he sometimes did). He murmured an order quietly: the quartermaster at the wheel yelled it: all hands sprang to their stations. They all had their stations for wearing ship, and they were the same posts for tacking. Now down came the mizzen on the run. The quartermaster, at a nod from Hamed, who was standing up on the cutter by the davit heads, eased the helm down. She responded at once, putting her long nose into the wind. By that time we were perilously close inshore, right in the shallowing water and watching the shelving sand, just outside the breakers' line. But she came all right. She answered her helm beautifully, and the big lateen sail proved a well-balanced rig. She turned on her heel and carried round with her own way, even when the huge sail was full aback.

This was an awkward moment, for if she gathered sternway she was finished then. She did not. She kept her head and came round handsomely, though the business of handling the backed mainsail and the awkward tripping of the great lateen yard with all the pressure of the wind trying to break it were extremely difficult maneuvers. The mainsail, which like all Arab sails had no gear on it whatever, wrapped itself in huge awkward folds between the yard and the raking mast and did its best to become entangled with all the gear—the mast tackles, the halliards, the shrouds. Out of this mood of wild recalcitrance the sweating crew had immense difficulty in getting it: they kept up a savage chanting and singing the whole time while the canvas boomed and the mast creaked and the yard swayed, and the noise of the breakers close by was ominous and unending. I feared that the lateen yard must break, for with the sail aback all the pressure of the wind was against it, and the unsupported mast could easily have come down. It was a complicated and exceedingly dangerous piece of seamanship, and nothing but sheer manpower got that great mainsail back under control. It was a piece of canvas 130 feet on the head, with a luff of well over 90 and a foot a hundred feet long. It was well over six thousand square feet of canvas—an enormous sail, as it had to be when it was the main motive power of a ship of 150 tons. I was glad then that we had such a large crew, for there was work enough for all of them. Only the fighting spirit of the crew curbed and controlled that fighting, thrashing piece of canvas; and it had to be done carefully, too, lest the weak seams split, and the ship should be left there in that dangerous situation with her sail unfit for use.

It was well done and I was glad I saw it, but I did not wonder that we never tacked again. I could appreciate the Arabs' reluctance to go about head-to-wind, and I began to think the lateen a useful sail only in fair winds. That is the way the Arabs try to use it: with any winds other than the monsoons, lateen-rigged ships could not safely keep the seas.

The next day we were at Mukalla, coming in late in the evening. We had been, so far as I could discover, twelve days on the passage and by that time I had settled down comfortably. It was just as well, for we did not again enjoy so peaceful a passage for some months. The first thing we saw was Nejdi, waiting on the jetty, and with him was a collection of the wildest-looking Arabs I had yet seen.

Chapter 3

ON THE HADHRAMAUT
COAST

M U K A L L A at first sight is a picturesque and romantic place, and after Aden, which is British, and the Red Sea places, which are dull, it is so perfect a picture of what one expects an Arab port to be that it is difficult to accept it as real. Ashore it does not quite live up to this high promise. The principal port of the Hadhramaut, Mukalla is today as ever the place of merchants, the port from which the wandering Hadhrami set out for Java, India, and Africa, and to which they return. The Hadhrami has always been a wanderer, going out from his largely barren land to get a competence elsewhere and returning always to spend it. It was to pick up a shipload of these wanderers that we had come to the Hadhramaut port, for though in these days they usually travel to Java and the East Indies as deck passengers in steam—Dutch liners call regularly at Mukalla to take them—they still voyage to Africa and India by dhow.

Mukalla is an interesting place of white buildings struggling timorously to keep foothold between the great mountains of the Hadhramaut and the sea. Round the waterfront of the small unprotected bay the buildings cluster stout and tall and prosperous, with the minaret of a mosque here and there. But farther back—not so far—they become dilapidated and gray in their efforts to struggle up the almost precipitous sides of Mukalla's brown mountain. It is the mountain one notices more than the town, the frowning mountain with its white tower forts which are now unused. The possibility of using mountain forts to protect the port from attack from behind probably led to its situation there. The mountain sits above the town as if wondering whether to push the whole thing into the sea, which it could do with one brief shrug: its precipitate bulk and alarming proximity are at first sight overwhelming, and in the gorges great rocks lie, waiting. Here and there one sees where a fall of rock has slipped down, with fatal consequences to any building that chanced to be in the way. If I lived at Mukalla I should hate to see a heavy rain.

The harbor is interesting, and the bay is quiet in the northeast season. The southwest wind would blow directly into the bay and then it would be untenable. When we came in, we were one of twenty Arab dhows at the anchorage, and there were others on the beach. In a small sheltered place east of the city there was a dhow-yard on the beach, and here men were building two large sambuks with square, picturesque sterns. The Hadhrami dhow-builder likes to decorate his craft, and the sterns of some of the sambuks on the beach and at the anchorage were elaborately carved and painted. They were usually decorated with several rows of geometrical designs in triangles, stars, and crescent moons, done in blue and red and green, and adorned with appropriate texts from the Quran carved along the sides of the poop. Many of them had rows of dummy windows carved and painted on their quarters, one row on each side, finished off with half-drawn curtains painted in white. This was a favorite design. Other ships had a row of stern windows painted on them, in addition to those on the quarter. Many of them were covered round their whole sterns with brightly painted designs, from the waterline to the deck. The effect was sometimes striking, especially with the reflection of the pretty sterns shimmering in the clear blue sea. Their freshly limed under-water bodies gleamed and their hulls, where they were not decorated, shone with oil. They were a good-looking lot. There were also several old Aden sambuks there under the Italian flag, sailed by wild big crews of Somalis with many boys.

These Somali sailors had a wildness lacking in the Arabs. Even the men who pulled about the harbor in small boats, selling fruits and dates to the ships, seemed afraid to go near the Somali sambuks. The Somali sailors were very tall, with wild locks bleached and reddened: they wore white sarongs, very long, and threw folds of unsewn calico loosely over their shoulders when they went ashore. They strutted about as if they were content with life, and very well pleased with themselves.

There were other queer craft in the harbor, including some small vessels from Seihut and ports along the Mahra coast—long, low vessels with very low, raking bows and their masts raked more than any I had seen before. Hamed said these were exceptionally fast. The largest of them did not look forty feet long, but he said they sailed to Zanzibar. There were others, manned by sullen-looking men in brown shirts and Suri shawl-turbans, which had straight sterns, ramlike low bows, and high vertical masts. These Hamed spoke of as *Bedeni*: they were very small and appeared most unseaworthy, but Hamed said they went down to Zanzibar, too.

The harbor was always picturesque and interesting, but after some days I began to wonder what we had come there for. Nejdi brought out a wild gang of Beduin the first day, fierce-visaged men in black with their hands and legs and bodies covered with heavy indigo dye. This, they said, was protection against the heat and the cold, which was a comforting belief, for they appeared to have few other clothes. These men were armed with large curved daggers which they carried in silver scabbards lashed round their waists, before the pit of the stomach. The same belt which carried the dagger seemed to carry all their other possessions, and thrust in beside the dagger might be another knife—a smaller one, for finishing off the stabbed victims and for working—or a reed for music; and in pouches on the belt might be a few coins, and their tobacco. These Beduin went without head covering. They wore their hair long and smeared heavily with butter. They had no sandals. They were thin, lithe, gaunt, and wiry, and they had alert and very watchful eyes. They came aboard with Nejdi, who looked curiously unlike them (though he was descended from the desert people himself, the hill desert people of Nejd), and they ran about the deck like children. They were, I saw, being shown round the ship, and they seemed as excited about her as if she had been an ocean liner. These were Nejdi's prospects, I guessed—our passengers. They included a small good-looking man who was described by Hamed as chief of a Beduin tribe from somewhere inland. It was mentioned in the most casual manner that he was considering taking his tribe to Africa, but I still refused to believe that they could come with us. He was aboard often, always scampering about peering into everything. He and the others seemed most pleased about the size of the ship, and they did not bother about appointments. Size was enough for them: to them, she was a very large ship.

I was very puzzled by the time they all spent down in the loathsome great cabin, for no matter where else they did not go, they all gazed long and earnestly into that horrible place, while old Yusuf Shirazi dilated upon its merits. Down they went, through the small hatchway on the port side aft, and after a while came out again murmuring *Taiyib*, which apparently meant "very good." What was very good about that place? I asked old Yusuf. What did the Beduin want with it? Were they going to ship some cargo down there? But Yusuf murmured something about the compassion of Allah—a comment the appropriateness of which I did not appreciate at that time but realized later. A "cargo" we were certainly going to have there, and all Allah's compassion would be needed to soften its hard lot. Once I got a hint from Yusuf: if I had known something more of Arabic I might have learned. He said something about *bints*. *Bints?* Women? (Even in Australia, a bint is a girl.) But surely Arab dhows never carried women. Migrating Arabs never took their women with them, according to the books I had been able to read. But all I could get out of Yusuf was a reiteration of his belief in the goodness of Allah, and even when the great cabin was being cleaned Hamed knew nothing. Not that that foul den was really cleaned. Some of the stuff in it was thrown into the small cabin right aft, and this was as far as the cleaning went. There might have been a clear space of eight by ten feet in the center of the great cabin, when this restowage was completed.

During this time Nejdi came to the ship only for the feasts, of which there was one every second day. We just stayed at that anchorage, and nothing happened, and we had feasts. It was a pleasant existence provided one had no business elsewhere, and I had none. Every day we had a sheep for the midday meal, it was made the occasion of a feast. These functions were simple. Abdulla, the nakhoda's brother, would go ashore the evening before to buy a fat Somali sheep or a skinny Hadhramaut goat, which would bleat the night away on the little forecastle head and bite the dust at the crack of dawn next morning. Apparently all hands were expert butchers. They cut the sheeps' throats with gusto and efficiency, and the poor beasts would be dragged right out of their skins into the pot. The pot was one of those big round black tubs which are traditionally represented as suitable for missionary-boiling in the wilds of Africa and the more remote South Sea Islands. Into this thing, simmering on Jassim's brushwood fire, would go the whole sheep, or lamb, or goat, with various delicacies from it scattered in smaller pots on lesser fires. On such occasions Jassim could fit five fires into his small fire-box, and really he could do wonders at turning out a feast. The principal ingredients were always the same—sheep or goat, and rice. Sometimes the rice was flavored with raisins; sometimes there were chickens as appetizers. There was melon to follow the main course, for melons were plentiful at Mukalla and the Arabs loved them. When everything was ready, Yusuf would bring up the Persian carpets from somewhere down below and spread them over the whole poop, placing a large eating mat of Swahili design over the center carpet. Then the sheep and rice would be brought on by the quartermasters, and all the delicacies. By this time strangers would be coming aboard in droves.

Nejdi gave good feasts and was profligate with his hospitality. It always seemed to me that he was too profligate. Every other nakhoda in port, all the port officials, all the passenger agents and half their clients, a group of Suri and Mahra people; a Yemeni Seyyid who was thinking of going to the Congo to collect some dues; customs clerks, merchants—all these piled on board, until the place was like a Rotary club, and the only way they could all get at the eating-mat together was to sit sideways, like sardines spliced into a box, each with his right shoulder in the solid phalanx of human anatomy that faced the food, and his right hand working on the feast. There was no room for any one to sit squarely at the mat, and tear in. They could only sit sideways. The *pièce de résistance* of all these feasts was always the sheep's head, which sat on the tray of rice nearest to Nejdi. When the feast was about three parts over Nejdi would nonchalantly reach in for the head and, using his two hands, get to work on the skull, breaking it up and rending out the eyes and tongue, and splitting the thing on the deck to get at the brains. These he would distribute to the guests of honor. By that time Nejdi's right hand would be covered with ghee and rice, and the forearms of all and sundry would look as if they had been working in a rice mill, for at the feasts some of the decorum of our daily eating was dropped. I was always sorry for the sheep. Its head always looked so inoffensive, and its gaze was so sad. After all, it had been working on the sheep only a few hours before: the thing had bleated that dawn. And here was Nejdi smashing it on the deck and plucking out its brains.

After the feast we had coffee, then sleep: after the sleep, the midday prayer followed, and after that Ismael, our musician, would play on his damned guitar. Then all peace was ended. In six months I never came to like that music. So far as I could see, there was not a thing to like about it. One can become accustomed to Scots pipes and Siamese reeds, to Balinese and Javanese gongs. Even the Swahili, banging on their drums, produce some kind of rhythmic noise, and the Beduin's reeds were not wholly unpleasant. But Ismael on his guitar was and remained an affront to the ears of mortal man. Given the slightest encouragement, he also sang, which was worse. His songs were interminable, plaintive, and most repellent, sung horribly in an unnatural and dreadfully unattractive voice. Yet everybody insisted that Ismael was a musician of note in Kuwait, and ranked among the supreme attractions of the vessel. Nejdi, I learned, had gone to great pains to induce Ismael to ship in the *Triumph* and had bought the guitar for him, as well as giving him privileges on board. I soon noticed that the musician, besides being let off work for the day, was accustomed to collect bakhshish* from the more important of the guests. He added lines in his songs with this in view, though the songs were mostly about love so far as I could gather. At any rate they were full of references to *bebes,* and ludicrously soulful looks. A bebe, I gathered, was just another bint. We heard of them only in song. That these songs were all highly moral in tone I saw reason to doubt, and there were often occasions when I much regretted my lack of Arabic. Ismael must have had something to put into those songs to hold his hearers, for the melody was always atrocious and the delivery abominable. He never got any bakhshish from me for his music, though he pointed out now and again his great desire for a gold wrist-watch. Whenever possible, I gave him bakhshish to stop. This was usually wasted. It was, I suppose, inconsiderate of me to want him to stop when everybody else so enjoyed him. But he used to go on far into the night. Sometimes we had drums with the guitar, and this was better, for they helped to drown the music. Often there was dancing but it was always the same dull shuffling, agitating, finger-cracking, hopping and jumping I had first seen in Ma'alla Bay. We never had any dancing girls: they were kept ashore.

We stayed at Mukalla for days and days. Nothing happened. The first day we had discharged some deck cargo for the Sultan. Each day some woolly Beduin came and wandered over the ship, finishing up in the great cabin from which they emerged smiling and murmuring *taiyib.* Whatever was *taiyib* about that place? What was this all about? Well, questioning would not find out for me: I could only wait and see.

Other booms from Kuwait and from Kungk and Lingeh in Persia came and sailed, and still we stayed. We saw little of Nejdi apart from the feasts: apparently this gathering of the passengers was an arduous business. He came very little to the ship. Whenever he did come there was a feast, and about fifty men came with him. Our crew, who never missed a chance to trade anywhere, added to their goods here, buying large quantities of small straw fans, and basketwork which was quite attractive. They bought this in bales, cheaply. Yusuf said these baskets were much sought after by the Europeans in Mombasa and Zanzibar. The ship loaded a consignment of cooking-stones, and the pestles and mortars, things which the

* Bakhshish = tips, largesse.

Hadhrami use for crushing corn in the preparation of the daily bread. These things, a little Hadhramaut tobacco, some ghee in kerosene tins, and some dried shark seemed all we shipped at Mukalla. The whole lot might have been five tons.

The crew also watered the ship. This they did with skins in the long-boat, pulling away to a creek at the western end of the town at dawn each morning. Here they grounded the boat and marched to a pool in an oasis, about a mile from Mukalla's western gate. It took about three days to water the ship in this manner, but there was nothing else to do. The water got in this way cost nothing, and I hoped it was reasonably good. I should have to drink it. The sailors sang the morning away at this employment, and slept in the afternoon. On most days they did not bother to go ashore, for they had no money. Sometimes Ismael went off with his guitar to be a public nuisance somewhere, and on such occasions I was glad.

So the days passed. Coastal sambuks, Somali dhows, Persian booms came and went. An Indian kotia, with a cargo of tiles from Mangalore, came in: she was very similar to an Arab baggala but more heavily rigged and better built, and she had a much smaller crew. She had only eight men: an Arab of the same size would have had at least twenty. The kotia flew a large flag of dark red silk, with two narrow white horizontal bars: she moored alongside a Persian baggala named the *Hope of Compassion*. Most of the Arab dhows had these mellow religious names, but often when I went aboard and asked the name, nobody knew it and the nakhoda would have to look it up in the certificate of registration. No names ever appeared on them. I learned later that there was good reason for this when, for example, the vessel was running a cargo of mangrove poles out of the Rufiji Delta, or skipping out of Mogadishu with a few thousand lire. The Arab does not like his ship to be too easily identified and he knows that to European eyes all dhows are alike. In their own talk, they were accustomed to speak of the vessels by the nakhoda's name: our ship was always the boom *Nejdi* and was rarely referred to by her own people as the *Triumph of Righteousness*. She had at least two other names, as was usual with the big dhows. The Arab hates official identification. It was the same with the others: Abdulla Kitami's small boom had two names but was always known to seafaring people as the boom *Abdulla Kitami*, Ganim bin Othman's big *Mercer al-Baz* was the boom *Ganim bin Othman*, and so on. This applied, however, only when the nakhoda was at least the nominal owner.

During this time I stayed on board, for I could not walk. It was always interesting on board, sitting up on the nakhoda's bench abaft the wheel watching what went on. There was always plenty to watch, if not aboard our own vessel then aboard the others by which we were surrounded. Usually four or five dhows came and left each day, bringing cargoes from Aden, Seihut, and the Mahra coast, and loading for Somaliland, the Yemen, and Eritrea. Most of the ships lying in the harbor, like all the Arab craft I have ever seen anywhere, just stayed at the anchorage and did nothing while their masters were ashore trying either to get paid for the cargoes they had delivered, or to collect fresh cargoes to take elsewhere. We did a lot of this waiting at anchor ourselves, and sometimes I found it a little exasperating. However, it was pleasant to know that we should never go anywhere without staying at least a week there, perhaps a month. One had a chance to look about and really to see the ports we visited.

Christmas came while the ship was at Mukalla. On the day I thought to be December 25, I was at last able to go ashore. I went in the gig with Abdulla, Nejdi's young brother, and the passenger Said who was off on some mysterious errand, looking more wily and intriguing than ever. We landed at the small stone jetty and Said disappeared at once. His fellow passenger, Abdulla, had gone the first day, so quickly that I did not see him go. Nejdi's brother and I wandered slowly along the road that leads past the dhow-yard, with its piles of ship's timbers and knees from the Yemen and planks from Malabar, past a new sambuk being built under a screen of date mats to protect it from the sun. This was the way to the bazaar, always the most interesting part of any Arab town. Abdulla had said that Mukalla's bazaar was good, and he was going to see if it offered any goods for sale along the Benadir coast. Before we had reached the bazaar, however, my leg gave way again, and Abdulla and I sat for a time in a coffee shop near the dhow-yard, watching the scene round us and the passing crowd while we sipped hot goat's milk flavored with cardamons. It was not bad: and it was not very good.

The scene was good, though, for the streets of Mukalla teemed with strange human beings dressed in all the colorful costumes of the East— Banyan merchants in their flappy diaphanous trousers and little black hats, Yemenites in sarongs and big turbans, Beduin in black and indigo, leading soft-stepping great camels laden with firewood and goods, Persian, Somali, Kuwaiti, Suri, Batini sailors and nakhodas, wandering half-castes with blood from all the East in them, half-Malays, half-Turks, half-Africans, half-Egyptians, half-Baluchi, half-Balinese. The Hadhrami wanders far and takes his women where he finds them, bringing back the

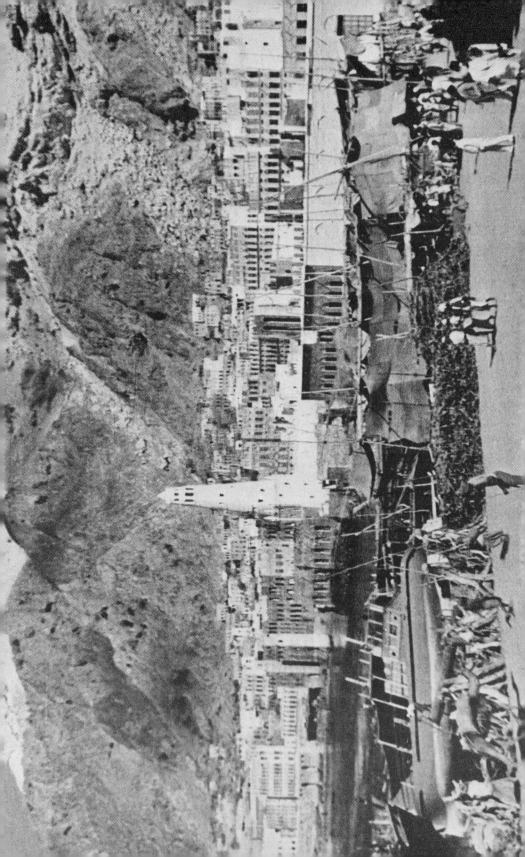

male offspring to his native land, and the blood of the whole East pulses in those busy Mukalla streets. The pure-blooded desert Beduin are the most striking of them all, walking always fearless and erect, gaunt and half-starved and poverty-stricken as they are, oily-haired and half-naked. Many are armed with the Hadhramaut dagger, and a few carry ancient muskets and other guns, though this practice is by no means so general as it was before the British forced peace among the warring tribes, very recently.

We sat there cheerfully in the coffee shop, Abdulla now and again calling for fresh embers for his hookah while the crowd milled round. The coffee shop was a rough open place more on the street than off it. It was just a shanty of three walls and a mat roofing, with the earthen floor liberally spread with benches on which squatted Arabs of all ages. The Arabs were in small groups, carrying on earnest conversation. They looked romantic as they puffed at hookahs, or tossed off tiny cups of black coffee. Now and again a Kuwaiti or Persian nakhoda dropped in, for this was the nakhodas' coffee shop. Coffee shops in Arab coastal towns are sharply zoned: they are the clubs, the meeting places, and the exchanges, where most of the business is done. I was to see a great deal of these interesting institutions before my voyage in the *Triumph of Righteousness* was over.

I was finishing my third cup of the flavored goat's milk when Mr. Ingrams, the British Resident Adviser in the Hadhramaut, walked in. Asking why I had not been to the Residency before, he took me off at once in his car. Well, it was Christmas Day, I thought: and Christmas Day is a man's own. I was not going to intrude on the Ingrams on such a day and that was the first time I had been ashore, the first time I could walk. I did not care to go to the Residency when I was so lame and generally helpless: but I was very glad to be taken. As a matter of fact, it was not Christmas Day, but Christmas Eve. I was one day out of my reckoning.

I was comfortably established in the Residency, a handsome white building which was once a rich Arab's town home, within an hour; and there I stayed for several days. It was pleasant at the Residency and it was good to have a meal. I had a room which once belonged to one of the former occupier's several wives, and I could look across over the Residency garden, where in the mornings the new constables were drilling, towards the palace of the Sultan, where the bands played. The harbor sounds came in through the open window, and I could hear the booms' crews singing in their longboats as they pulled in for water. I could watch them wa-

Mukalla, port of the Hadhramaut

tering, carrying the quivering skins, black and wet and shaking as if they were queer headless beasts somehow alive, and I watched the west gate of Mukalla, with its constant stream of interesting life.

At that time Mr. Ingrams was pushing ahead, for the first time in history, with a comprehensive road program for the Hadhramaut. He was constructing motor roads to Shibam and other important places. The Beduin who carried on the business of camel transport did not like it; nor did some of the tribes through whose territory the roads passed. The Beduin, accustomed to do something about the things they do not like, smashed up the roads. On such occasions Mr. Ingrams, being a wise man, did not send punitive expeditions against them. He went out himself, met the disgruntled, talked with them, and promptly enrolled them in the road protective police. These were the wild creatures who now drilled in the square every morning, and happy citizens they were.

I had a look with the Ingrams at some of the hinterland of Mukalla, along the wide beach at the town's western end. Camels plod along this beach, sedate and serious, and heavy-laden asses amble. The camel park by the west gate is always full of life: here the camels from the interior

West Gate, Mukalla

British Residency, Mukalla

bring their burdens, sit back upon their haunches and wait for new ones. Beduin often came and spoke while we were out on these tours: often we saw the women tending the flocks and herds, and gathering brushwood for the tent fires. Much of the Hadhramaut, though I saw little of it (for my eyes turned ever towards the ships), had a wild grand beauty. We went one day along the new road over the ironstone hills, and watched the evening rest in a bowl of brown and reddened beauty among those wild rolling hills, and darken them: the stars came quickly, and the night softened all the outlines of the hard land. Beduin drivers padding by with a camel caravan sang some ageless chant of the hills, and the sea rolling in along Mukalla Bay murmured a lullaby.*

We dined one evening with the Sultan in his palace, in a room within sound of the sea. The service, the clothes, the dishes were all more European than Arab: the Sultan himself seemed more Indian than Arab. He

* The interested reader is referred to Miss Freya Stark's *The Southern Gates of Arabia,* for a comprehensive and most interesting description of the Hadhramaut.

was a very tired-looking man in the middle fifties, looking much older: he sat in a European chair at the head of his large table, wearing a fez and a long close-fitting Indian coat, and we sat and ate and ate. The Sultan's son, the Crown Prince of the Hadhramaut, sat happily at the other end of the table, smiling because he had that day remarried a favorite young wife whom for political reasons he had earlier been compelled to divorce. The political reasons, whatever they had been, now no longer held, apparently, and he had wasted no time about remarrying.

Late that night, Abdulla, Nejdi's brother, came to the Residency, saying that the boom was outward bound and would be gone before morning. Would I come, or should I prefer to ride with Nejdi on a camel to the port of Shihr? Damn the camels, I said. They stink, and they make me seasick. So I went with Abdulla to the ship. I was very grateful to the Ingrams for my stay with them, and I left Mukalla with my leg strengthened, and fortified with good food enough to keep the scurvy away for six months.

I was aboard the ship at midnight, to find the poop and the maindeck so crowded with passengers that there was scarcely room to walk. Cloaked and turbaned figures sat about murmuring quietly, and everywhere I looked were forms stretched out on mats asleep. The coming of these people had changed the whole ship and she now so teemed with life that I wondered where I could sleep. But my place on the bench aft was still there for me, with my chest beneath it. There I turned in for a few hours' rest, ready to watch the ship sail out in the morning. Abdulla whispered that a few of the passengers had come on board. A few? I asked. They seemed to be about a hundred. Yes, he said, business was not good, and reports of depression down the Benadir coast and in Zanzibar and Kenya had kept many at home. No matter, his brother was going ahead to Shihr, along the coast, and we should get more there. More? Where would they fit? Abdulla smiled. I had to walk upon six Beduin, a Seyyid, and a lesser Hadhrami sheikh to reach the place where I slept, and I could not get at my chest for the recumbent forms all round it. Yet we had shipped only the first of our passengers.

I began to wonder about this voyage down to Africa. True, it is no great distance from the South Arabian shore across the Gulf of Aden and down before the monsoon to Mogadishu, in Somaliland. Abdulla said Kuwait ships had sailed from Mukalla to Zanzibar in less than eight days. But we were not bound directly towards Mogadishu, Mombasa, or Zanzibar, so far as I was aware: we were bound on a trading voyage, and Allah alone knew when we might be rid of these passengers. They snored; they took up a great deal of room; their possessions took up more. Under the light of the moon I could see that already so much baggage had come aboard that many bundles were lashed along the poop rail, outboard. We must have taken some merchant of standing, for along the port side of the poop, just forward of the toilet box, were lashed a folding-bed and four cane chairs. I went to go down into the great cabin to bring up something of mine from there, but I could not, for Yusuf Shirazi was sleeping with one eye open across the hatch: he motioned to me with his open eye that my gear was all on deck, and I would find it abaft the wheel. There it was, but why this removal from the great cabin? What *was* the mystery of that place?

But on that subject, for the time being at least, I had to hold my peace. I should find out in due course.

We were gone from Mukalla in the first light of the morning, before the sun rose. We had a light fair wind out of the bay, and we sailed in company with the Persian baggala and Abdulla Kitami's small boom. Our position at the anchorage was a crowded one, with ships all round us and a way out only ahead, a narrow way between a ledge of rock and the small boat in which a hurricane lamp burned at night to mark the port—its only light. I was interested to see how Hamed bin Salim would get the ship out of this congested place, but he managed with surprising ease. First, as usual at anchorages, he hoisted the mainsail on its yard, fast in light stops so that a tug at the sheet would bring the canvas fluttering down. Then he unmoored, passing a line to a sambuk astern, and heaving short to one anchor. Then a puff of air came faintly marking the surface of the bay, and, as the air struck us he shouted an order: down fluttered the mainsail, out broke the anchor, and the sambuk astern let go our line. There we were slipping slowly along under way. We were so close to a Bombay kotia on the one side and an Omani baggala on the other that once we had sailed from our place in the tier it was impossible to see where we had been.

Hamed handled her very well, I thought, and the sailors did their work splendidly. It was made no easier by the crowd of Beduin on deck and the gang of ancient Sinbads on the poop. When it came to maneuvering the ship, however, little attention was paid to either of these. Any one who got in the way was simply knocked down, and the passengers learned quickly to flee to the other side of the deck as the sailors came rushing and chanting. Those sailors of ours never went at a real job of work quietly. They rushed at it, singing lustily, and fought it until it was done: this was Nejdi's style, and even when Nejdi himself was not there it was continued.

So we sailed from Mukalla Bay that bright morning and the town was picturesque and beautiful as the sun rose. Later it was calm, and we were within sight of Mukalla all day. It was a hard place to leave, and the Beduin looked back at it sadly. Some of them played mournfully on their reeds: others, in spite of the calm, were already seasick. Others again jostled and crowded about on deck stowing what little gear they had, and getting out their firepots. They brought their own food, but the merchants on the poop ate with the ship. Some of these merchants looked rather tough, and some of the Beduin were tougher. They were an unprepossessing lot, and first impressions of them were far from favorable. I wondered more about this voyage down to Africa. How long would this wild gang be on board? I asked Hamed. Not more than ten days or so, he said: and Allah was compassionate. They were going to Mogadishu, most of them: the Italians had work for them down there and in the interior. Had they permissions from the Italian Consul, passports, and all that kind of thing? No, said Hamed, they had not: but this movement of the Arabs down the African coast had gone on from time immemorial, and even the foolish Europeans could not stop it. A few of the merchants, I gathered, had some sort of identity certificates, and the ship was supposed to have a passenger list. Perhaps she had. If she had, it must have been thrown overboard, for I never saw it and I know that when she arrived at Haifun, the first port of call in Somaliland, there was none on board.

The wind was quiet all that day and we made little progress: but the way from Mukalla to Shihr is short, and we came to the Sabæan port next morning with the baggala ahead of us—she ghosted beautifully—and the Kitami boom behind. We were twenty-four hours between these ports. At Shihr we found ourselves one of ten booms at anchorage. Eight were Kuwaiti, and two from Persia: we were all bound to Zanzibar. The harbor at Shihr is nothing but an open roadstead, and the ship rolled there more heavily than she ever did at sea. This made the Beduin very sick, and the maindeck was a bedlam.

Landing on the beach at Shihr was dangerous and difficult, for a high surf ran and we could not bring our longboat in. The quartermaster in charge anchored her outside the breakers and the sailors, rolling their long shirts on to their shoulders, ran in through the surf. Zaid, the freed slave from Kuwait, carried me on his great back—Zaid had always been very good to me while I was blind and lame—but as we were almost safe a sea knocked him down and sent us both sprawling. I hurt my knee, and rose wet and cursing. I cursed the Queen of Sheba for choosing such a place for the town of Shihr (if she ever did; which I doubted). Hamed had said that here the fabled queen built her ships of war to attack somebody or other, but I doubted that too. Now with the pain in my knee I remembered only that the Queen of Sheba was a woman and womanlike had made a port of this fool place, where there was neither wood to build ships nor a place to launch them. Shihr seemed to me then nothing but a walled piece of sand facing the Arabian Sea, and I wondered what excuse it had for its existence. It stretched for about a mile along the shore but at no place was there a decent landing: the town itself was mean and poor with unmade streets and unfinished houses, a good many of them apparently going to ruin. The Sultan's palace, a huge white building, and the bastioned wall were, so far as I could see, the only buildings of importance in good repair. The bazaar was small and offered very little.

Fishing seemed the only industry, and I saw that the fishermen still used the ancient sewn boats. Some of these were small, but others, used for cargo lightering, were larger. The smaller ones had sails and the larger oars: they were built roughly of planking fastened together by a stitching of fiber, and there were no other fastenings. They were pretty boats, shapely double-enders with good lines and a handsome sheer, and they were elaborately painted in white stripes, with one black and one green triangle at bow and stern. Some were steered with paddles; others had small rudders, balanced so that they were always under water, and manipulated by a piece of cord leading to the helmsman's foot. This he held between his toes, steering the ship by a gentle movement of his foot. The small sewn boats used by the fishermen spread one square sail, and they could scud along beautifully in anything of a breeze. Fine edible fish seemed extraordinarily numerous off that coast, and all day long the fishermen were landing their heavy catches through the surf. They were very cheap, a boatload of splendid fish bringing only a few cents. Drying small fish for camel fodder was going on almost along the whole length of the beach. I saw nothing else being carried here but fish and some dates, for a Persian boom from Basra was discharging dates at the anchorage. A poor bazaar, a few rough mosques, some tumbledown buildings, a sultan's palace, camels, donkeys, goats, chickens, some lesser merchants, few soldiers, Beduin, a coffee shop or two and a lot of fish—this was Shihr. Except for the poor houses it remained largely as nature made it and I wondered why it had been considered worth putting a wall round. I went back aboard.

We stayed at Shihr for days and days. There was no sign of Nejdi, and nothing happened, except that the Beduin made a bedlam of the anchorage. We loaded no cargo and discharged none. Nejdi ought to have been back from his camel-ride, but he was reported to be looking for more passengers. I wondered where we could put them. Already we must have had more than fifty, though some, apparently, were coming only as far as Shihr to see their tribesmen leave.

On the third day, just at dawn, a big soldier came out in a sewn boat asking for me. What now? I thought; but it was only His Highness the Na'ib asking me to come to the palace. What exactly a Na'ib was I was not sure, but he lived in the palace and he was Mayor of the town, if nothing more. Sultans, Emirs, Na'ibs, Sheikhs—they are much the same. The only variation is in the name. At any rate, when a Na'ib asks you, you go: and I was glad to go though my leg hurt rather badly when I moved. There was noise and confusion on board, and some of our Hadhrami had developed a horrible capacity for quarrelling. A day with the Na'ib in his great white house would not be so bad, so I went off with the soldier, expecting to be back the same evening. It was a week later before I returned.

The Na'ib himself was waiting on the beach with an ancient car, and we drove to the palace. The Na'ib of Shihr was a slight thin man with a fiery red beard. He was a very pleasant soft-spoken gentleman, dressed strikingly in a bright green turban and a sarong with green and red stripes, surmounted by an old coat. Round his waist was a fold of cloth with a large ivory-handled dagger in a silver sheath. The ivory was adorned with gold. He wore rough sandals of colored leather, and chewed incessantly at something which looked like snuff. Though I could not talk to him (for my few words of Arabic were purely maritime, and had been picked up from the sailors) we got along very well. He made me comfortable in his palace, which was a large handsome building overlooking the town and the sea with some picturesque ruins topping the square before it. Once in, there I stayed. We entered the palace through a gateway where some Beduin soldiers reclined on easy guard with their rifles beside them. Other rifles and large swords hung round the walls, and a group of citizens squatted outside the doorway. These rose as we entered, with salutations. We seemed to climb a great many stairs. I was accommodated in a pleasant room furnished with a sofa, several armchairs, a table, and a large bed, with carpets on the floor and on the white wall nothing but an Egyptian calendar three years old.

We fed very well in the palace, breakfasting always on chickens, omelets, eggs fried in ghee, unleavened bread fried in God knows what, and black coffee. At noon we ate again, very sumptuously, on roasted lamb and boiled rice, and fresh bananas and canned pineapple from the Malay States. In the evening we had fish and rice. This was the substance of our meals invariably, though sometimes we had the fish at noon and the lamb at night. After every meal, the Na'ib had the ingredients for his chewing stuff brought to him. Mixing up leaves and lime and whatever else went into the concoction, he chewed loudly and methodically for some time, with frequent expectorations into a spittoon on the table. In the afternoons we drove round the town and outside it, to an oasis where a small ox, working on an inclined runway in a pit, hauled up water in a leathern bucket. We visited the Beduin camps, full of babies and yelping dogs, and saw all there was to see in Shihr. This took about ten minutes. The rest of the day I sat in the Na'ib's palace looking out, and before long, pleasant and hospitable as the old man was, I began to suspect that this was a worse occupation than sitting on the outside looking in. But, being his guest, I could not leave.

I missed the ship. I missed old Yusuf Shirazi and Zaid the freed slave, and Abdulla, Nejdi's brother, silent old Hamed bin Salim, morose little Jassim the cook, and all the rest of them. I had grown to like them all, and I wanted to know what was happening aboard the ship. I might have solved the mystery of the great cabin if I had stayed aboard. There was nothing to read in the palace, and I had brought nothing, not expecting to stay there. Indeed, I had very little to read with me on the ship, for I had not wished to have anything which might tempt me away from the fascinating observation of all that went on. I had only five books and, except for a book of poems, these were all about Arabia.

On the fourth or fifth day, when the *Triumph* had been in port perhaps about ten days—I was always hazy about times and no one else cared about them—Abdulla came up to the palace to say that Nejdi was coming back that night, and the boom would sail before the morning. She was, he said, probably going to call at one or two other places along the coast before turning away for Africa: he mentioned Hami and Seihut. We wandered down to the beach in the Na'ib's wheezy old car, about four o'clock—the Na'ib, Abdulla, and I. I liked the old Na'ib though I had never exchanged an intelligible word with him. He was very good to me, but I looked forward to returning to the ship, and to the voyage down to Africa.

When we came to the beach, we passed a large crowd of Arabs of all shapes and sizes, waiting with a vast collection of battered old tins, ancient carpet bags, and household goods done up in date matting. I did not know what these migrants were and I did not look at them very closely, for I presumed they were probably for some other boom. We had our own contingent. I asked Nejdi's brother what ship they were for, but he only smiled. Out at the anchorage again, I found the ship a pandemonium of noise with all the passengers from Mukalla settled down—settled down so well that there was no longer place for me on the bench aft (this, Hamed soon changed)—and there were some new faces among them. What a madhouse the ship was! It was late in the afternoon, and the sailors were getting the ship ready for sea, bending the big mainsail along the long yard with singing, chanting, and yelling, now and again stamping their feet. Half the booms at the anchorage were similarly engaged and bursts of song, clapping of great horny hands and stamping of rhythmic feet, came from all parts of the roadstead. It was a quiet afternoon with no swell: now no one was seasick.

As the day ended and the sun set I saw a fleet of sewn boats coming out; the surf was now quiet. I watched them with mild interest and no thought beyond the reflection that possibly this was the last time I might see them in action, but after a while I saw they were coming towards us. I saw, too, that all the boats were filled with human beings. They were bringing out all that great crowd of Beduin I had seen on the beach, and they were bringing them to us. Good Lord! Our decks were already so crowded I thought that there was no room to move, and the longboat which we had towed from Mukalla had still to be hoisted aboard. There must have been over a hundred of them. On they came, the whole wild mob, some chanting in the sewn boats, others yelling, babies crying, children screaming, Beduin looking up stolidly in their black rags.

As the sun went down and throughout the brief twilight, while the sailors prayed in the pandemonium of the poop, the embarkation of our passengers went on—on and on and on, far into the night. The poor illumination of a hurricane lamp threw a bizarre light on the scene as hordes of the wanderers scrambled up the side and clambered aboard. There was not so much as a rope ladder to assist them: nobody checked them.

All who came simply clambered up the side the best way they could, threw their belongings down (if they had any), and sat where their belongings landed. In this way they made room for themselves, for first they pitched their bundle aboard, over the side before them, and then ran and placed themselves where other passengers had scrambled out of the way. If you had no baggage, you had no place, in that first scramble. Before long there was a line of them sitting along the mainyard, though Hamed and Abdulla chased them down from there saying there was plenty of room. They filled the open space beneath the break of the poop; they piled into the carpenter's new dhow; they packed themselves between its ribs and the side of the vessel; they streamed along the fore part of the poop; they sat upon the capstan, the forecastle head, the sailor's chests. Those who were experienced among them made at once for the sheltered space beneath the poop, on the fore part of the great cabin bulkhead; while those who were making their first voyage—and they seemed the great majority—mooned about like sheep and did not know what to do with themselves. Chest after chest was passed up on the poop, bale after bale, bundle after bundle of bedding, until the sea chests stood six deep on each side and the tins and bales and bedding were massed over them. I could not understand how the mess would ever be cleared. Old men, blind men, lame men, men in bandages, men in black, men in white, children, boys, merchants, camel-drivers still with their camel canes, a Seyyid with his staff, fierce-visaged men who looked ready for anything, mild-looking men, thin men, fat men—still they came, piling on board. The surge of humanity swept over the vessel and threatened to engulf her, until I felt crowded even on my six feet of the officers' bench and wondered, not for the first—or the last—time on that strange voyage, what I had really let myself in for.

But what was this? Something strange, even in this extraordinary scene, was happening. I saw that they kept on passing up queer long bundles swathed in black, one after the other, which were immediately passed with some deference into the blackness underneath the poop. Here they promptly disappeared. They were being stowed away in the great cabin. At the fifth or sixth bundle I became really interested, for the bundle moved. What *was* this? I asked old Yusuf, who was swearing and running round trying to keep order, making way for those bundles and seeing to their safe stowage. Yusuf did not hear me. I repeated the question: what were these bundles he was passing so carefully into the great cabin? Bints! Yusuf said as he rushed by, bints. Women! Great Heavens! They must have passed up about fifteen of them. So that was what the great cabin was for. Poor devils! Most of them were very slight, like girls. I saw one dropped, later: she leaped to her feet and, holding the black veil before her eyes, ran lithely towards the place where a doorway led into their prison. My own recent memories of a week in that ghastly place gave me a shock, and I wondered how fifteen or twenty women or girls were going to survive a voyage cooped up in that foul and loathsome den. So that was what the Beduin had been so pleased about, always coming up out of that inferno grinning and murmuring *taiyib:* they were going to ship their women there. What was so *taiyib* about it I still did not know, if not its excellence as a place of segregation. They could scarcely have regarded the place as good accommodation. In Arabia the sexes must be segregated at all costs, though they die for it. Some of them did, aboard the *Triumph of Righteousness*, before that voyage was over.

Just before midnight, after the last of the passengers had come aboard, a headcloth which belonged to no Bedu suddenly appeared at the rail. It was a white headcloth, touched with gold, and it was bound by head-ropes of black silk. One fold was wrapped about the wearer's face as he came over the rail, dropping a stick and his sandals before him, but even if only his great hawk nose had been showing all hands would have recognized Nejdi. It was Nejdi, back from his camel-ride, in from the desert; Nejdi, who had driven in all these passengers by fair means or foul, from God knows where, and now was come aboard to sail this great ship with them, again God alone knew where.

He came aboard silently. He took one look at the crowded decks, and strode aft, walking on the tops of the chests, for there was no other place. With him was a turbaned perfumed sheikh in silks, who remained awhile squatting on the bench aft, conversing in long whisperings. At length, with a soft "Fare ye with God!" the perfumed one departed, going down silently over the side into the boat which had brought him. Nejdi still sat there aft, watching the weather, his brooding dark eyes on the wind and the sea. He looked tired, as if he had come a long way, but he was alert. The sail had been made ready before then, and all was in order for departure. Before four o'clock there was a breath of air from the land, and we sailed. Silently the ship passed out into the night, unlit and ghostlike, with her great mast seeming to rise unaided from the sea of humanity sleeping there bewildered in the shadow of the sail. The women in the great cabin were silent, and no man stirred. The mainsail fluttered down, the wheel kicked quietly: we were off.

Chapter 4

DELIVERING THE BEDUIN

WE DID NOT GO to Hami and we did not go to Seihut. Nejdi, who had scoured the countryside on his camel as far as Seihut, had decided there was nothing to be gained by visiting those ports. His must have been a great camel-ride, for Seihut is more than a hundred miles from Shihr. Whether he was pleased with the results of his mission I did not know, but he did not seem to be. On general principles Nejdi rarely seemed pleased with anything. He complained that there were not enough passengers, and that the boom could have accommodated a hundred more. This I did not at first believe, but after the passengers had settled down I had to admit that it was probably so. There was room for more. The Arab passenger takes up very little room and asks nothing but a place to throw himself down. The *Triumph* had a beam of 29 feet, and her maindeck from the great cabin bulkhead to the forecastle head was nearly 70 feet long. The poop had a maximum beam of 26 feet and was 27 feet long. The maindeck, then, had an available area of something like 1900 square feet, and the poop perhaps 300. This gave actual deck space, giving each passenger twelve square feet—six feet by two, which was much more than they needed—for over 180 persons, without counting the score or so who could be put into the great cabin. In addition, there were the longboat and the new dhow, and there was space beneath the forecastle head. There was no doubt that, at a pinch, the boom could carry as many as 250 Arab passengers: but I should hate to be on board among them.

The longboat and the dhow took up some deck space, but Arabs slept beneath them and all round them, in them and over them. No space was lost. Chests, bundles, everything was slept upon. The Arab slept always on his side and did not ask even for space enough in which to turn. Only the merchants on the poop had any real belongings, the merchants and two young sheikhs who were going to Lamu in Kenya for business experience. Forty of the Beduin had only one wooden box between them, and a bale of sheepdung as fuel for their tin firepot.

Exactly how many passengers we had on board at that stage of the voyage I never discovered, though I tried every day to count them. Like everything else to do with the vessel, this was a closely guarded secret. The Arabs never volunteered any information, and though Nejdi and Hamed bin Salim sometimes asked me to identify certain of the ship's papers for them, and to examine and translate them—this was later, when I had picked up more Arabic—I rarely learned anything in this way. I never learned by questioning. There was no passenger list from Shihr: my daily totals varied by as many as twenty persons, and I could never count the women and children beneath the poop. That place was now strictly out of bounds, and no one went there but old Yusuf Shirazi. Abdulla the Suri and Said, our two passengers from Aden, were still with us, though Abdulla had gone missing in both Mukalla and Shihr. We appeared to have embarked several others of their kind, including a burly big Suri named Majid, which they pronounced "Mide" and the poop under the officers' bench on the port side was full of their merchandise. We now had some forty persons on the poop alone, and the daily prayers were a scramble, for there was not room for all to bow and kneel together.

Our passengers from Mukalla included an old blind merchant from somewhere in the interior of the Hadhramaut, a man who had long been settled down inland and now was coming out, at the age of sixty-five, to wind up the affairs of a dead brother buried somewhere in the Congo. He was a fine old man with a handsome, drawn face: he had a servant with him, and five times a day he was led up on the poop to his ablutions and his prayers which he recited in a thin quavering voice. Hamed and Nejdi and the rest were very kind to this old gentleman, though ordinarily there was not much human consideration about them. How could there be, in all that crowd and in such a life? The old man led the prayers, standing in front of the long line of the strange congregation with his drawn tragic face sightless towards Mecca. That old face could be extraordinarily moving. When he was not praying he sank in reverie at the bole of the mizzenmast, his hands clasped together, and was lost in thought, heedless of the teeming life all round him. He was dressed always in purest white with a long white turban wound upon his high forehead, but how he succeeded in keeping himself so clean in all that mess and bedlam I could not understand. Before we had been a day at sea the maindeck was a filthy morass

Nejdi checks the passengers

and it could never be cleaned, for so long as the passengers were aboard no one could get at it. How our sailors lived during this dreadful time—these conditions went on for six weeks—I never quite understood. When the last of our passengers had left the vessel, at Mombasa many weeks later, somehow and from somewhere the sailors emerged again, worn and thin and tired. As far as I could discover, they must have slept in tiers on the anchors and cables, and on top of the firebox.

On this first day of the voyage down to Africa we beat along the Hadhramaut coast, making to windward of Ras Asir. Though it was now mid-January and the northeast monsoon should have been long established, the wind was flukey and more from the east than the northeast. Nejdi made a series of short tacks along the coast, never getting far away, exactly as Hamed had done on the beat to Mukalla. If he stood too far from the land we should be caught in the set to the westward, and lose ground: inshore the countercurrent helped us, and we came on slowly. We passed close by the picturesque village port of Hami, and the place looked so fresh and interesting I was sorry we did not stay there. Here three sambuks were anchored, but no deepwater booms. The Kitami boom and the Persian baggala had sailed before us and we were now alone. Abdulla Kitami was bound direct for Mombasa.

The Hadhramaut coast in the neighborhood of Hami and towards Ras Sharma had great beauty, with the high flat-topped cliffs of the *wadi* sides away in the distance, and from them, rolling down towards the sea, all the lesser hills, marked with sunlight and shade like shadowed folds in cloth. Now and then we saw a pleasant little village, picturesque and seemingly quiet.

Still Nejdi crept along the coast, determined to get to windward of all Africa along this Arab shore before falling off towards Haifun. His purpose was the sound one of getting to windward while he could, and afterwards using the east wind to run directly for Ras Asir light* upon which he would have to come by dead reckoning, for he knew no navigation and I had brought no instruments. It was not far, and visibility was good. He always came that way. When an Arab shipmaster spoke of knowing the waters and the way on the sea, he meant exactly what he said. He was not speaking of a theoretical ability to make a voyage with the help of astronomical observations, wind and current data, the latest Admiralty charts, leadlines, patent logs, and all the rest of the long list of ordinary paraphernalia. Nejdi coaxed his ship along by his knowledge of local

* Our Cape Guardafui is known to the Arabs as Ras Asir.

conditions, and the coasts of South Arabia (and the coasts of the Persian Gulf, Baluchistan, and all Western India) were an open book to him. He showed his knowledge now, and the benefits of it, though I admit I was puzzled by his short tacks. If I had been trying to get a ship out of there I should probably have made long boards, on the assumption that the monsoon would be truer away from the land and would haul fair. I should have been wrong: Nejdi knew his winds and waters.

At last we drew to windward of Ras Sharma, and fell away abruptly to head towards Africa, laying a course inside the island of Socotra, to pass within ten miles or so of Ras Asir. I was interested to see Nejdi rule off his course. He did it properly, from the compass rose of a comparatively modern chart: but he had no parallel rules and he used a straight frond of date and his thumbs. Though scarcely a method likely to be approved by the Board of Trade, this was effective, but his fatalistic belief in the compass, which he always insisted in regarding as true no matter where the ship was or how much iron might be thrown round the binnacle, might have been fatal to the vessel in conditions other than those we encountered. To him the compass was always true: he had bought and paid for it. I learned more of Nejdi's navigation methods later.

A hundred of our passengers were sick, and the ship was a mess. The Beduin did not bother to go to the rail. Some of our migrants, indeed, when they sat on the rail would lean back inboard to spit, and no amount of shouting at them would induce them to change their ways. Perhaps they saw that the sea was clean and the ship dirty, and therefore spat on the ship. The more experienced travellers adopted all kinds of strange devices to keep the seasickness away. They prayed frequently and with great devotion. They smelled at small green lemons, and stuffed wads of paper into their ears and nostrils. Some of them presented a ludicrous appearance, with large wads of newspaper protruding from each nostril, the ends of the paper attached round their necks with string. This did not save them, and many of them were very sick. They all kept eating, which was wise. The ship's motion was not bad and the weather was ideal. The sea was slight and the breeze a pleasant sailing air which, once we had got to windward, was fair, and the ship had only to fall off and run towards Ras Asir light. Conditions could not have been better. This was as well with such a welter of humanity on board.

Actual living conditions aboard the vessel during this stage of the voyage were very bad, though I doubt whether they seemed so to any of the Arabs. Right aft on the poop, we had the first-class passengers—the mer-

Rigging the bulwarks

chant Sinbads Said, Abdulla, and Majid: the Seyyid from Mukalla who
was going down to Africa to collect dues: the blind old sheikh, the two
young sheikhs, and several others. These ate the ship's food, paying a rupee extra for that privilege for the voyage. The fare from Mukalla or
Shihr to Africa—it made no difference which was the port of embarkation—was eight rupees without food, nine with, and twelve rupees for
women. Nejdi explained that he did not want women, who did not usually come—Abdulla Kitani had only three in his 150 passengers—and
that was why the rate was higher for them. They had to be sheltered and
segregated. It was better, he said, to have none of them, for they often
made trouble. But he had to bring some that voyage. The fare was the
same whether the passengers were bound to Mogadishu, Lamu, or Mombasa. It was customary that it should be paid in advance, though this was
not strictly necessary. The first-class passengers, who included, apparently, several old friends of Nejdi's, did not pay in advance, and indeed
several of them never paid at all.

On the fore part of the poop were a group of young half-caste Ha-

dhrami, many of whom seemed half-Malay. Some of these looked villain-
ous, and occasionally there were fights in this section. Here also were
the two young sheikhs travelling to gain business experience. The elder
of these may have been twenty-two: he was born in Surabaya, he said,
and spoke Malay as well as some Dutch, and his own Arabic. He was a
fine-looking young man who prayed far more than any one else on
board. Long after all the others had finished their daily ritual he was still
praying, on his knees in all that welter of humanity, praying with his
hands across his chest and a rapt expression on his youthful face. When
he was seasick he prayed more than ever. With him were his brother, aged
perhaps eighteen and by no means so ardent a Muslim, some servants,
and a half-caste Malay who was one of the noisest and most obnoxious
people on board. This half-Hadhramaut-Malay had an ancient gramophone with him and some terrible records from Cairo and Damascus,
and whenever there was no other noise—which was seldom—he brought
these things out and raised havoc with them. Also he sang, in a voice worse
even than our musician Ismael's, until that worthy was disgusted and
lapsed into a painful silence.

At night other odd passengers came up on the poop and reclined dangerously along the edges of the chests and wherever else they could fit
their bodies. Down on the maindeck, beneath the overhang of the poop,
were some forty wanderers, who seemed to have formed themselves into
small cliques. One of these cliques was made up of fellows from a village
near Shibam, in the interior of the Hadhramaut, and there was another
of young men from Sur. I don't know how they had managed to get to
Shihr, but probably they had wandered round the coast in one of the small
Suri or Mahra vessels. When an Arab begins to wander he may turn up
anywhere. Our curious old Seyyid on the poop, for instance, had been an
automobile worker in Detroit and had spent eight years in the stokeholds
of ocean steamers. For a man who had served so long under the British
flag he knew very little English, but he used frequently to address me in
a queer language. It was not Arabic. I was not sure of that, but Abdulla
said so, adding that it was neither Swahili, nor Persian, nor Hindustani,
nor any other language known in India. It certainly had not the slightest
resemblance to English or to any other European tongue that I could
recognize. It took me a long time to find out that he was really speaking
very bad Polish, which he had learned in Buffalo and Detroit under the
impression that it was English. He had lived in Hamtranck, the Polish
suburb of Detroit, and his fellow workers must have been Poles.

The young sheikh who prayed so much was a courageous young man. He read every day to his entourage, usually from the Quran but sometimes from other books, and he read aloud even when he was seasick. This takes courage. He was one of the most likable of the whole group, and I liked his brother, too.

The Beduin on the maindeck led wild lives and there was always yelling and arguing going on down there. I noticed, however, that it was never the real Beduin who began the arguments, though they often continued them. The quarrelsome ones were the half-castes, and the worst of all was a half-Somali with three children, a dreadful little boy named Abdulla, another much smaller boy who was even worse, and a little girl with her shrew face painted stupidly with black lines beneath the eyes and across her brows. This shrew-faced little girl used to go about with her big father all day and disappear into the great cabin by night. She pinched and scratched all the boys smaller than she was, when their parents were not looking, and she always shrieked if anybody touched her. She made life a hell for the small boys in that ship, but one day three little mites of about four years of age got together and gave her a hiding which she thoroughly deserved. She was perhaps seven years old: she wore long dresses and longer trousers, but her little devil of a face was covered with nothing but paint. It would have been better veiled, and the ship would have been quieter if she had been gagged, together with the rest of her family. All day long the decks resounded with piercing yells for her elder brother, Abdulla, to do some job. He was loud-mouthed, noisy, quarrelsome, and bullying. Abdul-lah! Abdul-lah! All day that infernal half-Somali yelled, when he was not fighting the other passengers. He never had room enough for his firepot: he never had water enough from the ship: his children were for ever in trouble. He had brought all his household possessions and was moving for good down to Mogadishu. His household goods were in a box, and he had brought two goats. These stood throughout the voyage tethered to the side of the wooden water-tank forward, and they were the best behaved and quietest members of that family.

This dreadful creature was not typical. By far the greater number of our passengers were quiet and decent people who, once they had settled down to the life on board—and this took them very little time—sat and slept and yarned and cooked their few victuals, and did their best to keep out of trouble and out of the sailors' way. The chief of the Beduin was a small, wiry man named Aura, an attractive, clean-faced Arab who had his small son of about three years old with him. I liked Aura, and the little boy, who took a constant delight in the ship and all that went on, was a great favorite with the sailors. The little child, who had a huge belly and an extraordinary coiffure—his head was shaved at the sides, and across the middle a tussock of black locks stood up like a row of palm trees on a beach—knew no greater delight than to follow the sailors at their work and pretend to haul on ropes with them and sing their songs. Sometimes he became so interested in this that he would dash about the decks for hours by himself, hauling with his baby hands on the great ropes and lustily chanting his own version of the sailors' songs. Another of his favorite sports was fishing, though I never saw him catching anything. He was a sturdy little fellow, and the dreadful shrew-faced little girl knew better than to pinch him when nobody was about. She tried once, and ran away howling with a clout on the ear. That little devil of a girl seemed born with a desire to avenge Muslim womankind on Muslim men and, though the manner of her revenge was restricted to sly hits, kicks, pinches, and scratches, and the only men she could attack were children smaller than herself, she kept to her purpose with a vixen's tenacity and ceaseless en-

Booms on the beach

ergy. Aura's little son, however, was a match for her. The little boy had
a tiny black sarong perhaps four inches deep, and that was all the clothes
he had. Sometimes his father put butter on his jungle of hair, or renewed
his belly-band of indigo. They were a good pair.

We had a great many children. Some seemed to be travelling by themselves: I never saw anybody looking after them. Most belonged to families,
and all were at least nominally in the care of an adult. I found out later
that several of them had been hired by beggars to go with them down to
Africa: they did the work, and the beggars begged. There was a bad-
tempered blind man who had brought two boys with him, aged perhaps
eight and nine. Apparently the arrangement was that they were to work
for him, and he provided them with the passage to Africa and back,
their clothes, and food. He was not among the first-class passengers and
he had to bring his own food. After a few days it became obvious that he
was not feeding the children at all. He was a morose man who played
mournfully on some battered reeds, nearly all day. This apparently was
his manner of begging, and if I was ever near he set up a whine for alms.
The children, who had not been away from Arabia before, put up with
his ill treatment for several days. Eventually the matter came to the attention of the nakhoda, when it was at once dealt with, for Nejdi was
judge and jury in all disputes.

In addition to sailing the ship and seeing that the passengers were delivered to their destinations safely, Nejdi had complete charge of them:
he ruled them with an iron hand. He judged in their disputes; he led them
in prayer; he controlled their comings and goings; he quieted them and
tamed them when necessary, and attended to all their needs, except their
medicinal and surgical needs. There were no medicines on board, and
no dressings.

Whenever they had anything to bring to his notice, the passengers
came to the break of the poop, stuck up their wild heads, shouted "O
Nejdi" and began straightway to recount their wrongs. It was a free and
democratic life. Nejdi was king, but he had no craven subjects. Everybody else was a king too, and Nejdi had only his natural ability to keep
them in order. This he did by force of character: and he never shouted.
He was in command because he was the natural commander, and for no
other reason. Life on board the *Triumph of Righteousness* with our passengers was far from being a picnic but, without Nejdi, the ship would
have been nothing more than a madhouse. As it was, if it had not been
for the rigid observance of the first rule of the ship, I do not see how life

would have been tolerable. The first rule was just this: that whatever happened and in all circumstances, the passenger was never right. This was an effective and thorough principle, which I found pleasing. In spite of the inconveniences and the hardships of the life, the opportunity to observe the application of this sound and workable principle in regulating the conduct of passengers at sea would have made up even for a month of dysentery. In all arguments with the crew the passenger was in the way and he had to get out of it. This may seem harsh when, after all, the passenger had paid his fare; but he had paid only to be carried in the ship as she was, to be allowed to come along and take her as he found her. He had nothing to say about her running and he could not be allowed to become an inconvenience. The only way to run that ship, with her huge unhandy lateen sail—the only way to run any ship with any kind of sail, or sails, or even ships with engines—was efficiently, thoroughly, with alertness and competence. There was no opportunity for pampering passengers. The passengers could only be on the deck because there was nowhere else to go: if they were on deck they must sometimes be in the way. They were only there because the ship needed the revenue she earned from them. Being allowed to come was the beginning and end of their privileges. Once aboard they were live ballast, or worse, for the ship was deeply laden and had no need of ballast. They were a noisy and dirty inconvenience to be got rid of as soon as possible, and this fact was soon impressed on them. If they did not like it, they could go riding on camels. To them the conditions were tolerable enough.

The day the two children complained about the blind man's treatment of them was typical. Every day Nejdi was called upon to deliver Solomonic judgments in all kinds of disputes, except with regard to the women. These were shut up, locked up, and forgotten, and never allowed even a breath of fresh air on deck. This might have been hard on them, but in such a world it was unavoidable and indeed it was the best fate that could have overtaken them. As Nejdi pointed out, they would probably not be kept below for longer than two months, at the most. (He had told them two weeks.) On this day—the day of the dispute—things were much as usual; a group of Beduin were delousing their indigo-stained sarongs on the deck of the longboat, the Somali's goats bleating by the watertank, and the Somali yelling at a group of fang-toothed half-Malays by the break of the poop. The quarrelsome little girl was prowling about looking for a chance to vent her sadism on some male baby, Aura the Beduin chief playing with his small son, Beduin and Hadhrami la-

borers chatting, sitting, sleeping, cooking, eating, praying, reading
the Quran, applying grease to one another's hair, pawing pieces of shark
as hard and dry as basalt rocks and looking about as palatable. Suddenly
this fascinating and comparatively peaceful scene was disturbed by a loud
yelling, followed by fierce imprecations and a string of oaths in Arabic
that would have startled a camel. Incidents like this were too commonplace to excite remark, for the half-Somali began such scenes ten times a
day. The only thing strange about this one was that he had not started it.

In a moment, other noises subsided sufficiently to make it clear that the
new row was originating somewhere beneath the poop overhang. In a short
time a yelling and general commotion burst out on the main deck, where
firepots and trays of rice spilled in all directions, and a goat ran bleating,
while the shrew-faced bint, scared for once in her life, scampered for the
great cabin. The central figures in the disturbance, which was becoming
more general every moment, appeared to be the blind beggar, his two
small boys, a fang-toothed half-Malay, an old man in half a sarong, and a
broad-shouldered Arab silversmith from Mogadishu. As far as I could
make out—and it was difficult to make out anything very clearly—the
blind beggar was trying to attack the two boys, who were yelling and
fighting each other; the fang-toothed one and the silversmith were fighting to decide who should restrain the blind man from his attacks on the
boys, while the old man had got in the way and could not get out again.
More people joined in the fray, and sailors ran aft to stop them. They
tried to run aft, but, even at the best of times, it was difficult to run along
those decks, and now that the whole after part of the main deck, between
the stern of the longboat on the starboard side and the bow of the new
dhow on the other, was a seething, yelling, milling mass of Beduin, it was
impossible.

At this moment Nejdi, who had been reclining on the bench aft reading from the Quran to two Suri merchants, leaped to his feet faster than
I had ever seen him move before, picked up a camel-driver's cane and,
leaping over the low rail at the break of the poop, was down on the deck
like a shot. Wielding the camel cane like a flail, the only one silent in all
that mob, he cleaved a way towards the contestants, who by this time
numbered at least a score, while the sailors fought through from the fore
part to reach him and go to his aid. Not that Nejdi needed aid. He was
doing very well alone. In almost the flash of an eye he had stopped the actual hostilities, if not the commotion—that never died down all day. He
had the blind man by the scruff of his neck in one hand, the fang-faced

Malay and the old man in the other, and the two boys at his feet. Then the sailors reached him and everybody went to the poop where a court of inquiry was constituted to deal with the case forthwith.

Nejdi was the whole court, and the only other man—apart from the contestants—who dared to open his mouth was the Seyyid from the Hadhramaut. Since he had the blood of the Prophet in his veins, the Seyyid was privileged, and he often intervened as peacemaker in the ship's disputes, though seldom to much purpose. Now all began to yell at once, together with about fifty other passengers who streamed up on the poop, until Nejdi quieted them and chased them down again. It appeared, after some time, that the blind man had hired the two boys to help him on the voyage to Africa and in such other countries as he might visit. He was to clothe and feed them, and pay for their transport. But once he had got them away from Shihr, where he had posed as their father and safely on the voyage, he had chosen to forget his bargain and refused to give them anything to eat. The two boys, disgusted—naturally enough—with this, had left his service. They declined to make his meals ready and to look after him, or even to lead him about the deck. They claimed that as the blind man did not feed them they were not obliged to work for him, and it took them all their time to ensure their survival in the crowded and hungry vessel. They had sought, then, to attach themselves to the Mogadishu silversmith, a kindly Arab named Ashuan, but Ashuan already had a family and had no place for them. Their situation was becoming desperate and, that morning, after being hungry for three days, they had mutinied and tried to raid some of their original employer's food. The blind man caught them at this—for he was very sharp in spite of his handicap—and was beating them when the silversmith intervened. Then the engagement rapidly became general.

The discovery of these few facts took half the morning. There had been several further skirmishes, though none of them was very serious, between supporters of the fang-faced Malay and others to whom, apparently, they had taken some objection. Nobody supported the blind man, because he was so obviously in the wrong. In the end Nejdi's judgment was that the blind man must keep to his bargain and feed the boys properly. He objected that they were lazy boys, good for nothing, who had foisted themselves on him. Why then, asked Nejdi, had he pretended to be their father? He had done this, to get them aboard. It was purely out of the kindness of his heart, the beggar said. But would not the same kindness of heart send them out to beg for him on the streets of Mombasa,

Dar-es-Salaam, and wherever else they might get to? The blind man admitted that it would, for he hated the idea of children being without employment. The boys, he said, had been homeless and friendless on the Shihr beach, and he had befriended them. As a reward for this great generosity they now turned on him and, refusing to work, accused him of starving them. But he *had* starved them, hadn't he? The blind man said he was short of food. The silversmith then produced the beggar's box of dried fish, and his half-sack of rice. It was clear that he had no case. Nejdi said that if he did not feed the children properly the ship would feed them, and the beggar be held aboard and not allowed to land until he had paid for all their food. The beggar whined that he was a poor man, but everybody knew that he was one of the richest men aboard. Nejdi also made the boys apologize to him for their disturbance of the peace, and made them promise faithfully to serve the blind man so long as he fed and clothed them. After some demur the children did this and the matter was ended.

By this time new trouble was brewing in the waist of the vessel, where the loud-mouthed half-Somali was yelling that somebody had milked his goats while the fight was in progress. Somebody had.

I was surprised that the starvation of the two children could have escaped attention in so crowded a vessel, and wondered that no one had bothered to look after them. I had not seen them before. The reason probably was that, when all were so poor, the need of others was apt to go unobserved. They were all ready to help when the need was brought to their attention. Afterwards the silversmith saw that these children were properly fed, and Nejdi kept his eagle eye on the bad blind man.

Nejdi kept his eagle eye on many things. From the moment his great hawk nose showed above the rail until the last fold of his headcloth disappeared down the Jacob's ladder into the boat, he was in command of everything in sight. He knew all that went on, and directed most of it. He never seemed to be sound asleep. As soon as he came aboard, Hamed bin Salim ceased to have anything to do. The direction of the ship was in Nejdi's hands, and the responsibility was unshared. Hamed was not even a mate. He was a stand-by, an officer to look after the ship in port, and to sail the ship when Nejdi was not there: when Nejdi was there Hamed kept the accounts and did little else at sea. Nobody opened his mouth except to repeat what the nakhoda had said, and this often went unheard because of the continual din of the passengers about the decks and also because the sailors, whenever there was work afoot, sang and chanted with so much vigor that they could not hear the orders.

I often suggested to Nejdi that he should use a whistle to break in effectively upon the clamor, and I bought one for him once. He never used it. He said it was unseemly. He liked things as they were, and was opposed to change. Sometimes this disregard of orders seemed to me as if it might be dangerous to the vessel and her gear, for when twenty stout mariners got on the end of a line and swayed away they were apt to do damage if they were not checked in time. They never watched what they were doing: they rushed at the work and waited for the orders they did not hear, and they never stopped their chants and yells so long as the work continued. At the slightest murmur of an order, they were up on their feet and singing. They sang continually; they sang as they ran along the deck to the job, scampering over and upon the boats and knocking the passengers down: they sang all the time they worked, and when the jobs were really big—such as hoisting the lateen yard—they stopped occasionally and danced.

I often wondered about the women imprisoned in the great cabin. Only once did one appear on deck, a slight small figure swathed in black who came up the first dawn at sea to pray at her husband's side. What induced her to do anything so unusual I never did discover, but she was allowed to pray briefly before being chased below. The husband, however, was warned that he must keep his women under better control. Nejdi seemed to think the episode very improper, and several times I heard him talking to the Seyyid about the worrying forwardness of females in these days, as exemplified by this and other incidents. Nejdi had very definite views about the status of women, and often gave them expression. He praised the system which maintains women in the strictest seclusion, and had nothing but scorn for our European ways.

When there was trouble on deck, or anything really interesting happened, I wondered how our women were able to curb their curiosity, for they could not see out of their prison. I discovered that they employed the shrew-faced bint and other young girls to carry reports to them, and they knew most of what went on.

By night we sailed very well upon our course to weather Ras Asir, with the moonlight bright on the swollen sail, and the ship's noises, apart from the Beduin snores, pleasant to the ears. All the passengers stretched themselves on the deck, some wrapped in sacking from the cargo, some in indigo and wretched rags, others with blankets. Some of the merchants had elaborate beds which their men spread for them each evening on six feet of the poop, beds bright with tasselled rugs and gay cushions. I lay on the starboard side of the reclining bench aft on a Turkish carpet Nejdi gave me, and though sleep was sometimes hard, I was well content. But in the grayness of the mornings, when the muezzins seemed to try to see who could make the greatest din; when the bedding and the carpets were wet with dew, and there was no prospect of breakfast other than unleavened bread; when the Beduin and the half-castes noisily sluiced themselves with sea water and the children yelled—I sometimes wondered why I had come.

Day succeeded day and in the fascination of the voyage I forgot little troubles like these, forgot the traces of fever that still remained from the Hadhramaut coast, and the lameness that still made walking painful. The ship wandered southward in a welter of noise and discomfort as we carried our Beduin for delivery in Africa. The monsoon blew true and our progress was steady, if not always pleasant.

Chapter 5

ISMAEL SAVES A CHILD

ON THE MORNING of the fifth day after leaving Shihr, the ship coasted close in by the base of the precipitous promontory of Ras Haifun. Nejdi was cutting the corner and we were very close indeed, for the conditions were excellent. The breeze was fresh and fair, from the northeast, and there was little sea. The current here sets towards the land and it is not a place to fool with, but Nejdi knew what he was doing. The promontory's eastern end is without dangers. We were cutting the corner not to save time, which never mattered in Nejdi's existence, but in order to be able to point for the anchorage at the town of Haifun immediately the ship drew off the southern tip of the promontory. It was a picturesque place with great yellow cliffs towering above the ship, which slipped along quietly in the blue sea. If we did not hug it closely, we should have to beat to reach the anchorage tucked behind it.

On board everything was much as usual except that it was a little quieter, and for the moment there was no serious row in progress. The half-Somali, the father of the shrew-faced bint and the little brat Abdulla, was asleep, and this automatically reduced the noise on board by half. Our group of half-Malays, or whatever they were, lay in the shadow of the mizzen taking their ease, in spite of the noise of forty-seven Beduin sitting round them, singing. Each Bedu had a hand over one ear as he sang, and I wondered why he did not have his hands over both ears, as I had, and wads of cotton wool thrust deep in them besides. Kaleel the carpenter banged and drilled at his new dhow, now and again calmly turning over a sleeping Beduin so that he might get a fresh plank. Little Jassim the cook was drowning the livestock in a basket of rice with a bucket of water hauled up from the sea, while his assistants Abdul-wahhab and Mishari pounded corn for the unleavened bread. Other sailors, with Abdulla the nakhoda's brother, crouched like apes over a large basket of Iraqi dates. The dates were a congested sticky mess and looked as if they had been trodden into that basket by a camel some years before. Abdulla and the sailors were picking out the soundest fruit, pitting them with their teeth, and re-stowing them, more or less neatly, in little paper cartons labelled "Fresh Clean Dates, Produce of Iraq." These dates were to be trade goods for the Somali at Haifun, who were the only people who would eat them.

On the poop the Suri were seated in a group and Said was going through some haberdashery which he appeared to be making ready to land. Said was a smuggler, and he would soon be busy. Majid the big villain, in a long brown shirt, examined the haberdashery with interest and offered suggestions, in a very loud voice, as to the best manner of smuggling it, while Abdulla read to himself quietly from the Quran. Nejdi, who had been discussing subjects as diverse as the growth of Islam in Japan, the great days of science in Arabia, the property laws of the Hadhramaut, and the best way to make a passage in a dhow from Mandalay to Cutch in June, now was quiet, for the moment, puffing at his hookah. Ismael the musician, that ballad-whining reprobate with the guitar, had stowed away his music and was going through the contents of his chest, round which a group of Hadhramaut half-castes had gathered. He was trying to sell them some inferior ready-made Japanese coats, which they were scrutinizing but not buying. Yusuf Shirazi, his eyes, which had been paining him for a long time, half-covered in a visor-fold of his white headcloth, was engaged in some mysterious occupation the nature of which I could not understand. I watched him with interest dimly conscious of the scene all round. Children scampered along the bulwarks, playing merrily, the little son of Aura leading them.

Suddenly I heard a splash. Nejdi started. There was a scream—a child's scream. Some of the Beduin rushed to the side. "Child overboard!" they shouted, pointing. I leaped up. The child, a bawling bundle with his white gown streaming in the sea round him, was rapidly being left astern. Instantly, before I had time to collect my thoughts, there was another flash of white and one of brown. Two rescuers had leaped across the poop and were over the side before I could recognize them. In a few moments I saw that they were the musician Ismael, who went first, and Abdulla the Mysterious.

It was a brave deed. We were making about five knots, and there were sharks. The boy fell rapidly astern. We were perilously close in under the cliffs, and the wind, filling the huge lateen sail, was right behind us. The ship was not equipped for such an emergency. There were no lifebelts nor lifebuoys, or any other kind of lifesaving apparatus. The cutter was at the quarter-davits, fortunately, but it was securely lashed there. The ship herself was in a bad position. We were so near the cliffs—we could hear the breakers and watch the backwash gurgling at the cliff-base —that to throw the ship aback would be extremely dangerous, for there she would be in grave danger of driving on the rocks. To bring her up and let her shiver by the wind on the port tack, keeping the way off her, would be equally dangerous, for the set could easily put her ashore.

I wondered what Nejdi would do, for now he had to get back three people instead of one. I could not see a move open to him that would not gravely endanger the vessel. He showed himself, in those circumstances, an alert and skilful seaman. He knew what to do more quickly than I did. Without the least excitement, without as much as rising from his bench, he rapped out one curt order, so rapidly that I did not understand it. The sailors understood it. They had always worked splendidly, but in this emergency they worked like demons. In response to Nejdi's command they swung the huge mainyard midships. The quartermaster slammed the helm down, and Nejdi threw the ship across the wind, aback, so that her stern was seawards and her sternway carried her from the cliffs, instead of towards them. It was smartly done, though the situation of the vessel was still critical. We must have been within fifty yards of destruction. It was a question which would affect the vessel more—her sternway—which was not much, for half the sail was now useless—or the set. Her sternway took her from the cliffs. The set put her towards them. It was a fight between them, with Nejdi, compelled to wait for his sailors and somehow get them back aboard, unable to help. But he did not seem to doubt the result, nor did the sailors. They rushed immediately to the poop and began to clear the gutter. In the *Triumph*, as in all Arab vessels, nothing was ever quite ready for use. The Arab policy was to cope with emergencies when they arose, not to prepare against them beforehand. I had been inclined to scoff at this. Now I had a lesson. Those stout fellows were as splendid throughout this whole situation as any sailors on earth could have been, and they had that boat cleared and away into the water as rapidly as any smart liner might have been getting an emergency boat overboard, starting with the boat ready. They all worked: they all chanted; they all sang—even in this predicament, with the ship five minutes away from disaster, the child drowning, and their shipmates fighting for their lives in the shark-infested seas. No one was excited. No one,

except the Beduin passengers, now yelled. The sailors worked magnificently, with Nejdi and Hamed bin Salim leading them. Ismael and Abdulla by this time were far astern, specks on the blue expanse of the African sea; but we could see that Ismael had the child, and Abdulla was
helping him.

Now the cutter was down and away immediately it touched the water, with Abdulla Nejdi's brother at the tiller and old Yusuf Shirazi and
the serang at the oars. They pulled lustily, though without excitement.
The cutter was only 16 feet long. It was very small in the ocean, but
there was no sea. The sharks were the danger—the sharks, and the rocks.
The ship was slowly, but very obviously, being set in towards the cliffs,
which now seemed to tower above her masts. When she rolled we saw
the cliffs above her mastheads, not the sky.

We saw the cutter reach the trio, struggling in the sea. They picked
up the child. We saw them take all three aboard—the child, Ismael and Abdulla the Mysterious. Nejdi stood by the davits on the port side of the
poop, watching everything, gauging the chances for his ship, cursing the
Beduin child and all the Beduin, and all the other passengers; sometimes
he signalled to the man at the wheel to give her a spoke this way or that.
The cutter began to pull back towards the ship, coming very slowly
though they were doing their best (the oars were short and bad). She
seemed to come slowly because of the obvious danger in which the ship
herself now lay. To make things worse, the Beduin, unable any longer to
control their excitement, began to rush the poop in their anxiety to see all
that went on. There was now nothing more to do than to get the cutter
and its people safely aboard, and then to let the ship fall off from the wind
again, but true to all the instincts of passengers the world over, the Beduin
who had been helpless and useless before now clamored and scrambled
and stormed and yelled.

"Get down off this infernal poop!" yelled Nejdi, in its Arabic version. (I assume that is what he yelled.) "Get down off this poop, you
bunch of scum!"

The Beduin, as Beduin will, kept on coming; those in the front ranks
being driven on by the impetus of those behind. Nejdi and Hamed bin
Salim snatched up camel canes, and Majid the Suri and Said the Smuggler
advanced behind them. Nejdi wasted no time, but slashed into the midst of
the advancing Beduin, driving them down from the poop so that the cutter might be hoisted in safety, and the child, if he needed attention, receive it without further risk to his life. Still the mob behind came on. The

cliffs of Ras Haifun gave back yell for yell from the excited passengers, and the scene aboard was pandemonium. The cutter came on; the ship drifted: the Beduin stormed the poop. They were trying to climb up by way of the stem of the longboat, to leap over the rail, to jump from the carpenter's new dhow. What they hoped to do or to see or to gain by this maneuver was incomprehensible. They did not get far. Nejdi, who never wasted words in real emergencies, slashed about him with the cane, and behind him was his able lieutenant, Hamed bin Salim, also slashing. Gradually they made an impression on the hysterical Beduin, and the opinion seemed to gain some ground that it was not such a good idea to storm the poop.

All this time the sailors, who had been forward attending to the sail, were fighting to reach the poop again, but the intervening wedge of stampeding human beings prevented them. Abdulla bin Salim, the second serang, seeing that things might become desperate, ran hand over hand and foot after foot up the main halliards. Swarming from the masthead on to the yard, he ran out along the great yard and swung himself by means of the long vang out and down again on to the poop, in this way coming in over the heads of the Beduin. This would have been a good piece of climbing even for a monkey, but his example was immediately followed by the others one behind the other. Though this was a climb, and a feat excelling most of the ordinary performances offered by highly skilled acrobats, one and all accomplished it with a speed and seeming ease that was amazing. Down they swarmed on to the poop, hand over hand, forming a living wedge behind Nejdi. In a twinkling the situation was under control, and the Beduin began to retreat before the mariners down from the poop. The situation was so bizarre and events moved so rapidly that it seemed at the time like a kaleidoscopic dream. Looking at this scene with my own eyes my mind could only respond, This isn't happening: this *can't* be happening! The stampede of those Beduin made no sense: the rescue of the child made no sense: the bravery of the musician Ismael was of no apparent intelligence whatever, and (by me at any rate) utterly unexpected. I had so disliked his music that I had, I fear, also disliked him. After this piece of heroism, however, I tried to suffer his music, and I liked him a great deal. He was a good fellow, after all.

Now the cutter was alongside and the noise ceased, as suddenly and as completely as it had begun. With no excitement and no sound other than the chanting of the sailors, the boat was hauled aboard and the child taken up, and the ship fell off again, and upon her course. She had drifted within thirty yards of the backwash of the breakers at the cliff's edge. Ismael the musician and Abdulla the Mysterious were left to take care of themselves. Neither Nejdi nor Hamed nor any of the Beduin looked at them. Nejdi cuffed the child, who beyond the wetting and some fright was none the worse for the adventure, and told him that if he fell overboard again he would be left there. The child went forward, grinning, and Nejdi, who was a fierce man when roused, and a hard man always, went back bright-eyed to his bench, his hawk nose high and sniffing. He did not look at the cliffs or speak to Ismael and Abdulla. He left Hamed bin Salim to superintend the resetting of the sail. The emergency was over, and that rush of the Beduin had been very undignified. Nejdi hated things to be undignified.

So we sailed on, having narrowly escaped destruction. In the evening, when it was time for the daily salutations after the fourth prayer, Aura the chief of the Beduin came and said briefly "Thank you, O Nejdi, that you saved the child." Nejdi returned the salutation with quiet dignity. The storming of the passengers upon the poop and the manner of their driving from it were not mentioned, nor ever mentioned again. Nor were Abdulla and Ismael thanked. When they had come aboard Ismael went on with his work, without even attending to his clothes except to wring out the bottom of his shirt, and Abdulla the Mysterious, more mysterious, more handsome, and more gaunt than ever, changed his brown shirt and returned to his Quran-reading. But after that I looked upon them both with different eyes. I liked both Ismael and Abdulla after that, and forgave Ismael his dreadful music and Abdulla all his mystery and whatever nefarious employments might have gone with it.

We hauled our wind at the south of the promontory, and headed towards Haifun, the first of our calls in Africa. We were anchored there in a few hours. The passage so far had always been most interesting, if somewhat trying, and the sailing conditions had been very pleasant. I already had some never-to-be-forgotten images from the wandering of the big boom, pictures of moonlight upon sails, the murmur of the quiet turning of the waters at the low bow, the drowsy figure of the seated helmsman aft and the alert and bright-eyed image of Nejdi behind him, that quiet and small tornado, driver of ships and ruler of men; the softened light of the binnacle's glow falling upon the figures of the sleeping merchants, while Said the Smuggler, perhaps dreaming of some pretty slave-girl in far-off Asab or the northern borders of Baluchistan, turned in his sleep and groaned.

So we came to Haifun, which is called Dante by the Italians. By any name that place is objectionable, for it is nothing but a saltworks surrounded by sand. Once it was a famous market, and the trade of the Eastern mariners down to here is very ancient. Haifun, which is a bay tucked in the farthest corner of the southern side of the gaunt promontory of Ras Haifun, was once called Opone, and under that name the anonymous chronicler of the *Periplus of the Erythræan Sea** (supposedly writing in about the year 60 A.D., not long after Hippalus had stumbled upon the Arab's knowledge of the monsoon winds) has something to say about it. Exactly how much that chronicler or compiler knew about some of the places he describes on the African east coast is open to doubt, for his estimates of distances are so confusing and his descriptions of places so vague as to leave some doubt as to whether he ever saw them. In the thirteenth paragraph of his very brief *Periplus* (his Directory of the Indian Seas covers the whole of the Red Sea, the Gulf of Aden, the Gulfs of Oman, Persia, and Cutch, the Arabian Sea, the Swahili coast and the west coast of India, in sixty-six paragraphs, none of which is very long) the compiler says:

"And then, after sailing four hundred stadia along a promontory, toward which place the current also draws you, there is another market-town called Opone, into which the same things are imported as those already mentioned, and in it the greatest quantity of cinnamon is produced (the *arebo* and *moto*), and slaves of the better sort, which are brought to Egypt in increasing numbers: and a great quantity of tortoise-shell, better than that found elsewhere."

The author of the *Periplus* goes on to say:

"The voyage to all these far-side market-towns is made from Egypt about the month of July, that is Epiphi. And ships are customarily fitted out from the places across this sea, from Ariaca and Barygaza, bringing to these far-side market-towns the products of their own places: wheat, rice, clarified butter, sesame oil, cotton-cloth (the *monache* and *sagmatogene*) and girdles, and honey from the reed called *sacchari*. Some make the voyage especially to these market-towns, and others exchange their cargoes while sailing along the coast."

It is interesting that this cargo, listed in the year 60 A.D., was precisely the same as that which we carried down to Opone alias Haifun alias Dante in the year of grace 1939, and though Opone in these days is far from being the prosperous market place it once was and it is now difficult

* I quote from Schoff's translation. (*Periplus of the Erythræan Sea*, translated and annotated by Wilfred H. Schoff, A.M.: Longmans, Green and Co., 1912.)

to sell these things, our group of Sinbads did their best. There were a few differences. Our girdles (by which I suppose is meant the folds of cloth the Somalis love to wrap about themselves, and not the feminine garments of the same name) were made in Japan, and our "honey from the reed called sacchari" was plain Javanese sugar from the Dutch East Indies, transshipped at Aden. Most of our ghee was in the Standard Oil Company's rejected containers. We had not made the voyage "especially to these market-towns," for the markets have long been run down: we were among the "others exchanging their cargoes while sailing along the coast." We saw nothing of cinnamon and tortoise-shell: all we got out of Haifun were some very dead sharks. As for those slaves of the better sort, the only thing I learned about them was that they could scarcely have been of the same tribe as the present-day Somalis. The Somali is rarely a slave, and would never be a slave of the better class.

Our stay at Haifun was, I suppose, typical of the carryings on of the average dhow today. I had a few surprises, none of them particularly pleasant ones. When I had thought of this trading voyage before it was begun, I had visions of a succession of pleasant ports up African rivers and in romantic bays, staying in each while the ship exchanged her goods: but I had dreamed of these things without any knowledge of the Somali coast. Now we had come to our first port and it was nothing but a semi-circle of dull sand, the beach covered with sheep dung and the entrails of fish, the center of the scene a very modern saltworks sending out salt in steel buckets along an endless conveyor to a berth offshore. To the right of this salt plant were some Italian bungalows and the house of the Resident, with the Italian flag. To the left, a mean Somali village straggled along the hot beach, nondescript and squalid, soon giving up the hopeless attempt to find sustenance in such a place.

Out in the bay, one of a tier of three Kuwait ships and two Persians, we swung to our anchors, while the offshore wind blew the filth of the maindeck back over the poop and life aboard was hell. We stayed there two weeks during which very little happened. For days nothing happened at all. Our first welcomers were a boarding party of two Italians, a Somali dispenser, and several soldiers. The Italians, having learned from long experience the necessity for it, at once proceeded to draw up as comprehensive a list as they could manage, of the persons on board. They tried hard to complete this day after day, but it was a farce. All the Suri and various other mysterious travellers had disappeared over the side as we came in, and the list, even after four days' hard work, was far from complete. It never was complete. The Somali dispenser, looking very depressed, went through the lot scratching their arms with a piece of sharp steel and wiping in some smallpox antitoxin. I should not blame the Italians very much if they did not feel particularly welcoming about these visits of the Arab dhows, but, after all, they took the place, and this Arab trade is very old. The Arabs bring goods for Arab stores to sell to the Somali, and do not compete with any Italian trades: they could not if they wished, and they are not interested. I noticed then and always that our trade was with Arabs only, just as later I saw that the Indian kotias from Cutch and Bombay traded only with and for their own people.

Day after day, we swung there in Haifun Bay in a welter of filth and flying smuts, while the Beduin fished and fought and yelled, and nothing else happened. No one was allowed ashore (apart from the ship's own people), and I wondered what we had come there for. Being a European travelling with Arabs I was a suspect, though of what I did not know. I appeared to be taken for a British Agent or a subversive influence of some kind. Perhaps I was going to stir up trouble in Abyssinia, or spread a little unrest among the Somali, who never are very restful. I was inclined to laugh at this suspicion, but it worried Nejdi seriously. It was real enough. He said if I was suspect, so also were the ship and himself, which was bad for trade. The Italians have agents themselves—or did have—in Iraq and the Yemen, and elsewhere, none of whom spread the gospel of peaceful acceptance of this best of all possible worlds. Perhaps their own use of these perfidious propagandists helped to make them suspicious of me. Nejdi said they were always very suspicious. He added that they refused to believe Lawrence was dead—he called him Yawrens—and that they were dreadfully suspicious of all Britishers and also of most Arabs. The idea of being mistaken for Lawrence, though highly flattering, scarcely held water, even amongst Bedu. Lawrence was a small man, short, and very fair: I was six feet high and even after two months sailing with the Arabs, still weighed 160 pounds. Lawrence was dead, as all the world knew: there was nothing mysterious about the manner of his passing.

However, there it was, and I certainly was a prisoner on board. My arm was scratched with the steel and the antitoxin rubbed into the wound by the Somali, and that was that. There I stayed. More booms came, more sambuks lay in idleness at their anchors, some of them seemingly deserted. This Arab trading was the most casual business. We just stayed there and nothing happened. Nothing, that is to say, with regard to the trade of the ship. Said and Majid and the other smugglers, who appeared again when the census of our passengers had been completed (in the meantime they lived quite unnoticed aboard other ships which had already been cleared), began their smuggling without delay—Hamed bin Salim, Abdulla Nejdi, and nearly all the crew followed their example, and there was a great movement of haberdashery, gay rags, and diluted perfumes in little bottles to that dung-strewn beach. More often the Somali came out and themselves took the stuff. They came by night, in dugout canoes, or slipped by in the shadow of the ship in their fishing boats, and stowed a bundle of sarongs beneath the fish as they passed. They were very smart. Other regular traders were whiskered Sinbads from the Suri ships who had no money and always asked for credit. They took a great deal, but what they did with the large stocks they were continually taking away, I was not sure. I think they often landed it elsewhere, at smaller ports along the open coast between Haifun and Mogadishu.

It was always very interesting for me on board, and the scene was always diverting. I did not mind not being allowed to land. Even in a dreadful place like Haifun, no day on board the *Triumph of Righteousness* was ever wholly like another. After some days I saw beauty in Haifun itself, for the encircling sandhills could be very beautiful in the sunsets and dawns.

I was still very lame and could scarcely walk, but I was happy enough on board. The monotony of the awful food did not really matter, and if the water was bad, I must have gained immunity by that time. If I were to catch any illness from our Bedu, it was a risk I had to take. A few of them showed the early stages of some minor form of leprosy.

I used frequently to marvel at the taciturn acceptance by the Bedu of whatever happened, whether expected or not, planned or not. When they came aboard in Shihr they had been told that the whole passage would take not more than ten days, yet they had been three weeks aboard before we even thought of leaving Haifun. They did not seem to mind. It is doubtful whether they even noticed the passing of so many days, for to them Allah's compassion was ever sufficient. They met no troubles halfway. I wondered what they did about food, but they could survive on very little, and fish were plentiful. They could usually get a piece of *khubz* from the ship, though most of them preferred to make their own. They liked theirs done in ashes, with plenty of the ashes left on.

Our days began long before dawn, and the muezzins began their calls to prayer some time before I could detect the faintest tinge of grayness in the eastern sky. The sheikh from Shihr, who had deposed our sailor

Sultan from his monotonous job, insisted on making several extra calls each day, and his timing was too preposterous even for the Arabs. Though the Arab may not have very fixed ideas about time, at least there are fairly well-defined periods for the announcements of the five daily prayers—dawn, with the first lighting of the sky; morning, a little after the sun has passed its meridian; third, or afternoon, when the sun has lost its glare and its redness is whitening and the shadows are long; fourth, or evening, immediately after sunset; fifth, or night, any time between sunset and dawn, but usually, for the convenience of the ship, about two hours after sunset. Our sheikh from Shihr, who was a most scurvy creature and as unsheikhlike as a Brooklyn longshoreman, delighted so in his muezzin calls that he used to make them three and four times in the same morning, sleeping between calls and waking with a conception of time so hazy that he obviously did not know it was still the same day. He became so bad that Nejdi, who hated doing anything active about anything, had at last to rig up the ship's bell on a beam before the quartermaster's seat, and have the quartermaster strike the bell at the right time for the prayer calls. The bell, which looked more as if it should have been round a cow's neck than aboard a ship, had been bought from a junkyard at Bombay, whence comes so much of the Arab dhows' seagoing gear. This new system worked for a few days, but then the quartermasters forgot. Things went on as before and, after a while, the bell disappeared down below again.

Prayers, breakfast, cooking, eating, sleeping, catching fish, cleaning fish, looking at what went on aboard the other vessels, fighting, yelling, picking off lice from sarongs and shirts—so the days passed for our Bedu at that hot anchorage, while the first-class passengers from the poop smuggled industriously.

One bright morning I watched the scene on deck. It was typical of what I might have observed any morning. On the port side—upon the small forecastle head which was really only a working platform for the anchors and the fore tacks—Jassim the cook and a passenger were methodically killing and skinning a Somali goat, a large beast which had stood tethered to the port cable during the night. On the other side of the forecastle head, three sailors cleaned fish caught during the night by Hassan the helmsman and Mohamed Amiri who, having fished all night, were now snoring in the lee of the firebox while the Beduin milled all round them. This fish-cleaning was anything but a hygienic business. No time was wasted on such nonsense as stripping the scales, or washing out the fish: they were split with a blow from an axe, the backbone slit with a rusted knife, and the flesh pounded with coarse salt liberally mixed with whatever else might be blowing round on deck, stamped in by the sailors' feet. The deck was bloody and unscrubbed, the salt grubby and uncleaned. I lost all interest in fish, and firmly resolved to avoid all dishes with fish in them from that time onwards. (For that matter, any visit forward was enough to put me off the ship's food for all time.) When the fish had been opened and salted, they were threaded on a piece of light coir rope and hung in the sun.

In the meantime the goat-slaughtering was completed, and Jassim and the Bedu his mate were coiling the dead goat into the big pot. Watching them was a young Beduin boy with long hair and soft gentle features, who looked, but for the straightness of his lithe body, very like a girl. He wore a silver bracelet on his right wrist, and a dagger was thrust into the folds of his sarong. He was a gentle boy and he and the old chief Aura were the quietest persons on board. I wondered what had brought him down on this long voyage, bound towards Zanzibar. Once I asked him, but he did not know. He did not seem to know even where the ship was going. He was a very shy and reserved youth. I gathered that there was a famine in his tribe, and not food enough for the young men. He had heard the elders speak of opportunities in Africa: therefore he came. He was from the far interior of the Hadhramaut, near the borders of the Great Desert. Would he return there, I asked him. Most certainly, he said, for Allah was compassionate. He hoped he might not remain in Africa more than three or four years. I wondered where he would be allowed to land, and how he paid his fare, for even a few rupees are a fortune to such as he. He told me that he and some of the other young men of the tribe brought frankincense to Mukalla on their camels from the borders of the desert, and in Mukalla they sold both camels and cargo.

By the messy, smoky firebox Jassim, looking sadder and blacker than ever, squatted on the tiny fore hatch and stirred the goat-pot with a piece of wood. The hatch itself was a dreadful sight, covered with pieces of goat's entrails and fish's scales, and littered with firewood, utensils, date stones, and scraps of *khubz*. Abdulla Nejdi and his gang, regardless of all else, continued their packing of "best" Basra dates. If these really were best Basra dates, Basra dates must be extremely bad, and I wanted none of them: but the label was libellous. They were very old dates which the Arabs wanted to sell to the Somali, who were not particular, and they disguised them in the new packages the better to make a sale. We had sixty large packages of these dates, shipped from some merchant's go-down in Aden. There they had lain for years, awaiting a rising market. Now, if they could not be sold to the Somali they might as well be dumped in the sea, for no one else would have them.

Beneath the poop of the new dhow a tiny girl lay sleeping, a fat little mite in a long print dress with a black hood, her chubby small hands and her chubbier small face liberally decorated with lines of black and henna. From her ears hung silver ornaments, about ten to each lobe, which jingled when she walked. There were two heavy silver bangles round her ankles, and she looked as if she were acting as transport for the family jewels. These little girls were seen on deck only in the daylight hours, for by night nothing female except the ship's cat was allowed outside the confines of the great cabin. Stretched along the rough planks of the dhow's bottom some of the Beduin lay asleep, their heads protected from the sun by the light folds of their black girdles, for the Bedu had no headcloths nor turbans. Others on the main deck, crouching wherever there was space, were preparing food over tiny fires, frying fish, boiling rice, frying *khubz*. Some ate. Some made coffee, in long-spouted brass pots designed to extract the maximum heat from the minimum number of embers. Some drank coffee. The poorer the coffee the more elaborate the manner of serving it, some of the Beduin handing round the thimbles' full of black mud as if it were nectar from the gods, bowing and clicking the porcelain cups against the spout, as though they were headwaiters at the Ritz. Some answered the calls of nature in little pews along the ship's side: one cleaned out a pot, rather perfunctorily: two small boys fought and no one interfered with them. They were doing no harm. Elsewhere on the maindeck, Beduin oiled themselves, and buttered one another's hair. Aft on the poop a Suri merchant wrapped a couple of new sarongs about his waist and two more above his knees before going ashore, for Aden sarongs brought good prices there, and he could sell them to the Arab stores. Near him a Hadhramaut child, not without viciousness in his coarse face, wolfed at a dish of rice as though he feared some one would take it from him. A dispute broke out, somewhere near the watertanks.

Old Yusuf Shirazi, squatting on a chest near me, was very busy at something, and did not even look up at this new outbreak of noise. I watched what he was doing. He was still at the same mysterious occupation I had observed off Ras Haifun. He was making medicine, though it looked like witches' brew to me. He had a number of tiny packages of seeds and things and some herbs tied up in corners of old turbans. Twisted pieces of weeds, odds and ends of leaves, dried and very ancient seeds, pieces of bark and lengths of something that looked like string—all these went in, and Yusuf pounded and mixed them industriously. What was it for? I asked him, but he replied only that it was medicine. He pointed to his eyes, which were running. Allah was compassionate, he said: it would be good medicine. He added that he was making a brew to drink, not a lotion. He was mixing the stuff in the lower half of a broken Basra pot, and he stirred it with the point of a Beduin dagger. I wished I could have done something for his eyes, but I could not. It was an old infection. It dated from his pearl-diving days, he said. He had been a pearl diver from Kuwait for years, and thanked God that he was finished with that life. It was hard on the eyes and on the lungs, to say nothing of the stomach. He stirred his brew methodically. It was the most extraordinary medicine I had ever seen.

I learned later that the "medicine" was a concoction for increasing the flow of milk from the breasts of Beduin matrons. What Yusuf wanted was milk to bathe his eyes, because milk was good for them. The "medicine" was a secret of the harem he had learned in Kuwait. It was to be used to induce a copious flow of milk from the breasts of a Beduin lady in the great cabin, a matron of ripe years who had offered her co-operation.

In the background, fourteen sambuks, mainly from the Mahra coast and the smaller ports near Sur, lay at anchor as idly as ourselves, and the crew of a Suri drummed and danced while their water came on board. It was bad water, from a stagnant well. Perhaps the noise was to scare the jinns out of it.

The days passed at that Haifun anchorage, and the decks which were never cleaned grew filthier and filthier until the maindeck was a morass on which I was almost afraid to go. The sun shone, the Beduin yelled, the fish stank, and we still worked no cargo. Nothing happened. I began to think we might have dropped in there by error. But if we were there by mistake, I wished the mistake could be rectified and we would go, for Haifun was no ideal anchorage and to stay there on board an Arab dhow cooped up with a horde of Beduin had its less pleasant features.

While we lay there I had many opportunities to examine and to visit the lovely Persian baggala anchored near us, for the ban on my landing did not apply to visiting other vessels in the harbor. This was the same baggala which had sailed from Aden and Mukalla with us. She was called the *Hope of Compassion* (a name which, like our own, was sometimes changed), her nakhoda was a Persian named Sulieman Radhwan bin Said, exiled to Kuwait, her crew numbered thirty-three, and her capacity was 3000 packages of dates. She was a lovely vessel of about 200 tons. I was surprised to see that, though she was larger than we were and had much roomier decks, she had no passengers. Nejdi said passengers would not go in baggalas: they preferred booms. The baggala, he said, was becoming extinct: baggalas were less seaworthy than booms, and their carved sterns, though stately and picturesque, were apt to be dangerous in a pounding sea. Perhaps the evil reputation of Sulieman bin Said had something to do with the baggala's lack of passengers, for I was told that the Persian exile had a hard name. He was a small man with very bright black eyes set closely in a parchment face, and his chinstrap beard made him appear almost devilish. Though he was Persian he dressed always in the Kuwait fashion, in a long white gown, with headcloth and *aghal* on his head. Other Persians wore their turbans wrapped tightly round their heads, bound in a smooth, almost geometric, manner which was quite distinctive. I gathered that Sulieman Radhwan no longer felt any pride in his nationality.

In the baggala were the nakhoda's two sons, cheerful boys about eight and twelve years old who clamored to be photographed whenever they saw me. They were apprentices, but what they learned was a matter left entirely to them. They appeared to have learned a great deal about skylarking.

The *Hope of Compassion* had been a week at Haifun before we arrived, and Sulieman gave a feast for us the next day. I was at this feast. It consisted of the usual goat and rice, served under an awning on the poop. It was at least better than our fish, and the baggala was most interesting. She was the largest of the surviving baggalas, and in many ways the most picturesque. To sit on the bench abaft her wheel, high in the afterpart of the steeply rising poop, and to look from there along the picturesque romantic sweep of her ancient decks, from the worn planks of the poop to the curved horn at the low bow, never failed to stir me, and though we saw that baggala many times again and I was aboard her on countless occasions, I always left her with reluctance. She was beautiful from outside, and she was beautiful on board. Her windowed stern was especially lovely. Its elliptical area of ancient teak was covered with intricate patterns of excellent carving, and her curved bow swept up from the sea as gracefully as the breast of a swan. She was big, for an Arab. Her oiled teak hull sat prettily in the water with a grace and strength and sweetness of line that sang of sea-kindliness, despite all Nejdi's comments on the vulnerability of her stern. I wondered how, if her stern was so vulnerable, she had managed to survive so long, for she dated back to the slaving days. She was very old—more than half a century. Like so many Arab vessels, every line of her flowed and blended perfectly into a harmonious and lovely whole, though she had been put together on the beach at Sur by carpenters who could not understand the most elementary plan. She was built by eye, and she was built beautifully, though she was but a heap of indifferent teak poorly fastened with weak iron; and, here and there, an ill-butted plank had warped, and all her fastenings wept with rust-stains from every pitted head, and caulking of poor cotton-stuff poked from her sides. Her quarter-galleries were latticed delicately, like the narrow windows of a harem court: her five stern windows were protected by iron bars, and a teak shutter swung from the central window richly carved in patterns of crescents and stars.

To step over her high bulwarks on to that spacious main deck was to slip back five centuries, for aboard as overside she was a craft of the Middle Ages. Her deck layout was almost exactly a counterpart of our own, even to the carpenter working on his new dhow. She had the same low forecastle head; the same heavy beams for belaying halliards and cables; the firebox with its crouching smoke-grimed cook; wooden watertanks, one on each side, the great bole of the raking mainmast rising from the forward end of the long narrow main hatch, though her masts were higher than ours. Her maindeck was made of worn old planks unfit to keep the water out, and her heavy bulwarks were made even higher by washboards raised two feet above them, fore and aft. She had a number of great ringbolts in the deck capable of lashing a liner's bower, and a big capstan that looked as if it might have come out of Nelson's *Victory* stood near the poop overhand. She was much more ornate and elaborate than our own new *Triumph*; and was obviously the product of a more leisured age. Whenever carving and embellishments could be added they had been, and the precincts of the poop were liberally decorated in this way. The break of the poop was low, and there was not headroom to walk under there, but the deck of the poop sheered high, and in the after part of the spacious great cabin there was seven feet of headroom. (This was the only Arab vessel I ever boarded which had good headroom in the poop.) The whole break of the poop was carved with a delicate tracery of involved patterns into which texts from the Quran had been worked. The reclining bench for the officers aft was not as ours was, a rough construcion of unfinished wood, but an elaborately finished and well-joined piece of built-in furniture, protected by a carved teak railing, low enough to vault over and high enough to be of protection to the sleeping men—high enough at any rate, to prevent them from being rolled outboard or flung inboard by a heavy roll. Aboard our *Triumph* we had no such protection. The baggala's poop was very different from our own, though like it in essentials—the small working capstan, the inevitable rows of chests, the rising mizzenmast towering above, the binnacle, the wheel, and the helmsman's chair. It differed in its air of hallowed age and its deep but indefinable attraction, its caressing song of untold romantic voyaging. It sang in every worn old plank of those ancient decks, and all its songs were stirring.

That poop and that whole ship put their arms round any sailorman who ever stepped aboard, and he had to love her, though she wept her caulking from her poor old planks and a fourth of all the sea over which she had ever sailed had leaked through her, and she reeked of fish-oil. Upon that poop I found my mind turn easily down channels that led to pirates and slaves and all those long-gone far-off things, and I could see again all the wondrous ships of my pre-maritime youth, when all the sea was wonderful and every ship an ark of grand adventure. How different had the reality been! Yet here, on board this ancient Arab dhow lying at that stifling anchorage, hundreds of miles from anywhere upon that forlorn coast, it was easy to dream again of the sea there never was, knowing so well the sea there is. Pirates and slaves, doubloons and gold, song and merriment, women and rum. The strange thing was that they *had* all been there—the pirates, the slaves (Swahili from Zanzibar and Mozambique), the pretty dancing girls and the travelling harem, the little slave virgins for the merchants of Sur and Oman and whoever else could buy them: and the song of Ismael and all his kind. In place of rum there was arrack from the Tigris dates, though Sulieman, a bigoted man, touched nothing of this kind. Aye, aye, pirates and slaves: both had walked here. For that matter, both walked there now. Down on the maindeck, after the meal, lately freed slaves chanted and danced merrily, and on the poop Sulieman Said was by way of being something of a pirate himself. For Sulieman Said was planning to steal a cargo in Haifun Bay, and he wanted —I believe—our Nejdi to help him.

Chapter 6

THE SONS OF SINBAD

MYSTERIOUS THINGS happened on board that baggala. She was half-empty when we came in and I wondered where her cargo had been landed, for it was not sold in Haifun. It was sold somewhere in Somaliland. That at least was certain. In the nights, when there was no moon, I often noticed Somali dugouts and sewn boats moving silently over the harbor, making towards the place where Sulieman's big vessel lay. They went out deep-laden and they returned empty. What were they bringing out so mysteriously? None came to us. Their paddlers never chanted. They slipped by silently, unlit, furtive. After five nights of watching I began to wonder what was going on. What were they taking off so furtively to the baggala? I racked my brains and thought of many things, from skins to ivory. The ancient trade round those parts in skins of leopards and of lions is now regulated and under government control; besides, it would have taken several thousand slaughtered beasts to fill all those boats with skins. But what were their cargoes? Ivory? That was still good stuff to smuggle—dangerous, though. I would put nothing beyond any Arab or any Persian, wandering Africa way in a dhow. Whatever trade, legal or otherwise, might bring some rupees to his deep pockets he would try.

Night after night the canoes and the sewn boats continued to flit by. Yusuf said they were fishermen. The others pretended not to see them. Sulieman himself was often aboard our boom, usually coming in the mornings, very early, and going ashore with Nejdi.

One night the canoes stopped coming. The baggala was deep in the water then, and the sailors were bending her big lateen main. Yusuf said she was to sail in the morning, bound directly for Zanzibar. But in the morning something had very obviously gone wrong. The baggala did not sail. Instead, a boat full of Italian and Somali police came out and arrested Sulieman Said.

Even then I could learn nothing from my taciturn shipmates, who were, however, not so uninterested that they did not rush about and in five minutes effectively hide all the haberdashery and other trade goods which, after the first casual customs inspection, had been openly left in the chests and tied up in bundles all about the poop. Yusuf Shirazi disappeared hurriedly down the hatch of the great cabin. What he was doing down there I did not know, but I heard a great deal of yelling and shoving. I found out later that he was arranging the women on their mats, very carefully, so that they hid the tiny hatch leading to the secret chamber deep below, right in the bottom of the ship. What was in the chamber I did not know, but I could guess. Part of it was probably wads of Italian paper lire.

All these efforts were, however, unnecessary, for the Italians did not bother us. We saw them pull by in their boat, with Sulieman Said looking very sorry for himself, seated in the stern sheets between two large Somalis. After the Italians had gone, Nejdi rushed ashore, taking all his henchmen with him—the muallim Hamed bin Salim, the Suri smugglers Said and Majid, the Seyyid from the Hadhramaut, and another red-bearded man who was prominent among the first-class passengers, one Abu Ali, who was generally vociferous on these occasions. Off they dashed in the longboat, with our sailors singing. We could see a Somali guard over the baggala. Yet even that morning, when our friend Sulieman had just been apprehended for something serious, Hamed, Said, Majid, and the others still smuggled. As they dashed over the side into the longboat, they all had sarongs, money-belts, and turbans lashed about them beneath their robes, round their waists, their thighs, and their knees, and their pockets were full as always of tiny bottles of blended perfumes.

But what was all this about? What had Sulieman been caught doing? I took my binoculars and kept them fixed on the baggala all day, determined to solve the mystery. I could find out nothing from my shipmates. Grins, shrugs, cheerful expressions of profound belief in the mercies of the All-Highest—this was all they granted me. It was useless to ask questions. So I watched, hour after hour, and before the day was out I learned that the Italians had discovered aboard the baggala a hold full of stolen salt, taken from the beach under their very eyes—two hundred tons of it. The unromantic nature of the cargo was somewhat made up for by the audaciousness of its theft—two hundred tons. My first feeling was one of regret that Sulieman had not sailed with it, for to purloin all that salt was a fine gesture of contempt. The last canoe-load, apparently, and his own anxiety to be gone, had proved his undoing. He had gone along the beach by night to see that last boat-load go, and he finished with the business. A customs officer chancing to be down upon the beach to take the air (or more probably with an eye upon some shapely Somali wench) saw the nakhoda, and followed him. After that, discovery was simple. The Somali were caught redhanded, and Sulieman with them. He blustered, but it was no use. Worse still, he was caught with the lire on him with which he was to pay for his cargo, and he had not got those lire from an Italian bank, as the regulations require. They were smuggled lire, bought illegally in the 'black' market at Aden. It looked as though Sulieman would come badly out of this business, for the Italians are even stricter about currency smuggling than the stealing of salt. The situation was rather bad.

We were not left very long in doubt about Sulieman's sad fate. I thought it might have been sadder. His lire were confiscated, the salt was taken back to the beach (this took three days of hard work, in five or six boats) and the baggala was fined one thousand rupees. This was stiff, for a thousand rupees is a large sum in the East. Sulieman had borrowed most of the lire from our ship, from whom I did not know. These were gone, and he had not a thousand rupees. In this emergency, an emissary was sent from the shore to appeal for our help. I was interested to see the instant response of all on board. Nejdi himself, Hamed bin Salim, Abdulla Nejdi's brother, Said, Majid, and the others, the quartermasters, the serang, Kaleel the carpenter, even Jassim the cook, all went at once to their chests on the poop and, diving into their inmost recesses, brought forth all the rupees they had. Some had only two, others four or five. Hamed bin Salim had about 400, but these included some belonging to the ship. All were made available, and within twenty minutes we had over 600 rupees collected, thrown carelessly on to a headcloth by the capstan. I made up the balance for they appealed to me as one of their shipmates. Then off went the emissary, looking relieved but still worried to get Sulieman out of the jail. It was a bad jail, he said, and I can well believe it. I never saw it. Sulieman was freed that night and he sailed next morning. He went out from Haifun a sadder but no wiser man. What he proposed to do next to recoup his fortunes I did not know, but there would be something. Later—considerably later—we heard of the baggala being up to something down the Madagascar Channel.

It was a quiet day with a gentle breeze off the land when Sulieman sailed. The baggala showed no flag and her crew gave no cheers. The sailors hove her short, raised the peak of the lateen main, broke out her hook, and she turned upon her lovely heel and went. She was a picture of grace and beauty as she turned her carved and galleried stern to the sand of Haifun Bay and, though she went out without the cargo she had come to take and her nakhoda had to be considered an ignominious failure in his attempt at bare-faced stealing, she looked a ship of romance and real adventure as the land wind filled her great sail that morning. It took them a long time to masthead the sail that fluttered out golden in the morning air: her burnished hull slipped slowly through the blue water as if loath to depart from the scene of her shame.

What Nejdi had to do with this incident I should never have discovered by asking him, or indeed by seeking information directly from any Arab. But it was something. I saw him add some lovely Persian carpets to the pile with which Sulieman finally bribed himself out of the jail, and he would not have done that without a direct interest. Our Nejdi, like all the other wanderers with dhows, was ready for whatever turned up, though he was clever enough usually to keep his own hands out of the dirty work. It began to occur to me that perhaps the legitimate trade which we carried on so haphazardly was not our main source of income but I did not know, at that stage of the voyage, what was. We had the villains for any perfidy—the Suris Said the smuggler, and Majid the loud-mouthed, and Abdulla the Mysterious who even then was skulking somewhere ashore never seen by the eyes of European man. What *did* that fellow get up to? Whatever it was, I looked on him with favor. His prompt and able assistance of Ismael when the Beduin child fell overboard showed him to be a brave man. He could do what he liked in Somaliland, so far as I was concerned.

I suppose it was wrong of me to take that attitude: but I had grown to like the Arabs, especially this scoundrelly group of old Sinbads who dwelt on our poop. Sinbad himself, liar that he was, could not have concocted adventures such as were commonplace with them; Sinbad himself, that old Arab scoundrel, would not have been ashamed to ship out with us. I sometimes tried to imagine the old reprobate as one of these merchant-adventurers of ours. He must have been much the same kind of man. All our wanderers from the Gulf of Oman and the Persian Gulf were potential Sinbads, even the sailors, each with his chest of goods and his readiness for any sort of profitable adventure. Sinbad, for that matter, appears to have been more merchant than sailor; but the two callings go together in Arabia. Our smuggler-in-chief, the Suri Said, was a Sinbad, if ever there was one. So was Nejdi. So were Hamed bin Salim, Abdulla the Mysterious, the other Abdulla Nejdi's brother, the Hadhrami Abu Ali, the Persian Sulieman Said.

I looked across at old Said, wily, wizened old devil, as he prepared himself for the shore, and thought of the many occasions when that old Sinbad must similarly have prepared himself. Said was bound on a smuggling expedition. It was amusing to watch him prepare himself for this. First, he wrapped six money belts around his waist. Then he covered these with three sarongs of good quality. Then he added two of poor quality. A cape of tasselled and decorated turbans he slung over his bare back. That done, he wrapped more sarongs and turbans round his thighs, four to a thigh, and two more round his knees. When all this had been done, he pulled on a new gown. Over that he drew an old gown, the pockets of which he stuffed with small bottles of perfume. Then he carefully wrapped a new turban round his head. On top of that, he placed his old one, first having wrapped a parcel of hashish in a knotted corner. He looked rather fat by this time, though he was naturally a very lean man —he added a few spare strings of prayer beads, made of artificial amber manufactured in Germany, to his pockets, and called loudly for his boy Mohamed, who was next loaded. Mohamed grinned delightedly during the performance, while he was dressed in four sarongs, eight turbans, two shirts, and three money belts. He grinned if only for the pleasure of having such finery to wear, for it was the only time the boy had it. Said, his master, dressed him well only when there was nefarious work afoot. Mohamed knew his part. When he had been dressed, he shuffled down into the longboat lying alongside, and took his place in the bow away from the merchants, who sat aft. It would not do if he landed with them. He was always the first ashore, hurrying off to the rendezvous with his load of haberdashery and then, an hour or two later, wandering back aboard again to pass the morning swimming with Aura's baby son and other cronies. Mohamed was a bright boy. He was one of the best smugglers aboard.

In the meantime Hamed bin Salim, Abdulla Nejdi, Abu Ali, and several strange Suri from a sambuk near by were similarly robing, and by the time the longboat was ready to go ashore it must have had several hundred rupees' worth of dry goods on board. The sailors did not have much, and preferred to keep their best goods for the better markets farther south. But they took enough. The only people in the ship who did not smuggle, so far as I could see, were the carpenter and the cook, both of whom were far too busy.

All this was doubtless illegal and ought thoroughly to be condemned, but it interested me. The Arabs made a game of it. They went off like a group of school-children, happy and carefree: this sort of thing was their life. Said, the ringleader, was such a thorough and unscrupulous scoundrel, so absolutely without pretence, so genuinely and wholly what we call bad that I rather admired him, if only for the complete straightforwardness of his perfidy, and I always watched with fascinated interest to see what he would be up to next. There was no nonsense about him; he did not play at being bad, though he made a game of his smuggling. As for his obvious contempt for our regulation-ridden world, I confess I could not bring myself to blame him. We Europeans have never made the Arabs' life easier, and much of what we do was utterly inexplicable to them. They came down that coast to trade, and trade they did, and it would take more than the Italians to stop them. They had their own philosophy of life, and so long as what they did conformed with their own standard, I would not condemn them.

Said was a smuggler and, according to European standards, a bad man. Majid, by any standards, was even worse, but each day I found myself liking that cheerful old reprobate even better. If a man is "bad" there is some merit in being wholehearted about it. Abdulla the Mysterious, too, was probably a public menace wherever he appeared, and the most innocent form of activity in which he would have been engaged was the collection of dues for some religious sect. This is an occupation disliked by the Italians and the British alike, for it is a drain upon African wealth to no good purpose. Abdulla was an agent of some kind; that at least was certain. But I liked him, too, though I rarely spoke to him, and he shared no thoughts not expressed by the prophet in the Quran.

The list of our "criminals," I suppose, might be continued. Nejdi himself, if his iniquities were ever brought home to him, might languish for years in some Italian jail. Yet I hope he will keep out of one. Our Nejdi was a smuggler, too: he was an adventurer with a wandering dhow ready for whatever might turn up, and scrupulous about nothing except the tenets of his religion. Any enterprise which promised profit he would follow, but our own sea commerce surely developed much along those lines. Were not such qualities the envied merits of our glorious pioneers? Our own adventurers, wandering the globe in tiny ships, had opened up sea routes and laid the foundation of empires; poor Nejdi was trying only to lay the foundation of a competence for himself, and none of the Arabs had much interest in empire. To him and to Said and all their kind, the complex and unworkable system of hide-bound regulations by which we seek to control our world, and their world too, was a bad joke.

If the Arabs are contemptuous of our regulation-ridden world, I cannot find it in myself to blame them. According to their own lights, they are doing no wrong, and they are ready to face the consequences of any of their acts. They cry for no consul to aid them. They have no consuls. They are wandering seafarers doing their best to make a living, and they find that hard enough. They have a great contempt for all things Italian, for they complain that the Italians send propaganda among them in Arabia and yet harry them when they come to Somaliland. A people who cannot permit trade in their own colonies, they argue, ought quietly to withdraw from the field of propaganda.

I often yarned with our Sinbad Said, during the long evenings in Haifun when I was cooped up on board. He had trodden on a splinter of rock somewhere ashore and had an infected foot. I treated this, and he was grateful. In this way we became friends and he talked to me about his life. It took a long time to get him started, and he soon stopped. Said was not a man much given to yarning, perhaps for fear of giving away trade secrets. He was reticent, like most of the Arabs. One night he told me of his youth, when he used to go down to Africa with his father Feisal, who was a trader in slaves. Said seemed rather to regret that those good days were passed, for, according to him, there was nothing wrong with the slave trade until the British came and stopped it. He frequently sighed to think that this lucrative business had come to an end. His father had run slaves from East Africa up to the Gulf of Oman, he said, generally landing them in Sur. He prospered greatly at this, for it was a good business. He had many wives, and many sons. (Said was the fourth son of the seventh wife.) Said himself had started off early, for he had no liking to stay home when the big baggalas were sailing. When he was about six years old—Said was hazy as to ages and years—he went with his father down to a place called Bagamoyo, on the coast of Africa opposite the island of Zanzibar. That trip they went up into the Congo.

At other times they went into Abyssinia, from Assab and a place near Djibouti, but that was only to buy girls. Lovely girls, Said said with a sigh: but he had been too young to appreciate them. Eventually they drifted to other trades, finally running Baluchi girls from Baluchistan across to Oman: but fate, in the shape of the British navy, caught up at last with them, and they had to go into other fields. The father died. Said drifted about. He went here and there, buying and selling, always travelling in dhows with his cargoes. He smuggled; he ran contraband; he ran arms; but he never stole. He had, he said, done well out of the European war, from 1914 to 1918. He had been in the arms business at Muscat then; it was a good business. He ran arms up the Persian Gulf and landed them for the Beduin to carry to the Turks, to help them in their fight against the Arabs under Lawrence. I ventured to suggest that this activity was unpatriotic—were not the Arabs fighting for independence and unity? Said did not see the point. Profit was his motive, and he was not ashamed of it. If he had not run the arms, he said, somebody else would have. It was a good business. It was money from the infidel, which any of the faithful might lawfully take. Later, he ran arms to Afghanistan. That was even better. He seemed to like the arms business, not only for its profits but for its danger. Said seemed to delight in a job of smuggling or a piece of arms-running well done, and he certainly had the temperament for both occupations. But what about arms now, I said. Were there no more to be run anywhere? Well, I'm here, said Said: and I've got no arms here. I gathered that arms-running had fallen on evil days.

The old smuggler rubbed henna into his beard to redden it, while he squatted on the officers' bench of that romantic boom, and now and again shouted for the boy Mohamed to bring embers for his pipe. Astern of us Sulieman's baggala lay swinging to her anchors (for this was before she had been caught), and I thought as I looked at her dark shape and glanced from her to the profile of old Said beside me, what a wealth of exciting adventure still exists in this seemingly dull world: There, under the African sky, at that quiet forlorn anchorage, this smuggler talked to me of slaves and slavery as a going business—his relatives, he said, still carried it on somewhere in Oman—and I found myself liking him. According to him much of the British anti-slavery propaganda was overdone, for the conditions in slavers such as the big baggala then astern of us were, he said, no worse than those aboard our own crowded boom. It was a mistake to look at these vessels and their goings-on only through European eyes. Africans carried off to Arabia were invariably better for the change. Did I not see this, on board the boom? For she was half-manned with the descendants of these people. A third of the population of his own Oman, he said, had African blood—and a good life they led, or at any rate a satisfactory one.

When we had been ten days at Haifun it was announced that we should sail on the morrow. When we had been there twenty days, I was listening to the same announcement with less and less interest. We had watered the ship—I didn't see why we hadn't just filled our tanks from the sea, for Haifun water was so salty that I could not drink it—we sold a boat for a hundred rupees to some Somali fishermen; we tried to sell the bad dates from Aden, and failed, because the port medical officer, an Italian, would not allow them to be landed: and we exchanged a little of our rice and sugar for some very high dried fish. This was the sum total of our proceedings at Haifun, so far as the regular business of the ship was concerned. Beyond these things, and all the hashish and haberdashery and whatever else our Sinbads smuggled, we left nothing behind us at Haifun.

Nothing, that is, but the body of a girl who died in the great cabin. She was a young girl, aged perhaps fifteen, but by Arab standards she was a woman and she was going to Zanzibar to be married. One morning Yusuf Shirazi came quietly over to me where I sat on the poop watching a small boom come in from Batina, and said in Arabic, "Come, O Nazarene; a woman has died." He said it so calmly that for the moment I did not grasp the message: what, a woman dead? From what, and how? But Yusuf did not know. It was a young woman, he said: she died. That was all he knew. She was in the great cabin now. Would I come? The faith of the Arabs in my inconsiderable medical knowledge, merely because a few clean dressings I had put on some wounds did good, was pathetic. Here was death and they thought somehow I could cope with it.

Nejdi was ashore. So were Hamed bin Salim, and Abdulla Nejdi, Said, Majid, and the Seyyid from Mukalla. I asked Yusuf if he was sure the girl was dead. He answered that he was, in a manner that permitted no doubt. Then there was nothing I could do about it. When I heard of death and serious illness aboard that dhow I always feared for epidemics and grave infections, for the conditions were such that had any bad illness come the prospect for all of us would have been serious. Yusuf said the girl had not been sick: she just died. How? I asked him: did some one kill her? He did not know. She had taken a little *khubz* and some sweetened tea, and she fell back and died. She had not said anything. He was there at the time. He had not noticed, for he was doing some work and paying no attention to the women. One of the older women saw the girl fall back, and then they saw that she had died.

I told him to send a boat ashore for the doctor and Nejdi, for I would not go down until Nejdi came. If the girl was dead I could do nothing. Even if she had been seriously ill, I could have done nothing. But I would have tried. No one else was ill, according to Yusuf. All the occupants of the great cabin had been healthy enough, until then.

After about an hour, Nejdi came with a Somali medical dresser, and we went down. The news had been kept quiet, though somehow the report of death had spread and, for once, conditions were fairly peaceful on board.

In the great cabin the scene was unforgettable. I had not been there since the women had come aboard: no man had, except Yusuf. They had now been cooped up there about a month. The place had been cleared a little, and the stores and ship's gear moved to the sides, well aft: the bulkhead across the fore part was firmly secured. It was so gloomy that even with the hatch open, it was impossible to see when we first came in from outside, for the hatch was very small and gave little light. Through the small open port on the starboard side one ray of sunlight came, losing itself rapidly among a pile of blocks, and tackles, and empty ghee jars, piled in that corner. After a moment or so, I could see. I saw the women grouped about. There must have been twelve or more, sitting bundled up in black on mats and Beduin rugs. Only their eyes showed, and their eyes watched us. I felt all those eyes on me. In that dull gloom I did not at first see the place where the dead girl was. Then I saw that she was in the center, lying on the floor. Her face was uncovered, now that she was dead. I looked at it and saw, to my surprise, that she had been lovely. It was a startling face to come upon in a place where I had not imagined anything lovely to be. Though I had been with the Arabs for some time, this was the first time I had seen the face of a marriageable young girl. I had not known they could be so lovely.

The ship swung to her moorings, and the light from the port, diffused and golden, swung across the gloom, reaching to the girl. Poor child, even in life she had never belonged down there in that dreadful place, among that crowd of older women who huddled from her, suspicious, almost animal-like, watching not her but us. She ought never to have been in that frightful travelling prison, delivering her to a harem in Zanzibar, to a husband she had never seen, in an island far from her home. Her skin was like ivory, her features delicate, her little profile gentle and very lovely. Her small mouth was firm and well formed. Her black hair was rich and beautiful, and her eyes were closed as if in sleep. Her dress was of black satin decorated with hand-sewn wire of gold, for some one had put her in her bridal gown. Her small hands lay folded on the half-formed breasts, which were small and delicately rounded. The light moved from her and left the place in which she lay under a dark pall of gloom, but I found myself unable to take my eyes from that dead face. The other women huddled there, silent. One old woman, veiled with the Beduin eye-slitted mask instead of the all-covering veil of the town harem, moved closer, stared at the Somali dresser, and stared at me.

"From what did she die?" she said.

Merely from being there, I should have thought: Such loveliness could not survive that fetid, frightful gloom. Yet they said she had been happy. Accustomed always to hardship—she was from inland, near the desert's edge—she had not found the great cabin so bad as it seemed to me, but she must have missed fresh air. The fact that she was going far from her home to marry a man she had never seen had not troubled her, for that is a woman's lot in Arabia. The stench of the place was nauseating—the fumes of the bad ghee and all the other mysterious things of the ship's stores, the ship's own aroma of foul bilgewater and fish-oil, the unpleasant odor of the cramped-up human beings. It was as much as I could do to stay down there at all, with the hatch open and the two ports, and the ship quietly moored at anchorage. Yet here this poor girl-child had lived a month. No wonder she was dead: I do not see how she could have stayed alive.

The Somali could assign no cause for death other than heart failure.

"All hearts fail at death," Nejdi said: "do you know no more than that?"

But the Somali did not. Neither did I.

In the presence of the dead girl Nejdi seemed awed a little, and he swept a look of scorn at the other women. I discovered later that he suspected one of them of having poisoned her, for there was a woman there from the same harem, a woman sent from Zanzibar to collect this pretty virgin. Perhaps an older woman little cares to see fresh loveliness come to her lord's harem. It was all fantastic to me, like so much of what went on in that dhow. Nejdi was relieved that it was not smallpox or anything like that: a simple case of heart failure was straightforward enough. It was not his business to find out what had caused it.

In the late afternoon they buried her, taking her ashore in the stern-

East Coast of Africa, showing the voyage of the Kuwait boom

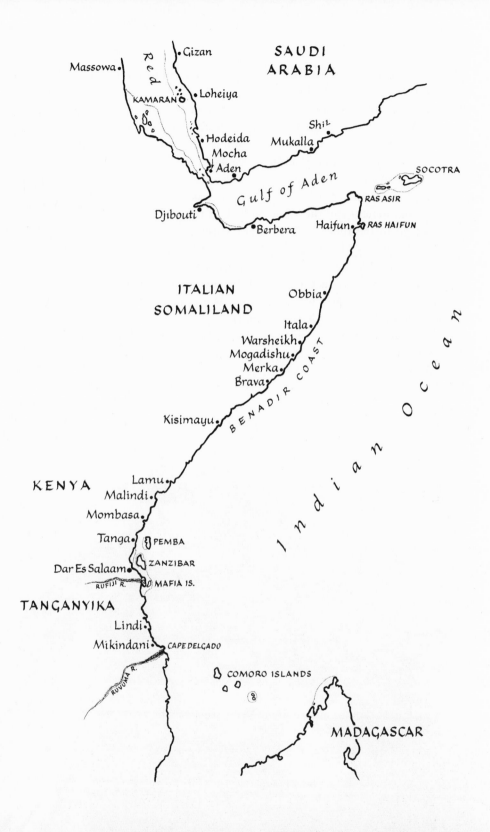

sheets of the longboat. Nejdi had gone then. Hamed bin Salim had charge of the boat and, even in that funeral procession, he still smuggled. He was not the only one who put a few extra money-belts and sarongs about his waist and knees before he went down into the boat, for Said, Majid, and the others were also there, and the boy Mohamed, not grinning now, sat in a new gown and turban up in the bow. The slight small body was covered with a black veil and wrapped in a date-frond mat. It lay in the stern-sheets in the midst of life, for the boat was crowded, and with the Beduin singing quietly and the sailors pulling at the oars, the boat was gone. I did not go to the funeral. These were Muslims and this was their ceremony. But I was sorry for the poor girl, and wondered long about her.

The following day she was apparently forgotten. In the next port I heard Nejdi deny that there had been any deaths on board.

A few days later we left Haifun. We came out from the harbor past a German steamer loading salt, and four other Arab vessels sailed with us. The wind was light, and we passed a boom coming in which was more crowded with people than any vessel I had ever seen, even among the Arabs. She was a small vessel, very decrepit, and her teak hull looked as

Sleeping mariners

Hymn of praise

if it had been long without oil. Her sail was tattered, her mast spliced in two places, and her rigging festooned with Irish pennants. But she came in bravely in the morning sunlight, her white sail bellied in the easy breeze, and the white-bordered red flag of Trucial Oman fluttered at her staff aft. Her decks were so crowded that the lowered sail looked as if it must smother a hundred people, and the sailors had to run across the passengers' shoulders. That boom could not have had a waterline of 60 feet, for she was very small, yet she had at least two hundred passengers, 90 per cent of whom were large, bearded men. They were hanging over the rail and jostling one another, all dressed in long brown shirts and loosely rolled turbans. She passed close by us. Nejdi exchanged greetings with her nakhoda, an old man with a long gray beard. He said he was twenty-one days out from Sur, and had met nothing but light winds.

That little boom was an extraordinary sight. She was so crowded that four men sat across the nakhoda's bench, which was large enough only for him, while six more sat on the rail behind. Men sat along the mizzen yard and out on the stemhead. Men hung all along the rails on both sides, and the decks were so crowded that it must have been impossible for any one to sleep. All round the rail outboard hung bundles and bales of belongings, very poor. Up forward the crew were banging Indian drums. How so small a ship could be cleared from any port with so many human beings on board I did not understand. Why, I asked Nejdi, did so many Arabs wish to leave their country at once, in so poor a vessel? Nejdi said there was trouble between Sharjah, the next port up the coast, and Dabai, whence the boom hailed—political trouble, bad enough to culminate in a local war. He left me to gather that perhaps these people from Dabai crowding that boom were fleeing from the war: but Hamed bin Salim said there was a famine round Dabai and all the Trucial coast was so poor that any one might gladly leave it, even in a 60-foot boom crowded with two hundred people. Old Yusuf Shirazi said that it was just an excursion from Dabai to Zanzibar and they had all come along for the ride.

We sailed on slowly down the Somali coast, which seemed nothing but a reach of dull sand, and the way was so easy and the conditions so good that it was like walking down a street. All the navigating we did was to sail merrily on before the northeast wind, with Africa on our right-hand side. At first the wind was very quiet, but afterwards it began to freshen, and we made nine knots. There was no way of measuring the speed, for there was not even a chip-log on board, but I could get a good idea by noting the times when we were abeam of the different points. By day we kept close in beside the coast, which was everywhere monotonous and dull: by night we hauled out a little, though not much, for it was obvious that Nejdi feared to lose sight of the land.

When it breezed up, the Beduin were seasick again and the conditions were bad. They went about again sniffing at lemons, with their noses and ears caulked with paper-wads, but it did not help: they were violently, noisily, horribly ill, and the sailors laughed. The breeze freshened on the second day until it was blowing really strong, so that we were unable to carry the big sail. The seams began to split. The *Triumph of Righteousness* could not stand much weather. The conditions, though fresh, were those only of a good trade-wind day, such as would be perfect for any grain ship or any reasonably well-kept European vessel; but the boom began to show weaknesses. The mast worked on its step, and jerked with the rolling; the mizzen halliards carried away; the mainsail split its seams so badly that in midafternoon Nejdi ordered it lowered, and unbent. The only way the area of that sail could be reduced was by changing it, by lowering the big sail, taking off a piece at both ends of the long lateen yard, and bending a smaller mainsail to the shorter yard. This the sailors now did, and it was prodigious labor. It took about two hours. With the sail down the boom rolled and pitched, though not badly. Though she had then no canvas set and presented little windage to the breeze, I was glad to see that she kept a little way and was controllable. When the new sail, which was several cloths smaller than the old and had a much shorter hoist, was being set, it blew out some seams, too, and had to be lowered again and repaired. This all hands did by sitting on it and stitching away at the seam with their inadequate bent iron needles.

Afterwards, as long as the fresh wind lasted, this was a daily occupation. Yet it never occurred to Nejdi to make a better sail. I ventured to suggest a few minor improvements which would have prevented much of this work and loss of way, but he replied that Allah was compassionate. The breeze would die down: the sail was all right. Hamed bin Salim admitted, however, that they liked their sails that way, poorly sewn with the round seams, because then the sails would always give in the seams first in strong winds. Not only that, but if the sail were too strong it might carry the mast away in a puff of wind. It was better to lose an indifferent sail than a good mast. There was sense in this argument. But the

Sleeping child

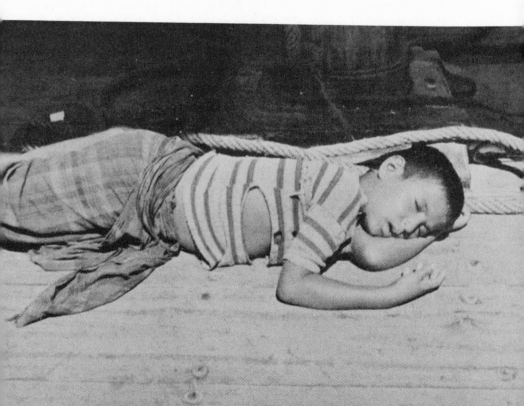

constant inefficient repairing of the weak seams and the frequent hoist-
ings of the heavy yard made a great deal of unnecessary work. This reflection, however, occurred to no one but me. According to the Arab
mariners all work was unnecessary, on general principles, but that which
Allah in His wisdom made unavoidable they would do.

During this stage of the voyage we often saw other vessels similarly
engaged in repairing their sails, and we once passed a small jalboot from
Sur which had been dismasted. Once by night we even saw a dhow showing a light, which was most unusual: actually she was showing three lights,
but they were all hurricane lamps in the maindeck to light the mariners
at their work of repairing the sail.

Sometimes the ship labored heavily, but even under these conditions
she ran very well and did not make much water. I was surprised to see
that the Arabs never made a move towards securing anything, or fore-
stalling any emergency. Whatever was going to happen they allowed to
get started before they did anything about it. For instance, the rows of
sea chests and passengers' belongings on the poop, which stood there all
through the voyage, were never secured, though it was apparent that the
ship's motion must dislodge something. I got some lashings and secured
my own chest so that it would not hurt anybody but, even when they
saw me do this, the Arabs made no move to secure their own. Perhaps
Nejdi thought that, with so many human beings packed between them,
the chests on the poop could not find room to move; but they did. In the
middle of the night the ship, lifted by a quartering sea, took a violent roll,
and all the chests on the starboard side rolled down alee. Instantly there
was a wild yelling and screaming, followed by some groans. Chests
rolled with a wild clamor; tins rolled with an even wilder banging; the
first-class passengers pitched across the deck; Beduin yelled. There
might have been a serious accident, but fortunately no one was hurt, and
in a little time, the barefoot sailors, chanting as they worked, had succeeded in getting the chests back again in their rightful places. Then they
lashed the chests there, at last, but very badly. They lashed only those
which had moved.

No sooner had they finished this and the ship settled down again
than she took another bad roll, and the carpenter's new dhow, which
also was never properly shored up or otherwise secured, fell over on
twelve Beduin who were sleeping beneath it. Now there was a screaming.
One of the Beduin was pinned underneath and he, poor wretch, began to
roar very loudly. The sailors moved the dhow in time, and got all the

Beduin out. The one who had been pinned beneath was not even bruised, and in the morning when I looked for him I could not find him. Not that he would have accepted medical attention, for the Beduin were all scornful of that.

About this time Nejdi began to complain of a bad back. There were very severe pains in the back of his neck and below his shoulder-blades, he said, which was not to be wondered at, for he always slept in the dew and insisted on removing the slight protection of the awning long before nightfall. He said the awning interfered with his view of the sail and his sense of the wind by night, and therefore it must come down. He asked me to remove the pain from his back, and I tried, using liniments; but he slept again in the dew and the pain returned worse than ever. Then he poured scorn upon all Christian remedies and called for a good Muslim from the maindeck, a Suri who lived under the break of the poop. This man went to work in great style, and I watched with interest what he did. He stripped Nejdi down to an Indian sarong and placed him in a clear space on the poop. Then he poured hot ghee on to the nakhoda's back. After that he got really down to work. He pounded, punched, smacked, twisted, pinched, and flogged Nejdi's back until even the stolid Nejdi almost shrieked. He picked up the flesh, of which there was very little to spare, in handfuls that he must have been tearing from the bones, and Nejdi started violently. He rolled handfuls of it in the hot ghee, and Nejdi squirmed: he punched and pounded up and down the nakhoda's backbone, and Nejdi had to hold himself up with his hands braced against the deck. How that Suri worked. He pounded Nejdi for a good two hours. After that, Nejdi pronouncing himself cured, dragged on his long shirt and staggered to his bench, but I ventured to suggest that the treatment was so drastic it had made him forget the ailment. He now had to recover from the treatment, as well as the ill. At this he scowled, saying that Arab medicine was vastly superior to European. In this instance he was probably right. The application of hot ghee and the very thorough massage of the affected parts were both good treatments, though two days later poor Nejdi was just as bad again.

At Haifun we had embarked several new mysterious passengers, all Suri, who came out from different hiding-places when the ship was at sea. One of them was a blind man with a young son and a one-eyed servant. The one-eyed servant saw but poorly with his surviving eye, which was the only one between the two of them. They had come from Muscat, and were bound down to Zanzibar to see some relatives. We also

Holy man

shipped an English-speaking Suri who said he had business in Mogadishu. He took his place as one of the first-class passengers, eating the ship's food: and I soon saw that his business was smuggling too. He had his merchandise with him, tied up in bundles, and joined in the daily conferences which were led by Hamed bin Salim and Said. These worthies frequently counted large sums in paper lire, which they tied up in the corners of sarongs and turbans, and stowed away. They always counted the money and stowed it away in full view of all hands, for they had no fear of theft.

I took a hearty dislike to this new Suri of ours, and he remained one of the few Arabs that I did not like. He spoke with a whining voice: he had enough English to be a considerable nuisance (for he knew just enough never to get anything right and to misinterpret everything, at the same time holding the opinion that he had no more to learn) and he always called me his "very dear friend." This I was not, but I had to put up with him. He said his father was a merchant of Sur, owning two baggalas which he sent trading to India. He himself—his name was Mohamed—usually commanded one baggala and his brother the other. This year, however, his father had laid up one of the ships and had sent Mohamed down the African coast to look over the prospects there. This at any rate was Mohamed's version of his voyage, but Nejdi, who also did not like him, had another. He said Mohamed, being a very bad nakhoda, had lost his baggala, and that now having been kicked out of his home, he was making a smuggling voyage on his own. I don't know which version was correct, but my natural prejudice led me to prefer the second. Mohamed the Suri was no addition to the amenities of the vessel, and to try to follow him in English was much more wearying and considerably less effective than to cope with any one else's Arabic, though I still had but little of that difficult tongue.

One Friday we sailed past a place called Obbia. Friday being the Muslim Sabbath, no unnecessary work was being done and no necessary work looked for, and all hands had their fill of looking at the roadstead. All we could see were a radio station, a resident's house complete with flag, and the inevitable sand. Obbia is about 350 miles from Haifun and some 260 from Mogadishu: having been then only two days at sea, we were not doing badly. Off Obbia, and all the way down this coast, we caught large numbers of fish, especially big bonita, albacore, and those bull-headed lovely fish that sailors know as dolphin. We also saw many flying fish, and a considerable number of these fluttered over the side. The Beduin

Beduin girl

promptly pounced on them and the unfortunate ship's cat hadn't a chance. The cat was a poor little thing which had been sired by a Suri tom out of a stray at Berbera, and it led a miserable life on board. Its principal duty was to keep down the livestock in the great cabin, but that place was so depressing that even the cat turned up its nose at it.

We caught our fish by the simple method of trailing lines astern— seven of them, no less, trailing from the cutter, the davits, the quarters, and wherever else on the after part of the poop they could be attached. At first small flying-fish were used as bait, large hooks being threaded through them, but as soon as the fish began to bite, the sailors used pieces of the white skin cut from the bellies of the fish. This seemed to be a better lure. Some days we caught as many as twenty or thirty large fish, when conditions were good and the ship was making the right speed: sometimes, too, a fish was roasted in the ashes. Compared with the rest of the food we had, these ash-roasted fish were grand.

We passed other Italian outposts—Athelet (otherwise Itala), and Warsheikh. These were poor places, seen from the sea. They were mainly distinguished from the sand around them by an Italian flag flying over a bungalow, though Warsheikh had an Arab house or two. We did not go into any of these places, for Nejdi said it would be waste of time. It seemed to me that was right.

All this time the filth and dirt on the squalid maindeck had been steadily accumulating until the place was frightful and I wondered that any human beings could survive in such surroundings. I kept to my six feet of the bench aft, behind the Sinbads and the other first-class passengers, and thanked God there was a fair wind to blow the maindeck rubbish forward. During this stage of the voyage I found the disadvantages of the life increased rather than diminished. Yet those Arabs were a good lot, and, with a few exceptions, likable. Those few I actively disliked were not Arabs—the quarrelsome half-Somali, the noisy Hadhrami-Malay with his infernal gramophone, the shrill, despicable, little shrew-faced bint, who still ran about the deck all day and maltreated the little boys.

If the general capacity of the Arabs to tolerate squalor far exceeded my own, and they could create hardships at sea of which I never before had dreamed, they were men. Even in the midst of noise and filth and squalor, the stately bearded Beduin from the desert maintained the little courtesies of their daily lives, the greetings, the mannerly respect towards one another, the proper decorum at the tribal eating mats, the ceremonious serving of the dreadful coffee. The constantly cramped quarters, the crowds, the wretched food, the exposure to the elements, the day-long burning sun and the night-long heavy dews, if they continued to be disadvantages, were far offset by the interest of being there, and the voyage never became monotonous. There were occasions when I wished it would, if only for the sake of a moment's quiet: but it never did.

As we came nearer to Mogadishu our passengers, thinking they were to land there, preened themselves and got out clean clothes. As we ran on past that Somali sand, Said and Majid and Abdulla the Mysterious and the others got out their mascara and their henna, reddened their beards, and hennaed their palms and the soles of their feet, the Seyyid from Mukalla and his henchman Abu Ali leading in these arts. One of the quartermasters shaved Nejdi who, being a nakhoda, never shaved himself, and another shaved Hamed bin Salim. Said the smuggler was a lavish user of henna, and of mascara for his eyes, and when dressed to go ashore looked rather like a nightmarish version of a chorus boy with a beard. Doubtless he felt very good. The sailors shaved off all their hair and beards, keeping only their moustachios, as is the Kuwait and the Persian style.

In the sunset on the fifth day we picked up Mogadishu light. It was hazy and we ran on, though it was blowing fresh. It was long after nightfall when we headed towards the town, the lights of which were bright and numerous. Mogadishu seen by night from the sea looked a big place, and interesting.

Chapter 7

TROUBLE AT MOGADISHU

MOGADISHU, or Mogadiscio, or Mogdishu, or Magadoxo, to give the place but a few of its many names, is a poor harbor under any of them, for it is a mere indentation in the northeastern African coastline fronting the Indian Ocean. There is a breakwater sheltering a lighter basin for the landing of cargoes, and this is also used as an anchorage for native vessels. We came into the Roads on the Saturday night, and all that night it blew hard. The sheltered basin of the dhow harbor is difficult to enter in the dark, and Nejdi fetched up off the breakwater's end, with the ship rolling and pitching in the open sea and the shelter of the breakwater close under her lee. I did not blame him for not going into so narrow and congested a place by night. It was difficult to see, and it would have been easy to put the ship on the rocks. The margin of safety for making that entrance is small: I wondered that he even thought of trying it.

All night the wind increased and the sea got up until it was breaking right over the breakwater and our situation there in the open sea was anything but pleasant. At first we lay to two anchors, then three. Before the morning it was five. The big Arab dhows go plentifully supplied with ground tackle for most of the harbors where they lie are foul. I had never seen a ship lie to five anchors before. She had so short a scope of cable to each of them that their number was no guarantee of her safety, and I watched apprehensively lest she should drag. I was not alone in my apprehension, for neither Nejdi nor Hamed bin Salim slept that night, and before the sunrise when I saw that she had dragged a little and the rocks alee were perilously close, I put my few valuables in my pockets and prepared to swim for it if necessary. Those rocks under our stern were nasty things, jagged and ugly: we should have been on them in a minute if our cables had parted, and the cables were nothing but cheap ship-laid coir made out of coconuts from India.

However, they held, and we lay in safety through that wild night. Dawn showed the sea still rising, though the wind quietened a little then, and though we plunged and rolled all that long day the ship was not again in danger. By mid-afternoon we were able to take up two of the anchors, and lay then to three. These anchors were let go from different places on both sides of the low forecastle-head, and being each to so short a scope of cable, and the wind being constant and strong enough through-out to overcome the force of the tide, they did not foul. The *Triumph* normally had three anchors ready at her bows and two more stowed on deck there, handy enough—though often beneath the ship's firewood and all the sleeping crew—and another large bower aft. With her sails low-ered and the lateen yard stowed fore and aft the ship presented little wind-age, apart from the high poop, for her masts were bare and she had very little rigging.

With the daylight, in spite of the weather, a small longboat from one of the Sur dhows in port came out to us. Her nakhoda came on board. He reported that the Italians were not allowing any Arab passengers to land. This was bad news, for here we were with over a hundred of them who imagined they were bound to that place. At last we had arrived only to be told they could not land. Nejdi, who never believed in meeting trouble halfway, kept this knowledge from them, and though many were now seasick again from the violence of the motion at the anchorage—it was far worse than being at sea—they continued to prepare to land. Nejdi went ashore with the Suri, though this was probably in defiance of all port regulations. Afterwards I noticed that Abdulla the Mysterious had gone too, though I did not see him go. Others of the Suri were also miss-ing, including Majid, Said the Smuggler, and the blind man from Haifun. Mohamed, the small boy, always disappeared on such occasions. I saw none of these go, though I was watching.

There was no need for them to hurry, for no boarding officers came out to us. We stayed there, pitching and rolling, and life aboard that day was almost completely miserable. Sprays drove over the vessel wetting the whole maindeck, the fresh monsoon blew cold in that exposed place, though it was almost directly under the equator; the Aden water had all gone, and there was very little left to eat. Fish which had been caught the previous day was already high, though we ate it: and the half-caste

Somali from Shihr yelled and fought all day while he assembled his possessions for landing. When we anchored the rudder was always immediately allowed to swing, and now it banged back and forth until I feared it would burst from its gudgeons. No one else was worried, but poor Jassim at the firebox spent a day of torment. The wind blew the smoke of his camel-thorn fires back over him and all the ship.

With the ship head to wind, dust and dirt and debris and filth blew everywhere. That day was a bedlam and, before the day was out, I wondered how much more I could stand of it. The Beduin and the others from the Hadhramaut, in their intervals of seasickness, chanted words of praise to Allah for their safe deliverance, though they were still by no means safe, and they had not been delivered.

Nedji came back before nightfall, coming out in a small Diesel tug which he had hired to tow us behind the breakwater. This ought to have been a simple manoeuver, but it was a mess. By that time Hamed bin Salim had disappeared (I think he went off with some merchandise in a Somali fishing-canoe): Nejdi stayed in the tug, and only his brother Abdulla was on board. It was typical of the Arabs that though they had been expecting a tug all day they had no towline ready, or anything else. The tug barged and bumped into the ship heavily alongside waiting for a line. Nejdi yelled; the passengers yelled; the serang and the sailors ran and chanted. Hassan the helmsman, sent to connect the rudder chains, became so interested watching the tug bump into us that he did not do his job, and no one made him, so that we started off behind the tug with only one chain connected and had to stop and drift until the other was made fast. Kalifa, the other helmsman at the wheel, murmured "As Allah wills" in response to every shouted order until I felt like swearing at him, for Allah was not steering the ship, but he was. He insisted on sitting in the chair at the wheel though he could not see over the passengers crowding the poop and all the deck, and when I suggested he should stand up he was grievously insulted.

"Starboard, starboard!" Nejdi would shout from the tug, waving his arms violently.

"Starboard, starboard!" repeated Abdulla standing on the bench aft.

"As it pleaseth the Lord," Kalifa murmured piously, shoving the wheel hard over the wrong way and causing the ship to take a horrible sheer, while the water shoaled and the little tug, puffing and panting, was having hard work to hold us. The passengers kept up a constant din, and the small boys raced everywhere, while one of the Somali's goats got loose on the deck and began to eat up the halliards. A wire hawser used for heaving in the last bower, led to the capstan aft, carried away and hit the sailor Sultan across the head, laying his skull open until the blood poured into the waterways. They brought him to me and I marvelled that he was still conscious. The blow would have fractured the skull of any lesser man, and it made even Sultan depressed and thoughtful. I cleaned it up, stopped the bleeding, and bandaged it hurriedly and temporarily, hoping he was not seriously injured. He went back to his work. When the hawser carried away the capstan took charge and threw out its bars, which scattered with murderous force in all directions. How they avoided striking any of the passengers who pressed around I cannot imagine. For my own part, if they had been struck then I should not have minded. Now the anchors were away and the tug moved ahead, dragging us slowly from the rocks. Nejdi yelled again. Abdulla yelled in answer, the passengers shrieked, the Seyyid prayed, the goats bleated, and the astonished and depressed kitten scampered out of the way of galloping bare feet and hid behind a ghee-jar.

From our exposed and dangerous anchorage to the shelter of the basin behind the breakwater was only a short distance, and the Arabs aboard the other twelve or fourteen dhows already there watched us with interest that turned to apprehension as we came, for we bore down right upon them and there seemed nothing the little tug could do to keep us straight. The wind was still fresh, the *Triumph* was a large dhow, the tug very small and its handling most inexpert. Finally as we came in close among the tiers of anchored vessels the tug coughed and gave up the struggle. The serang threw three anchors overboard, two of which, unfortunately, were no longer connected to their cables. The tug made off, taking Nejdi with it and, in the predicament which followed this unorthodox maneuver, the ship was in the charge of no one. She took complete charge of herself, for the single anchor could not hold her, and she drove down upon the tier of anchored vessels. First we crashed into a small ex-pearling jalboot from Bahrein, and having given her a resounding thwack 'midships which made all her timbers creak and groan and carried away a considerable part of her bulwarks along the starboard side, we drove next into a Suri sambuk with a deckload of cows. The cows fast in little stalls on top of the cargo became frantic and tried to break out: our mizzen boom caught in the rigging of the sambuk's main, and the protruding end of the lateen yard carried away, falling on a cow. The passengers yelled and stampeded; the serang and the sailors worked furiously to get the longboat over the side—a thing which should have been done hours earlier—to carry out moorings; and the whole of the waterfront looked on with interest. Still we charged about that congested harbor, next sideswiping a Batina boom with fish and passengers.

It was a thoroughly bad show, and, when at last the tug brought Nejdi back, he was in a frightful temper. It was not the damage done which bothered him, but the loss of prestige caused by such a public exhibition of poor seamanship.

Apart from the damage to the ex-pearler, the carrying-away of part of the mizzen yard, and the breaking of Sultan's head, nothing really serious had happened. The anchors which had been thrown overboard without cables were easily recovered, for all the Kuwait sailors are also pearl-divers. Long before midnight the ship was moored, the cows astern of us slept soundly, and all was peace and quiet again, except for a conference of Suri, Persians, and Nejdi, which went on far into the night all round the place where I wished to sleep. What this conference was about I did not bother to learn then, for after that long day and the preceding night I was tired. It was easy enough to guess. It was about landing passengers, and restrictions on trade, and the misdemeanors of the Italian shore officials. In this conversation I heard many references to rupees and lire and many uncomplimentary remarks about the Italians. What method of overcoming the difficult restrictions of the port was being planned by those bearded, hooded conspirators I do not know, but I later learned that it was effective.

Nejdi presided over this meeting, as he was to preside over similar ones during our stay. He had taken the *Triumph* into Mogadishu the previous year, homeward bound with cargo and passengers from the south, and he knew the ropes.

In the morning (by which time a considerable quantity of the trade-goods the ship had brought, but had not manifested, were already delivered to the Somali and other vessels) the boarding officials came, and after curtly shouting from their launch, without even bothering to come aboard, that no one could land, left again. This news fell upon the ears of our multitude as a sad and bitter blow. What, not land? After coming all this way? After paying their fares, and making this sea voyage of many days? The Beduin who had not travelled before appeared bewildered, and the Hadhrami and the others who were not making their first voyage were incensed. Some of them stormed up on the poop and began to shout at Nejdi who, saying it was the Italians' business and not his, went ashore.

After a while most of the passengers quieted down, and they began to murmur again that Allah was compassionate, and to express the hope that the Italians would return and lift the ban on them at least partially. Though it must have been a very serious matter to all of them—some of the Beduin had even put on clean clothes, bought carefully from long savings in the Hadhramaut for this very occasion—the resignation with which most of the Arabs accepted this bad news was admirable. Exceptions were the quarrelsome ones, particularly the half-caste Somali, who kept up a constant screaming, and a number of the Hadhrami who scowled and said that the Italians had been glad enough to impress them for labor on the Assab road and other enterprises. For the rest, *inshallah*, either a day would straighten things out at Mogadishu, or Allah would see them safely delivered somewhere else—Lamu, Mombasa, or Zanzibar. Many were beginning to run out of food, and there was no fishing at those moorings. During the day a small boom came in from Batina, the one which had been with us at Haifun, and her two hundred passengers were added to the list of the unwanted.

It might be said, on the Italians' behalf, that it is difficult for them to enter Arabia, and except perhaps in parts of the Yemen, they are given no encouragement. It must be admitted, moreover, that one look at half our passengers would condemn them as undesirables anywhere. The Italians, pouring money desperately into their East Africa in the attempt to get some back again, and pouring still more into their new Abyssinia, look askance on wanderers from Arabia whose only aim is to take money out instead of contributing to the national wealth. They are scarcely to be blamed if they look upon the average Arab as not the best kind of immigrant. Whatever their propaganda agents may have said elsewhere, in Mogadishu they made it clear that they look upon the Arabs as a dirty, dishonest, and disunited horde, avaricious, fanatic, and quarrelsome—unskilled, covetous, lawless, and undesirable migrants from almost every point of view. They accused them of being at the bottom of every illicit trade, and of rarely producing anything other than schemes for the furtherance of various forms of intrigue and smuggling. They feared the Arabs as possible sowers of discord among the Somali and the Abyssinians. In short, except as coolie labor for such enterprises as the Assab road, the Italians had no welcome whatever for the Arabs, either as migrants, merchants, or masters of trading ships. The Arabs, in turn, heartily disliked the Italians, for they had no respect for the European who possessed so many of their own faults and, so far as they could see, none of their virtues. The petty officials with whom the Arabs came in contact were too often just as noisy, irascible, avaricious and some-times downright dishonest as any smuggling Suri or cunning Kuwaiti knew how to be. Some of them could be bribed and the Arabs, knowing this, had little respect for any of them. The Somali hated them, and none of them for-gave them for Abyssinia. The Arabs respected the English, who could do things they could not do, and the Germans, who were thorough and ef-ficient. But they laughed at the Italians in Somaliland.

Mogadishu is now more an Italian than an Arab town, though it was an Arab settlement for many centuries, and there is still a very large Arab section. Throughout the town now one sees stencilled profiles of Signor Mussolini, that "Defender of Islam" so mistrusted by the Mus-lims themselves, adorning the columns and pillars and buildings every-where, and in the center of the town a large mosque, more ornate than usual, overlooks a café-bar on the opposite corner, and a super-cinema.

At first it seemed as if I should see all I was going to see of Mogadishu from the ship, crowded in her place in the tier of Arab vessels. The ban on landing applied equally to me, and there I stayed. It was more in-teresting than Haifun, and I did not mind. Each morning the official launch came alongside and sometimes officials came on board to carry out in-spections, though they always did this with considerable distaste. I did not blame them, for the conditions on board were deplorable. One morn-ing they lined up all the passengers they could find and checked them carefully. The Suri and others had disappeared, and our numbers had considerably declined. For the first time I was able to witness an accurate count of those bound to Mogadishu: there were seventy-three men, five women, and two babies. These were not all our passengers by any means, for we had another thirty for Mombasa and Zanzibar, not to mention the Suri and the other "merchants."

The port doctor went over all the passengers carefully, and his inspec-tion brought to light some nasty cases of which I had not previously known. There was a small boy with rickets; and a tiny mite of a girl of the same family who was going blind. When I saw these I could not help feeling that a little less reliance on the compassion of Allah and a greater readiness to accept the benefits of science would save much misery in Arabia, for the causes of these two cases were obvious. Wretchedly in-adequate diet was to blame for the boy's condition, and some venereal in-fection was blinding the little girl. These two children were taken ashore, and I hope the doctor was able to do something for them.

In the end some of the passengers were allowed to land, but only those who could prove they had had previous residence in Italian Somaliland. To my great relief these included the father of the shrew-faced bint, who went ashore yelling as always, leading his family and goats and carrying all his possessions. The shrew-faced bint, horrible little thing, was dressed in a new ankle-length dress of red and yellow, with her face, hands, and feet painted red and black, and her hair more buttered than ever. She had six silver bangles on each wrist, two more above each elbow, and round her neck a number of suitable extracts from the Quran— if they were really suitable they would have burned her—fastened into tiny silver containers. She had a heavy silver ornament round each ankle. She kicked the son of Aura as she went by, while her father yelled from the boat. The mother, shrouded in black, and on deck for the first time, added her share of invective, and the little boy Abdullah, who had done all he could to make life a misery for everybody on board, sat back in a new sarong and clean cap and grinned from ear to ear. They were a dreadful family, and I should hate to meet them again. With them gone, the noise dropped at least 50 per cent, and the ship was almost peaceful.

Other passengers disappeared, though Nejdi was careful to see that no one who appeared on the Italians' Haifun list was allowed to leave the vessel. He allowed the Suri and the older Hadhrami to come and go as they wished. Yusuf told me that his reason for this was simply that these men, long-experienced travellers with no desire to stay in Mogadishu —or anywhere else away from their own Arabia—could be trusted to look after themselves and to return to the ship in time for sailing. They would not be left behind and get the ship into trouble, whereas the others, the Beduin and the migrating Hadhrami and Shihri, wished only to land and stay. If they got ashore they would stay, and since they had all to be checked on board before the ship could sail, Nejdi took no chances. There on board they remained, cooking, praying, sleeping, yarning, as always, looking at this promised land so close and never setting foot on it.

The Suri seemed to be allowed ashore in Mogadishu more freely, probably because they could be trusted to leave—most of the Suri were bound to Zanzibar and made their headquarters there—but also because it was not possible to tell a Suri passenger from a Suri sailor, for all wore the same beards and clothes. Sailors had daylight leave, being allowed to land and go to the bazaar or to a mosque, so long as they returned to their ships before nightfall. It was easily possible for the Italians and their Somali police to distinguish our passengers from our sailors, for the Kuwaiti dress and look quite different from other Arabs. Many Kuwaiti would pass as Montenegrins, Spaniards or Greeks, if they used European clothes, but the Suri, in brown smocks alike even to the tiny embroideries at the neck, with hennaed beards, fingernails and toenails, their heavy turbans kept on by light head-cords with tooth-sticks always dangling at one end, could never look anything but what they were. They had very distinctive faces.

Their ships, like the men who manned them, had many features peculiar to themselves—their liking for decorations in blue and white, for example, which reminded me of the Finns and other Northern mariners; and their fondness for the big square-sterned sambuk and the carved baggala. While we were there, more than five or six hundred Suri and Omani Arabs must have passed through Mogadishu. Some of the ships they came in were almost incredibly small and decrepit, though the worst were from small ports along the Mahra coast and Trucial Oman, and not from Sur. Nejdi said they were ex-pearlers from the Gulf. Pearling was a depressed industry, he said, because of the competition of cheap Japanese cultured pearls, and many vessels formerly used only for pearling now voyaged to Africa and wherever else they could find employment. There were ships in Mogadishu from Seihut, Mukalla, Sur, Kuwait, Muscat, Haifun, Massawa, Bahrein, and Persia. Some were only about thirty feet long, but they had all made long voyages. The strangest craft of all were the straight-stemmed, sheerless craft from the Mahra coast, with high upright masts and large single sails. These were always crowded, and the conditions aboard them were appalling. Though I found life trying in the *Triumph* while we had passengers aboard, I doubt very much whether I could have survived an ocean passage in one of these smaller, crowded vessels. Aboard the Suri sambuks and baggalas the crews were largely Negro, descendants of slaves and many of them still slaves themselves. They danced and chanted and clapped their horny hands all day. We often gave feasts aboard our ship, but I never attended a feast aboard any Suri. Sometimes we went calling, Nejdi and I, and then we would be entertained with black coffee, always very bad, and some dreadfully sweet stuff of which the best quality came from Muscat and Zanzibar. For my part I wish they had stayed there, for though Nejdi praised this stuff and said it was unrivalled for its vitalizing qualities, I always felt that I could do very well without it.

The days at Mogadishu went by pleasantly, and I was glad if only because we were not at Haifun, and because the quarrelsome Somali no longer shrieked about the decks. I could now walk fairly well—not that

that was much advantage when I was not allowed ashore. Italian officials, always very minor ones, were always coming to interrogate me. They seemed to suspect me of some dark purpose unknown to me. This worried Nejdi. Their questions were always the same and none of my replies seemed to satisfy them. Why did I come to Somaliland in an Arab dhow, when there were steamers? When I said that I sailed with the Arabs because I liked doing things like that, and that I did not care in the least where the dhow chanced to go they frankly disbelieved me. One day an unusually officious Italian finding an old notebook from the voyage to Gizan in the *Sheikh Mansur* pounced upon it. There were some rough sketches in it, one an outline of the waterfront at Gizan and the other a plan of the sanitary arrangements in a pilgrim sambuk. These the Italian ripped out of the book and took ashore. What he expected to find in them I don't know, but he did not bring them back. These are sad days for a European to wander about the earth, and the Arabs observed these antics with scorn. Later, I was allowed daylight leave in the city, but Nejdi swore that seven secret police watched me all the time. This was very flattering, but I doubted it. They would not have seen anything. I liked Mogadishu, which was a clean and orderly place, attractive and busy.

The same official on going through the sailors' chests found a package of Japanese merchandise in Ismael the musician's. This he bore away in triumph. His triumph would have been short-lived if he had known that every one had contributed something towards it and that it had been left there for him in the belief that it would be as well for him to find something. The real goods were either already landed or stowed away below the great cabin, where no European would dare to go. When the searcher carried off this planted bundle of merchandise, Ismael protested loudly, so loudly and for so long that I began to think he meant it. He even carried on the farce to the extent of going ashore and to the customs house to demand the return of his package because it was for Mombasa, not Mogadishu. Much to his astonishment, he actually was given back the package an hour or two before the ship sailed. But that was not until some time later.

Meanwhile we stayed and stayed in the Arab tier at Mogadishu, and if we had any reason for being there, apart from the forlorn hope of getting rid of another hundred or so passengers, I could not discover it. Said, Majid, and all that ilk, who always turned up once the ship had been safely cleared inwards and the passengers looked over, were busy smuggling, and the conditions were good enough for them. Indeed, the conditions

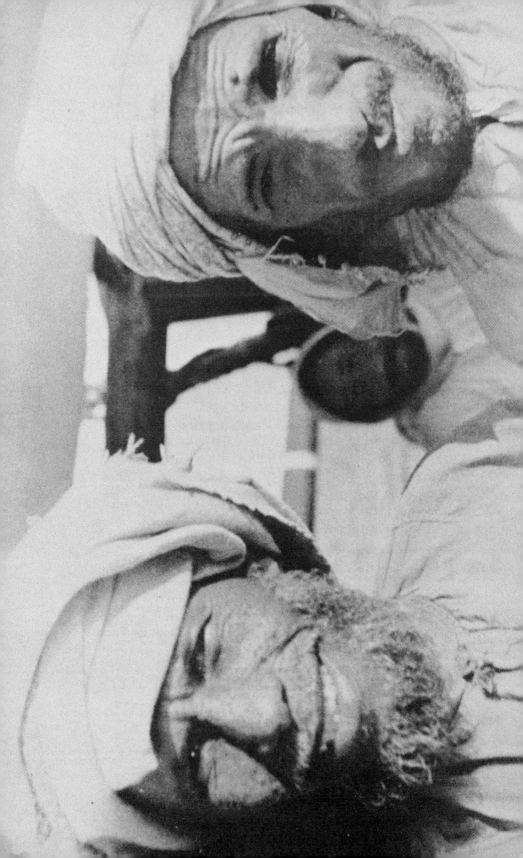

were excellent, for the ship lay close to the landing jetty, surrounded by other vessels, and there was communication with the shore by longboat all day long. They had to go out past Italian and Somali guards through a closely watched gate, which was the only way from the docks, but each time they went ashore their brown gowns covered large stocks of sarongs, money belts, perfumes, Aden cigarettes, new turbans, and all sorts of things.

As at Haifun, it was amusing to watch them preparing to go ashore. A corner of a sail had been drawn across the afterpart of the poop, partly to keep some of the maindeck dirt from blowing back there but really to screen the nightly conferences, and this acted also as an excellent screen for our Sinbads. Said was even more thorough here than he had been at Haifun, and always wore at least three gowns and eight sarongs, and tied more sarongs around his knees. Wherever he left the stuff ashore he kept an old gown and an old turban, and he returned always to the ship in these. He often made six trips in a day, off in the longboat loaded down with his haberdashery, and Mohamed his helper seated in the bows. They never went through the gate together but made their way separately to the bazaar. In a couple of hours he was back again wearing a ragged gown and an old turban. How he continued to do this without arousing suspicion I had difficulty in understanding, but Yusuf, who did his own share of the business, said it was a matter of distributing the right bakhshish.

This was not the whole story, however, and Said was caught occasionally, for sometimes a suspicious gateman made him strip. Then his goods were taken from him, and he was beaten. He would return at once to the ship worried but not contrite. In no wise deterred, he would immediately load up again, for he said the Italians could not tell one Suri from another —which was true—and the Somali, having been "fixed," would not give him away. Sometimes he might be caught twice in one day, but if he got four cargoes through he was doing very well.

It all went to the native bazaar. Yusuf said almost every merchant there was prepared to make a deal; every stall-holder in the *suq* was in the market for all the smuggled goods he could get, for duties were high and the Somali very poor, and the restrictions the Italians had been compelled by their home government to impose on trade made ordinary lawful business virtually impossible.

Smuggling was carried on on a large scale at Mogadishu, not only with haberdashery. I watched our Persian carpets go ashore, and did not see them come back. Everybody aboard but the Beduin passengers, who had

The smugglers: Majid and Said

no funds to finance the business, and our cook and carpenter, was some sort of smuggler, and so were all the others in every other ship. It became so bad—for merchants who still had to buy duty-paid goods protested—that after a week or two the Italians insisted upon searching every Arab who went through the gates. This was not enough, for there were other ways. After we had been at Mogadishu only five days Mohamed the Suri came whining to me and said he had got all his goods ashore, being caught only twice. He seemed to think that being caught at all was a grave injustice.

The economics of this smuggling, so far as I could make out, worked out somehow like this. After a year or two of indolence and the enjoyment of his women in Sur, a wanderer such as our Said made his way towards Aden or Muscat—Aden is the better—and there spent three or four hundred rupees, preferably on credit. A Sinbad loves credit. Because he has no banking system he regards credit as a means of making a living out of somebody else's money. He lays out this small fortune with great care upon such goods as he knows will catch the Somali and the Swahili eye, colorful sarongs, turbans, headcloths, girdles, and things like that. He prefers haberdashery because it is always appealing, and it is easy to carry and

Passengers at Mogadishu

to smuggle. Then he buys a passage, again on credit if possible, in some such dhow as ours, though many Kuwait nakhodas will not take these merchants because they compete with the ship, frequently fail to pay their fares, and are often undesirable. When he has found a nakhoda who will take him, he sets off towards Africa, perfectly content to go where the ship goes, and trade where she does. His goods are with him; he eats the ship's food, he knows his way about. He has been everywhere, and is often useful to a young nakhoda. He is not on the passenger list and never appears anywhere on the ship's papers. He has no passport. He does not wish to be identified, or identifiable, for it is easier to carry on his trade that way. He passes as a sailor in all ports: the Europeans cannot tell one Suri from another, and he has nothing to fear from his own kind. Because he visits all ports in transit and never officially lands anywhere—never, indeed, having any official existence—he never has to produce any baggage or clear himself through any customs, and in all ports he smuggles systematically and thoroughly. He knows merchants, and he knows where to sell his stuff. Indeed he brings some on commission, and sometimes carries mail and messages surreptitiously. He is ready to undertake business of every kind, and knows how to do it. His voyage takes perhaps eight or nine months of the year, and in that time on an expenditure of four hundred rupees he will make a clear profit of a thousand. This is good; but sometimes he has to face losses. If he buys on credit, he must often sell on credit too. When he has cash he is always profligate with it, if not also always generous. It is doubtful, in spite of the high percentage of profit, whether he really does so well. If he did as well as he should, he ought to be able to retire ashore after a few voyages, but these modern Sinbads never do—not the Said type, at any rate. He had to extend credit himself, and he also had to take losses. I doubt whether he made very much. A great deal of his time was taken up with endeavors to collect debts owing from previous voyages. Like so much Arab business, smuggling appeared largely to be erected on a structure of debt.

Nejdi also had smuggling to do, chiefly in harem veils from India. Being a Kuwait nakhoda he never sank to actual smuggling himself, so far as the landing of goods was concerned, and always got Suri to do his work for him. Perhaps this was one reason why Suri were so prominent among the *Triumph*'s first-class passengers, if not upon her Italian passenger lists. Every morning, after the dawn prayer and the daily *khubz*, there would be a gathering of Suri round the transom aft—always the same Suri, always for the same purpose. They talked, smoked, shouted a little, and departed laden with odd merchandise. Nearly every morning there would be a dispute over something, usually about the proceeds of the previous day's business. Many of these Suri were not sailors but odd mates and wanderers in small jalboots and sambuks, and baggalas, and they lived by scraping up whatever they could on these annual voyages down to Africa. They had no money of their own to buy trade goods, and seemed glad enough to work with the Kuwaiti on a commission basis, though old Yusuf Shirazi disliked them and said they were not to be trusted. He landed his stuff himself, as did all the sailors. Only the afterguard did not. These Suri were a dirty crowd in greasy turbans and brown gowns which looked as if they had gone unwashed since Sur was founded. Many of them had infected eyes, and partial blindness was common among them.

Among these smuggling Suri our pock-marked Majid was prominent if not respected, and he was smuggler-in-chief to Nejdi. Nejdi had brought a large parcel of elaborate veils for the harem, which he had bought in the bazaar at Bombay on a previous voyage. They were curious-looking things in red and black. Though they did not look very attractive to me, and I could not understand how they could be worn, they were, apparently, much to the liking of Somali ladies, and brought a good price in the *suq*. Nejdi had hundreds of them. Majid's method of landing them was to stuff as many as possible inside the deep hem of his brown gown, to wrap three or four inside his turban, to fill the commodious pockets of his waistcoat with a couple of dozen more, and to lash another twenty or thirty in a sort of triple money belt which Nejdi lent him. So loaded, Majid marched ashore every morning and off through the gate. He was never stopped there. He was out like a shot and up the street, brazen and confident, and he strode through the hot sandy streets like a racer. How he could walk barefoot on the asphalt sidewalks in the heat of the equatorial sun, I do not know; but he did. I don't know where Majid went in the *suq* and it was not my business, but he promptly got rid of the veils. Some days he would land two cargoes, but generally he was content with one, and perhaps that was why he was not caught. He was a striking man, even among the Suri, with his gaunt face, handsome and distinguished despite its pockmarks. Once he attracted attention he was easy to remember: but to the Italians he looked like any other Suri nakhoda. So they let him pass. After once passing through the gates, I am sure Majid must always have been recognized, but he knew his work, and on the third day I overheard Nejdi remark that he had never had stuff landed for him so efficiently.

Hoisting the yard

On the eighth day, however, he began to wonder when he would receive the first instalment of the money for the veils. This was a detail
which his friend Majid had so far overlooked. Majid landed the veils and
he got them to the *suq*, but he never came back with any cash. He always
had a plausible explanation for this, but in the course of time no expla-
nations could suffice to hide the fact that Majid would never bring that
cash.

By this time all the veils were landed. That was several thousand lire
gone. Then there was trouble. Abdulla, Nejdi's brother, commissioned to
go to the *suq* and find out what had happened, returned with the report
that the merchant who had received them had paid Majid for them. Majid pretended to be grossly insulted and vociferously denied this, but
there was a very great row far into the night. Nejdi had trusted him,
and was not accustomed to being defrauded. Apparently, if a man was a
Muslim that was sufficient guarantee of his honesty. Majid may have been
a Muslim but he never produced that money. Towards midnight, when
the dispute had reached a noisy climax, he was summarily ordered out of

the ship. He went at once, shouting in the night, but in the morning he was back again as brazen as ever. He had come back only for his belongings, a small tin trunk very old and battered, and a piece of blanket wrapped in a Swahili mat. With these things, still shouting his innocence to the assembled vessels at the anchorage, he departed in a longboat belonging to a baggala near by in which he had found refuge.

With him went the other Suri smugglers, Said and his confederates and the boy Mohamed, and their belongings. The offense of Said and the others, who were thrown out of the vessel with him, was that when they were asked for some payment on their fares—they had then been eating the ship's food for two months and had travelled 2000 miles with us—they pleaded poverty and refused. At this Nejdi lost all patience, and there was a general clean-up of the Suri. If the ship really lost all those fares, I could only conclude that there was something wrong with Nejdi's business methods, at any rate in his handling of the Suri. Said must have had some lire, for every one had seen him counting them, and he still had a large store of haberdashery. Why Nejdi didn't seize some of this I don't know, or why he did not punch Said on the nose and make him pay, but to take direct action of this kind was never his way.

When I talked over the incident with Yusuf Shirazi, Yusuf said it was enough that an Arab should lose his reputation for honesty. The whole coast would know that Said and Majid had acted dishonorably, and their name would be bad. Yusuf admitted that it was bad enough before; and it seemed to me that the pair had escaped remarkably easily after what really was a piece of bare-faced fraud. Later I found that Mohamed the whiner, who always called me his very dear friend, was of the same type. He, also, landed goods for the Kuwaiti and did not bring back the cash. But he was still trusted temporarily, and remained at Mogadishu to collect the money owing on his promise to produce the money at Mombasa or Zanzibar. We saw Mohamed again, but we never saw the money.

It was a bad business, and considering the losses at Haifun, the failure to get rid of the bad dates, the enforced acceptance of Haifun fish for the Aden rice, the waste of time trying to get rid of the passengers, and the loss of so much of the Suri revenue, I could not see how the voyage thus far had been very profitable. It cost nothing, it was true, to keep the Beduin and the other deck passengers on board, but they were a nuisance. Probably, though Nejdi had lost the proceeds of the sale of his valuable veils, much of the other smuggling had been quite satisfactory.

I missed old Majid, who, though a thorough scoundrel, had the merit of being a picturesque one, and I had had many entertaining yarns with him about Sur. If my Arabic had been better I might have learned something of that place: as it was, I learned only about Majid. He, too, had been once a nakhoda, but his reputation for slippery dealing in business ventures had caused him to lose command of one ship after another until at last no one would give him a ship at all, and he was reduced to wandering up and down the coast, living by his wits. He had no money of his own, and never would have any, but he knew his way round the whole east coast of Africa and the west of India. He was a pilot for the Rufiji River, the Comoro Island, the Madagascar coast, and the Gulf of Cutch. He had two old quadrants, both of which were badly warped—neither of them had an eye-piece—and a general chart of the Indian Ocean corrected up to 1746. I tried to get this museum piece from him but he would not part with it, though I offered him three modern charts in exchange. The old one was decorated with Arabic script giving landmarks, distances, and other information of importance to the Arab mariner. Majid spoke Swahili, Persian, Hindustani and several Indian dialects, as well as some Somali and his own Arabic, and he could curse well in English though he did not know what the words meant. I missed old Majid, for he had been a good friend. I had cared for some cracks on his big feet, and given him pills for his chronic constipation. He neglected to return the carton in which I kept the pills, and he kept the contents too, but he probably regarded this as a gift. He frequently addressed me at great length on subjects of speculative theology, of which I understood not one word. No matter. I had only to mutter *Taiyib*, very softly, whenever he paused for breath, which was not often. At each *Taiyib* Majid would smile, take breath, and begin again. We got on famously. The ship was the poorer for his going, I thought, though it is quite possible I was the only one who thought so.

Nejdi's troubles were not yet over. Some passengers still held him responsible for bringing them to Mogadishu and not getting them ashore there, and twice there were stormy deputations of the Hadhramaut half-castes on the poop. These incidents, however, did not matter very much. There was nothing Nejdi could do and the situation was not of his making. He would never have accepted the passengers if he had known there would be so many difficulties in landing them, and, as he said, they could land in Kenya or Zanzibar. What was the difference?

Then an utterly unprecedented thing happened. The women mutinied. For many weeks then the unfortunate women had been imprisoned in the great cabin. It was February and many of them had been there since December. I wondered that they had not mutinied long before. We never saw them, and day followed day with no one ever giving them a thought, unless one died. Yusuf often went down into the cavernous gloom and came up again with various stores, and sometimes I observed that he looked worried. As for the women, their fares were paid and there they were. The Italians would not have them in Mogadishu, or anywhere else, and there was nothing to do but wait and take them on to Kenya. The women were supposed to accept their fate. I do not doubt that most of them did; but one day they mutinied. Such a thing had never been heard of before.

They chose the right time for their revolt. We had a feast on board that day, for it was a holiday and we had two sheep. It was the day of the Feast of the Pilgrimage, the *Idd el Haj*, and some of the poop had been cleaned. After the feast, Nejdi, very quiet and dignified with his hawk nose in the air, sat back on some cushions placed round the bench, engaged in earnest discourse with various Persian and Omani nakhodas from the other ships, and the relatives of shipowners who were guests at the feast. Ismael strummed softly—for once—on his guitar and did not sing: the water pipe passed from mouth to mouth, and every one was well content, filled with rice and sheep. The Beduin and other passengers lay asleep on deck and on the chests. Najdi was appearing at his best.

Suddenly the hatchway of the great cabin burst open with a wild bang and out rushed the women. Horror of horrors, what was this? Nejdi, who could face most situations with unperturbable calm, almost started from his cushions and let the cane of his water pipe drop from his mouth, but he quickly recovered himself and sat staring. The others looked amazed, caught off guard for a second: then they gazed on the scene with frigid dignity. First came a large Beduin lady, she who had supplied the milk for bathing Yusuf's eyes: behind her were some other women, all ancient. The large Beduin lady began at once to yell and, having begun, continued to yell. She never stopped for breath, and she never said anything pleasant. She screamed questions and paused for no answers. She stormed, she raved, she shrieked until the whole harbor was looking on and Nejdi, though he still preserved a stony silence and looked on with his usual statuesque dignity, must have been perturbed. What exactly the lady said I should hate to have to repeat but the gist of it was obvious. She had booked a passage to Mogadishu, and this was Mogadishu. Then what in the name of all this incompetent man-run world was keeping her

on board? Who, if not Nejdi? This and much more—much, much more—
she shrieked, freely interspersed with appropriate vituperations. The other
women stood about and, so far as one could tell from their veiled faces,
looked their approval. They were all Bedu and they wore the slitted veil
of the desert; their flashing eyes gleamed dangerously, and now and again
three or four of them broke into a supporting chorus of the stout one's
harangue.

At the end of some fifteen minutes the stout lady was compelled to
pause for breath. Nejdi murmured *Taiyib*, which I suppose signified his
agreement with all that had been said. This only loosed a greater torrent,
and it looked to me for a while as if one or two of those women might
even think of violence. In this I wronged Arab women and under-
rated Arab men: there was no violence. When matters reached the stage
at which any ordinary female citizen of colder climes would long have
been throwing everything in sight, the clamor suddenly subsided. The
women had had their say, and apparently that was all they needed. They
wanted food; they wanted to know when the ship would sail; they wanted
to know where they would really be landed. Nejdi replied in a quiet and
thoughtful voice that they would get food; that he would sail on the morrow; and that if they were not landed at Lamu—where he thought next of
going—they would certainly be landed at Mombasa. More than that, he
undertook to get them there in less than two weeks.

He was so shaken by this utterly unprecedented episode that we actually did sail on the morrow, though this had not been his intention. It
was extraordinary.

Chapter 8

A CALL AT LAMU

OUR DEPARTURE from Mogadishu was preceded by a bad scare. The Italian boarding officers, after they had cleared us, were suddenly seen coming back to the vessel just as we had re-embarked our lire and our score of unlisted passengers from a Persian boom near by. This was serious, for if we were caught trying to smuggle Italian money out of the colony it would be bad. Nejdi watched the Somali guards and the Italian officers board the ship again in considerable alarm, though he showed no sign of it and greeted them with quiet dignity. He must have been immensely relieved to discover that they came only in search of an Arab from Brava who, apparently, had been wrongly allowed to leave. They took this Brava merchant ashore again, but it was a long time before Nejdi dared retrieve his lire from the ghee jar into which they had been hurriedly flung, and stow them away properly below the great cabin. Our unlisted passengers were cheerful, for we had not yet sailed, and they could always pretend to be visitors from other vessels. Since none of them had ever been officially entered into the country, it would obviously have been only a tiresome formality to clear them out. The Arabs always sought to lessen the work of European port officials by keeping from them the knowledge of troublesome problems of this kind, and I must say that their system worked admirably. Our unlisted wanderers had not so much as one identity certificate between them, and they had been travelling about the Indian Ocean like that for years. I thought it would be a shame to stop them now.

We were away before daylight, with the last of the near-full moon setting behind the cathedral towers of Mogadishu. Outside, as the day came, it was cloudy with a high swell, though there was not much wind. Our Beduin were seasick again and miserable, but they appeared to have forgotten any disappointment they might have felt at not being allowed to land in Mogadishu. Now they looked forward to going ashore at the next place we came to, wherever that might be.

We came out from the harbor with a little sambuk so incredibly mean and poor that she merits description. She looked as if she had not been oiled since she was built, or even beached for cleaning. Her topsides were a warped and weeping mess of indifferent teak very poorly fastened, and her underside was mossy and weed-grown. Her masts were fished in several places, and her main halliards, which were made of plaited straw, were one long and very ragged splice. The sail she set was so threadbare and decrepit that it looked as if the mere act of setting it would shred it in pieces. Her few ancient blocks were battered deadeyes, and her high bulwarks looked as if they would fall back inboard at any moment. She was about sixty feet long, flush-decked, with a sort of small platform built across the afterpart of the poop above the wheel, and the reek of fish oil and stinking fish from her hold was abominable. The crew were dirty-looking in their greasy gowns, and the passengers sat huddled in rags round the bole of the mizzenmast. There were about twenty of them, and the sambuk also carried some women. The arrangements for these were exceedingly primitive. The sambuk had no cabin aft and no enclosed space anywhere, so the women were housed in a kind of makeshift shelter, if it could be called that, built round their toilet box. The box itself protruded from the side of the ship on the port quarter, and was covered with old sacking. A shelter of date matting, supplemented, here and there, by pieces of torn and threadbare tarpaulin, kept the women out of sight. The whole tent hardly covered ten square feet of that uneven deck, yet Yusuf said at least five women huddled in there. They had been there since Sur, and they were bound to Zanzibar. The only cooking arrangements on deck were a battered sandbox with a few stones, more primitive even than the "galley" in the *Sheikh Mansur*; the longboat looked as rigid as a concertina.

I marvelled not only that such a vessel had sailed from Sur to Mogadishu, but that it had ever been allowed to set out. Later, however, I saw even worse ships. Ideal as are the sailing conditions which the Arabs ordinarily encountered in these summer runs down the African coast, yet ships can be lost there, no matter how azure and balmy the general run of the days. It had blown fresh enough on some days we lay in Mogadishu and quite a sea ran outside—sea enough, I should have thought, to trouble such craft as that decrepit sambuk from Sur. I must add, in fairness, that most of the ships I saw from Sur were sound enough, and some of them were splendid vessels.

We came on slowly down the coast, passing close by the ports of Merka and Brava but not calling at them, for Nejdi had had enough of the Italians. Getting out of Mogadishu with all the lire he had—I don't know how much was on board, but it was a good deal—and the unlisted passengers was enough. To go into any other Italian ports would be unwise, particularly as they offered no trade. We wandered down pleasantly to the southwestward, with the barren sand of Somaliland along the starboard beam, and the monsoon quiet. We were past Merka before noon and had the Brava light abeam soon after sunset, with the wind fresher and a full moon to light our way.

That night was very beautiful, with the ship all quiet and the bright moon astern of us throwing graceful patterns of the masts and rigging on the sail, and the dip and roll of her rhythmic and peaceful. On the poop the children and the merchants slept, and the sailors, hooded in the longboat, kept their silent watch. Right aft, on his place on the officers' bench Nejdi sat, muffled in his headcloth and his desert cloak, puffing at his hookah and carrying on a conversation in low earnest tones with the Seyyid from Mukalla and the merchant Abu Ali. Abdulla the Mysterious listened. He was now our only surviving Suri from the early stages of the voyage. Perhaps he had not heard of the exodus at Mogadishu until it was too late to take part of it, or perhaps he was mysterious enough not to care. The Seyyid from Mukalla had been ashore in Mogadishu, going off dressed as a Suri on the tenth day of our stay there and not returning until the ship was to be cleared.

Snatches of Nejdi's words came to me as I reclined on my carpet and dreamed pleasantly, watching the motion of the ship. It was the same old discourse—mostly about Japan, and the iniquities of Europeans. According to Nejdi, our world was about due for eclipse: his hope was in the growth of Islam in Japan. Some of Nejdi's views were disquieting, and it was interesting to listen to him expounding them. Unfortunately he spoke Arabic so well, in comparison with the sailors, that I had considerable difficulty in understanding him, and it would often be a week before a point would sink in. To acquire a knowledge of good Arabic ought to be the concentrated work of at least three years: at that time, I had had three months. Nejdi droned on to a muffled chorus of throaty *Taiyibs:* about him the tree-mast creaked, and the lateen sail bellied windful in the moonlight. I wondered whether, with all our boasted progress and our scorn of his poor ship, we Europeans were really far ahead of such clear-headed mariners as Nejdi, wandering Eastern seas. The thought disturbed me: I let him drone on, and the gurgling swish of the sea was soothing.

On the second day the wind freshened again. This day we passed a body in the sea. It was the body of an Arab man, partially wrapped in date-frond matting. It was floating face down, and there were fish. I saw it after the morning meal, at the time of the first fiesta. I looked over the side, the ship foaming along, and there it was. I called no one's attention, but Yusuf's. It was a buried passenger, he said, dead from some crowded Batina boom. It was commonplace enough. They often died. Yusuf was not interested. He said the small boom we had seen at Haifun and again at Mogadishu would lose at least ten persons through death before she reached Zanzibar. They just died. If there were smallpox on board many would die; but smallpox was now unusual. A few years earlier there had been smallpox at Kuwait, and thousands had died.

We left the body dipping quietly in the sea among the fish; our passengers did not see it.

Yusuf told me that another small boom, one of the very old ones, had driven ashore during a day of strong monsoon somewhere north of Warsheikh while we lay in Mogadishu. She was carrying some sixty passengers. He thought some were not drowned. In such casual manner the Arabs would announce serious and important news. But surely, I said to Yusuf, the loss of a ship full of passengers was a serious thing? Not a Batina boom, he answered. They were no good anyway. Nobody seemed to care what happened to the little ship, and if Allah in His wisdom chose to claim one for the sea, He had His reasons. The act seemed half-expected of Him, and I must add that this did not surprise me.

The passage from Mogadishu towards Lamu was uneventful. I was not sure that we were going to Lamu until we came off that place on the third evening, and, the conditions being propitious, went in. Nejdi had not said definitely that he was going in until we got there, though the previous day I had seen him examining a chart of what he imagined to be the harbor. Unfortunately this was Port Durnford and not Lamu Roads, and when I pointed this out to him he was not pleased, saying that charts were no good anyway, and he knew the way. South of Kisimayu the character of the African coast though still dull changed a little for the better, and we saw some trees along the foreshore, for the first time in weeks.

There had been some calm that morning. It did not last long, which was well, for when the wind dropped it was very hot, and the stenches from the maindeck and the well abaft the mainmast, whence the bilge-water was bailed, swept round the ship instead of being blown away. This was dreadful: for after many months on board I never got used to that smell of bilgewater. I had served an apprenticeship, I suppose, as hard as any, for I had been in whaling ships and leaky grain-carriers; but the stench of whale and the smell of sea-rotted grain were gentle fragrance compared with the bilgewater and the odor of Beduin aboard an Arab boom.

By mid-afternoon we had a light air from the northeast which grew steadily. We were able then to fall off and head towards the sand-bluffs of Lamu, and we sailed in in the evening with the conditions excellent. Our entrance into the arm of the sea which leads pleasantly to the pretty township of Lamu was as ludicrous as our tow into Mogadishu. Ab-dulla, Nejdi's brother, was at the wheel, snatching a puff at the water pipe at every opportunity, seated so that he could not see. The muezzins all made the sunset call to prayer with the competition among them stronger than ever, and the poop was so crowded with praying passengers that the helmsman could see nothing at all every time they rose from their knees. Rows and rows of praying upturned backs alternated with mumbling turbaned heads, and orders went unheard. So we came in through the difficult passage, not without dangers. At the hour of prayer the changing bearing of Mecca mattered more than the pilotage of the roads. But Nejdi knew his harbor, and we were anchored off Lamu in three fathoms of water as the moon rose over the low land.

That pilotage of Nejdi's into Lamu Roads was one of the most amusing occurrences of the whole voyage. The mixture of prayer, ceremonial ablutions, orders to the helmsman, the excitement of the passengers, and the general activities of the scampering sailors preparing for arrival, was extraordinary.

The entrance into Lamu harbor, which is an arm of the sea between Lamu and Manda islands, is properly indicated by a series of leading-marks: the harbor itself is full of shoals, and a ship not expertly conned would soon be aground there. Nejdi paid no attention to the leading-marks, knowing his own. He conned by eye from personal knowledge, and I noticed that the Arabs always did this, even in a place like the Rufiji River. (There, incidentally, it is the only way.) The fact that we came to the most difficult part of the winding entrance just as the sun set was an awkward complication, but the prayers could not be delayed no matter what happened to the ship, and the muezzins began at once with their calls to prayer. This in itself made considerable noise, but it was only the beginning. At once all hands began the noisy and thorough ablutions without which no self-respecting Arab would dream of praying, and Hamed bin Salim advanced to his post facing Mecca at the head of the assembled worshippers and, having discarded his worldly thoughts, began to intone the melodious prayers. Behind him stood the blind sheikh in the middle of a line, fifteen strong, which included sundry mariners, quartermasters, Beduin, and the wilful Malay. Behind this was another line, filling all the space between the chests. Others stood on the chests, in the boats, on the water-tanks, everywhere. Because we were at last arriving safely—so as far as they knew—at a port in Kenya, the prayers of the passengers were even longer, louder, and more general than usual, and dozens who customarily prayed alone now joined in the general worship. As every worshipper had to have space in which to get down on his knees and touch his forehead to the deck, the praying took up a great deal of room.

With the ship just straightening up for the roads, Nejdi rapped out an order to his brother and turned his back before it was obeyed, for he had to climb over the reclining bench down to a little platform right aft, where his jar of washing water was kept, in order to perform his ablutions, and when he did this he could not see where the ship was going. This did not appear to trouble him. Abdulla, his brother, had been in Lamu before, though only once. I suppose he knew the way, too. (Abdulla once told me that anything he had seen once he knew for ever afterwards, which was a comforting piece of optimism, though difficult to share.) Now and again Nejdi, spluttering with the sea water on his face, thrust up his black head from which half the headcloth was thrust back—he never allowed his head to be completely uncovered—and shouted a fresh order which would go unheard. Then it would be shouted once more and Nejdi in exasperation would climb up from his ablution platform and yell the order yet again. At last Abdulla with the usual response "As Allah wills" would nonchalantly obey and the ship, which fortunately was very responsive to her helm, would swing in the last second of time.

The chorus of worshippers, intoning loud and solemn *Amins* to Hamed's recited prayers, rose high while the mangrove swamps loomed perilously close along the starboard side and a sandpit showed alee, and two Suri sambuks moving in ahead echoed incantations across the waters. It was a wild and picturesque scene, and Lamu Roads was such a place as I had dreamed of when first I had heard of this African voyage. The light darkened swiftly as it does in these tropical parts, though not before the romantic hamlet of Shella showed to port, with its ruined mosques and tumble-down buildings. The importance of this once proud port has long departed. Shella standing on the foreshore on the landward side below Lamu's bluffs is now decayed, but it looked romantic in the day's last light with the big Arab ships sweeping past, their decks crowded with white- and brown-gowned figures intoning the evening prayers. It was romantic enough for anybody, though we shaved some of the corners very close, and I did not think much either of Abdulla's helmsmanship or his attitude towards the task in hand.

"Starboard! Starboard a little!" Nejdi would yell.

No answer from Abdulla.

"There is no God but God and Mohammed is the Prophet of God," from Hamed.

Amins very loudly from all and sundry.

"Starboard! Starboard!" again from Nejdi.

Still no answer from Abdulla, who bent down to get a quick whiff out of the water-pipe left there by Yusuf, while the embers still glowed. At last Abdulla, looking up again, perceived that his brother, standing in the gig at the quarter davits, was shouting something.

"As Allah wills," he replied, and put the wheel this way or that, usually the right way but sometimes not.

The ship swung: the prayers continued: the darkness deepened over the heavy green of the mangrove swamps of Manda Island low along the starboard side, and the lights of Lamu showed beyond an island in the channel. But here the going was tricky, and there were awkward turns. Nejdi, busy with his prayers—for they must be said in the brief interval between the setting of the sun and the end of daylight, and there is no twilight here—looked up a moment to con the ship in, and yelled at his brother to stand at the wheel instead of sitting there. Abdulla, aggrieved, obeyed. Now that we could fall off for the anchorage only a mile away, the sheet could be eased and the yard allowed to fall midships a little. The sailors chanted and ran in response to the order.

The ship was then a scurrying bedlam of running feet, praying forms, and frantically rushing passengers, for the Beduin on the maindeck must get out of the way of the sailors when they work or be knocked down. The mainsheet eased too much, took charge and had to be got in again. Though we had only a mile then to the anchorage—for the ship came in handsomely and the evening wind was fresh—no one had seen that the main halliards were clear or even that the hitches had been taken from the turns round the beam where the two hauling parts are crudely made fast forward. The serang, who had not had time to complete his prayers, had not yet attended to the anchors. Now the ship had way enough, and Nejdi shouted for the sail to be lowered for, as usual, we should come up to our anchor with the masts bare. The sailors rushed at the halliard-ends, sending Beduin, children, goats, and Jassim the cook flying in their path, and while all chanted and yelled Yusuf Shirazi, Saqr bin Hamoud, Sultan the muezzin, and half a dozen others wrestled with the hitches and turns. At the last conceivable moment of safety the halliards were let go, and the great yard came creaking down while the sail billowed out over the vessel covering the Bedu at their prayers, and the ship carrying her way moved on slowly towards her appointed anchorage.

Let go! Nejdi cried, and an anchor went over to which, fortunately, a cable had been attached. Startled Beduin came out from under the sail by the score. The worshippers on the poop finished their prayers; the sail was unbent, and the evening salutations passed quietly from man to man. The excitement which flared up so rapidly was all subsided. Abdulla, having finished at the wheel, puffed contentedly at the water-pipe, and his brother, hunched behind him, called for the longboat and a fresh pipe. So night came to the now peaceful ship: we had arrived.

We stayed at Lamu a peaceful week during which an Indian merchant came once to look at the carpenter's dhow, for which Nejdi asked a thousand shillings and was prepared to take seven hundred. The Indian found much fault and offered six hundred. Then he went away—without the dhow: after that—some days after—we also sailed.

Lamu is a good place. From the harbor it appears as a group of pleasant white houses, all with spacious verandahs arched beneath red roofs and set amid trees on a gently rising slope from the sea. On either side of the small town are Swahili huts, and stacks of mangrove poles merging into the palms. By the waterfront, mirrored in the still water, lie the small Lamu and Bajun boats, squat and fleet and able, and with them, moored in the stream, some Omani and Batina ships, booms, sambuks, and small baggalas just in from sea.

Ashore, the town and its surroundings are even more attractive than they appear from the sea. The narrow streets of the old Arab town teem with life, and the whole place is enchanting. Lamu is the northernmost port of Kenya, a British colony on the east coast of Africa, but it is almost entirely an Arab town. The buildings, the background, much of the language, the customs are Arab: half the little stalls in the bazaar are run by Hadhramaut Arabs. Lamu's streets are the narrowest I have seen, with hardly room for a water-laden ass to pass. The tall flat-roofed Arab houses lean towards one another, with their upper windows open, welcoming. Many of them have beautiful carved doorways.

Here and there in Lamu one may still find some treasure of the ancient past—a piece of Chinese or Persian pottery, delicate woodwork from India, or Damascus steel. Lamu is off the beaten track and still unspoiled. In the streets a lady from the harem sometimes hurried by, heavily shrouded in her black cloak and veil, but not so heavily that something of her charm could not seep through. The beauty of some of these Lamu girls is very striking. Many wore old American gold dollars in their ears and on their cloaks. When we were there, American gold dollars could still be bought on the beach at Lamu. American gold came there half a century ago, when American trade in sailing-ships was important on that coast, and the United States was one of the first countries to send a consul to the Sultan of Zanzibar.

Outside the town I visited the dhow-yard, where Swahili carpenters were rebuilding an Arab dhow. This they did by the simple process of carefully removing, first, all the old ribs and replacing them with the new. Then, when they had put in new ribs, they took off the old planking and replaced it with new. In this way they were making a new ship with exactly the shape of the old one. It was warm on the yellow sand near the sea, and the shipwrights worked beneath a shelter of rough thatched palms. Near by were the hulls of all kinds of small dhows, most of them the familiar Lamu boat with its low freeboard, its fast, fleet lines, its sharp straight bow and European transom stern. Arabs build these; and Swahili sail them. They carry on most of the native coastal trade of all East Africa from Juba down to Madagascar. Lamu is the home port of the most of them, the most important native dhow port of all East Africa excepting perhaps only Zanzibar. There is a tradition that much of the European appearance of these Lamu dhows—for the hull is more English than Arab, though the lateen rig remains—is due to the foresight of a local sultan of fifty years ago, who asked the captain of a visiting English frigate to show his carpenters how to improve the local shipbuilding standards. At the time of the change Lamu was famous for its ancient sewn *Mtepe* boats, with their curious matlike sails. These were more picturesque than useful, and were certainly not Arab. The *Mtepes* have all gone now. The last hull was rotting to pieces on the Lamu beach, a sweet-lined dhow from Kuwait beside it, built and carried there aboard some boom. A Cutch boat from India was lying on its bilge near by.

I watched the keen lined double outrigger canoes come rushing in with their fish, and a Bajun boat, manned by a horde of picturesque and stalwart Bajuns, went out to sea with her orchestra of swing instruments playing wild, stirring music. I liked Lamu tremendously and wished I could stay a while to learn something about it. There were the Pyrale Islands; within a stone's throw are the great ruins of Patta and Manda Islands. Here are the Bajuns, a mysterious people; here a great slave-mart thrived for centuries. The Chinese came, the Arabs, Indians, Malays, Portuguese, British, each adding to Lamu's story and going on. Lamu is a quiet place now, thrown back upon its timber and cattle trades, and a little depressed, for few tourists come and the palmy days are gone. Shella is a ruin and Lamu's trade is declining, though it improved a little when supplies were run in from there to the northwest for the Italians' Abyssinian war. That is stopped now, and neither the Italians nor the Ethiopians buy anything they can do without.

Lamu has coconuts, shipping, beef to sell to Mombasa and points south, and the mangrove poles called *borities*, cut from the low islands. Arabia is a treeless land and any wood is at a premium there. The cheapest wood, and the strongest for many uses, has always been the mangrove pole. It can be had simply by cutting it from its swamp. Up and down the east coast of Africa these great swamps cluster and the mangrove thrives. There is something in the soil washed down from the interior which puts iron into the heart of these coastal trees, and long use of them in Arab building has proved their worth. The dimensions of many an Arab room are fixed on the beach at Lamu, for the ordinary Arab house, away from centers like Aden and Bahrein, is built of coral rock fastened with mud and lime, and roofed with earth-covered matting spread on mangrove poles. It is cheap, and satisfactory on a dry land.

All along the Lamu waterfront stand piles of these mangrove poles, red with their heavy gums and tan. Picturesque small dhows discharge them from upstream, and Swahili guards grade them, count them, and brand them with the government hammer. The ring of hammers of the government's forestry guards is a familiar sound all day, and the stacks of *borities* grow until they tower over the Swahili huts.

Behind the waterfront, in the straight narrow streets which are parallel to the sea, are the romantic stores where dark-skinned traders deal in Turkish delight and hookahs and coffee pots from Syria, or Persian carpets and Indian brass. Here are the sandal-makers, who provide stout shoes of an amazing cheapness, the embroiderers of Hadhrami caps, the makers of mats and weavers of cloth, the ropemakers, and the sellers of sherbet and fruit. Here, too, are the native hotels, always lively and picturesque, open to the winds, with the habitués reclining on benches in front noisily smoking tobacco from some bubbling hookah, or passing the ceremonial coffee cup.

Sailors from the Arab and Persian deep-sea dhows walk along barefoot and erect, their weather eyes lifting for the *bebes* of whom the town offers a plentiful supply. Lamu is a place famed throughout coastal Arabia for the attractions of its women. I saw Zaid, our ex-slave, and all our serangs and quartermasters and sailors stepping out, their bold wild eyes searching the harem roofs, and little Jassim the cook, not morose any longer, was fetching up the rear.

At such a place as this our Beduin stared in amazement, for this could be heavenly if they were allowed to land. They were properly counted on board and then they were allowed ashore to exercise, but not to stay. Officially there were 104 of them by this time, but this official reckoning by no means included all. For the first time I was able to examine what purported to be our passenger list, and I saw that the number of women left in the great cabin was now 8. Twenty-four passengers were said to have landed in Italian ports, and a total of 12 others had joined us. The crew list showed 27 names. This gave the total number of persons officially on board, when we arrived at Lamu, as 131. Actually there may have been 150. Nejdi and all the Arabs hated these official accountings. Even if he had tried to have them correct, they would still have been wrong. He did not try at all, and the more wrong they were the better he was pleased. Nejdi regarded all forms of government control as unwarranted interferences with the liberty of mariners and the will of Allah. Had not Allah ordained all things? Then why make lists of them on foolish forms, and attempt to control what could never be controlled? Nejdi's contempt for a regulation-controlled world was deep, bitter, and abiding.

After they had been checked, our passengers were allowed to go

Lamu roads

ashore, and it was a great relief to see the decks clear of them at last, if only for the time being. Nejdi had the poop cleaned and scrubbed for the first time in my experience, but he left the filthy mess of the main-deck. It was no use cleaning it when the Beduin would be back aboard so soon. The Beduin had not been ashore since Haifun, for they were not allowed to land at Mogadishu, and they wandered through Lamu's streets and round the countryside like men in a happy dream. It was the mango season, and every fruit stall was full of these luscious fruit. The Arabs are inordinately fond of them. Nejdi thought nothing of wolfing twenty or thirty large mangos at any moment and ate all that came on board, no matter who brought them. Lamu was, indeed, a good place, for fish teemed there and vegetables and meat were plentiful and cheap.

The principal occupation of our mariners and the few Sinbads we had left was smuggling, though the amount they smuggled was not very great. As in Italian Somaliland, the main items were haberdashery and the tiny bottles of cheap perfume, but here cigarettes bought cheaply in Aden were good stock in trade. At Aden, apparently, there are several manu-factories which specialize in cheap cigarettes with trade names very like those of well-known brands. These sell for a few rupees a thousand in the bazaar in Aden Camp, and there is a high duty on them in East Africa. They were ideal for smuggling, and most of our people had laid in large supplies. The only drawback to this trade was the bulk and the awkward nature of the cartons in which the cigarettes were packed; it was diffi-cult to elude the guards with anything so conspicuous. The subterfuges which the Arabs used were sometimes amusing, but not always effective. Brazen effrontery was their main weapon. They were allowed to bring in a few of the cartoned dates which they had been packing so carefully from the large packages, and, when they brought these in to sell—they were allowed only a few each—they carried them in large baskets which always contained something else. The guards, being Swahili, and well aware of most Arab tricks, always examined the baskets and found the goods. Not being hard-hearted men, they did not confiscate them but or-dered them to be left in the longboat. From here it was an easy matter for the Arabs to get them ashore, for they kept coming and going contin-ually, always with little baskets with fish and meat and fruit and vegeta-bles. Between the baskets they brought and the baskets they took away, sooner or later those goods were landed.

Our sailors landed only the few things necessary to purchase their enjoyment in brothel and *suq*. Sometimes I sat in the shade of the commissioner's verandah, by the waterfront, and watched them. It was always an instructive, and often an amusing sight. One day I saw Zaid, caught redhanded with 2000 cigarettes and, after a long harangue, he was led away. The Arabs, like most other people, considered that to be caught in wrongdoing was a most unwarranted intrusion on their liberties, and everybody was upset by the arrest of Zaid. Zaid, however, was not as badly treated as he might have been. He was kept in the prison until morning, and then brought before the local magistrate, very frightened, and tremendously relieved when his night's incarceration, together with the seizure of his cigarettes and the payment of a small fine, were deemed sufficient punishment. He returned to the ship and was cheered by his brethren.

If his arrest was meant to be exemplary it failed utterly, for that same day the tribe was ashore again smuggling more furiously than ever, and I saw Abdulla, Nejdi's brother, hawking an armful of beads in the *suq*.

Days passed. Our Beduin still wandered wide-eyed through the shady streets, dressed in their yellow-and-red finery and buttered hair. After five days the finery was becoming a little thin and the butter rancid. One day on the waterfront I met Said the Seyyid from the Hadhramaut dressed as a Swahili, and he borrowed two shillings. I wondered at this, for Seyyid need not ordinarily seek funds from Nazarenes: but Lamu was full of these descendants of the Prophet, and pickings were lean. Elsewhere on the coast, at Mombasa and the other larger towns, the younger Arab had become suspicious of some of these claims to near-divinity and scornful of the absence of ambition which often accompanied them. Consequently there had been an influx of the holy into Lamu, which is more backward and less in contact with changing ideas. This was regrettable from the point of view of Said the Seyyid, and he found himself short of ready cash. I never saw my two shillings again. I never saw the Seyyid, either, and I did not miss him. He and several of our Hadhrami merchants went missing at Lamu, where only those few who could establish Kanya Protectorate residence were officially allowed to stay. The bulk of our wanderers would have had difficulty in proving residence anywhere, for they were without official evidence even that they had been born.

Nejdi seemed worried at Lamu. It was obvious that the world depression had made business very bad, and the chances of a satisfactory rate of profit on the voyage were dwindling. In ports Nejdi was always a harried man, and the thought occurred to me that an Arab nakhoda had a great many worries which are spared the ordinary shipmaster. Not only

On a fresh monsoon

does he sail the ship, and navigate and pilot her, but he controls all her spending, all her people, all her papers. He buys and sells the cargo without benefit of agents; he finds the passengers and suffers them too, and rules them; settles their disputes, and gets rid of them, which is not always easy. He is a businessman, astute and capable, a judge of timber, of sugar and rice and ghee and frankincense and dried fish, an appraiser of dhows small and large, a master shipwright, a master sailmaker, a master maker of ropes. He knows the best place to sell things as diverse as a cargo of Malabar logs or Rufiji mangrove poles, of sesame and coconuts and Berbera goats, cotton-goods and salt. He knows a good agent from a bad, even in Sur; a solvent Arab from an insolvent. Sometimes he errs. He has much on his mind, conducting his great ship over the face of the Eastern waters, tending her people and her trade, and bringing her back safe to her home at the head of the Persian Gulf. Nejdi was a man with a man's job; and if he was sometimes, by our standards, a bit of a ruffian too, I did not blame him.

Without the passengers it was like paradise aboard the ship. Unfortunately it was a paradise that had to end, and on the seventh day Nejdi sent for his Beduin. Deep-sea dhows are allowed seven days free of port dues in Lamu Roads, but on the eighth day they must pay. So they sail on the eighth day, and this was Nejdi's intention. What mysterious emissaries went out and collected our passengers I do not know, or in what devious ways they were collected; but in the Eastern world there never was a problem so complicated or so mysterious that Nejdi could not solve it immediately if he wished to. Our passengers were constantly taking advantage of the freedom of movement made possible by the inability of Europeans to tell them one from another, and frequently we changed as many as twenty persons in a port, always going out, so as far as the officials knew, with exactly the number we had brought in; but not always with the same persons. If Nejdi had sent me to the *suq* to look for passengers I might, after a time, have returned with two; now Hamed bin Salim waved his hand and they came back in droves.

But they did not all come back this time, as the Arab immigration inspector unfortunately discovered. This inspector was an Arab converted to Christianity and therefore, according to Nejdi and the rest, no longer

Dhows at Mombasa

any good. This convert noticed that we were three women short. The dreadful truth burst on Nejdi that three of the women from the great cabin must have run away. I must say that, if he blamed them for that, no one else did. This was a serious thing, for we had to leave with the passengers we had brought. If the inspector had been willing to co-operate it might not have mattered, for we could easily have covered three of the children with the women's black veils and gowns, and slipped them into the cabin. First they could have been counted as children, then smuggled into the cabin to be counted again as women. Such things can be done. Unfortunately, this inspector was too conscientious, and he demanded at once that the women should be found. Nejdi said they were ashore. There was no doubt they were: but it was also sadly probable that they were then halfway to Mombasa.

But Arab nakhodas are brought up coping with problems of this kind. Nejdi sent his brother ashore with instructions to bring off any three women he could find and, since there was a large supply of Swahili wenches of far from impeccable moral character who were ready to welcome an opportunity to try the gay life of Mombasa, he had no difficulty in returning to the ship within half an hour in tow of three of these. Giggling bundles of sheathing black, they were promptly stowed away in the great cabin. Our passenger list was now complete, and we could sail. We went out to sea before dawn the following morning. The three Swahili damsels, used to a freer life than that led by their Arab sisters, raised hell down below before we had gone five miles. They had, they said, come as guests and not to be cooped up in a dungeon, and they shouted through the hatchway throughout the passage of the Kenya coast. Nejdi clamped down the hatch, locked it, and paid no attention, but the Arab women resented the characters of their new companions and there was a general uproar down below.

It lasted only a day, for the wind was good and it was a short run to Mombasa. What the women did, so long as they did not get the ship into trouble, worried nobody: down below they stayed.

Chapter 9

MOMBASA'S STORY

WE DRIFTED slowly in calm with Kenya's dark green coast alee pleasant in the sun, and the passengers aired their belongings on the rails. Aft Nejdi, who missed several of his best listeners now that the Suri, Said the Seyyid, Abu Ali, and most of our other Sinbads had gone, held forth at length to the few who remained. What a man he was! I looked at him, for the five-hundredth time that voyage, as he waved at the air with the cane of his bubbly-pipe and punctuated his remarks with many pious exclamations and exhortations to the All-Highest to witness that he spoke truth. Near him, some forty of the Beduin sat, listening. I looked at these wanderers of ours also for the five-hundredth time, and hoped devoutly it might be the last. They were interesting, but I felt that I had seen enough of them. Nejdi's monologue droned on and on. He was on his familiar subjects—the decadence of the Western World and the coming rise of the East. On such occasions Nejdi spoke of us in Europe as if we had already ceased to matter, though we still dominated the world. He took a long view: day-by-day events neither concerned nor worried him. By his long view our day was ended: the glory of Islam would rise again soon.

It was curious to be there and listen to him, for me, a European, one of the envied. Now and again a chorus of low *taiyibs* burst from his listeners. They paid no attention to me, for by that time I had become too much one of them.

The calm continued, and we did not sail. No matter: it did not worry Nejdi. We should come to Mombasa in good time. He was not one to fret when the conditions were adverse. He could always talk, or just sit there, on the nakhoda's bench, a brooding hunched-up silhouette in white. The calm was Allah's and, having brought it, Allah would take it away again in His own good time. The calm was Allah's and troubled no man: the satisfactions of his discourse were a man's own. So Nejdi talked, and the ship lay lifeless in the flat sea while the stench of bilgewater and the reek of the Haifun fish rose to heaven. The sailors, worn and emaciated from their past seven weeks on the hopelessly crowded deck, were repairing drums and stretching new kids' skins on tambourines, for our arrival at Mombasa would mark the end of an important section of the voyage and it was traditional that we should be drummed in to the anchorage. Every drum in the ship was being made fit for service. I looked forward to seeing this, for we had not yet been drummed in anywhere.

When Nejdi suddenly said, "There is Mombasa," on the second day, I scarcely believed him at first, for I saw no great port and indeed nothing to break the shoreline—nothing at all, except a few houses and a water-tower. Mombasa comes upon you suddenly, bound down from the north, and for such a good harbor succeeds in tucking itself effectively away. Moreover, it seemed that we had only just left Lamu. But ports on this coast, south of the Benadir, are close and good: it *was* Mombasa. The fish-traps and the plantations along the shore were more numerous than any we had seen on our long run down and there was a prosperous settled look about the land. Now we were opening up the entrance to the harbor, and Nejdi made a wide swing to avoid the reefs at the northern point. He called me over, saying it was a bad place, and showed me how the Arabs conned their ships. The northern point was dangerous, he said: there were sets and rips there, and a nakhoda coming in had to know what he was about, for all the apparent simplicity of the place. There was a wreck in the middle of the channel, but this was marked by a buoy. As we turned and came in, we could see the remains of another wreck on the southern point. The weather was good and the breeze fair, and Mohamed the serang came scrambling over the passengers, yelling for the drums. The sailors snatched them up, and ran forward banging as they went, and singing.

The passengers, more accustomed by now to arriving at places at which they were not allowed to land, watched our entrance into Mombasa with more calmness than they had shown at Mogadishu or Lamu; but many of them ran about and were excited enough to get in the way. Now we were coming in, past the hospital on the one side, and on the other a rising point with coconut palms. The ancient Portuguese fort of Jesus towered above the waterfront. We were headed for the Old Harbor, on the northern side of the town. Mombasa stands on an island in a deep bay, about 600 miles southwest of Mogadishu, and both the northern and the southern arms of the bay afford excellent harbors. The southern arm, known as Kilindini, is now reserved for steamers: the northern arm remains much as it always has been, and here the native vessels congregate —the little Lamu boats down from the north, the Swahili from Zanzibar and Dar-es-Salaam, the Persians and the Arabs from the Gulf, the Somali under the Italian flag, coasting down from Haifun and from South Arabia, the Indians with their tiles and pottery from the Malabar coast, from Mangalore, and the Gulf of Cutch. Kilindini is a place of wharves and cranes and tugboats and regulations, like any other modern port, and as such it is a good one. But it was the native anchorage which appealed to me, this picturesque and romantic place into which we sailed that quiet Sunday evening, with all our drums beating and the sailors singing their age-old chant and, as we came in, the other Kuwaiti in the harbor breaking out their flags and cheering us to our anchorage. It was a good arrival, and I found it pleasantly moving. The green trees, the gaily colored Arab and Indian houses, the squat strength of the old fort, the picturesque assemblage of dhows at the anchorage, the clear blue water breaking gently along the beach by the swimming club, the boats, full of ragged mariners, which flitted across the harbor with rhythmic splash of paddle and lilt of sailors' song, all these made the port interesting and colorful. We brought up to single anchor off the swimming club. It was late afternoon.

We found ourselves one of a fleet of four newly arrived vessels, one of them a Persian boom which had brought a cargo of tiles from Mangalore, the others Arabs from South Arabia. We kept our colors at the staff aft, which is how the big dhows customarily announce their arrival. Remembering our experiences at Haifun and Mogadishu, I did not think that the ship would be cleared that night, but in less than twenty minutes the port doctor, a cheerful Irishman, was aboard. He had a good look at everybody and particularly examined recent vaccination and inoculation scars, for the big dhows are much dreaded as possible carriers of smallpox. They must be watched carefully, for no Arab, Persian, Indian, or Somali nakhoda will ever admit that he has had sickness on board. I heard Nejdi deny that there had been any deaths or illness, though there is scarcely an Arab craft which brings passengers from Oman or from the Hadhramaut without losing some of them. It is usually of little consequence, if they have not died from something infectious: but from a port doctor's point of view the trouble is that, when sickness does occur, the Arabs always do everything possible to conceal it. The Arabs regard all illnesses with their usual fatalism, as manifestations of the will of God, and quarantine to them is nothing but a hindrance wished upon them by Europeans and therefore to be avoided at all costs.

We were quickly cleared in, for we had no sickness, and I looked about me again at the picturesque harbor there in the tropic dusk. Other Kuwait nakhodas were on board—Ganim bin Othman from the big boom *al-Baz,* with whom we had shared the anchorage at Haifun; Bedar bin Abdul Wahhab of the baggala *Bedri,* a sweet old vessel moored close in by the stone quay among a group of Suri; and some other Kuwaiti I had not met before. Bedar was a young man, very tall, dignified in his long white gown and brown cloak. His gown and his headcloth were of white, heavily blued, as is the style of the Kuwait nakhodas on their voyages. Ganim bin Othman was dressed in the same way. Nejdi chatted with them, about conditions in the port, the chances of selling cargo, and similar topics of importance. He learned that the passengers could be landed without difficulty—Ganim had already landed 150 of his own—but the market for Arab products was not good. It was better at Zanzibar, Bedar said. The trouble, said Ganim, was that the Suri always undersold. If a man had a chance to make a sale, some Suri would undersell him. It was very difficult. He had been a month at Mombasa and had not sold all his cargo yet. He planned to go down to Tanga and some smaller ports and buy sesame and general cargo for the run home: he would come back to Mombasa for passengers. Bedar said he was tired of trying to sell his cargo at Mombasa and would go on to Zanzibar on the morrow.

I liked these conferences which went on round the transom of our *Triumph* on these first nights in port, with Nejdi silent and dignified puffing away at his tobacco and Yusuf attending him, good old Yusuf who never had much chance of rest while Nejdi was aboard, and round Nejdi the other nakhodas, all equally silent and dignified, though sometimes they all became far from silent when some subject dear to heart and pocket caused a flare of interest. Sometimes there would be as many as sixteen perched round the reclining bench, with a crowd of passengers and quartermasters and serangs from the other booms' longboats crouched on the deck at their feet. Often in the periods of silence nothing would be heard but the creaking of the ship at her anchorage and the distant drums of the Suri sailors, and the gurgling and bubbling of the water pipes, or the splash of passing oars. Their gowns and close-wrapped headcloths, their gold-embroidered cloaks and their black wool head-ropes, imparted to the Arabs a becoming air of solemnity; their faces were strong, and showed up well in the ember glow from the pipes. As always I was struck by the air of conspiracy which seemed constantly to surround these conferences, though there was usually nothing furtive or conspiring about them. The dignified silences of these gowned men seemed fraught with threats. I well knew this impression to be erroneous, for if I sat among them myself in robe and aghal—it would not have been courteous for me to dress otherwise—I too felt a conspirator and, curiously enough, almost equally dignified. I put this down largely to the robe and the flowing grace of headcloth and cloak, and thought how frequently man arrays himself in such garments when he wishes to create an impression of dignity. Ashore in a tropic suit I soon felt quite ordinary.

The conference had no outcome beyond the usual crop of rumors, and I turned in upon my carpet under the stars reflecting upon odd reports that things were good in Mombasa and we should stay there ten days; that things were bad in Mombasa and we should go on to Zanzibar the day after the morrow, probably with a cargo of bullocks (which would be better than Bedu); that after unloading we should return to Lamu to load mangrove poles for Bahrein; that we should go to the Rufiji Delta and load mangrove poles for Kuwait, that we should go down to Mikindani and ferry maize to Zanzibar. It was also suggested, at varying stages during the evening, that we should beach and clean the ship at Mombasa, Zanzibar, the Rufiji, Lamu, and the Seychelles Islands. These were only a few of the rumors which drifted about that evening. Which of them if any might prove later to be true did not worry me, for I had learned by then to accept what happened and never to hope to forecast anything. This, after all, was not such a bad way to live.

I awoke in the morning to the sound of Suri drums, and saw a tiny Mahra boat warping in to her anchorage close beside us. She was one of the curious straight-bowed, double-ended, ugly little craft hailing from the Mahra coast of southeastern Arabia, or the type known to the Arabs as Bedeni. The distinguishing features of these are an air of general unkemptness and a curious straightness of line, unusual among the Arabs. The bows, sterns, and mast are usually as near to bolt upright as the indifference of their timbers will permit. The method of steering them is the most primitive of all Arab craft, a cumbersome arrangement of yoke and ropes led to a light beam. Their freeboard is invariably very low and, altogether, they are the most unprepossessing of dhows. They are without sheer and their lines are ugly, though they sail well enough. They have generally only one mast, stepped a little forward of midships, higher than the usual Arab mast.

Though it was before sunrise, the day was already warm and deathly still, and the poop was full of praying passengers, with Hamed bin Salim leading them in the dawn prayer. Behind him stood a line of sailors and passengers, the Beduin with their scarred cheeks, the Baluchi from Lamu in their voluminous blue trousers, and the lesser merchants already dressed in their best clothes to go ashore. Nejdi, his praying done, had requisitioned the Malay's gramophone and was grinding out some fearsome tunes. He was in a gay mood for the moment. All the passengers were milling about in their shore-going finery and gathering up their possessions, which now seemed even fewer than they had brought on board.

The longboat from some Suri baggala drummed by, manned entirely by stalwart Negroes, with a pink-turbaned mate seated in the stern, who rose to his feet and waved as he passed us. The seafaring Arab makes all his salutations standing: it is unbecoming to wave or to hail from a reclining position. The longboat was laden to the gunwales with sacks of salt. Three Suri nakhodas, in pink turbans embroidered with blue and red and lashed on with the light headrope of Oman, were already on our nakhodas' bench even at that early hour, and Abdulla, Nejdi's brother, squatted there sucking at a water pipe, "drinking" tobacco, and making a frightful noise over it. Yusuf came up with the morning meal, a few rounds of unleavened bread washed down by cups of very sweet tea. But this morning we were in port and our arrival was celebrated by serving freshly made *khubz*, instead of the half-sodden stuff from the previous day which is more usual. Moreover the *khubz* had been sprinkled with sesame seeds for flavoring. Prepared this way and served hot, the meal, though frugal, was satisfying. The Suri joined us, for guests must always break bread. The tiny Mahra boat warping by burst suddenly into a tumult of handclapping, rhythmic and loud, though what it was for I did not know. The small craft chose to moor right beside us, and I saw, though it could not be forty feet long, there were more than sixty people on board. They stank, and the stench from the dried fish cargo blew over us horribly. Ugh! Even Nejdi could not stand this, and yelled for the serang to take the longboat and tow the Mahara dhow away. The reek of her fish was offensive and violent, making our own bilge seem like rosewater.

During the night we had moved in at high water to our place in the tier of ships, and were moored then bow and stern not thirty feet from Bedar's baggala *Bedri* with two Suri and a Persian on the inshore side of us. Beyond them, two boats from Cutch and the Lamu boats were lying in a pool of tan-stained water where their mangrove poles and firewood had been dumped on the shore. All round us were booms, Lamu boats, Indian kotias discharging fragile clay pots, Swahili cutters with their holds covered with a roof of thick thatch, Suri baggalas and sambuks. From the waterfront the sickly odor of copra came across the harbor, to mingle with the hundred-odd odors competing there, a competition in which stale fish won easily. A little farther on the red flag of the Sultan of Zanzibar flew over Fort Jesus. Like its sister-fort in Lamu, this is now a jail; but it stands stalwart and picturesque as ever, and some of its old bronze guns still point out to sea. On the other side of the harbor, the coconuts straggled across the blue skyline, fringing the green rise beyond the beach. Outside an oil-tanker passed distantly, bound elsewhere, and a liner moved in slowly towards Kilindini. Our passengers were jostling and crowding about worse than ever. It was not yet seven o'clock, but we could see the immigration officers coming out in a boat and there was great excitement.

The examination was almost perfunctory. All the Arabs produced for inspection had papers of some kind or other, but what the papers were and whether they applied to the Arabs who had them, I should not like to say. The immigration officer, a young policeman in spotless white, sat on the nakhoda's bench aft with his Swahili clerks beside him, and carefully went through the list checking off names. Our Arabs were allowed to land freely. As the officer said to me afterwards, what else could be done? They were usually good citizens who caused little trouble. They could be trusted to take care of themselves and not to become public charges, and that, put in a nutshell, was all he had to care about. The Arabs had been accustomed to come down to Mombasa and Zanzibar from time immemorial, and though it was true that opportunities for employment grew less and less, they could scarcely be turned away. It was known that many of them had used up their last resources in coming down to the Kenya port, and perhaps they were ill-advised to do so; but if the worse came to the worst they would always get themselves away again. They never came asking to be repatriated. A few rupees brought them down, and a few rupees took them back again. If they were without money themselves, they could usually go back on the credit of some tribesman or of some tribe in South Arabia, or one of their organizations.

There they were, ships full of them, every northeast season, and they landed—blind, beggars, musicians, hawkers, porters, women, children and all. Everybody we had was allowed to land at once, and there were whoops of joy. It was a strange scene, as Beduin after Beduin came up on the poop to have his name checked by the Swahili clerk, who seemed ready to check anybody, and stood for a moment beside the Scots constable, bewildered now that at last they were to be allowed to land. Many of them hesitated to go away, thinking that so brief an interview could surely not end so long and wearying a passage, remembering, too, other interviews in Haifun and at Mogadishu which were only preludes to further weeks on board. But this time it was real: they could land. They rushed away and dragged out their best clothes, if they had any, and there was a wild buttering of long black locks, a hasty donning of clean sarongs and cotton shirts. Boats from the shore came off and our passengers scambled over the side, though not so quickly that Hamed bin Salim, who always watched the ship's accounts, could not keep careful check on them to see that no one left who had not paid his fare and any sums he might owe the vessel. The Shihri from the Hadhramaut had all paid their fares in advance, but some of the passengers from Mogadishu and the wanderers we had brought from Lamu had not paid. Others owed a little for food, supplied by the ship after they had used up their own. Hamed watched them with eagle eye. He was good at that kind of thing. No arguments and no promises meant anything to him; whoever had not paid his debts in full could not land, and that was final. I was amused to see the lengths to which one passenger from Mogadishu went, to impress Hamed with the vast amount of wealth which would be forthcoming from him the moment he stepped ashore. He did not step ashore, though his protestations and his laments filled the harbor. He had to send for some one to bail him out of the ship before he could go. He owed about fifty cents. The sailors, being paid on the share system, had a keen interest in seeing that no one left without having produced his fare, and we had already lost enough over the Suri.

I did not recognize some of our passengers as they went down the side into the shore boats, so completely had their appearance changed. A frightful old man with one eye and a most unpleasant profile, scraggy, miserly, wizened, and almost entirely repulsive, who had never changed his gown from the evening he had boarded the dhow at Shihr until that morning—he who called himself a sheikh, and competed crazily in the muezzin calls—now came to the rail spick and span in a new white headcloth and long flowing gown of Japanese silk, with a black camel's wool cloak edged with gold wire on cuffs and lapels, from which hung two tassels heavy with more gold wire. The old scoundrel looked almost presentable, and though he had long become an object of derision on board, the Beduin and the others now looked up to him. The blind piper who had quarrelled with his two boys was also there, dressed in a sarong of green-and-white stripes, with his pipe in his belt ready for use. The two boys with him were in clean shirts. Many of the Beduin had brought out bright sarongs of yellow and red, and some of the Hadhrami even wore coats. They had coats made of shoddy cotton, sewn in Japan and sold in the Arabian bazaars. There is scarcely a bazaar in all coastal Arabia which does not offer these wretched garments for sale, at prices from about four annas* upwards. Most of the Hadhrami looked smart in clean sarongs hanging to their knees, clean singlets, money belts and colored sashes about their waists, bands of narrow black wool about their shins, and a large and gaily colored turban wrapped round their heads. There was very little in their money belts and even less in their stomachs, and what was to become of them in that strange place they did not know. But they went fearlessly, in the spirit of the pioneer, determined to make their way somehow or other.

I asked the immigration officer what became of them. He said that many became lesser porters, though they had lost much of this work in recent years. The African bushboys, brought from the interior, had proved much better at it—stronger, more able, and less prone to intrigue. More than that, the bushboys kept their money in the country, and this the Arab often did not. The Arab's ambition was always to make enough money to go home again, and though he was prepared to work at anything, he rarely came prepared to make his way in the country. He was more apt to look upon it merely as a source of wealth, a place of temporary residence whose only real value was to provide him with the wherewithal to return to Arabia and live a life of ease. Many of the Arabs came and went in this way, coming down to Kenya and working hard there for a year or two, or even five years—for they had patience—but always going back to Arabia when in funds. Some went home each season. It was cheap: the journey from Mombasa to Mukalla and back might be made in any dhow for less than fifteen rupees, both ways—little more than an English pound. Life was cheap for Arabs in Mombasa, and even easier in the Hadhramaut. The wandering Arab asks no roof above his head

* Four annas, a fourth of a rupee, is less than sixpence, or ten cents.

and carries his bed with him. He can live on very little food. His total living costs do not usually exceed two or three annas a day, less than five American cents. This is in the towns: in the country with his tribe, the costs would be infinitesimal. A few presents brought back from Africa and wisely distributed, a few *pice* spent at a coffee-shop, a little generosity with the water pipe, a good name in the mosque—these would suffice to make him welcome indefinitely. When all his money was gone he would return to Africa, or wander somewhere else, to Java, India, Singapore. Just as there was a large settlement of Hadhramaut Arabs in Mombasa there was also one in Java, in all the coastal towns. I had noticed that several of our younger Sinbads brought with them newspapers published somewhere in the Dutch East Indies, printed half in Arabic and half in Dutch.

In Mombasa, I was told, the Arabs used to have practically a monopoly of stevedoring, especially in the native harbor. That also is now lost to the Africans, and the Arab must content himself with lesser burden-bearing and with the fresh-water trade, carrying and delivering water in skins and tins to the Arab homes. He finds work also as a night watchman, sleeping on a rough stretcher before a building or shop; as a coffee seller, hawking his wares through the streets with a brass-bound urn and a tiny charcoal fire, clinking his porcelain cups; as a petty hawker of basketware or veils or cotton stuffs through the *suq*; or as a minor shopkeeper, though this is an envied profession. It seemed to me that most of these coastal Arabs wished to be shopkeepers. It did not matter how small the shop might be, or how few its wares: so long as there was a space to spread things and to squat on top of it and puff at the bubble-pipe, they were content. These tiny shops crowd every Arab *suq*, and the stock in trade of any half-dozen of them might be bought for five dollars. A few mangoes, oranges, limes, and coconuts: some shallow baskets of rice, chilis, and grain: some stalks of coarse Arabian tobacco; a bright collection of trash from Japan—any of these was enough to stock a shop, by Arab standards.

I saw some of our passengers ashore, during the *Triumph*'s stay at Mombasa. Several of them were hawking things through the *suq*, carrying small bundles of sarongs, singlets, shawls, and turbans which they offered to every one they met. I did not see them finding many purchases, but they looked content. Some varied their stocks with cheap imitation amber beads, in the familiar thirty-three-bead Muslim rosary, with tiny bottles of smuggled perfumes, with playing cards bought at Aden, or violently perfumed toilet preparations. I saw others already established as helpers in tiny shops, probably the property of relatives. There is a considerable traffic in these shopkeepers between East African ports and South Arabia: one kinsman goes home for a year or two, and others come down to carry on the shop. Others were competing in the already overcrowded street coffee-selling business. They wasted no time. They were at work the day they landed.

Our beggars also wasted no time. There had not been much opportunity to beg on board, and they had not been allowed to ply their ancient trade in Mogadishu. The first afternoon I was ashore I saw our ill-tempered blind man wailing on his pipes on a pitch in the *suq* near an Indian cinema. One of his boys was begging, and the other was gathering scraps of wood to make a fire. The blind man moaned for alms as I passed by, but I gave him none. He was one of the worst men we carried down from Arabia. Others of our passengers who were not beggars were not so well off, for porterage work was scarce and Africans were preferred. Those who had been in East Africa before seemed to settle down quickly enough, for many had relatives, or tribesmen, who kept places for them. Our Beduin, who had not been away from the Hadhramaut before, did not find it so easy, for they had no relations so far from home—no relations, and no friends. I saw several of them while the ship remained in port. They were conspicuous even in the international welter of Mombasa, with their unmistakable Beduin faces, their gaunt lithe bodies, covered with indigo and clad only in short black sarongs, their wild black locks smeared with ghee. They wandered about like children who had lost their parents, staring at the strange sights as if they were unable to comprehend them. Barefoot and erect, they passed along, hungry for the sight of a camel and a swirl of sand from the desert. They did not sit in the coffee-shops, for they had no money. They did not loiter in the *suq*, for its delights were not for them. They were to be found in the clear spaces, or down on a field by the Portuguese fort by the side of the harbor, with their puzzled eyes fixed on the north. They had come so far in that big ship, sailing for many days: and now what kind of fate awaited them? I hope it was a good one, for there was much that was fine in their simple characters.

One day as I wandered in a side street going back to the ship, suddenly a baby voice piped with the Arab salutation, "Peace be upon you, O Nazarene!" I looked down, in surprise. It was the baby son of Aura. He sat on the hot pavement in his tiny sarong, smiling with his limpid great eyes, a tiny mite to be alone there in Africa. He looked happy though a little tired, or perhaps hungry. He was playing with a piece of stick which he kept banging on the asphalt for the pleasure, I suppose, of hearing the noise, and he looked about him at the marvels of Mombasa. He had never been able to bang a stick on a sidewalk before. I stopped, to ask him how he fared, though his Arabic baby chatter was beyond my depth. He was waiting for his father, he said: that much I gathered, when Aura his father silently padded into view. Aura looked tired, too, and bewildered, as if the city were too much for him and its noisy mysteries too confusing for his clear and simple mind. Barefoot, his jet-black locks smeared with grease, his only clothing a black sarong and a cloak of black-dyed calico thrown across one shoulder, he still appeared dignified and self-possessed, in spite of his bewilderment, for a desert warrior of South Arabia was no man to be fooled by a crowd of heartless city streets.

Aura told me he could find no work, and did not know where to look for it: he and the baby were sleeping in a field. A pleasant field, he said; it had trees, and it was green. He was sure they would be all right. Allah was merciful, and they had come a long road. He asked nothing of me. The two of them were uncomplaining. Allah had brought them to Africa where they wanted to go, and that was enough. I discovered they were hungry only when I gave the little boy some coins as a parting gift, and he gave me his man-to-man thanks and said that now they could buy a little food. Just then a camel ambled by, looking almost as much out of place as the Bedu: the little baby rose and clapped his hands, and the coins fell in the gutter.

They were a brave, grand pair, Aura and his son, hungry and alone in that Mombasa street and yet sufficient unto themselves and fearful of nothing. Their faith in the boundless mercy of Allah was in no way shaken, and their hope for the future was bright and undimmed. The pair of them, as I left, waved to me and wished me Allah's blessings, and the last I saw of them Aura and his little son passed hand-in-hand down the road behind that camel. I liked them well: they were such good companions. I wish them luck, and hope that fortune has smiled on them somewhere in Kenya. I never saw either of them again.

We were to have had a big dance of celebration the night after our passengers had left us, but Ismael the musician was missing and the mariners, though they had not been given any money, were off hunting the local *bebes*. So we had the dance several evenings later. It was a particularly good dance, though by that time I felt I had seen all I wished of such celebrations. The decks were clear, for the first time since I had come aboard. Both the longboat and *Afra,* the carpenter's new dhow, were overside. The decks had been swept clean and even scrubbed, so that they shone with an unusual cleanliness. A sail was spread over the maindeck, from the mainyard, as an awning. Every carpet in the ship had been spread, and others borrowed from neighboring dhows also adorned our maindeck and poop. The whole of the ship was given up for this party, the guests being received on the poop by Nejdi and Hamed bin Salim as they came up the Jacob's-ladder and took off their sandals. Then they came down to the maindeck, by the poop ladder, and sat in state beneath the awning on carpets and leaning cushions which had been arranged along the top of the hatch. It was a dignified and pleasing sight. The sailors sat round the bulwarks in two long lines, dressed in their cleanest and best clothes. Their moustaches were carefully trimmed, and Abdulla bin Salim, the serang's mate, had his tuft of black beard in a state of geometric perfection. They squatted quietly round the sides of the ship, and Nejdi and the guests sat along the main hatch in the middle. The hatch was low, and comfortable. Ismael strummed his guitar and for once played some quite attractive melodies. Some of his songs seemed to consist largely of passionate dialogue between a *bebe* and her paramour, and the listeners would smack their thighs and roar with delight.

A fiddler had been brought from a Suri baggala, whose black-bearded nakhoda sat silently by Nejdi throughout the night; and there were some tambourines, a triangle, and at least nine drums. Two of these were large Indian drums, stretched with new goatskin warmed frequently at Jassim's fire. The others were small cylindrical things, made of Basra pottery, and covered at one end with a piece of goatgut. These also required frequent warming. They were played with the hand, the sailors taking turns with them, striking them with fingers and thumb alternately. The rhythm they could keep with the tambourines and drums was very good and sometimes stirring: they all seemed to have a perfect sense of rhythm. The maindeck was lit by the soft glow of two lantern lights which I never saw used at any other time, and the red glow from Jassim's wood fire forward was reflected on the polished teak of the solid mast. The brightly colored carpets, the stately cloaks of the men, the burnished brown of the heavy mast, and the dark canopy of the sail above made a romantic and pleasing scene. The sailors looked their best, and their singing was splendid. Along the top of the main hatch sat some twenty guests, including the nakhodas from the other Kuwait ships, and the Suri, a Persian or two, and a number of Arabs from the shore.

Abdul-latif, the sailor, led our singing. That was his job. He always led the singing at the hoisting of the yard and in the boats. He was given bakhshish for that, and signed on on that understanding just as Ismael received bakhshish for his music and old Yusuf for his excessive work. Abdul-latif sang well, but I preferred the throaty bass of the Negro Zaid and his compatriots. Ismael was the worst singer of them all. His caterwauling became almost unbearable as the night wore on, until once when no one was looking I gave him some bakhshish to stop.

About midnight—these parties always went on all night—the Swahili immigration clerk came noisily on board in a state of considerable intoxication, and he immediately gave Ismael a large sum of bakhshish to sing again. This Swahili was a man of importance in the Arab world, but it was unfortunate that he was so drunk. He could not stand up, and he insisted on singing. He sang very badly and danced worse, and he kept getting up and trying to dance, and falling into the musicians. He was the only drunkard I ever saw aboard our dhow, or aboard any dhow. Some of the Arabs drank a little, though not much. When they did drink it was in secret and very quietly, and they did not dare to get drunk. This was a condition to be avoided at all costs, for the good Muslim seen intoxicated could be a good Muslim no more. But this Swahili was frightfully drunk and careless who saw him. No one remonstrated with him or led him away; no one seemed even to notice that he was drunk. The party and the dancing went gaily on and his antics were unheeded. Next day, however, he heard about it. Drunkenness is not lightly forgiven by the devout Muslim, for the drunken man forgets his prayers.

It was the best party we ever had. Nejdi danced with several of the other Kuwait nakhodas, though not with the Suri. The dances consisted mainly of the usual shuffling to and fro on the carpet along the port side of the deck, with great solemnity and dignity though without much grace, keeping step with the rhythm of the drums. After about twenty minutes of this the rhythm would quicken and the pace of the dancers quicken, until with a final burst of wild music from the guitar and a furious drumming, the dancers would stand before the musicians and shake their bodies violently. This part of the dance was always very exciting to the sailors, and several of them, unable to contain themselves, would jump up and rush to join the dancers. There they would stand, perhaps a dozen of them, shaking their bodies and looking tremendously pleased. With a last flick of the guitar Ismael would bring the music to an abrupt end and the drums would thump out a last beat, at which the assembled group of dancers and sailors would jump high and turn round, yell, and go off laughing, to sit down. This was great fun and they never tired of it. I was however never able to follow either the rhythm or the meaning of this dance. My untrained ear could never determine when it was time to turn, or jump, or anything else. There seemed to be no order in these proceedings, and I soon gave up the attempt to look for any.

This dance was a celebration for the delivery of the passengers, and an entertainment for the friends of the ship in the town. It was also a chance to exhibit the musical skill of our friend Ismael, who apparently was a man famed for guitar and song throughout the Persian Gulf. It was a feather in Nejdi's cap that he had been able to induce him to make this African voyage. The Suri, and Ganim bin Othman, whom Nejdi did not love, were supposed to be green with envy. Whether they were or not I do not know; but it all added to Nejdi's stature among his kind. And that, to him, was everything.

Far into the night and indeed all night long, our party went on. The sailors never tired. The Swahili clerk fell asleep about three in the morning, and was promptly lowered into a boat and removed ashore, snoring. Hamed bin Salim, who never danced and who appreciated Ismael about as much as I did, betook himself to a carpet in a far corner of the poop shortly after midnight, and tried to sleep. Old Yusuf Shirazi, who also was not keen on dancing, tried to do the same, but Nejdi shouted for him so loudly and so constantly that he might as well not have tried. Yusuf, however, regarded five minutes not spent asleep as five minutes lost and, though he could take his rest only in three-minute spells, still took it. From time to time trays of sherbet in various colors (none of them looking very drinkable, for they were mainly bright reds and blues), or oversweet tea or bitter coffee were passed round, and dates, and figs, and the yellow sweetmeats known to the Arabas as *halwa*. This was dreadful stuff, almost sickening. It stuck to fingers and to tongue, and tasted like paste made of molasses and bad sugar flavored with spiced honey. Nejdi could eat it by the pound and so could all the others: they were welcome to my share. As a change from these delicacies we had bowls of Italian canned fruits, bought very cheaply at Mogadishu, and Belgian biscuits made for the African trade. When I rolled in my carpet on the starboard side of the nakhodas' bench aft, about five o'clock in the morning, Abdullatif and Zaid were still leading the sailors in song. I went to sleep to the beat of drums and bursts of laughter and melody. They were singing a Persian boat song which was quite good. I awoke an hour or two later to Sultan's dawn muezzin call, and I saw that the sailors though they had danced and sung through the night were as fresh as schoolboys. The Swahili came early, and apologized for his drunkenness of the evening; but he was not forgiven and the episode was not forgotten while I remained in the vessel.

Mombasa was a good place, and all hands enjoyed it. I never tired of the native harbor and the native town. The heavy scent of copra at the customs steps, the singing of the sailors aboard their ships in the harbor, the picturesque and so varied ships themselves, the setting of the pretty harbor with Fort Jesus and the Arab houses in the background, the blood-red water round the Lamu wood which the matted little ships have brought, the palm-fringed green arm across the bay, the white lateen sails which seem always so piratical and picturesque, the graceful bows of the big booms and the stately sterns of the big baggalas, the crowded streets with their Indians, Baluchi, Swahili, Arabs, Punjabi, and Japanese dentists, and many other Easterners—all these were good to look upon and made Mombasa interesting. It was the sort of port I liked.

I was interested, too, to find out all I could of the trade in dhows. There is no sign of any falling-off in the dhow trade at Mombasa. While we were there, never less than thirty deep-sea dhows lay in the harbor, of which the majority were Suri and other southeastern Arab vessels. During 1937, port statistics showed 214 foreign dhows entered the harbor. In 1938 the number was 241. In 1939 it promised to be even higher. With the setting-in of the northeast monsoon they begin to come, first the little Suri and the Bendeni from the Mahra coast hurrying down to Zanzibar with dried fish and Mango Arabs; then the big Kuwaiti and the Persians, with general cargoes and passengers from the Hadhramaut. Then come the Indians from the Gulf of Cutch and the Malabar coast, and an odd-Somali flying the Italian flag, down from Haifun. The Arabs bring passengers, and salt in bulk from Aden, where it is cheap. The Suri bring fish, which is sold in the Swahili marketplace. The Arabs also bring carpets, though not many, for they are luxury articles, and the genuine product of Persia is both hard to get and hard to sell. They bring cooking stones and ghee, and other Arab products. The Indians bring tiles and earthenware pots. The Indians do not make trading voyages as the Arabs do, but usually come on charter with goods for Indian importers in the East African ports.

Compared with the expense of getting a European vessel about the ports of the world, the expenses on one of these Arab voyages are very low, and this doubtless is a main reason why their trade continues. Our stay at Mombasa cost less than four dollars—less than one English pound. The Arabs ask little in the way of port facilities. They have a bay to lie in and a stage at which to land their goods and that is all. They lie to their own anchors and never come alongside, and they land their goods in their own boats. If they need repairs or cleaning they beach themselves and do their own work. Pilots, tugs, dockmasters, waterside workers, watermen, stevedores—all these would starve were they dependent on Arab employment, for the Arabs do not use them. The Arabs indeed declare that they could get on quite well without any European supervision and object to paying such dues as are charged: but they know very well that if Mombasa were not in European hands they might be made to pay considerably larger sums by their own countrymen. The Arab has a rooted objection to the payment of any fees or government charges, because he has a firm tradition that all fees and dues are a form of graft. To him dues are unwarranted and the upkeep of ports unnecessary, for he can find his own way where he wishes to go and choose such ports as will float him. Harbor works, breakwaters, improvements of all kinds mean nothing to him and he strenuously objects to being expected to pay his share of them. He has always been able to sail in those seas, he says: why should he pay to make them safer for the Europeans, who do their best to drive him out of them?

One point in the harbor regulations struck me as interesting. That was the requirement, under the Native Vessels Ordinance, that "no native can be engaged as a seaman without having previously been questioned by the port officer with a view to establishing that he has contracted a free engagement." Nobody is to be shipped either as crew or passenger without supervision; both crew lists and passenger lists must be complete and they are very important documents. These requirements, I learned, which still stand, are to prevent the Arabs from shipping extra Swahili seamen who sail for Arabia cheerfully enough and are then sold for slaves. I wondered that it was still necessary to take such precautions, but it was considered to be. The Suri, said Nejdi—the poor Suri were blamed for everything—would still sell slaves, if they could: there were markets in Oman. If they could get some good stout Africans up to Sur they could still dispose of them. At Lamu I had heard of the case—well authenticated—of a sambuk from somewhere in Oman which, running through the back passage towards the open sea, had deliberately run down a fishing canoe and taken the two Africans in it to Arabia to be sold as slaves. This was recently. The Africans are still wary of the Arab in his ships, though, so far as I could see, the Kuwaiti never tried to recruit any of them. Nejdi said he could not give a slave away in Kuwait, where they had only to go to the British Political Agency to be freed. Of course, if he could turn up with a cargo of bewitching virgins he might find a market anywhere; but where would he get such a cargo? He had been looking for years and had not yet found one. According to Nejdi, the Kuwaiti had never been slavers: that was a trade carried on from Muscat and Sur, from the Batina coast and Trucial Oman. It may be true that the Kuwaiti never carried African slaves, for they are comparative newcomers to the East African trade; but how much holier they really are than the much maligned Suri I should not like to say.

In the shipping office at the head of the ramp above the landing stage, I found one day a curious volume in which there was much recorded that gives an insight into the proceedings aboard Arab, Swahili and Indian dhows. It was the Casualty Book, always grim reading. I read through it one morning, sitting in the customs room of the shipping office, looking through the open windows at the shipping anchored in the Old Harbor, where Suri, Kuwaiti, Indian, Hadhrami and Persian jostled one another and the small Lamu boats came and went. Now and again a Bajun came foaming in with a burst of music. They were drumming up water aboard a Suri ship at the anchorage near our *Triumph*, and the ancient *Bedri*, which had taken herself to sea in tow of her longboat earlier that morning, lay miraged in the calm outside. There was a good breeze inside the harbor, strangely enough, and apparently no wind at all outside.

The Suri were making a lot of noise with their triangles and drums, and every few minutes they would all stop to clap their great hands with a thunderous noise that could be heard all over the harbor. Inshore, her crew were grounding a Muscat jalboot, at high tide, leaving her far in on the flat to be dry at low water. They, too, danced and sang, and the distant sound came pleasantly to the high windows. On the landing stage a gang of bushboy coolies toiled with sacks of salt. They were a stalwart and magnificently muscular gang, so wet with sweat that they looked as if they had come up from the sea. They sang a chanting song as they worked. Everywhere was this deep-throated chanting of muscular men, forming a background to the intense toil. Overhead the sun burned and the sky was of cloudless blue. Inside, in the cool of the customs room, a group of Arab passengers were checking their baggage. Occasionally an Indian merchant would hold up these proceedings, very briefly, while a chit was signed. The customs office and the shipping place seemed smoothly run, and the Indians in charge were helpful and courteous. I saw our friend the Swahili clerk who had been drunk on board at the dance. He hurried by sheepishly when he saw me.

In this Casualty Book were accounts of strandings, dismastings and other losses of vessels set out in a precise handwriting as if they were entries in a merchant's ledger. The accounts seemed to have no relation to the events they narrated and, seated there even with the panorama of the ships outside, it was difficult without a conscious effort to picture the struggles, the grief and the tragedies so prosaically listed. I was impressed by a curious similarity of many of the accidents. It was amazing how often some hard wind just "suddenly came up," or some rocks suddenly got beneath the vessel. Some of the laconic accounts of shipwreck were almost amusing. Consider, for example, the case of the Lamu dhow *Amantulla*, outward bound from Mombasa towards Dar-es-Salaam. Everything was going well, according to the sworn statement of her nakhoda, when "all of a sudden a terrific gale swept over our dhow and dashed same against a rock." She was lost. She had a cargo of 250 bags of maize and six cases of umbrellas. The crew, apparently, swam ashore each holding an umbrella, for they salved ten. Then there was the Lamu dhow *Violet* (nakhoda Mubarak bin Khamis) which suffered a similar fate. She left Lamu with seven crew and one passenger bound south for Zanzibar, and a cargo consisting of 125 bags of beans and 18 sacks of moong, whatever that is. The little *Violet* was going quietly along the coast somewhere off Kilifi when "all of a sudden our dhow was carried over and dashed against a reef with the result that the rudder came out and two planks from the bottom were broken and the sea started coming in." She was lost, too, and they did not salve anything—not even a sack of moong.

This sudden springing up of bad weather from calms became monotonous. It is true that the neighborhoods of Malindi and Kilifi, and outside Mombasa itself, may at certain seasons breed sudden bursts of bad weather: but these can usually be seen coming and prepared against. It seemed to me that many of these vessels had been lost in squalls. Their unwieldy lateen sails and their too close proximity to a dangerous coast, in addition to an inadequate lookout and too great a faith in Allah, had been their undoing. Not that it always took a squall to sink them. The dhow *Admiral*, for instance—another from Lamu—was quietly entering the

port when "all of a sudden she struck the old shipwreck" right in the center of the passage. That was the end of her. The shipwreck has been there
a long time: surely the nakhoda knew the way past it. There is, too, the
sad story of the Zanzibar dhow *Fat-el-Khair*, which was sailing from Zanzibar to Pemba in bad weather when "all of a sudden the mast came
down," which would be a calamity aboard any vessel. The nakhoda, however, overcame this disability and ran for Mombasa in distress, where he
duly arrived.

Some of the dhows have simply gone missing. They sailed and never
came in anywhere and nothing of them had ever been found. Losses of
the small Swahili craft are numerous, but the big Arabs seemed to be mentioned rarely in that book. The Indians had their share of woe. There is,
for instance, the story of the Indian dhow *Kaalianpassa* (178 tons), master Moosa Ahmed, which, with a cargo of 2700 Indian mats from Pasni
towards Zanzibar, sprang a leak about a month out. The sworn statement
of the master, Moosa, duly recorded in the Casualty Book, goes on:

"We could not get at the leak because of the cargo. The vessel sank
quickly. We abandoned her and rowed three days and landed all safe at
Malindi. I took my map of India, my map of Africa being lost."

I like the picture of Captain Moosa, his ship going down, searching
for his map of Africa and, not finding it, taking the map of India instead,
on the ground, I suppose, that any map was better than none. But he was
a long way from India, if they had been at sea a month. He also, he adds,
took two saucepans of fresh water, a compass, six pounds of flour, and the
oars. It was just as well to take the oars. A sailor, one Othman Bachu, con-
firms his captain's story, adding only that it took fifteen minutes to clear
the boat, and the sea was over the decks of the dhow before they left.
He admits that the boat was not stocked with provisions and water. Judg-
ing by my experience, boats never are, for the fatalistic Muslim, be he
Arab or Indian, would never dream of doing such a thing. They had not
seen land but they knew they had only to pull towards the west and they
were bound to turn up somewhere in Africa. They are very prosaic about
it: the three days' pull in the open boat, in bad weather and beneath
a dreadful sun, seems to have inconvenienced nobody.

"We set a course for the west, and got to land on the third day," Othman says, adding only that they had no money. Beside his testimony is
his mark, a smudged thumbprint: Captain Moosa signed his statement in
the same way.

Then there is the Indian kotia *Din Ganja Pirpassa*, whose master was one Mohamed Hajji Jammohamed. His kotia was of 135 tons and had a crew of ten. "On the thirteenth of January, 1939," he begins, "I with ten able crew left Mangalore for Mombasa with 60,000 flat tiles and two tins pepper pickles consigned to Mombasa Hardware Ltd. The weather was fine until the twenty-second when the wind suddenly increased in force and the sea rose and it became tempestuous." They lowered the sail and let the ship drift: this is the usual way of meeting bad weather both in Arab and Indian vessels. They lower the sail and drift. The kotia "labored heavily and rolled seas on board." He thought she would founder and therefore jettisoned 12,000 of the tiles. This saved the day and the ship lived through the storm. Afterwards the weather fined, and she sailed on to Mombasa, reaching there on the eighth of February with the rest of the cargo.

This casualty record was an interesting book. I noticed that though accidents were frequent, loss of life was not. "They are all good swimmers," the shipping clerk said. It seemed to me that they have to be. I looked out through the window again at the animated scene down on the Old Harbor, where the longboats pulled with song and sweep of long oars among the Arab and Indian fleets, and the sound of drum and chant and triangle mingled with the stamping of feet and the clapping of great hands. I wondered how many of those great dhows might have wallowed helplessly in the trough of the sea, sails lowered and seas on board, on the way down from Arabia, how many of the sinewy sailors chanting and working there might have rowed three days towards the west with nothing but a useless map of India to guide them.

The shipping clerk was looking out, too. He was a pleasant young Indian.

"A queer life," he said. "Don't you think?"

The diversions on board and these yarns of dhows were interesting, but we were rid of our passengers and had sold no salt. After five days Nejdi announced that we would sail for Zanzibar on the morrow. This, of course, we did not do; but three days later we were gone.

Chapter 10

ON TO ZANZIBAR

AFTER Mombasa, Zanzibar. That was the way of most Arab-African voyages, and it was our way then. We slipped out from Mombasa before daybreak one morning with our hold full of salt, and thirty new passengers on deck going to Zanzibar. Though with them we were still sixty persons on board, the ship seemed almost deserted, and life was heavenly. Our new passengers were Arabs from the Hadhramaut going south on business, as well as some citizens of Mombasa making an excursion, and a small group of Suri merchants who looked as if they might have been prominent in the hashish trade. The Suri clustered about the officers' bench aft listening to a monologue from Nejdi and I began to wonder whether that worthy had not shipped them simply to have an audience, for they sat at his feet most respectfully and never were behind with their *taiyibs*.

We were passing pleasantly down the channel between Pemba—which the Arabs called the Island of Green—and the mainland long before evening, with a good sailing breeze and the conditions perfect. We were well in mid-channel, for we were not going in anywhere in Pemba and we gave the place a good berth. As we sailed along, steadily nearing this Zanzibar which had been our goal for so long, excitement mounted in the ship, and the sailors ran bright-eyed to their work with a greater alacrity and more zest in their singing than ever before. Now that the passengers from Mukalla and Shihr were gone, there was room to dance on the maindeck again and they danced there to every order, as if they were making up for lost time. As soon as each piece of the work was done, they danced, with hand-clapping and rhythmic stamping of their horny feet; there was a greater sense of anticipation among them and air of excitement than I had ever observed before. This place, Zanzibar, this haven of the East

African seas, meant a great deal to them and not only because it marked the end of our outward voyage. From there, even if the ship continued to the southward, as she must if she were to load in the Rufiji Delta, they would be homeward bound. But I gathered that the prospect of the delights of the *bebes* of Zanzibar exceeded even the pleasurable thought of shortly being homeward bound, for these *bints* of Zanzibar, they told me, were the best in the Indian Ocean. There were enough and to spare for all comers, and they were exceedingly ready to afford delight to the virile Arab sons of the sea.

The way from Mombasa to Zanzibar is short and comparatively easy, and on the second morning we were off the northern end of Zanzibar island. The dawn was of that lovely kind which only the Indian Ocean knows, and the ship, running on upright and graceful before the quiet wind, had never looked better. The mellow tones of the predawn prayer were musical and the chorused *amins* of the sailors and the passengers ushered in the lovely day. The ship wandered onwards quite upright in the sea, for once, for the breeze was behind her and there was no sea to make her pitch or roll: she had no motion other than her own way. Flying-fish skimmed away from the side of the hull as she ran on: the wooded beaches of Tumbatu Island slipped by to leeward. Our drums were lying on the firebox ready to be warmed to drum us in to Zanzibar, for we should come in there with more noise even than we had brought to Mombasa.

The day was perfect and even the breakfast of unleavened bread tasted well that morning. On board, when the prayers were done, all was quiet and peaceful, in contrast with the conditions on the rest of the voyage. Swift little double-outrigger canoes manned by Swahili fishermen flashed rapidly by: here and there, on the land, we opened up a fresh prospect of some pretty beach as we ran on. Zanzibar is a pleasant low wooded land, with golden beaches.

I thought, as we sailed there that bright fine morning, of all the great ships that had passed that way and of the sea history which had been made in those waters. The Arabs, the Persians, the Indians, the Chinese and the Malays, too, before fierce Arab rivalry had driven them to their own waters, then Vasco da Gama, the Portuguese, and after him the rest of the Europeans. We had passed in the night the reef off Pemba where da Gama had left his ship *San Rafael*, during that famous passage to India at the end of the fifteenth century. The *San Rafael* touched on a reef off Pemba and was abandoned for lack of seamen to get her home. She was not badly damaged, apparently, but by that time da Gama had lost many of his men and could not get his three ships home. So the *San Rafael* was burned and her sailors taken in the other ships.

According to Nejdi, who like most Arab nakhodas had a wide, if not very accurate, knowledge of the history of the Indian Ocean, it would have been a better world if the Portuguese had burned all his ships on a Pemba reef, and himself with them. Nejdi saw nothing remarkable in Vasco da Gama's voyage, and a great deal to be regretted. According to Nejdi, the man was not even a sailor; and, as for the voyage, it was merely an overpublicized piece of carefully exploited good fortune. The success of the voyage to India, he said, had been made possible by the use of Arab pilots who were compelled to show the Portuguese the way, for they came in their well-armed ships and forced the Arabs to pilot them. Nejdi and the others spoke about da Gama's voyage as if it were a comparatively recent event. The man they honored was not da Gama or any other Portuguese, but the famous Arab pilot Ibn Majid who had, they said, shown him the way from Malindi to Calicut. They would have honored Ibn Majid more if he had thrown da Gama's fleet on the shoals of the Laccadive Islands. Why indeed he did not do this they could not understand, for he could have done it easily enough. Ibn Majid, according to Nejdi, was an Arab from the Persian Gulf, possibly from somewhere on the Hasa coast. He had been a famous pilot, and his safe conduct of Vasco da Gama from Africa to Calicut was the only crime against him. The Portuguese, however, had made him do that: Nejdi said he was a hostage delivered by the Sheikh of Malindi, when da Gama had so harassed the town that only an offer of safe pilotage to India would induce him to leave it.

It occurred to me that Nejdi would have found it difficult to pilot his ship from Malindi to Calicut even today, for the way lies over the open sea for many hundred miles, and Nejdi did not know the way across the oceans. He knew only the way along the land. I asked him if he could make such a passage. He said yes, of course he could. He would hire an Indian *muallim* to measure the sun. But this lack of proper navigational knowledge among the Arab nakhodas of today was a sore point with Nejdi, who knew well enough that in that field they compared poorly with the Arabs of old. No longer could a nakhoda of the Persian Gulf— such a man as Nejdi—take his dhow and voyage to China, Malaya and Singapore. He could not, without employing an Indian navigator, even undertake to deliver a shipload of pilgrims from Calicut to Jiddah, and on all his African voyages he had to coast.

It had not always been so and Nejdi knew it. In the great days of the Arab navigators Arab dhows covered the Eastern seas: now it was half a century since one had rounded the southern tip of Ceylon. Ancient methods, the old instruments, the old mathematics—in which the Arabs had so long excelled—all these were lost and nothing had come to take their places, nothing but discarded steamship compasses bought in a junk yard in Bombay, and uncorrected out-of-date Admiralty charts. Yet the Arabs still sailed, though they had lost much of their knowledge and some of their glory. Their voyages consisted largely of petty coastal trading and smuggling. Nejdi attributed their decline to their own softness and the heartless and efficient exploitation of their trades by the Europeans.

All this made interesting subject for conversation that bright morning as the big dhow slipped along the island of Zanzibar. I should have listened to Nejdi with greater patience if he had not always been so sure that he was right. According to him, we Europeans were all doomed and too stupid to be worth bothering about. We were no longer even the "people of the book," for we had obviously given up the teachings of our Book. The only advantage we had ever had had been our superiority in wealth and arms which, for some inscrutable reason, Allah in His wisdom had allowed us. Perhaps this had only been His way of administering a lesson to the softening Arabs and providing the Europeans with the means to destroy themselves. Yet Allah was wise and all-knowing: the day of the Europeans would soon be ended and the Arabs come again into their own. *Taiyib,* murmured all the Suri and Hamed bin Salim. I said nothing.

Nejdi liked to say that the Arabs had regarded the Cape as a sort of divine protection for the Arabs in their eastern seas. Good Hope in the south, with its storms; the Red Sea with its reefs and its dangers, in the north; the great bulwark of immense and unknown Africa, the deserts and the dangers athwart the path of the land caravan bound eastward towards the Persian Gulf—these things, said Nejdi, were Allah's bulwarks against the infidels. When they fell, it was a punishment for the too great softness of the Arabs who had held almost undisputed dominion over the whole Indian Seas from the sixth to the sixteenth centuries and had grown fat and soft from their profits. They had spread their settlements from Zanzibar to the Philippines, from Java to Canton, from the Malabar coast to the Sudan, from Siam to Mandalay, from Mozambique to Malacca. Now the infidel and the Nazarene had built far greater empires, but they, too, would fall and again the bulwarks protecting the

vast preserves of the Arabs would become effective and only ships propelled by the lateen sail would wander over Eastern seas. Allah was compassionate and the time for the punishment of the infidels was at hand.

Thus spoke Nejdi day after day. All his philosophy and all his arguments, all his hopes and all his views seemed grounded in fatalism and
faith in the compassion of Allah. According to him, God spoke and understood only Arabic. Nejdi was welcome to his views, which gave him
considerable satisfaction. I was not so sure of my own.

By this time it was mid-morning and there was more work going on
about the decks than I had ever seen being done in a dhow at sea before.
Kaleel and a gang were fish-oiling *Afra*, the new small sambuk, which
stank horribly. *Afra* had not been sold at Lamu or Mombasa, but Nejdi
hoped to sell her in Zanzibar for a satisfactory sum. She was a good-looking young vessel with a smooth bottom, a nice run and a saucy sheer to
her. It was a pity she had to be fish-oiled and could not be decently
painted. *Afra*'s price was still a thousand shillings, complete with mast and
sail and one anchor.

Hassan, the helmsman, was cleaning the brass binnacle for the first
time since Mogadishu. The serang and the sailors were scrubbing the poop,
on their knees, using their bare hands: the ship had no brooms. Yusuf
Shirazi was shredding tobacco for the hookah. Hamed bin Salim, who had
been awake all night, and Abdulla, Nejdi's brother, who had not, were
asleep in the shade of the mizzen. Ismael the musician was turning his
guitar beneath the break of the poop and Jassim the cook was boiling
Haifun fish. On top of his firebox were the drums, drying in the sun.
They would be warmed at the fire later.

Zanzibar Channel was a lovely place. By this time we were not far
from the town itself and we found ourselves one of a stately fleet of Arab,
Swahili and Persian vessels, big and small, sailing towards it. Round us the
last double-outrigger canoes were skimming, homeward bound with fish.
Once we overhauled a large Indian baggala lumbering along, rolling
slightly, for she was very light. Her huge carved stern, covered with elaborate designs, was very handsome. We passed close so that we could see
through the grills in the stern windows into her great cabin, where the
ghee jars hung and lots of mysterious things in raffia baskets: a silken flag
with red-and-white bars, very large, flew over her stern. She was a Por-
bandar ship, said Nejdi. A good one, I ventured to remark, to which Nejdi

replied that the Arabs were better, though he was surely too good a seaman to think this. He could not bear that anything Arab should ever appear at a disadvantage. True, his *Triumph* was much faster than the Indian and we slipped past her very quickly in spite of the fact that she was light and we were deeply laden. But I know in which ship I should prefer to face a blow.

We were in sight of the city of Zanzibar before noon. We were sailing then towards the pass in the reef not far from Livingstone's house, with our drums beating and the sailors gathered in a group on the foredeck, singing, and the red flag of Kuwait flowing out astern. We had our special flag out that day, the big one in red silk with "el-Kuwait" embroidered on it in Arabic characters, in white, and, vertically down the hoist, the familiar text of the Quran which adorns all good Arab flags— "There is no God but God: and Mohamed is the Prophet of God." Nejdi always felt and looked particularly dignified and quite noble when we flew that flag. We flew it only at Zanzibar, on this arrival day, and when we came back to Kuwait. I never saw any other Kuwait ship with a flag quite so ornate as ours. Our ordinary ensign was a piece of red linen about twelve feet by three feet, on which was plainly inscribed "el-Kuwait," in Arabic characters.

The scene was a grand one—the ship running in before the quickening breeze towards the palm-fringed beach, standing apparently right towards the land for a while, then swinging, in a wide curve, towards the anchorage: the great fleet of dhows assembled there, many of them with their colors out welcoming the Persians, the Suri, the Indian and the Kuwaiti which were coming in together; the blue sea; and in the background the pleasing silhouette of Zanzibar itself, shimmering in the haze like a line of ships under sail. Now we straightened up on the last leg towards the dhow anchorage, which seemed so filled with dhows that I could not see where we could fit in.

The buildings of Zanzibar, which had shimmered and danced in the heat, began to take concrete form, and the great white palace of the Sultan, coming down to earth, did not bulk so huge, though it was uglier. The other houses stretching red-roofed towards the point in a long straight line ceased their miraged dance, too, and now stood in orderly array. Nearer to us were booms and dhows of all kinds high and dry on the beach, and in the brief lulls of our own sailors' lusty singing we could hear the songs of their sailors careening them, and all the tumult of the harbor—Suri drums, Omani feet-stampings, Swahili songs, Lamu fiddles, Batina triangles. Still we kept running on towards the crowded anchorage, in which I could see no place where we could enter. It was like a war fleet assembled against us, a solid wall of oiled wooden hulls shining in the sun, with red flags flying and, here and there, the glint of burnished brass. Our own brass shone, too, and Nejdi and Hamed bin Salim were dressed in their flowing best. Nejdi wore his best aghal, the one with the half-twist in front which, I gathered, was the latest thing in Kuwaiti fashions. The passengers were standing about, also in their best clothes, all staring at the scene. Several of the Suri, in long brown gowns and embroidered turbans, were standing on the poop intently watching something. I saw that two of them had small parcels secreted in their cloaks.

Meanwhile our sailors continued to sing, and there was such a banging of drums as I never had heard before. The serang was leading them, an expression of ecstasy on his Negroid face. They sang and sang, banging on tambourine and drum. They sang so much that they could hear no orders and though they were far forward, as near to the eyes of the ship as they could get, they made so much noise that it was difficult for the helmsman to hear Nejdi's orders even when they were relayed by Hamed bin Salim in a very loud voice. Our mizzen had been made fast earlier, but the yard was still aloft: our largest mainsail was mastheaded, and the great area of that sail swelled with the freshening wind. We were coming in at eight knots. Now we were off the anchorage, our keen bow slicing through the sea.

"Port a little," from Nejdi, standing in the gig at the quarter davits.

"Port a little," louder, from Hamed bin Salim beside the wheel. "As Allah wills!" from Abdulla, giving her a few spokes.

> *Now we are coming in,*
> *And this voyage is ending:*
> *Thanks be to Allah,*
> *Always the merciful!*

Thus sang our score of mariners, to the accompaniment of loud banging on all the ship's drums and ecstatic whoops and cheers from Mohamed the serang.

> *Nejdi has brought us here,*
> *Nejdi, good master:*
> *Thanks be to Allah,*
> *Always the merciful!*

On and on and on, with never a glance at what was happening to the ship or the alarming nearness of the other vessels, the sailors sang.

Who helped our Nejdi?
Hamed, good muallim.
Thanks be to Allah,
Always the merciful!

"Lower the mainsail!" suddenly from Nejdi.

No answer from the mariners, singing more lustily than ever, hearing nothing else.

"Lower the mainsail!" screamed Hamed bin Salim, rushing to the break of the poop. "Lower the mainsail!"

Still no answer from the mariners singing away: no answer, and no obedience.

The ship was charging at the assembled moored vessels, as if she were going to break a way through them, since none seemed open by other means. There were fifty Arab ships swinging there. The wind was fresher than ever, and the short distance between the *Triumph* and the anchored fleet was becoming less with an alarming speed. We could see the faces of some Persians in the nearest boom watching with mild interest. I wondered why they did not fear for their lives, for it looked as though we should be charging into them within ten seconds. I reckoned without Nejdi. He excelled at such seamanship as this.

Hamed bin Salim was still screaming orders to lower the sail, while he dashed at the halliards to let them go. As always, nothing had been prepared and nothing was ready: the two hauling parts of the halliards were still thoroughly fast with turns and half-hitches round the forward beam. It was four men's work to let them go. At last the serang saw that the sail must be lowered and, leaping up, he led half the mariners to that job while the others still sang and banged the drums. It seemed minutes before the halliards were let go, but probably it was only a few seconds. The great parrals aloft began to creak and the yard to rumble down, while the cotton sail bellied out over the lee side and engulfed the singers. Down came the yard, creaking and protesting; on rushed the ship. Still drums banged and songs came from somewhere underneath the sail.

Now we were at the outer edge of the anchored fleet, inside the buoys marking the native vessels' anchorage. It appeared to me that we must certainly collide violently with at least three vessels, sending them skittling through the rest of the fleet moored behind them. But again I reckoned without Nejdi. He knew what he was doing. He held up his hand, to stop the drums, for the songs were ended and there was work enough for every one. He rapped out orders while the ship raced on. I saw that he had found a place, a very narrow place, into which I did not think our boom could enter, between a large Indian dhow and two Suri moored stern and stern. He was charging at that, while he signalled to his brother with his hand to give her a spoke of the wheel this way or that. Meanwhile when the sail had been gathered in and quickly cut from its stops the sailors under Hamed bin Salim and the serang were getting lines ready. I did not know then what they were for, since we were not coming along-side. Our long, oiled nose was already in the fleet: we were in the gap, bowling through. Nejdi shouted an order I did not understand, and im-mediately half our sailors were in the water, in their clothes, swimming for dear life. They were pulling ends and bights of the mooring lines with them, and they swam rapidly to the other vessels, boarding the In-dian and the outer of the two Suri. Here they quickly made fast the ends and bights of the mooring-lines, while other sailors aboard the *Triumph* gathered in the slack and checked the vessel's way.

She was coming in so quickly and she had so much way—for she was a ship of near 150 tons, and she still had more than 100 tons of cargo—that the sudden checking of her way made the Indian and the two moored Suri strain violently at their own anchors, and they ranged a little so that they brushed other ships. But they brushed them only lightly and did no harm. Nejdi, using these checks brilliantly, and very rapidly, eased his big vessel through the gap and alongside the Indian, bringing her here so quickly that the maneuver was accomplished almost as soon as I could perceive its aim.

At first I could not understand how he would take up his moorings, or even find any, in that crowded place, yet there he was, the ship in a good position, safe, and brought there without so much as rubbing against another vessel. The brilliant use of the two checks, and the fine waterman-ship of the sailors, alone made it possible. I was to observe later that feats of seamanship of this kind were common at the Zanzibar anchorage, where the native craft were herded together in a buoyed-off area not large enough to hold them, and certainly not large enough to give them elbow room.

The Arabs did not seem to mind this. They would probably have herded together anyway, for they loved that. They made use of the con-fusion which naturally surrounded such an arrival to evade the most irksome of the European regulations. No amount of strict inspection could possibly oversee all that went on when a ship came driving into a fleet like that and had, perforce, to take up her moorings cheek by jowl with half a dozen other dhows. It was a severe offense for a dhow to anchor beyond the limits of the dhow anchorage, and a motorboat from the port office would soon bring out officials to shout at her and shift her. No matter. The moment we came charging into that fleet, I saw our Suri hop over the side, on the side farthest from the town. One swam to a small boat astern of a sambuk, and this he quickly rowed back to us. The other jumped into it and rowed at once away. Within a minute they had disappeared and where they had gone into that fleet I did not know, though I had been watching them closely. With them went the mysterious parcels they had been carrying.

At the same time, some of the passengers also disappeared. It was too easy. Only those remained on board, I suppose, who possessed the necessary official papers, and were entered on the proper list. It was a bit of a farce, this seeming compliance with European regulations. The Suri grinned like happy schoolboys as they rowed away, and seemed to regard everything as a joke. What was in those parcels they so carefully landed? I asked Abdulla, not expecting to be told anything and knowing that I should have to disbelieve anything I might be told. Abdulla grinned. Hashish? I ventured, having heard that this was likely. Abdulla grinned again. After some time, he remarked that the Suri were no good, and grinned still more.

Later, ashore in Zanzibar, I was talking to a medical man. It was a strange thing, he said, that as soon as the northeast monsoon set in and the Arabs and the Indians began to come down, none of his patients asked for opium, until the dhows had gone again. Perhaps, he said, the Indians brought some.

Aye, I said, maybe they did.

Our arrival at Zanzibar marked the end of an important stage of the voyage. Outward cargo and passengers would be landed here, though the ship still must go farther south for her homeward load, to Simba Uranga on the delta of the Rufiji River, in Tanganyika. Our salt was sold and the rest of our cargo disposed of, except the bad dates, which by this time were fermenting horribly. With their sickly stench and the frightful odor of the Suri fish all around the harbor the anchorage was a foul place. Half the assembled fleet there seemed to be Suri, all laden with stinking

fish. Fortunately for us we lay on the outside of the fleet, and the wind blew from us toward the land. Our anchorage was across from the entrance to Funguni Creek, where the smaller ships were taken in and beached for cleaning.

When we came in, Abdulla Kitami's boom was on the beach, propped up on stilts. One of our first visitors was Abdulla Kitami himself. He came aboard all smiles. He had, he said, already been at Zanzibar a month. He had been fourteen days sailing from Shihr to Mombasa direct and had no trouble landing his 150 passengers, none of whom had died. The bulk of his cargo had been sold at Mombasa, where he had stayed ten days. Abdulla Kitami had then come on to Zanzibar, while we sweltered in Mogadishu and Lamu. He had now sold the remainder of his cargo. He was waiting until the northeast monsoon quieted, and it was time to go up to Lamu to load mangrove poles for home. It was not yet the end of February, and he had still some time to wait.

Abdulla Kitami seemed pleased with himself, but some of his sailors who pulled him out in the boom's longboat talked with our sailors, and were not so pleased. They liked Zanzibar, but two months there was too much. It was, they said, an expensive place, with far too many distractions. If they spent all their money there, they would have nothing left when they got home. Why, they murmured, had their nakhoda not gone elsewhere? Why had he not found it possible, as the Suri and many of the Persians did, to get a freight locally from some port to the south'ard, and earn a little with that instead of lying there on the beach earning nothing? A ship, they said, made her voyage to earn money. She earned nothing sitting on the Zanzibar beach. She could have gone tramping down to the Rufiji, to bring a cargo of poles from there for sale at Zanzibar, and then have gone northwards to Lamu for her second cargo. She could have gone for corn from Mikindani, as Sulieman Said was reported to have done with his big baggala. She could have found something to carry from Zanzibar, or to bring to Zanzibar, if only the nakhoda had bestirred himself and tried. The sailors, since they shared in its receipts, had a direct interest in seeing that the voyage was properly conducted. If Abdulla Kitami himself, they pointed out, wished to stay in Zanzibar and waste his money, he could do so. Saud the slave could take the ship. Saud was every bit as good a sailor and navigator. He had taken the small boom from Aden to Mukalla and Shihr, just as Hamed bin Salim had brought us. He was to have a boom himself the following year. Saud was a good man, not over-

Side of a boom

interested in the fleshpots, and not one to leave his ship rotting in the sun two months on the Zanzibar beach.

I listened to all this with interest, for it was only about that time that I really was beginning to learn the sailors' ideas about what went on. I mentioned the subject to Abdulla Kitami later, and asked him why he had not tried to earn some freights with his ship instead of waiting. Nearly all the other vessels were earning something. He said the Suri took such low freights that he could not compete with them; he could not, he said, possibly make any money hauling corn from Lindi or Mikindani or from Kilwa at half a shilling a bag, and the Suri accepted freights at less than that. He blamed it on the Suri; but I am not sure whether he was justified. He would not have lost money. At least he would have earned expenses, which was better than nothing. The sailors had to pay for all the food eaten in idleness at Zanzibar. He could have bought his own cargo in the Rufiji, if he had cared to. The cash could have been advanced by merchants in Zanzibar if he had none himself.

Nejdi made no mystery, for once, about his intentions. The *Triumph* was not going to be laid up, or even hauled into Funguni Creek and cleaned. She was going on to the southwards as soon as her cargo was discharged. If there were time, she would make two trips there, the first back with a cargo for sale at Zanzibar, and the second to load for the Gulf. Nejdi would not take her. Hamed bin Salim would do that. The Rufiji, according to Nejdi, who had never been there, was a frightful place, quite the worst place any Arab ship went to. It was nothing but a gloomy great swamp of ooze and mud covered with mangrove poles and jungle, in which the mosquitoes bit like dogs. It rained every day and the place was full of fever. The river teemed with crocodiles and other beasts, which overturned boats; the jungle was alive with snakes and chattering monkeys. Surely, Nejdi suggested, I did not want to go to a place like that. The ship might be there three weeks, or even a month: she would have to find her own cargo. It would be better, he went on, if I stayed with him: he had a place in Zanzibar, and we could go later to Dar-es-Salaam and Bagamoyo, and up to Pemba. I admit that this was an enticing prospect, and the idea of six weeks in Zanzibar and the surrounding ports was tempting. However, I decided that I would stay with the ship. I would go where she went, with or without Nejdi. He seemed to have some reason for not wishing me to go to the Rufiji: I must look into that. It was hardly likely that I should ever make such a voyage again, and I wanted to learn all I could. I should not learn much about ships with Nejdi in Zanzibar.

In the *Triumph*, it was impossible to foretell when something interesting might happen. One had to be there all the time, and enter wholly into the ship's life. It was no use being an onlooker. It was no use, either, to stay at Zanzibar, or to run across to Bagamoyo or any other place, for I should lose the thread of things in the ship. At that time, after being three months on board, I was only just beginning to find out what was really going on, for the Arabs, though not deliberately secretive, were expert at covering both their deeds and their thoughts. It was only by watching the proceedings of every day, watching and observing them carefully, and deciding for myself what really had been happening, that I came slowly to know what was going on. The obvious facts of the voyage stood out plainly—the wind and the weather, and where the ship was. But the more interesting things—the social and economic life of the sailors, the business structure of the ship and her voyage, the human side of things, the questionable activities of ship and crew—had to be dug out patiently, waited for, pounced upon, inveigled out of friends, discovered somehow in spite of the attempt to hide them. I do not believe that there was any deliberate or planned attempt to keep things from me. It was just the normal pattern.

It helped a little if I photographed the sailors, for they all took great delight in looking often at their own photographs if sufficiently flattering. The standard expected could be embarrassing, for I did not touch up negatives. It was difficult to make satisfactory photographs of some of those dark faces, handsome as many were. Often my subjects would profess not to recognize themselves at all when I handed them the finished results, and the lamentations were loud and continuous. They had their own ideas as to how they should look on photographs. Any shortcomings from this standard was my fault and quite unacceptable. It was useless to explain that my lens could see them only as they were and not as they imagined themselves to be. Many of them always posed very stiffly.

I found some of their importunities in this respect sometimes hard to bear, but when I saw the childish delight with which they bought themselves cheap picture frames in the *suq* at Zanzibar, and watched them going to the unheard-of length of employing public letter-writers to write letters home in which to enclose these things, I forgave them and tried to photograph my failures again. The photographs were handed round among all the Kuwaiti in the harbor—more than 200 men, for there were seven Kuwait ships there at one time during our stay, and their average crew was nearly thirty—to be admired, and I soon found sailors from the other ships hailing me in the street and coming out to the ship to be photographed. This, however, was an honor I declined.

I would stay with the ship, wherever she might go, and indeed looked forward to visiting the Rufiji. It was a place usually inaccessible. It was the place, too, where the destroyed German cruiser *Königsberg* still lay, and I wanted to see her. In the meantime Zanzibar was very pleasant. The harbor was always interesting, with its great fleet of dhows, and ashore the town was attractive and the hinterland more so. Zanzibar is still the center of Arab life in East Africa, though the influence of the Arabs has declined. The Arab Sultan of Zanzibar, descendant of the famous Seyyid Said of Oman, still nominally rules the island and its neighbor Pemba. His white-painted steamers, very smart, lie in the harbor: his uniformed band plays on the square before the English Club, and once weekly by the beach. His new white palace is a pleasant sight on the waterfront road, and almost any day one may see him come out of it in a large Rolls Royce with a red flag on the radiator, a bearded and benign old gentleman in a turban, going for a ride. Beside his palace stands the great House of Wonders which a former Sultan built and then lost because it was too expensive to keep up: this is now the government offices, and the old harem quarters near by have been made into a girls' school.

Not long ago Zanzibar was the headquarters of the Arab slave trade and here stood one of the last public slave-markets in the world. Where the market was there is now a cathedral. In these days Indians appear to own most of the businesses of any size in Zanzibar, as well as most of the coconut and clove plantations. Africans do the porterage and the stevedoring; the British do the governing. But the Arabs still crowd in their dhows with the coming of every northeast monsoon; and the Suri, brown-shirted and erect, still strut in the streets of the *suq*. They are allowed to carry arms, and hardly an Omani Arab is seen abroad who does not sport at least a curved dagger, silver-mounted in an ornate silvered sheath, lashed about his waist. The Kuwaiti bear no arms, for, in Kuwait, to carry arms is the mark of the Bedu; and the Bedu, according to the Kuwaiti, are uncouth. The *suq* of Zanzibar is considered satisfactory even by the Kuwait sailors, who regard nothing as approaching the standard of excellence set by their own town.

I found Zanzibar a good place, once away from the stench of the near-

Repairing the sail

putrid fish by the harbor. In the *suq* were all kinds of tropic fruits, and fish and meats and vegetables. The confection called *halwa*, melons, mangoes, sickly sweet cakes, and other Arab delicacies were there in abundance, and the confectionery-makers had the reputation of being second only to those of Muscat. There were arms shops in the *suq*, too, where one could buy an Omani dagger, though I saw none that was first class.

I gathered from our mariners that Zanzibar was also the first place on the whole coast for *bebes* and *bints* of all kinds, and for them the delights of Zanzibar's nights were boundless. In that port we had not even a dance on board, for the sailors were never there at night. Nejdi was away ashore, and often did not come near the ship for days. Everybody else was ashore except Hamed bin Salim, who went only on business, and old Yusuf Shirazi, who went to the *suq* to do the ship's buying by day, and landed for only two other reasons—to sell the last of the goods from his private chest, and to buy presents for his wife and children in Kuwait. Often, Hamed bin Salim, old Yusuf, and I were the only ones on board, after the day's work was done; and I was not there much. I liked the harbor but I also liked the town. Yusuf hawked Hadhramaut baskets to the shops, where he offered them for ninepence each, and they sold them for two shillings. Yusuf had several sacks full of Mukalla baskets and fans which he had been selling to shops at all our ports: he sold the last of them in Zanzibar. Ismael was much in demand as a musician, and was engaged to play at various parties and in the Arab night clubs. This pleased him and it pleased me. It pleased him because it meant cash, and it pleased me because it meant a quiet ship.

There was not much a sailor could not do in Zanzibar. To the Arabs and the other Asiatics, it was a wide open town and both the night life and the day life of the place were free enough for anybody. Our sailors usually worked all day, except for the siesta after the mid-morning meal which they took aboard, and they did not go ashore until the late afternoon. The routine was always the same. First they sold something—their stocks never seemed to give out—and then they spent the proceeds on the *bebes*. Any time between midnight and the dawn prayer, they came aboard again. Night after night it was the same: they were never satiated. Old Yusuf once confided to me that he did not think much of the goings-on at Zanzibar where, he said, the women were too free. He would hate, he said, to take a wife from that place. By the age of twelve the women had acquired an insatiable taste for variety which made them poor spouses for any man, most of all a sailor.

When they were short of money the sailors had not necessarily to go short of women, for I gathered that a lusty man of the sea was much sought after and, if his money was done, all a sailor need do was to go for a short walk out of town, across the plantations or towards some watering place, preferably at the time of the midday siesta when the men should be asleep. On such occasions he was sure to find some *bebe* on the lookout for adventure. The women must have been sad when the dhows sailed away, but some of the sailors remained behind. The sparkle had gone from the eyes of those Arabs who had been there too long, and they had obviously become soft. An Arab who had been five years in Zanzibar, Yusuf said, was no good in Arabia again. He had better stay in the island.

When the Arab was away from his homeland, according to Yusuf, his story was always the same. First he traded; then he settled. Then he went to ruin. Women, drink, easy-living—that was the way of it. Forgetfulness of the word of the Prophet, disregard of the daily prayers, non-observance of the severe fasts, an overpowering sensuality which found full play for its every wanton urge—so he went down the primrose path, and rarely fought his way back again. Less than half a century before, the Arab had been master in Zanzibar and of all that coast: now the Goanese sewed his pantaloons and made his coats; the Hindu had his business and half his plantations; the Indian took his thalers, his rupees, his pounds. The British told him how to manage his ship and where he might anchor her. The customs made him register his vessel, and compelled the nakhoda to have a certificate of competence. Every move of his ship was controlled and approved according to the Act.

The supervision of Arab dhows was far-reaching and at least nominally effective. It was enacted that all dhows must be properly surveyed and in possession of current registration papers. Crew lists must be complete and strictly correct. Crews must be engaged voluntarily, and not be in excess of the number of sailors reasonably required for the working of the ship. (This to prevent slave-running.) The number of passengers a vessel might carry was limited—ten for her first ten register tons, and seven for every succeeding ten tons. This would have restricted our *Triumph* to ninety-four, since she was registered there as 130 tons, which seemed to me a reasonable allowance. Vessels must be seaworthy: crew lists must be checked on entering and leaving—they were not—no one might be signed on without supervision; all passengers must be in possession of proper identity papers, and entered on the passenger list; dhows must sail when cleared, and have no further communication with the shore; no dhow might sail at night except with special permission. It was all very nicely laid down in the local Act. Dhows must carry proper navigation lights, including anchorage lanterns; they must fly their colors, entering and leaving; they must not dump rubbish in the harbor; nakhodas, if otherwise unlicensed, must pass an examination before the port officer for certificate of competency. The port officer, or his substitutes, must be satisfied as to the competency, sobriety, experience, ability, and general good conduct of the applicant, whose certificate when granted was subject to cancellation or suspension for reasonable cause.

And so on, almost ad infinitum. The lives of the Arab seafarers seem well defined and circumscribed by legal regulation—not that it mattered a great deal, for the regulations were intended to correct flagrant abuses rather than to control the Arab's every act. No one bothered the dhows much, so long as they stayed in their own anchorage and did not smuggle too flagrantly. As for the certificates of competency, though these were undoubtedly a step in the right direction, and the Arabs were proud of them when gained—they were accustomed to frame them and stow them carefully away in their chests—passing the examination was not unduly difficult. In theory, a satisfactory knowledge of the rule of the road, so far as it applied to them and to possible collisions with steamships, a thorough grasp of seamanship and of the intricacies of African coastal pilotage, and some elementary ability to cope with ordinary maritime accidents, were demanded of the Arab applicants. When it was discovered (as it was not always) that the nakhoda of a deep-water dhow from Arabia had no certificate, he was duly paraded before the port officer and "examined." The examination is by no means severe. As the port officers themselves point out, if a man has sailed his dhow from Arabia, it is reasonable to assume that he may be trusted to take her back again. The deep-water dhows are rarely in trouble: it is the small fry, the loosely built Swahili and the ancient craft bought from Arabia and sailed by local mariners, which figure far more in the casualty returns.

One day I was with the port officer, a pleasant young Scot who had been a ship's officer in steam, when one of the Arab nakhodas presented himself for examination. It was Abdul-razzaq, a crosseyed Suri. I knew him well: we had seen a lot of him. His baggala, a pretty little vessel of about seventy tons, was moored next to ours. Like most of the Suri craft, she had an afterguard of five or six old men. With these, and nominally over them, was the youthful Abdul-razzaq. He was a bombastic young man of about nineteen, over six feet tall, and very thin. Nejdi said his father owned the baggala and several more like her, and that was how the young man had become a nakhoda.

The examination of Abdul-razzaq was perfunctory and very soon over. The port officer, looking somewhat bored, first asked him through an interpreter if he knew the rule of the road. Abdul-razzaq certainly did not know it and never would, but the answer was "Yes." Well, then, what light should a dhow carry under way? None whatever, said Abdul-razzaq. To carry lights, he went on, was a waste of good money and good oil, an embarrassment to the crew, a disturbance of the slumbers of the after-guard, and a temptation to swordfish to ram the vessel. This seemed to me, even as it was passed on by the interpreter, a fatally incorrect answer; but at that moment the Indian master of the Sultan's Pemba steamer happened to come in. He usually conducted the examinations, for he had a good command of Arabic and a better knowledge of nakhodas. With a gesture of resignation, the port officer turned my friend Abdul-razzaq, who was still holding forth on the foolishness of carrying lights at sea, over to him. He implored the Indian captain to overhaul the Suri's unsound views about ships' lights, and the pair of them went into another room. The Indian took some small models to illustrate points in the rule of the road, and a chart of Zanzibar. A few moments later, they were back again. It was announced that Abdul-razzaq had passed. I saw a dubious look flit over the port officer's face, but he said nothing, and a certificate was made out. If masters' licenses could be handed out like that in Zanzibar I felt inclined to sit for one myself, for it was about time I had one. So I sat, and passed too, and was duly certified by the Sultan's government as fit to act as nakhoda of deep-sea dhows. The fee for this service was fifteen shillings.

In celebration of this event I decided to take Nejdi to the cinema. He had often expressed the wish to go, and there was a good cinema in Zanzibar. I inquired for him at the office of the agent, which was in a confectionery shop in the heart of the *suq*. It had a large verandah given up to the nakhodas of the more important vessels, and an inner sanctum in which the agent, a Seyyid of devout mien and very few scruples, conducted his business. There were many mysterious chambers upstairs. In one of these, on the third floor, I found Nejdi. He was sitting with Abdulla Kitami and the pair of them were casting sheep's eyes at a room full of girls behind an iron grill, across the courtyard, while a Swahili squatted on the floor entertaining them with a violin. Lunch was being put on a mat, though it was late, and they asked me to join them. We had a good meal of roasted chickens, fish, rice, chili sauce, and fruit, mainly pineapples and bananas, washed down with curdled milk. When the meal had been consumed, in surprisingly little time in spite of the fact that Nejdi ate three chickens and eight fish, we washed our hands in water brought by a servant, and went to sleep. By the time I woke, about an hour later, a group of Suri were squatting on the floor. We refreshed ourselves with tea and sweetmeats freshly made in the shop downstairs. I then had to sit listening to the Suri for another two hours, and at the end of that time Nejdi thought of playing the gramophone which stood in one corner. This was too much for me, though he assured me that Egypt's greatest singer performed on most of the records. I left them, and strolled to the waterfront.

In the early evening I met Nejdi and we went to the cinema, an Indian establishment not far from the *suq*. We took a rickshaw which hurried precariously through the narrow streets, with a Negro panting in the shafts and another pushing behind. Nejdi was in a pessimistic mood, and confided to me that things were not good in Zanzibar. Soon, he said, he would be pulling a rickshaw himself. There was no price for the salt, and the merchants had no money. The Suri would not pay for services performed, and he could not sell the small dhow. Nejdi was full of woes. The clove crop, he said, on which the prosperity of the island largely depended, had not been good, and in consequence money was scarce. Copra, the only other product exported on a large scale, was almost unsalable. He did not understand it. The previous year things had been very good, with a large clove crop and good prices: the Arabs had plenty of money, and trade was thriving. Nejdi, like most Arabs I knew, found it difficult to adjust himself to sudden changes, indeed to any change at all. If things had been good last year, he argued, why were they not good this year? It must be somebody's fault. If it were not, then it was his own great misfortune. In either case, it was most lamentable. But life was difficult in these days, Nejdi went on, as the rickshaw swung round a corner too violently and came into collision with a large Banyan seated on the step of his shop. It was the Europeans' fault. All the troubles of the world were due to them, because of the unnatural, unstable life they led, unprincipled, avaricious, violently jealous of all other peoples and of one another. They had made a mess of a good world. They should believe in God, and keep their women in order—these were the prime necessities, said Nejdi. These were the fundamentals—belief in God, and the ability to control women. By denying these two truths the whole European race had lost its balance and was dragging the rest of the world with it.

I did not pay much attention: Nejdi often spoke like that, and I was watching our progress with interest, for the Zanzibar bazaar was a striking place. It was very cosmopolitan. Greek, Goanese, Hindu, Punjabi, Sikh, Singalese, Omani, Hadhrami, Yemenite, Persian, Iraqui, Kuwaiti, Kurd, Swahili, Baluchi and Africans of all kinds jostled in the streets, or crowded to one side of the narrow way, making room for our progress, while Nejdi ranted on and I raised no arguments against him. What was the use? He was always so sure that he was right: and in this case, I did not know quite how to answer him. We dashed on through the streets, at full speed, at others slowed down to a walk on rising gradients, now passing a group of little Omani Arab girls in European frocks with red ribbons in their hair, or a dignified Hindu walking, followed by his young wife a carefully maintained six paces behind her austere master.

It was an unfortunate mood in which to take Nejdi to the cinema. It was also an unfortunate film. It was an American production, typical of Hollywood—a competent piece of showmanship, so far as it went, but uninspired. Usually I should have attached no importance to it, and indeed I should have found it dull, but, seen through Nejdi's clear eyes, it assumed a significance that was almost frightening. Before we got out of that cinema I began to wonder very seriously whether, after all, a great many of my Arab friend's views were not nearer right than some of my own. The film dealt with a New York stenographer and her efforts to escape, at least temporarily, from the monotony of her life and her work by spending a holiday in a vacation camp—a noisy, commercialized, completely vulgar and largely insane place which, apparently, was patronized mainly by large numbers of oversexed and repressed young women, and a few inane men.

If the film was intended to be a satire on these places it was without mercy upon them; but I do not think it was meant as a satire. It was just a film, made from a Broadway play, which had run long enough to catch the attention of the Hollywood producers, and it was no more than that. It was not intended, I am sure, as any sort of social document. It was intended to make profits, and nothing else. Nejdi read into it a very great deal indeed, and insisted on regarding it as a damning indictment of the white race. He thought it incredibly foolish. If he had had his way, the heroine would have been covered in black and kept within the four walls of a harem. She did not conform to any Arab standards of beauty in woman, for she had neither breasts nor buttocks worth mentioning, and her bearing was deplorable. She was like a limp rod. She had moreover a very large mouth, somewhat loose, and this was woman's greatest sin in Nejdi's eyes. With a large mouth no woman could be good, according to him. Why the amorous adventures of this uninspiring young woman, tame and commonplace as they were, should have been made into a motion picture he could not understand. Not that he looked upon it as a motion picture: to him it was a piece of European life. The crazinesses, the hollow shams, the inane futilities that paraded through that Hollywood production jarred upon him and disgusted him, until he got up, at the fourth clinch, and we went out. I was glad, for the evening was not successful.

He asked me again and again when we were outside, what did it all mean? The behavior of the curious persons who thronged that American vacation camp was utterly beyond his comprehension, and my description of them as New York Beduin failed to satisfy him, though he thought very little of Bedu. The standard of intelligence of those persons ought to have caused their confinement. How, he asked, could sane people live that way? At the first opportunity the heroine was in the hero's arms. There was nothing wrong in that, at any rate from the man's point of view, according to Nejdi, who was never against a little clean lechery. But didn't American men know a used woman when they met one? What was wrong with them? What sense was there in marrying such a person, there for the taking anyway and obviously co-operative? As for the woman, she had been tolerably attractive once. If brought up properly and reasonably fed, she might have developed a better appearance, though her big mouth would always be against her. Her family should have married her off when young.

It was indeed a silly story by any standards, but to Nejdi it was far more than that. He saw it as a mirror held up to what in his view could only be a thoroughly decadent society. He did not see it as a story, a "quickie" film to while an hour or two away and earn some revenue at the box office. Even if it were a story, he argued, it must reflect the society that produced it and paid money, apparently, to sit in seats and look at it. Didn't they accept it without protest?

After a while, it occurred to me that Nejdi had a point. Our visit to that Zanzibar cinema was not a success. Nejdi never forgot it, and for months afterwards he kept referring to its picture of what seemed to him the hopelessly stupid way of life he saw pictured in that film. American or European, it was the same to him.

I left him at the gateway of the house where he was staying, and went back on board. The anchorage was quiet and the stars were mirrored in the black water: there was no moon. Ashore in the distance somewhere I could hear the Swahili singing, and once there came a low sound of song from a Persian longboat pulling back to a Kungk boom. When that died away I heard the ring of laughter from a house ashore. I came on board to find all quiet, and peaceful, and the ghostlike apparition of Yusuf Shirazi rose to meet me at the gangway head. I looked about me at the silent anchorage and above at the raked masts of the boom, silhouetted softly against the stars, and I thought how satisfying it was to be there, a wanderer with those vagrants of the sea—satisfying, vaguely adventurous, pleasingly picturesque, a man's life in a man's world, which is hard to find anywhere in these days.

Was it not possible that these seafarers from Araby knew more of living than we did, for all our boasted superiority? Certainly they seemed to know a great deal more about contentment, and the acceptance of each day for its own worth and the pleasure of its own living. They were not forever wanting to be somewhere else, doing something else. They had no desire to be much wealthier than they were, to acquire vast possessions. They had not to be forever turning on radios lest their minds should think, to accept the thoughts handed out to them ready made by the morning's press, to fight and to crowd and to carry on the heartless, meaningless, pitiless enmity of city life. No! They lived, and were sufficient unto themselves. Now they were ashore with their *bebes*, and I thought nonetheless of them for that. Perhaps there are worse things than plain lechery.

It seemed to me that some of them were portrayed in that film.

Chapter 11

AT KWALE ISLAND

W E S T A Y E D two weeks at Zanzibar, though all the cargo was out after the first two days. After we had been there a week our departure was announced daily for the morrow. No one paid the least attention to these announcements. They were not even regarded as pious hopes. Tomorrow simply meant some time in the indefinite future. They might have said next week, or next month. The real cause of the delay, I discovered, was the difficulty in collecting payment for the cargo. It was easy to sell it, but collecting payment was a different matter. We had to have silver shillings to pay for our mangrove poles from the Rufiji delta, and it was no use to leave Zanzibar until we had a chest of shillings on board. In the Rufiji, nothing was done on credit. Once we had the shillings, we sailed quickly enough.

In the meantime, a very large boom came in from Kuwait via Aden, and took up her moorings close to us. Our sailors named her *el-Dhow*, and this was the only time I heard the word "dhow" used by Arabs. Though she could stow 4000 packages of dates in her big hold, *el-Dhow* was not an ungainly vessel. She had, they said, been built to carry 5000 packages and had been cut down, for her original size was too big. She had a crew of forty-five, and there was a new dhow on her maindeck, built on the way down the coast, which was forty feet long. Her nakhoda was the famous Abdul-wahhab al-Kitami, a stern-looking Arab with a mild voice and blue eyes. *El-Dhow* was kept up in style. She had a gangway, slung from the break of the poop, and the jackstaff at her steamhead bore an excellent model of an Imperial Airways flying-boat. This was a popular form of adornment among the Kuwaiti, who said that their port had recently been made a stopping place for the English aeroplanes. The big boom also had a small model of a biplane mounted as a wind-vane on a movable staff aft, where the helmsman could see it. Our sailors were very proud of the big *Dhow* whose own crew, I noticed, always swaggered through the *suq* with a special roll of their own. She was full of salt and rice, and general cargo. Abdul-wahhab announced his intention of beaching at Zanzibar when this was out of her, and then going up to Lamu to load. She could load over a thousand score poles.

We finally got away from Zanzibar on a Friday. Usually we did not sail on Fridays, for that day is the Muslim Sabbath when the sailors, if the ship was in port, liked to go to the public prayers in the mosques ashore. It was not a day of rest, and necessary work was always done. The ship's routine, such as it was, was not much affected. But it was a day for visiting, for calling on the other ships from Kuwait which were in the harbor, for drinking coffee and smoking the hookah. When we sailed on a Friday it was always late in the day for, according to the Arabs, the day ended with the sunset. By their reckoning, sunset on Friday evening ushered in Saturday, when it was proper to sail. We were ready long before that pleasant hour, with the yard mastheaded and the sail in stops ready to be sheeted home, and *Afra* and the longboat on towlines astern. The weather would be quiet for the short run to the Rufiji Delta, little more than a hundred miles south of Zanzibar, and we could tow our boats. We would take *Afra*, since she had not been sold, for she would be handy to ferry mangrove poles from the jungle to the ship.

Our anchors were aweigh, and we lay through the afternoon by a single line to Abdul-wahhab's *el-Dhow*, on the outside of the fleet. Hamed bin Salim was ashore collecting the last sack of shillings. Most of the crew, returned from the noon prayer in the waterfront mosque, were asleep in such shade as they could find. The anchorage was quiet and no one sang, for there was no work going on. Nothing was being floated into or out of Funguni Creek, or on to or off the beach, and the few boats which pulled across the roadsteads were bringing mates and quartermasters to their ships.

We were very high out of the water, for only the bad dates from Aden remained in the hold: these were to be our ballast down to the delta. Being so light, two sections were taken from the mainyard and our smallest sail was bent, for the ship, beamy as she was, could easily be blown over. Abdul-wahhab's crew helped us to masthead the yard, after the third prayer, and sixty men danced on our decks until the planks groaned. That sixty strong men should find hard work in hoisting the single yard of a 150-ton ship may seem unbelievable, but it was so. It is certainly an indication of the inefficiency of the gear. It took them little less than half an hour, though about a third of this time was taken up with dancing and singing. They stopped twice, once when the yard was two-thirds of the way aloft, and again just before it was mastheaded. How they worked, and how they danced and sang! Those Kuwaiti sailors never did things by halves. The whole of the deck was taken up by the hauling, sweating men.

There is a regular ritual about this yard-hoisting which was always religiously observed. As soon as the order to hoist the yard was given, the sailors at once began to sing. There was a special leader for this song —Abdul-latif the sailor, in our case, and he led off in a high-pitched voice. The rest, before the actual hauling was begun, answered with a chorus of the deep throaty growls which seem peculiar to the Kuwaiti. How they could get such a volume of thunderous and almost frightening growling out of their throats I do not know, but the sound always seemed to come from deep inside them. None of the other sailors ever made this noise, not the Suri, or the Persians, or any crews from South Arabia, or Oman, or the Red Sea. It was a deep, powerful, thrilling sound which the Kuwaiti seemed able to keep up almost indefinitely. I do not know what the origin of this habit was but I should not be surprised if it were very ancient, and had its origin in primitive attempts to scare off bad *jinns*. The sailors I asked did not know why they did it. It was the style, they said, and they like doing it. It had always been done. They would not think of hoisting up the yard without beginning that way, or of setting off in the boats, or of bringing a pearler to new moorings.

When all hands had answered Abdul-latif's verses, always about Allah and the ship, the wind and the sea, with a sufficient volume of menacing growls, the soloist, striking a yet higher note, suddenly quickened his pace and all hands fell at once upon the halliards. The deep growling stopped and the sailors took up the song while they hauled away on the two parts of the halliard. They hauled like athletes in a mighty tug of war. They did not just work: they fought the halliard down, and the yard up. They attacked those inanimate ropes as if they were living things to be subdued. The sweat poured from them; the song swelled; the taut yellow line, eight-fold in its huge blocks, stood rigid as steel as those great muscled arms brought it down. The blocks creaked protestingly; the loosened parrals groaned; the yard trembled and quivered along its length.

Up, up it went! The blazing sun beat down and there was no shade: the very sea burned with the sun's fierce light, and the sweat ran in streams. This was brutal work. It was difficult to keep foothold as they stamped and stamped again their great calloused feet on the wooden decks and hauled and sang. Up, up! The pace of the song quickened.

Oh, Allah! help us with our work:
Fill this great sail with wind.
Allah helper, Allah helper
Give strength to our arms
And all of us.
Allah helper, Allah helper,
Breathe thy winds bravely
On all this Sea.
Allah helper, Allah helper
And let us go.
Oh, Allah, let our good ship go!

So they sang, all of them, and the effort of the singing was enough for any ordinary strong men, in that fierce climate. Muscles strained and sweat ran unheeded on the deck. The sun blazed until the white beach hurt the eyes, and the glare from the white buildings was impossible to face. They sang with the deep power of virile masculinity. They sang lustily, with power issuing from their throats, itself sufficient to hoist that yard, had it better gear. But the blocks were inefficient and unoiled; the coir halliards were sticky, and full of friction; the parrals were unwieldy, and the yard huge. The leaning angle of the mast made the work heavier. But they worked on, worked and sang. When inefficiency can be redeemed by brute force, the Arab will never trouble about efficiency.

Their breath was not labored, though they worked so hard. They were all lean and sinewy men, in splendid condition despite the fleshpots of Zanzibar. They threw off their long gowns and stood bare-chested, with only their sarongs. Their head-cloths had long since slipped to the deck. Their great bare feet stamped, stamped, stamped into the deck. Yusuf Shirazi and Jassim the cook worked furiously getting the slack over the belaying beam for'ard. The muscles rippled on those brown backs like heads of ripe corn in a clean field, swept by a wayward wind. Up, up! The great yard came, slowly, slowly. The song swelled.

The yard was now half-way. Mohamed the serang saw this. As one man, they stopped, Yusuf and Jassim holding the ends fast by turns round the beam. Now they danced, three or four on the hatch with Mohamed the serang and the others round them. They still sang, though with a different rhythm: they stamped their feet and clapped their great scarred hands in time with the song, hands like great drums. *Allah si-i-idi! Allah si-i-idi!* they sang: and stamp, stamp, stamp went their bare feet until the whole ship shook. They sang and danced for some moments, with an air of complete abandon, keeping the rhythm sometimes with their whole bodies, sometimes only with feet and hands. Occasionally one would dash on to the hatch and execute some special step with wild yelling and whoops and shrieks. Mohamed the serang was a good leader.

Refreshed by the dance, the sailors rushed upon the halliards again with throaty growls, followed at once by Abdul-latif's song. If they had worked furiously before, now they were like madmen. Hassein the helmsman, Abdulla bin Salim, Ebrahim bin Sulieman, Nasir the pearler, leaped at the halliards on the forepart of the knighthead, swarmed aloft, and attacked them at the block, hauling and fighting that taut yellow line, forcing the unwilling block to descend and the yard to rise. Every muscle of their great bodies whipped and played. The song of Abdul-latif was even faster, broken into by warrior roars and shrieks from Saud and some of the sailors from the big *Dhow.*

> *Rise up, you yard!*
> *Think not that you can rest.*
> *Swell out, great sail,*
> *And gather to your breast*
> *God's wind,*
> *For we are bound for home.*

So Abdul-latif sang, his face contorted as his broad back strained to the work, for he hauled upon his share of the halliards as well as leading in song. The time was faster, faster, as the block descended. More sailors leaped aloft, running up the halliards like apes, hand over hand with the rope between their toes, old Yusuf again, and Mohamed, Kalifa the helmsman, Sultan the prayer-caller. Up they ran, and fought the halliard down, dropping, sweat-covered, yelling figures, into the crowd on deck by the knighthead, stamping, yelling, singing, straining. Round the knighthead, at the upper block, were knots of them, and two packed lines strung out along each side of the maindeck along its length from the break of the poop to the belaying beam forward. They danced again, and back to the work. So the yard went up. Now it was time to belay: but they sang so much and made so much noise they did not hear the orders, and threatened to pull the yard right out of the ship. But they heard in time, and the job was done.

Well done, I thought. It never failed to stir me. Sometimes I joined them at this work, but the pace was usually too much for me. A quarter of an hour of it was as much as I could stand, and I could never master either the throaty growling, or the thunderclap with the hands. Banging the deck with my bare feet hurt. My feet had been bare aboard that ship for months then, and my soles were tough enough to walk on flints, but jumping on that uneven deck was more than they could do.

The yard aloft, the sailors went to carry out further orders for the setting up of the parral tackles and the rigging, and trimming the gear. They turned to these new tasks like warriors who, having just repelled a great assault, hear of some minor breach in the walls elsewhere. Their song was different, but there was no pause. It was a quieter song, as they ran and gathered in well-trained groups. The work all done, they scooped up a hasty drink of lukewarm water from Jassim's tank.

Abdul-wahhab's men left us, when the yard was aloft, and returned to their ship. Just before sunset Hamed bin Salim came aboard, with a sack of shillings. With the sunset there was prayer and then, very quietly, the mainsail was broken from its stops, the line to *el-Dhow* let go, and we were off. It was a beautiful evening with a quiet sailing air from the north, and we went out from Zanzibar with a Persian boom, a small sambuk, and two jalboots from Sur. We stood past the point with the sunset behind us: the breeze held, and by midnight we were abeam of the light at Dar-es-Salaam.

Daylight found us off Ras Kimbiji, and the breeze which had been fresh all night was then quieter. Rain clouds clung heavily over the coast of Tanganyika, and before long some heavy showers passed over us. They left brief calms, after which the north wind came in again, and we sailed on. Throughout the morning the *Triumph* sailed quietly down the Tanganyika coast, steadily approaching the mouths of the Rufiji. We stood close by the shore and sometimes had very little water, though the boom was not drawing five feet. These were the most dangerous waters we had yet been in. Reefs and low islands abounded to windward, and to seaward of us, and often patches of the sandy bottom rose until they seemed almost to be touching our keel. No matter; we had with us Mubarak the Suri, pilot for those parts, who had been put aboard by Nejdi on the recommendation of the mysterious agent, the Seyyid in the *suq*. Neither

Hamed bin Salim nor Abdulla the nakhoda's brother nor any one else on board had been to the Rufiji before, for the Kuwait ships are newcomers in that region. The inside passage down called for accurate local knowledge. No other kind of navigation could get a ship through there. The actual navigation of the Rufiji itself, they told me, would be worse.

Meanwhile our sailors were overhauling the bad dates from Aden, bringing them on deck out of the hold until I began to think the ship would capsize. They threw overboard all the fermented packages, which stank abominably. Any that were not actually bad they kept, and stowed away again. There were perhaps sixty packages left when they had overhauled the lot, but even the "good" dates so remaining were exceedingly bad. I tried one, at Hamed's suggestion: it tasted like fermented molasses flavored with engine oil, and I wondered why we kept them.

When we had almost reached the northern end of the Rufiji delta, we passed close by a spit of beach running out from a low island. Suddenly, at an order from Mubarak the Suri, the ship hauled her wind and stood inside this spit. The sail was run down, and we anchored. On the inshore end of the spit two big baggalas were beached for cleaning. Hamed said this was Kwale Island, and we too would beach there for cleaning.

I had not known we were to visit Kwale Island. I had never, indeed, heard of the place until that moment. No one had mentioned it, and it was too small to be on our small-scale chart. Kwale is a low island close to the Tanganyika coast, by the northern end of the Rufiji delta. Though I had never heard of it, it is a place much frequented by Arabs bound to the south. The Germans used it when Tanganyika was German East Africa before 1914, and their stone Customs House still stands. It is a port of entry for dhows bound to Salale, Kilwa, and Lindi. A Swahili customs clerk enters the ships inwards, collects their small dues, and watches that they do not smuggle too much. This gentleman, a Mr. Timothy Anton, was soon aboard, pulling out in a boat from the beach, but even before he appeared our sailors had begun to make the ship ready for hauling out. I was interested to watch this operation. I had seen the big dhows hauled out before, at Aden, in Mombasa, and in Zanzibar, but this was the first time that the *Triumph* had been beached while I was on board. Our boom was a deep vessel with considerable deadrise, so that she would not stand on the beach unaided. She could not stand up like a Thames barge. Like all Arab craft, she would have to be propped on stilts. Even so, it would be dangerous to leave the heavy mainmast aloft, for she might easily topple over with the weight of that, in anything of a breeze.

It is the custom of the Arabs to clean their ships' bottoms and to effect any repairs which may be necessary by hauling them in to a shelving beach where there is a big rise and fall of tide. They float them in,
dismasted and empty of all cargo, on a high tide, and get them in stern-to
to the beach as far as they can be induced to float. The falling tide grounds
them, and they hold them up with a series of stout spars, eight or ten of
them, ranged along each side. Each returning tide floats the ship again and
often knocks down some of these props, so that tending the grounded
ship is an important, and sometimes also an anxious, business. The ship is
held securely in position with anchors carried out ahead and astern, one
over each bow and one from each quarter. The flood floats her and the
ebb grounds her again.

The ship usually remains on the beach only two or three days—longer,
if repairs are necessary. A comparatively new ship like the *Triumph* had
no bad planks and did not need repairs. On the first day, the old paying-
stuff is scraped off. On the second day, the new is applied, with a great
deal of work and much singing. On the third day, the ship is floated off
again, and rerigged, and the job is done. Only the ship's people join in
this work, and she carries her paying-stuffs with her. Ours were camel-
tallow kept in old paraffin tins, and coarse lime.

The first thing was to get the mainmast down. Ours was seventy-
eight feet high from the deck, with a girth at the deck of almost six feet,
a very solid and heavy piece of teak. I wondered how the Arabs would go
about the difficult task of unshipping so heavy a spar, but they had
worked out a system, perhaps centuries or even thousands of years old,
which made this a simple operation. First they got rid of the two long
yards, main and mizzen, and all the other spars lying about the deck, by
throwing them bodily over the side, where they were lashed together and
floated ashore in tow of *Afra* and the longboat. They were moored to
some bushes on the beach, and remained there until it was time to go.
Then, the mast-lashings and the wedges were unshipped. The mainmast
in our boom, and in all Arab dhows, was stepped in the forepart of the
trough-like main hatch, which forms a sort of bed in which the mast lies
back. When aloft, it rests against the fore end of the hatch: when down,
it lies back in the trough. It is raised and lowered easily by its own rigging.
To get it down, all that was necessary was to cast off the lashings where
the bole of the mast rested against the stout beam at the forepart of the
hatch, and then to heave the mast upright and cant it a little sternwards
with the main halliards, then carefully lower it backwards, steadying it

down with its gear. There was no standing rigging to send down. All the rigging consisted of purchases suited admirably to this maneuver. The mast lay back along the trough of the main hatch with its weight on a beam across the break of the poop, and the masthead projecting over the stern. Our mizzen was not unstepped, because it was a light spar stepped only in the deck, and we could take the ground safely with it up. If it were to be unstepped, as it always was at Kuwait, it was lifted out bodily by means of a simple tackle from the mainmast-head, the mainmast being held steadied by its tackles on its way down long enough to use it as a derrick to lift out the mizzen.

It was a simple method, and it worked well. Our spars were overside and beached, the mast down and along the deck, and the ship ready for beaching three hours after the sailors began. Baggalas, being sharper and deeper than booms, had not only to send both masts down but to get them off the decks before they dared trust themselves to be propped up on the beach. Ahmed Radhwan's big *Hope of Compassion* had once capsized on the Ma'alla beach through neglecting this precaution, and had lain there until the next spring tides floated her off. The two baggalas on the beach at Kwale had their masts overside. One of these baggalas was Bedar bin Abdul-wahhab's stately *Bedri*: the other was the Suri Abdul-razzaq's, he who had taken his master's license so recently at Zanzibar. We were to see a good deal of this crosseyed young man both here and in the Delta, for he was bound down to the Rufiji. So was Bedar.

With our spars floated away and our mainmast down and resting along the length of the ship, we were ready to be kedged in to the beach as the tide made. Our wheel had been unshipped and hung over one quarter, and the binnacle stowed away in the great cabin. On deck the ship looked rather a mess. Beaching her was a simple but extremely laborious business of kedging in at high water and being left aground by the receding tide. It took all night to do it, for the low beach ran out for miles, and the ship had to be kedged a long way. Again and again the long-boat shifted the kedges further ahead, until at last they were secured to trees along the point. The singing sailors danced and sang and hauled all night. When they hauled on the kedging lines they always went through the same ritual. The portside of the deck was clear, and they danced along this in a rough elliptical formation, half of them always hauling on the line, and the other half dancing back again to the forepart to take their turn. They kept up a continuous movement, round and round, each man hauling his section of the rope aft and then dancing and hand-clapping his way back to the front as he reached the break of the poop, ready to take up the burden again. This dancing, which they could keep up for hours under conditions such as these, seemed to refresh them, and they never dreamed of doing any heavy work without it.

I marvelled at the lung-power which could keep them going, to say nothing of the strength of arm which sent the ship along at a good rate to her two kedge anchors. It was all done in high good humor, though they sweated heavily even at night. It was full moon, and the work went on and on. We had to get in with that tide. As we came nearer to the beach we saw it would be a tricky business to thread the ship between the *Bedri* and the Suri baggala, for there was barely room for her to fit. Once there, however, she could not be in a better place. Hamed managed her well, and coaxed her into the berth, but the day was breaking over Kwale Island before the last of our supporting props was lashed in position alongside and the last line hauled taut to the anchors ahead and astern. Examination of our bottom showed it to be in first-rate order, though the paying-off was sadly in need of replacement. She had been cleaned and paid at Berbera four months before, but though the Arab method of paying with lime and tallow might be effective, it certainly was not lasting.

In spite of the fact that they had been up all night the sailors at once began to scrape the bottom, singing their old song for jobs of this kind:

> *A little at a time,*
> *Allah helper, Allah helper.*
> *A little at a time;*
> *Soon all is done.*

They sang the same verse for hours, but sometimes phrases more appropriate to the work in hand were introduced or little sallies about some incident or some one on board, in the manner of the old English chanteys. Scraping the bottom continued until it was finished, while others scraped away on *Afra* and the longboat, also grounded and propped up near by. By the time the scraping was done the tide was coming in again. Then we had rice and fish, and after that all hands coiled up in the shadow of the trees on the Swahili village green ashore, and slept.

Kwale was a good place, and I was glad I had stayed with the ship. It was pleasant to bathe in the early mornings from the long spit which ran out so far towards Tanganyika. It was pleasant, too, to stroll in the Kwale woods with Abdulla and Kaleel the carpenter and Said the carpenter from the *Bedri*, who was busy all day repairing the old baggala's rudder in the

shade of a sail spread from a tree across the beach. Kaleel helped him at
this work, and I liked to watch them. They were good shipwrights. They
had built booms together, back in Kuwait, and were old friends. We used
to stroll in the early evenings, between the third and the fourth prayers,
through the Swahili village and across the island. The two carpenters were
keen students of botany and took a delight in examining the trees and
shrubs. They also looked with expert eyes at the Swahili girls we passed
at the wells and in the fields and gardens: but the girls were far from
comely, and we never dallied there.

Kwale seemed to consist mainly of uneven coral, surrounded by mangroves. It is low and the soil is very thin, but water is plentiful. There are
some sheep and cattle. The village is of mud huts, rudely thatched. A
few small dhows are owned in the village, and the majority of the 200
Swahili inhabitants support themselves by fishing. Fish are plentiful in the
waters round Kwale, and the big shark and the dugong are dried. The
dugong is a favorite with the people of the mainland, and brings a good
price. There is one Indian store in the village.

Strolling along the beach one day, I came upon some interesting ves-
sels lying on their sides in a flat behind some gnarled old mangrove trees.
One was a Muscat jalboot about fifty feet long, and the other a small
Cutch boat, from India. They had come a long way to rest their old bones.
I should like to know what their records had been, before they had been
brought, no longer seaworthy, to rot out their derelict years on that
Kwale beach. They were both registered in Dar-es-Salaam. It seemed an
appropriate place to bury them, in that silent corner of the white beach,
with trees all round and nothing but the sighing of the wind in the forest
to sing their dirge. Across in full view was the mainland of Africa, with
some fishing dhows skimming over the blue water. Overhead, flying high,
a great airplane passed. It was a British Imperial Airways machine, recog-
nizable even at that height, flying the mails from Durban to London. The
Swahili with me did not look up. The air mail was a commonplace down
there and he was more interested in ships.

Outside the customs compound I saw part of the rudder of a deep-sea
boom, slightly worm-eaten, which Mr. Anton said had been washed
ashore recently from some wreck. Which wreck, he did not know. There
were wrecks fairly often, he said. In a squall only a few days earlier a
Swahili dhow had foundered not far from the island, and four men were
drowned. The salvaged cargo of copra was piled on the beach close to the
Triumph.

What I liked best about Kwale was the village green. This was a fine green patch near the point where the beached ships lay, at the northwestern end of the island. The customshouse stood on one side of it, and a path led across it to the village. In the trunk of a large tree shading the nearer part of this green was carved "Football Ground, 1933," but Mr. Anton said that little football was played now. It had led to too many injuries and too many fights, and the villagers had given it up. Beneath this sporting legend something else had been cut into the tree, but this was now difficult to decipher. All that could be made out was H.M.S. Something, and a date, which may have been 1889, or even 1839. Under this was an anchor. This may have been a relic from some slave-chasing frigate of the old days, for many of the slavers passed this way, coming up from Kilwa. According to local accounts, and the Arabs corroborated them, the slave-dhows, when the British were looking for them, were accustomed to sail up inside the reefs of Mafia, hiding in the mouths of the Rufiji if small boats came in search of them. Then they came up between Kwale and the mainland, and dashing through that channel by night, ran for the open sea and carried on from there, far outside, towards Arabia.

There are records of sharp encounters between armed boats from Her Majesty's ships and Arab slavers, off this Kwale Island. Many slaves freed by British sailors first tasted their freedom on the beach where we now were grounded. The Arabs knew the Rufiji very well, and apparently found it an excellent hiding place. Not only was navigation difficult on that reef-strewn, bad coast, but it was notoriously unhealthy. Kwale, now quiet, had known other stirring days, not only with slave-runners. It had been an outpost for the German cruiser *Königsberg*, when, in September, 1914, after her attack on Zanzibar, she fled for shelter to the Rufiji. For the *Königsberg*, too, the Rufiji was an excellent hiding place, too good, perhaps, for she still lies there.

I liked to sit in the shade of the old tree on the village green, and watch our sailors and the sailors from the *Bedri*, repairing their sails. Our sails were carried up and spread on the green, where they were pegged down and repaired. The green made an excellent sail loft. It was a good life, and I was glad that I had not stayed behind in Zanzibar. With my monkey Yimid for company—he was bought from a local Swahili for a shilling—and my good friend Mr. Anton to yarn with, I could stay there for hours. It was a grand spot. In the background, on the beach, were the big ships, Bedar's baggala very picturesque, like a galleon of Spain, with her carved and galleried stern towering over the trees and her low, sweet bow pointing out to sea. Every line of her was beautiful, except where she was hogged, and the stempost was a little out of true. The flowing grace of her lovely bow was as beautiful as anything I had ever seen. Every line of her blended sweetly towards that low, keen bow, and the flowing grace of her cutwater, rising from the comparatively short keel in a long, soft line until it became a carved stemhead, high before her, was a sight to delight the eye of any sailor.

She was a much prettier model than our big boom, which looked plain and almost ugly beside the *Bedri*. The boom's straight stem and straight sternpost, her sharp ends, the long stempost carried far out before the bows, the huge rudder, the lack of carving or embellishment—these things were products of a more utilitarian day. Baggalas cost more. The graceful *Bedri* was more than half a century old. What if she was hogged a little, and her fastenings wept a staining rust? What if the planks of her ancient decks were worn and old? What if her rudder was a little worm-eaten, and had to be patched before she could go on? She was a good old ship, beautiful to look upon; and when the day came when she floated off, I saw that she rode in the water with the grace of a gull. She was a ship, a real ship, in her own way just as lovely and as completely seaworthy (at her best) as any clipper. No one could say that she was wholly seaworthy now. Her day was done. So would the day of any iron-fastened wooden ship be, after half a century. Throughout her long life she had been in hard trades, bringing up logs from Malabar, carrying heavy dates to the Yemen, running down to Africa. She had not been much to Africa. She had been mainly in the trade between Kuwait, Basra, and the Malabar coast, the hardest which the Arab knows.

As I looked at that sweet old ship—I could hear her sailors singing as they paid her undersides—I thought I should like to get hold of such a vessel, and save her type from complete extinction in this humdrum world. There she was, one of the last carved-stern galleon-baggalas of Kuwait. There was only one other like her, for the Persian Sulieman Said's did not properly count. She was built in Sur, owned by a Persian, and registered in Kuwait only as a convenience. It seemed to me that some one ought to get hold of one of these old galleons and see that she remained in the world, with proper care. Some one? Why not me? I should be a good one for such a job as that, and the more I thought of it the more I liked the idea. The Arabs would never keep a baggala for historical reasons. Sentiment for ships meant nothing to them. They were fast changing to booms, and the carved stern would soon be extinct. To preserve a baggala would be of historical interest, for not only was the hull of the baggala directly descended from the best and fastest of Arab ships, but her galleried and lavishly decorated stern, I believe, was a survival from the Portuguese.

I sat beneath the tree and looked at the old *Bedri*, and at Abdul-razzaq's smaller galleon which was then being floated off. There was a terrific banging of drums and, every now and then, a thunderous burst of handclapping—more noise than work, by the look of things. It would be difficult to preserve a baggala. You could not keep her in Eastern seas. She would go to pieces. There was, moreover, little point in keeping her there when the people who would be most interested in her were on the other side of the world. She would have to be sailed either to England or to the United States. I thought about this and the possibilities of making such a voyage. With a well-found dhow it seemed feasible. One could go into the Red Sea with the south wind, about December, and with luck get halfway before running into the belt of calms which cushion the north wind between Perim and Suez. From then on it would be a dour beat to Suez, a beat of five or six hundred miles, for the Red Sea is long. But it could be done. Then would come Suez—her longboat could tow her through—and the Mediterranean, and after that, Gibraltar, probably another dour beat through the straits, for they can be very unkind to the westbound sailing-ship. Then, however, the worst would be over: for the northerly airs off the Portuguese coast soon bring a sailer down to the trade winds, and she has only to drift before them towards the West Indies, as Columbus did.

There were no great hazards to his voyage, it seemed to me, as I lolled on the village green at Kwale. Even the *Bedri* was as well-found as the *Nina*. If Columbus could do it, the Arabs and I could, I thought, do it too. True, the Mediterranean might not be so easy; the lateen rig is a hard rig to beat with, and there might be a lot of windward work on such a voyage. Still, it seemed to me that it might be worth trying—not, unfortunately, with the *Bedri*, which was obviously unfit for such an undertaking. But perhaps the other surviving baggala from Kuwait might be better. I resolved to keep my weather eye lifting for her.

It was a pleasing subject to play with, beneath that African tree, with the sound of the surf and the sailors' cries in my ears. Whether I ever could "save" a baggala or not, it was pleasant food for thought. One of the many difficulties I could foresee was that of holding an Arab crew. If I were ever to sail an Arab ship on this Transatlantic voyage, I must have an Arab crew. My Arabs, good fellows as they were, might take holding if they ever landed, say, among the *bebes* of Brooklyn, or even down in Florida.

I looked across at our sailors, sewing sail in the sun, and wondered what they would think of such a voyage. They were like merry boys. Sewing sail was the one job at which they did not sing, and at which they allowed themselves to sit down. They sat on the pegged-out sail and sewed rough round seams, with Hamed bin Salim and Abdulla Nejdi overseeing them. The sailors did not think much of Kwale Island, picturesque spot as it was. To them it meant much work, with more to come, for the collection of our mangrove poles in the grim Rufiji would not be fun. What was good about Kwale? Abdulla asked when I ventured to suggest it was a pleasant place. There was no *suq,* he said, and there were no *bebes.* There was not even fruit. But I liked Kwale, for all that; and most of all I liked that shaded village green.

We paid the bottom, sunny side first, on the third day, beginning as soon as the sunny side was dry. The tallow was heated at a brushwood fire on the beach and mixed with lime under the expert eye of the serang, and the sailors slapped it on with their bare hands. They worked in the mud and slime, and some of the stuff got in their eyes. Before the work was done they were covered with lime and tallow, and mud, and sweat; but still they sang. The bottom finished, they carried the anchors ahead far out over the flat to kedge her off, when the tide came in; and in the late afternoon we were afloat. She came off easily, and we kedged her into the bay.

In the morning she was rigged again, and we sailed towards this mysterious place, Simba Uranga, in the delta of the Rufiji.

Chapter 12

DELTA OF MISERY

THE RUFIJI is an impetuous African river flowing from the heights of Tanganyika eastward towards the Indian Ocean, which for countless years has been bringing down soil from the hills and depositing it along a hundred miles of coast. The sea outside is littered with banks, shoals, and coral reefs, which the mud swept down from the river makes it impossible to see. The entrances to the Rufiji are a rain-swept, wretched maze, as though designed by nature to make the passage of vessels as difficult as possible. Bars, banks, shoals, tide rips, eddies, unpredictable sets, rapidly changing channels, combine to propound a conundrum of navigational difficulties which would cause nightmares to any mariner.

Over all the vast area of the delta the water is only three parts water; the fourth part is mud. The soil of the islands and the banks is three parts mud, and one part water. Miasmic vapors, steaming swamps, rotting jungles, and pestilences of all kinds abound. The river is never stable, never sure even of its own channels from one day to the next, changing them with bewildering rapidity and without reason. The forces of the tide and the river's current change swiftly and beyond the range of human forecast, so that even the direction of the stream in any of the arms is unpredictable. Over the whole watery, wretched maze of the muddy, dreadful delta, the arms of the Rufiji constantly send out new feelers connecting and changing the charted streams. A mariner who knows the delta one year may return the next and not know it at all. It has defied all attempts at control. A whirlpool today may be an island tomorrow; a sandbank today may have been swept away by the morning. The whole river seems possessed of a spirit wilful, petulant, and destructive. Forever changing, it is never still. Always deceptive, it is never safe. The whole delta is gloomy, morose, and depressing almost beyond endurance. It rains almost daily, in heavy squalls which beat down like punishment, and leave clouds of steam in an atmosphere like a Turkish bath. When it is not raining the hot sun burns fiercely, and the fetid steam rising from the jungle swamps is fever-laden. It is hot, uncomfortable, and wretched without relief. The mangrove swamps and all the trees are a dark, dank green; the banks are muddy so that one sinks to the thighs in them at every landing; the whole place is tormented by the most savage, fearless, and horrible mosquitoes in the world.

If in all this world there is a worse place than the Rufiji Delta, I hope I may never find it. The list of its enormities is not yet complete, for the murderous crocodile and the clumsy hippopotamus lurk in the stream, ready to capsize a frail canoe and make short work of the occupants. In the jungle, monkeys chatter and scream, and kingfishers and herons, a splash of gay color, fly by the water's edge. In the high trees eagles perch, watching; and in the jungle there are snakes—boa constrictors, and small venomous things. The poisonous mud of the mangrove swamps abounds in leeches and ticks, ready to attach themselves to the foot: creepers beset the way, and thorns tear at the legs. Here only jungle beasts live, and there is no food. There are no gardens, for there is hardly a piece of dry land fit to put a hut upon, away from Salale and the few other villages. The banks are low, barely lifted from the swift waters when the delta is in flood: at high tide many of the islands are awash. The swift sets in the river pull at the moorings of ships with dangerous strength, and bring down great tree trunks from islands to hurl upon them. Pilotage in such a place is a nightmare: the whole delta is a bad dream. There is nothing to eat, and all food must be brought there.

The mosquitoes were worse than I had been led to believe, and I had frequently been reminded of their evil habits. They were unbelievably savage, and fell upon each Arab crew as the dhows came in with the ferocity of small flying tigers. It seemed to me that probably, never having tasted human blood before, the sweetness of it drove them mad. They bit and bit and returned always to the attack no matter how many of them one destroyed. Walking through the swamps one would brush one's forearm to leave it a solid mess of black and blood, the black the squashed bodies of a hundred mosquitoes and the blood from them, too, but not their own. The only defense was to cover oneself up, and it was too insufferably hot for that. Nothing else kept the mosquitoes back, but one could not go entirely covered. When there was wind and the ship was moored midstream they were not so bad, for they could not fly far

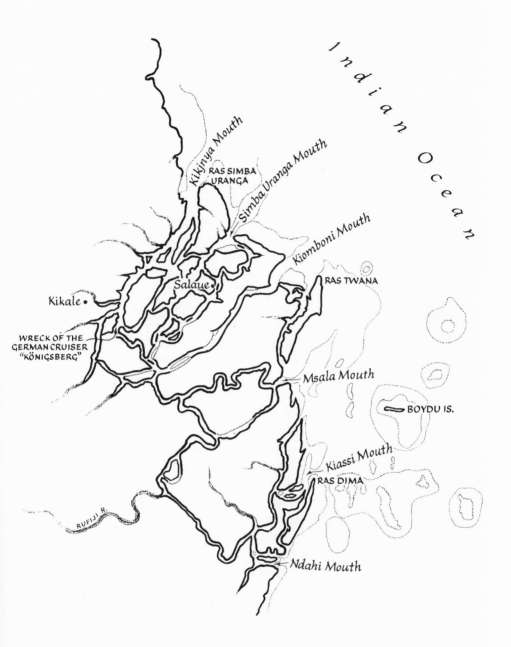

Indian Ocean

Kikinya Mouth

RAS SIMBA
URANGA

Simba Uranga Mouth

Kiomboni Mouth

Salaue

RAS TWANA

Kikale

WRECK OF THE
GERMAN CRUISER
"KÖNIGSBERG"

Msala Mouth

BOYDU IS.

Kiassi Mouth

RAS DIMA

RUFIJI R.

Ndahi Mouth

The delta of the Rufiji River, Tanganyika

in the wind; but when it was calm they were upon the ships like a locust plague in a rich field. Bees came, too—great stinging beasts, attracted by the strong smell from our spoiled dates; and when they came we had to forget the dates, for we could not go near them. The bees hummed and fought and stung all day long, and the nights brought the mosquitoes. The rain was penetrating; the river angry; the Swahili surly, silent and morose; our crew took fever; some from a Suri sambuk died.

In this awful place, this gloomy, wretched delta of the swift Rufiji, we spent a month. It was the worst month of the voyage.

I did not know what was in store for us when we came bowling into the gray Simba Uranga mouth of the great river early one March evening, with the ship cleaned after her beaching and so light and high out of the water that we dared not set the mainsail, but had the lightest mizzen aloft on the mainmast instead. Any greater press of sail might have capsized her, for there was nothing in the hold. We came out of a rain squall, with the tide at the flood and the wind fair, and Mubarak our pilot watched carefully as we swept wide round a point with casuarina trees and stood on past a coconut plantation on our starboard hand. Away before us a great reach of the river stretched towards the west, but Mubarak said that this was the most dangerous of all the Rufiji's many mouths and was not negotiable even by the Arabs in their dhows. We stood close by the bank on the portside of the Simba Uranga, which was the name of the mouth we entered, and swept round a bend almost at a right angle, so close that the branches swept the peak of our sail. We hauled our wind then, and stood across to the other bank for, though this was a broad reach, Mubarak said there were dangerous banks in it. There was also the half-covered wreck of a large cargo steamer, lying athwart the channel at the southern end. Something of the bridge, two masts, and two samson posts showed above the stream. This, said Mubarak, proud of his knowledge, was a German warship sunk by the British in the World War. Hamed bin Salim looked impressed, and so did I, for they could believe that if they liked. But unfortunately it was nothing of the kind. It was the wreck of the British collier *Newbridge*, which had been sunk there in an attempt to bottle up the German cruiser *Königsberg* when she was hiding at Salale early in 1915. The *Newbridge* had been brought from Zanzibar, and run in past the entrance through which we sailed: at that time the place was fortified by the Germans, and the *Newbridge* had a hot reception. Men had died in that swift stream, bringing the *Newbridge* in;

Salale, Rufiji Delta

and there she lay, an ugly blot on the gray scene, and the river had gouged a fresh channel beside her.

We ran close by the *Newbridge*, keeping well clear of her submerged bow—to touch that would have ripped us in pieces—and shortly afterwards followed another bend in the river inland. Herons watched us pass, standing in the mud by the riverbanks: monkeys chattered in the trees, and once we saw a family of them swinging through the forest. My Yimid from Kwale was wildly excited and chattered loudly. We twisted and turned round bend after bend, and at the turn of the tide fetched up at a place about six miles from the mouth we had entered, which Mubarak said was Salale. All I could see were coconut palms, one house, and a tumble-down jetty. Off the jetty were two small Swahili dhows, and Abdul-razzaq's Suri baggala lay moored farther up. We let go two anchors and the stream swept by, muddy and ill-natured. Then the mosquitoes found us, and it was hell. It remained hell for the rest of that month.

We spent most of that time moored in an arm of the delta, miles in-

land from Salale, near the place where the gutted hull of the *Königsberg*
lay broken-backed in the stream, not far from the village of Kikale.

Like the useless hulk of a dead hippopotamus the hull of the former
proud cruiser lay fore and aft in the Kikunya mouth of the Rufiji, close
by the landing place for the village of Kikale. Our sailors ferrying the
mangrove poles passed her daily, coming and going. To them she was
just another finished "man-o'-war Hitrar," as was every other wreck in
the delta. She lay on her side with little more showing than a part of a
splintered deck, a little of the hull, and some davits. Her back was broken,
and the hull was split in two somewhere abaft the bridge, as if she had
been blown up when the British monitors finally found her range. A
dull, desolate sight in the midst of the swirling water, against a background
of swamp and rainy sky, she lies in deep water at a place where the stream
makes a wide curve. Eagles watch from the baobab trees and the white-
winged herons fly by, and the Swahili, paddling past in their canoes, never
give the battered hulk a second look. She is too familiar a sight in the Rufiji now, for she has been there a quarter of a century.

At another bend of the river, in the Kiomboni mouth, about a mile or
two north of the village of Salale, lies another twisted wreck battered to
pieces by British shells in 1914. This is the cargo steamer *Somali*, once a
coaster for the German East Africa line, and later tender and store-ship
for the *Königsberg*. Now she lies a red, twisted wreck upon a yellow
sandbank, her mainmast and funnel askew, her foremast lying overside
like a crumpled tube, her back broken, and her hull virtually in two
pieces, with the jungle on the other side showing through.

From this jungle, and the swamps near the *Königsberg*, we cut our
cargo. But that took time. In the meantime, we waited.

The method of loading in the Rufiji was for the Arabs to come,
with their cash, and enter their ships and their requirements at Salale,
where there was a British forestry officer. He sent them on to the part of
the delta he thought would most quickly provide them with their poles,
for though the whole place abounded with these poles they had been cut
heavily from the more accessible places nearer the sea. Now the ships
were far back, for it was best to get a cargo as close as possible to the
banks of the stream. Cutting the trees down and trimming them took comparatively little time; it was carrying them to some landing place where
they could be inspected, graded, and marked, and from which they could
be ferried to the dhow, that took the time. Therefore the ships liked to

be in new places, alone, where the mangroves grew thick by the water's edge. (There were, I discovered later, other reasons why they liked to be alone.)

A dhow having been entered and assigned her place, moved upstream and recruited labor, which was sometimes difficult, for the district was not populous. It had no attractions to offer and the Swahili had no liking for the back-breaking, wretched work. For this no one could blame them. Sometimes it took two weeks to recruit a gang of cutters, for the dhows were all in together and the demand was considerable. When we arrived we were one of twelve dhows. The Swahili lived aboard, at the ship's expense, and they cut the poles by day. It took a long time to cut a cargo, though we soon had eighty Swahili living on board. Many of these were tribesmen, children, helpers; and some of them just ate. If you recruited a few Swahili to work, before long a whole tribe moved in to eat. They slept aboard, wherever they could lie down, and they ate the ship's food. Hamed tried the bad dates on them, but they would not eat them, and before long we were borrowing dates from the other Kuwait ships in the delta. The appetites of our Swahili were tremendous, and several times they ate so much that there was no supper left for the crew. The sailors suffered without complaint, because they knew that though their hunger might not be necessary, they must do nothing to displease the Swahili. Without them, we should never be gone from that miserable place. And they had to be fed.

The Tanganyika government controls cutting rights in the forests of the Rufiji Delta, but it is the practice to let them out to a private company on a royalty basis. The Arabs buy from the company, and the government's forester superintends them. No cargoes are ready, and each ship must cut her own. The poles cannot be cut and stored for the ships to come and load them, for not only would this cause much unnecessary work but it would lead to loss, because the banks of the river are nowhere stable enough to support a dump for long. Poles dumped today may be washed away tomorrow. The Swahili dump them a few score at a time, and the forest guards, under the forester's supervision, inspect them, see that they are graded properly, and brand them with the government hammer. No pole may be loaded without this brand. Tallies are kept, and when the ship is full she pays cash for what she has taken, and the labor is paid on a piecework basis. The Arab crews ferry and load their own poles. They may take dead wood from the forests for firewood, and water from the river to drink. Nothing else is free.

The Arabs have been accustomed to come to the Rufiji Delta for mangrove poles from time immemorial, and the trade is a very ancient one. Though, as a matter of policy, they appear, at least on the surface, to conform with the temporary regulations of what they regard as interloping governments, they see no reason why they should pay a European company for the right to take these poles. If they pay the Swahili, whose country the delta really is, they think that should be sufficient. It is a matter of great difficulty and some danger, to bring a big dhow from the Persian Gulf to the Rufiji and load her with mangrove poles, and it is only in comparatively recent years that the business has been more or less organized. It did not take me long to discover that the Arabs continue an effective campaign to ensure that, so far as possible, the organization has no more than the appearance of smooth working.

We bought some poles, certainly, and so did all the other Arabs in the delta. We had a forest guard on board, and so had all the other dhows in the delta. We were frequently visited by the energetic forester, a man from the Forest of Dean, with keen blue eyes and no intention of having dust blown into them; and so were all the other dhows in the delta. Our

Sailmakers at Kwale

poles were inspected, graded, and duly marked with the official axe. Our Swahili headmen seemed docile, law-abiding, anxious to please. We loaded, and paid for, 150 score poles. Yet we had loaded another 150 score before we left that place, though we were 2000 miles away before I could be sure of that, in spite of the fact that I had been there the whole time.

Every Arab ship in that delta, and probably the Persians, too, stole half her cargo in spite of every effort to check them. There existed, and I did not learn this until months afterwards, a widespread and very effective system for cutting and loading poles, unseen by the official eye. The headmen, the forest guards, the laborers, the Arab nakhodas and crews were all in it. It was a close-knit thing. No European could hope to break through the childlike front of these people: they acted in the whole affair like a group of school children organizing something against teacher, a teacher who was not so clever as he thought himself. How could one man control that vast area, and check these things? The Arabs loaded over an area little short of a hundred square miles, along a river front of more than a hundred miles. Even to visit each of them was the work of a week. In all that area, there was only one officer, and it seemed to me that he had in his department no native he could really trust. To pay guards to watch the Arab vessels, alone in their lonely reaches, was a waste of money. The guards, even if honest, were largely powerless, for they dared not stand against a machine as effective as that pole-stealing organization. It was like a racket in America, as well run and as unscrupulous. So far as I could gather the local Swahili headmen were the arch-conspirators, the leading racketeers. It was with them, and through them, that the Arabs received their unchecked cargoes. Great dumps of poles would be cut in secluded places, away from the river banks, for it was known that the forester had no time to prowl through the dreadful swamps and would probably have died of fever if he had tried. His predecessor had been carried away from Salale. Besides, he trusted his guards and looked after them well. The headmen cowed the guards and cowed the laborers. Not only did they take the Arabs' money for the stolen poles, but, in the tradition of the true racketeer, they withheld much of the laborer's share besides. There was one amongst those headmen who was a powerful man indeed, as powerful in his own way as any gangster in the United States, and even more unscrupulous. This man controlled the whole northern end of the delta with an iron hand. No laborer could be employed, no guard enter service, no poles cut without his command:

and he profited very handsomely by his power. This man, I discovered, looked after us, and Mubarak our pilot was the go-between.

He was a mysterious Arab, this Mubarak the Suri. A short, stout man of middle age, gray-bearded with bushy whiskers in the Suri style, he was an old Rufiji trader. He was always barefoot, and he wore the long brown shirt of Sur, with a red sarong under it. He generally carried a silver dagger, and his eyelids were darkened with mascara. He had a low, soft voice which could rise to a whine when he was excited; and he affected an air of great humility. He had a dhow of his own, back in Zanzibar, it was said: I wondered, if that were so, why he agreed to be a pilot for us. The truth was, of course, that though competent to act as a pilot, that was not his main function. He knew the ropes. He was a "fixer." He seemed to look not only after us, but after every other Arab dhow in our part of the delta. He was very seldom on board. He came and went mysteriously, and was the friend of most of the Swahili. He spoke Swahili fluently: it is a tongue easily managed by the Arabs.

Unfortunately for Mubarak, however, his own dhow arrived in the river from Zanzibar for a second cargo, not long after we had come in, and though her name had been changed and Mubarak was no longer the nakhoda, the forester recognized her as a dhow wanted for pole-stealing. Earlier in the year, with Mubarak in command, she had come in, asked for a ridiculous number of poles, and then sailed so deep-loaded that the forester's suspicions had been aroused. Unknown to Mubarak, he had the cargo carefully counted by the authorities at Zanzibar, when it was discharged there for sale to a local merchant. There was more than twice the number of poles Mubarak had ordered. Here was Mubarak, back again, our "pilot." Usually the Arab can rely on his general likeness to his kind —at least to inexperienced European eyes—as disguise enough. But Mubarak foolishly admitted his identity, and admitted—not suspecting anything—that he was also nakhoda of the wanted dhow. That was enough, and Mubarak was arrested. One of the Swahili headmen was implicated with him, having supplied the extra poles to his dhow, and the pair were taken for trial upriver to Utete.

Not that this inconvenienced us. Mubarak's work was too well done for that, by that time, and the organization too smooth. We had our fill of poles, and did not pay for half of them. So, very likely, did every other Arab in the delta.

For this dishonesty the Arabs, it seems to me, are not too greatly to be blamed. "If we complied with every regulation," Hamed bin Salim said, "we could not come. It is known," he went on, "that no ship here takes only that cargo she has officially paid for. If she cannot take the un-official balance, then she cannot afford to pay for the other, and the trade stops. The present system works smoothly. Nobody loses. Why interfere? The Europeans do not own the mangroves, for Allah put them there and they are for all men. There is timber enough in Africa; but we in Arabia are very badly off for wood, or we would not make so long and hard a voyage to get these poles."

So argued Hamed, who was seldom given to speech. (This was long afterwards. He said nothing while the ship was in the delta.) He pointed out, further, that the Arab dhows had slight encouragement to visit the Rufiji, for the loading delays were very bad, labor difficult to get, the river exceedingly dangerous, and not only had cash to be paid on the spot, but nakhodas were required to carry the cash with them over a dangerous and exhausting trek from the northern part of the delta to Dima, in the south, where the company's agent waited to collect it. So far as they could see, the company's agent existed to take their cash, and for no other reason. They made it a point of honor to see that he got as little of it as possible. If the trade were properly organized and poles waiting to be loaded, Hamed said, there would be no need to receive them from the Swahili. As it was, he did not think the *Triumph* would come to the Rufiji again. This was her first visit, and it would be her last. In future she would go to Lamu.

It was certainly true that loading was a slow, difficult, and laborious business. We lay ten days in our arm of the river without loading anything at all, while the Swahili ate. We had, we were told, to wait until they had got together a number of poles large enough for the guards to mark them. This they did, eventually: but in the meantime they had also collected a larger dump at a secluded spot not far from the wrecked *Königsberg*, whence they would be removed by night when the time came. As soon as the first of our cargo had been marked and officially released, we could load this dump. It was more than a hundred score, and the lot was put in in two nights. Neither the company nor the government, apparently, had any idea of the capacities of the Arab dhows. When we asked for 150 score it was presumed that that was our capacity, though if he had any suspicion, the forester could compel vessels to unload and check their car-goes at Salale or anywhere else he thought fit. But he was a forester, not a shipping clerk: and he had much to do.

When the loading began we were busy. The poles were ferried off at

Hulk of the Königsberg

high tide in *Afra* and the longboat, both of which were rigged with sails to make the work easier: two cargoes came by day, and two by night. I was sorry for the sailors, for the conditions were appalling. Throughout that wretched Rufiji month they led a life of incessant and excessive hardship, never dry, sleeping without shelter from the heavy rains, working all day and half the night wet with mud, water, sweat; bitten by the fever mosquito; their hands torn by the jagged, splintered wood and their feet by the tangled undergrowth and thorns, and the wounds of both infected, their only food a little rice and fish twice daily—sometimes only once. They worked steadily, never seeking rest when there was work to be done; and they sang while they worked. They did not sing at night, when they ferried the stolen poles. These came down the river in the rain, in silence, and were hurriedly stowed on board.

The days were either windless, heavy, and exceedingly hot, or it was raining. There was no recreation and no place even to walk: it was not safe to swim. The ship was covered with mud, though every one tried to wash the clinging stuff off before returning on board. A thatched roof was built over the after end of the poop, above the nakhoda's reclining bench, but this did not keep out the rain. Nothing could keep the mosquitoes down. They laughed at mosquito nets and seemed to delight in crawling inside them: one mosquito inside a net is worse than a hundred outside it. The sailors had no nets. They accepted the mosquitoes as they came. At first they tried to fight them off, but after a while they gave up the unequal struggle and let them bite, on the principle, I suppose, that if they were filled they would go away. If they fought them off they would only come back again, with others of their kind even hungrier. Better a comparatively few well-fed mosquitoes than thousands of hungry ones. I could never put this philosophy to the test. The mosquitoes bit so savagely that one's hands and arms swelled up.

Ashore there were sand flies and other pests, as a change from the mosquitoes. I was kept busy with my medical work and often wished that I had some real skill at it. There were many ills I had not seen before— tropical infections, bad skin diseases, outbreaks of discharging sores on the head, and fevers. Those who had been pearl divers in the Persian Gulf suffered terribly, for many of them had a skin disease which broke out here. It was a kind of rash of blind pimples, and they always had some signs of it, usually on their legs. As long as the pimples were not discharging it was not so bad, but in this wretched delta they were torn by thorns and splinters and jagged creepers. Every pimple that was opened became infected, either from the heavy tannin in the mangrove bark or from the poisonous river mud. I could do no more than try to keep the wounds clean, stop the bleeding, and prevent infection. Sometimes it was hard, and I ran short of medical supplies. I never had very many, and the demand was great. The sailors, too, contracted boils, as if they had not already ills enough. Some had small worms embedded in their knees and leg muscles, from which they had to be gouged.

The Arabs were good patients and, not for the first time, I had reason to be thankful for their immense powers of recuperation. But by the time we had been three weeks in the delta, they were obviously wearing down. They were thin and wan by that time, even the most stalwart of them; and I saw that many who were much less than thirty were now quite gray. It was a hard life; yet even here, old Yusuf Shirazi said one day that, bad as the Rufiji was, it was better than pearling. He thanked God, he said, that he would never have to do *that* again. I began to wonder about this pearling.

If it was hard for our sailors, it was hard also for the Swahili, whose moroseness I forgave when I saw the conditions under which they worked. Up to their knees in mud, cutting down mangroves with a small axe—those mangroves were iron-hard—stripping them, dragging them through the jungle to some creek or backwater where their dugouts were moored. Their small dugouts would hold only five or six poles. When they were full, the poles would have to be taken to the central dump, graded, and stowed. In places where the mangroves were plentiful, it was bad enough, but where other cutters had thinned them out it was exceedingly hard work. Early in the morning, immediately after the dawn prayer, which they always recited sonorously together, they left the boom, pulling in their dugouts upstream against the race. They pulled close inshore, keeping watch for the savage crocodile, which could easily upset their small canoes and drown them, before taking the bodies off to its lair to rot into a fit state for eating. They used the branches overhead to help them on their way. When bound downstream, they drifted in the middle of the river. That was easy. All day long they worked, with only a handful of inferior dates for food. Rain or sun made no difference to them.

They were picturesque, in spite of their surly looks. Most of them had tribal scars on the cheeks, two on each side. They were all dressed in Arab rags, mostly in very old Suri shirts, which hung on their great backs by threads. They were devout Muslims, at any rate while the Arabs were in port, and they recited their prayers with gusto. Indeed, those who worked the least prayed the most, sometimes keeping the sailors awake half the night with their sonorous mumbo-jumbo, and it is not fitting that the Faithful should rebuke the convert for saying his prayers. So they prayed on and on, until I often felt like rebuking them myself. The only excuse I could see for this exceedingly great devotion was that it was to make up for the rest of the year, when the Arabs were not there. Indeed, the Swahili confided to me privately that they did not pray much after the Arabs had gone.

If life was bad in the Rufiji for our sailors and the Swahili laborers alike, it must have been a nightmare for poor Hamed bin Salim. He had never been there before, and there he was, in command of a large and somewhat unwieldy boom, far up an uncharted arm of the impetuous Rufiji, charged not only with her safe navigation to and from Zanzibar, but responsible also that her cargo was secured in the least possible time, and half of it not paid for. He had eighty Swahili laborers in his care, to pacify, feed, and make work: he had the ship to tend—and that was job enough, in that swirling headstrong reach—and the boats to look after; and he had our crew to care for. During that month in the Rufiji I grew to appreciate Hamed bin Salim. I had liked him well enough before, but I had had little chance to get to know him on the run from Ma'alla to the Hadhramaut, and after that he was always overshadowed by Nejdi.

Hamed was an unusual Arab in some ways. He was thirty-six years old, and not yet a nakhoda. He was the muallim, the small nakhoda of Nejdi's boom, and it was very likely that he would never attain a command. He was a biggish man, for an Arab seafarer, with a close-clipped beard, high forehead, and a very large, straight nose. His father was from Nejd, and he had left there to settle in Kuwait. His strong face was marked by a great number of heavy creases, and bad teeth, very prominent, spoiled his mouth. He wore his iron-gray hair very short, shaving it off frequently. He usually wore a jawpoint beard, cropped very close and becoming. He was a big-limbed man, with brawny arms and powerful hands. He had a strong voice which could get excited at times. His voice was very sonorous in prayer, which he often led, for he was the ship's most devout Muslim. There was no question of this devotion, which was quite genuine. He was a high-principled man, scrupulously honest in all matters apart from such things as receiving Rufiji mangrove poles, and smuggling, and the like, all of which, in his view, were thoroughly proper; reserved, and very quiet, as became the second nakhoda of any ship Nejdi might command. He was a capable seaman and a good pilot. His visits ashore were concerned only with business, and he left women alone even in Zanzibar. He had been nineteen years at sea, beginning as ship's boy and rising to be quartermaster. From quartermaster to second nakhoda was a big step, and he may have owed his promotion to the fact that he had married one of Nejdi's sisters. Be that as it may, he was a good man and deserved the advancement, which was probably all he would ever get.

Hamed might have got a great deal farther if it had not been for his somewhat unfortunate personality. He had no knowledge of those little graces and ways and means by which men such as Nejdi commanded other men easily, and got them to follow him. No one could say that Hamed was born to command. Nejdi, from the moment his nose appeared above the rail until the last of his headcloth disappeared down the Jacob's ladder, was in undisputed command of everything in sight. Hamed did not succeed Nejdi; Hamed merely carried on in his absence. Hamed was capable, competent, energetic, and trustworthy. But he didn't know how to command. He was not popular with the sailors, who preferred the fault-finding, dashing Nejdi. Perhaps it was the old feeling against officers promoted from the ranks, for Hamed had been a working sailor with some of them, in other ships. But I think it was simply that Hamed lacked the personality to command. His ambition was to get money enough to buy a small plantation by the Basra River in Iraq, and there settle down and sleep while the dates grew. As things were, he had no idea when he might achieve this ambition, if ever. Plantations were expensive, and money was difficult to get. It was as much as he could do to keep his home going with the money he received as his share of the *Triumph*'s earnings, and the little he made from his ventures. He was a married man, with one wife and four children.

I grew to like Hamed, on those long Rufiji nights while the rain beat down on the thatch above the nakhodas' bench, and we huddled up together out of it. Old Yusuf Shirazi squatted by the wheel, puffing at his bubbly-pipe, and little Mohamed Kederfi, now and then, brought up a round of coffee or tea. Hamed and I yarned at such times, though usually he did not talk much. We yarned about all kinds of things, principally about dhows, and Kuwait. After a while he began to tell me things about the economic side of the voyage—what the voyage cost, for instance, and how much the ship could earn. She had, he said, been able to pay the sailors over 160 rupees a share the previous year, but he doubted whether she would be able to pay even 100 on this. Difficulties in Mogadishu, poor price for the cargo in Zanzibar, low rates on the passengers, and then all the extra time they had spent on board, the high cost of Rufiji mangroves—he said nothing about those received from the Swahili—and the probable difficulty of selling them in the Persian Gulf, these things made it difficult to earn profits. It would be better, Hamed said, to carry merchants' freights, but the merchants preferred that the nakhodas should take the risks. If the merchant sent his own cargo, he had to pay the ship, and support the investment of the cargo. If the ship carried her own goods, the merchants got them anyway, more often at their own prices than not, for no nakhoda could afford to wait long for a sale on a bad market, or give indefinite warehousing to his cargoes. So the merchants often received their goods without having to pay freight or run the risks of the voyage. It was an iniquitous system, Hamed said; but it was the way the Arabs worked. What could he do about it? Then he asked me about steamers, and how they were run, for Hamed was a man with ideas.

Throughout that bitter month Hamed worked dreadfully. Three

times we shifted ship, carefully watching the tides, now farther in towards the *Königsberg,* now out again towards another part of the river, for the boom by that time was beginning to draw a lot of water. We were loading her to the rails, and before she left the Rufiji we were drawing nearly thirteen feet of water. If we were caught in a far arm with a draft like that during a period of low tides, we might stay in the delta two months instead of one. Two months! The prospect was too dreadful to think about: though we knew that the Kuwaiti Abdul-wahhab bin Kalifa had already been in the river over forty days, with his big boom *Tai-seer.* Shifting ship down those swift streams was a dangerous maneuver, and often in some tide-rip we would swing right across the narrow channel and ground both bow and stern. At such times the sailors had to work extremely hard, even for them, carrying out lines to trees to straighten the ship again. Not even the greatest care would prevent such accidents. They did no harm, for we moved only with the rising tide, and all the banks were mud. But it was difficult, worrying, back-breaking work.

Meanwhile day succeeded day, and often no poles were brought at all, while the Swahili steadily ate all the provisions in the ship. Hamed knew that, whatever he did, Nejdi, sitting all this time at ease among the fleshpots of Zanzibar, would disapprove, or at least give the impression that things would have gone much better if he had been there. But if he were envious of Nejdi he never said anything, or showed his feelings. Hamed looked after the ship, and did his best always for ship and crew, and led the prayers. He overcame difficulties as they arose, and went on to look for more. He asked for no favors, and gave none. The sailors, when Nejdi was aboard, always came on the poop night and morning to offer their salutations. With Hamed, in the Rufiji, no one came. That was the difference between them.

When at last our cargo was on board, and the deeply laden ship lay at anchor off Salale again, with her maindeck below the level of the water, the tired, thin crew looked to the rigging and bent the sail. Hamed had then to set off on the trek to Dima to give the company its shillings. It took him two days to get there, for Salale is in the north of the delta and Dima in the south. It was the fourth day before he returned, looking thinner and more worn than ever. Much of the way had been by dugout canoe, and twice they were overturned, once by a hippo and once by a log which they feared for a moment was a crocodile. When they were not paddling along the moody river they forced their way across swamps, and through jungle. Hamed, who was barefoot, returned with his feet lacerated, and his legs torn by thorns. They had seen snakes, he said: once they passed a boa constrictor asleep after a meal. At Dima there was nothing to eat, and no rest, and he was worried about the ship. She was drawing a great deal of water by that time, and he wanted to get her out with the spring tide. So he stumbled back again, the shillings paid and the official receipt given, and the return was worse than the going, for it rained almost the whole journey. Sheets of rain alternated with torrid, humid heat; the mosquitoes were thick and fierce; sand flies tormented him, flying in his face. He floundered on up to the knees in the slimy ooze which was full of stabbing snags: foothold was impossible: the bush was full of thorns, insects, snakes. Crocodiles waited by the river, and bad-tempered hippos, to overturn canoes. Wet through, muddy, bloody, torn, hungry, with nothing to eat and only river water to drink, Hamed struggled on. When at last he returned to the ship and I ventured to say that it was not right the Arabs should face such difficulties to take a company its money, he said only that Allah was compassionate, and he did not complain. But he was very tired, and the spring tides had gone. A flood whirled in the river from heavy rains upstream, and debris of all kinds littered the broad stream, while logs, bushes, and tree trunks thundered into us. The stream was running a good six knots, and the deep-laden boom strained at her anchors. Mubarak was gone, led away for his trial upriver, and we were without a pilot. It was stormy outside, and the rain squalls over the river were frequent and depressing, and sometimes whipped up savage winds. But we had our cargo now, the company was paid, and the Swahili were gone. We could sail. Praise be to Allah! We could sail.

Hamed called all hands to special prayer, and in the morning we were gone.

It was the end of March when we sailed at last from Salale. We touched once, going down, but she came off easily, for we moved down with a fresh wind against the flood. The rising water floated her as she grounded, but we went carefully. Mubarak was in Utete jail, and there was no one else who knew the river. It rained that morning, and the dark and mournful river was a place of gloom. Our decks were full to the rail with wet and muddy poles. The ship floated sluggishly with her main-deck below the level of the water. The sailors, worn and thin, had no shelter and nowhere to go, for not only the space beneath the break of the poop, but the whole great cabin had been filled with poles. The bulkhead of the great cabin was unshipped, and the maindeck packed with poles to the rails. The top of the cargo was rough and full of unevennesses, splinters, and projecting ends which stubbed the sailors' toes as they ran. Every one had suffered, more or less severely, from the Rufiji stay. Abdul-latif and Ebrahim the helmsman were laid up badly with the fever. The others had heavy colds. Jassim the cook was worn almost to a shadow. Poor old Yusuf Shirazi was now completely gray, and so thin that his long gown hung on him like a bag and, where it was open at neck and chest, his ribs showed up like a skeleton's. All hands were in much the same condition. Even Abdulla, the nakhoda's brother, who did the least work of any one on board, showed signs of wear, and poor Hamed bin Salim was like a pessimistic ghost.

It rained all the way downstream. We swept past mudbanks and weeping trees, through rain and past mud, past always more and more arms, rivulets, backwashes, channels, and creeks of the swift-flowing turgid stream, past a clearing here that was the landing-place for Kiomboni, now again in sight of the sunken *Newbridge,* and the banks of the Simba Uranga mouth, where the Germans had their trenches and small guns. The wind dropped as we came towards the mouth, but the tide had begun

At Kwale Island

to ebb then and we continued. As we came out the rain cleared, stopping suddenly as we emerged from the gloomy river-mouth, as though, having done its worst, it was saying to itself: "Now, damn you, you can go!" The rain was like the spirit of that sad place and, having emerged from it, we thanked God and did not look back. Inside it still rained—rained and rained and rained. Ahead of us was comparatively open sea—not really open yet, for we had still the tortuous reef and bank-filled passage to Zanzibar to negotiate, and a call to make at Kwale to clear the ship. But the wretched Rufiji was behind us and the sailors smiled. Until they smiled, I had not observed how rare pleasure had come to be upon their faces. Hamed bin Salim did not smile.

We were not yet out of danger, and our troubles were not over. We drew a great deal of water—more than any other craft which sailed out that day, and we were one of seven. Shallows, reefs, sandbanks, sudden squalls abounded: it was the changeable period between the northeast and the southwest monsoons, when anything may happen. If we took the ground in our heavy-laden condition, we could do the ship serious damage. Any cargo we might have to jettison would be our loss, for it was all bought with the ship's money, or secured by her people's sacrifice. Simba Uranga mangrove poles sink: they are too heavy to float.

For that matter, we were not yet away from the delta, though we were outside the land. We were still in the narrow channel between the mudbanks beyond the Simba Uranga mouth when the breeze came again, from ahead, and we could lay our course only with difficulty. Ahead of us, almost hull-down, we could see the sails of six other Arab vessels which had sailed that morning. Hamed was conning us quietly when suddenly Abdulla, the nakhoda's brother, who had never been noted either for his abilities or his ambition at any other stage of the voyage, decided he would take charge. He began to give the helmsman orders conflicting with those given by Hamed. Seeing the ships ahead, he maintained that we could fall off and follow them. We could not, Hamed said, for there was a sandbank in the way. We could, said Abdulla, and ordered the helmsman to let the ship fall off.

"Keep her up!" said Hamed.

"Fall off!" said Abdulla.

"There cannot be two masters," Hamed said. "Let go the anchors!" And he sat down.

In this brief interchange, fraught with some peril to the ship, Hamed bin Salim was so obviously in the right that the helmsman paid no attention to Abdulla's orders. It is a poor pilot who can only follow ships ahead, and a poor officer who seeks command when the worst is over. Hamed was in charge of the ship, and Abdulla wronged him both by upsetting his orders and his command. Abdulla, being Nejdi's brother, was in a privileged position, and knew it. Hamed, being only Nejdi's brother-in-law, was in an unprivileged position, and he knew that, too. His duty was to take the *Triumph* to the Rufiji, fill her with poles, and bring her back to Zanzibar. He had to put up with Abdulla. Nominally no more than one of the helmsmen, Abdulla's position was not clearly defined on board, but everybody knew he was Nejdi's brother. Everybody knew, too, that he would probably get a ship for himself when the *Triumph* came home, if she made any money. Hamed would not: Hamed would not get a ship of his own, no matter how long he faithfully served both Nejdi and Abdulla, no matter how many weary voyages he made or how many bitter months he might tend their ships in the terrible Rufiji. The only way Hamed would ever get a ship of his own would be by accumulating enough money to buy one, and that he should ever be able to do that, try as he might, was most unlikely. He was a poor man with a large family. Abdulla was a young man with no family but a wife: he was a younger brother, and his home was provided for him. He lived with Nejdi, and they both lived with their father. His three children had died.

So Hamed sat down. Then he washed himself, and prayed, for it was the time of the noon prayer. He said nothing about the incident. Abdulla appealed to me. I said he was wrong, and that if Nejdi trusted Hamed to have command of the ship, then it was not Abdulla's place to make his command impossible. But, said Abdulla, Hamed was going a wrong way. There was no pilot. He knew as much as Hamed did. He could see the other ships. Well, I said, they drew less water than we did, and they were much farther out. They could fall safely off and stand towards the north when we could not. At that Abdulla appealed to one or two of the helmsmen, who said nothing. Then he, too, sat down. The breeze by this time had hauled a little fair again. We had been lying anchored with the mainsail aloft, gathered loosely to the yard which had been hauled in against the mast. From this condition it was easy to get under weigh again. Noticing the wind fair, Hamed weighed anchor and we went on. Abdulla took no further part in the pilotage of the vessel. We got an offing beyond the banks, and then fell off towards the northward.

After that the sailors, who had not greeted him throughout our stay in the Rufiji, came aft on the poop to greet Hamed night and morning. I was pleased at that. They had thought Hamed right, and this was their way of showing their sympathy. I had never known them to show much sympathy over anything or anybody; it was not a conspicuous virtue among them. But their quiet greetings night and morning to Hamed after this were very pleasing. If he noticed, Hamed gave no sign; but I think he was pleased.

For my own part, I knew the sailors better and liked Hamed bin Salim more, for that hard month in the Rufiji. I was glad I had gone with the ship, and I felt that I had learned a great deal more in that way, and had got to know all hands better. It pleased Hamed and the crew, I think, that I had chosen to come with them to that dreadful place, when I could as easily have stayed with Nejdi at Zanzibar. We were good friends before that Rufiji loading: after it we were shipmates.

Now we stood up towards Kwale, and the sun shone, and the sailors brought out their poor rags to air them, and try to get a little dryness into clothes which had not been dry for a month. My monkey Yimid, which had been hiding beneath the forecastle head for the past two weeks, came out again and chattered cheerfully, running up and down and jumping on Jassim's legs. Bizz the cat, which had found the combination of discomforts in the delta beyond even her infinite capacity for endurance— Bizz was used to a hard life—also came out again, looking woefully thin. I gave her some milk, which she lapped gratefully. Bizz looked round for mosquitoes, which had made her life a plague in the preceding month and, seeing none, almost smiled. Poor Bizz, there was not much joy in her life, and she must often have regretted leaving her native Berbera. She was very scared of Yimid, and never went near his end of the ship. Bizz lived aft, and Yimid for'ard: they never met if Bizz could help it.

Throughout the afternoon we looked back at the gloomy depression of the great delta where the rain lay heavy over all the Rufiji's mouths, and our crew again gave thanks to Allah. In the evening it rained again, and we fetched the anchorage off Kwale in a rain squall after dark—ticklish pilotage, for there was not too much water, and nothing could be seen. Hamed looked a queer sight piloting the ship in the dusk, with his skirts tucked up out of the wet and a Bombay umbrella overhead to keep off the rain. The sailors scampered about wet through.

It rained that night more than it had at any time during our stay in the Rufiji. It came down almost like a cloudburst, so heavy and so continually that the rainwater filled the cutter hoisted at the quarter davits, and the cutter became so heavy that it wrenched the forward davit adrift from its iron fastenings and tipped into the sea. *Afra* and the longboat, lying astern, were filled until they were waterlogged. More serious than this was the fact that the rainwater, pouring out of the sky, poured into the hold and came very near to foundering the ship at the anchorage, with the voyage back to Arabia not begun. With the maindeck under water, there was no way of draining any rain or any sea that might come aboard. It went into the hold. The ship was just a catchment area, drawing all the rain it could into its own hold, and the only way to get it out from there was to bail. During the cloudburst, bailing was sadly ineffectual: the water came in faster than it could be bailed out. Bailing was a laborious and diffi-cut process. A well had been left, as always, abaft the mainmast, and most of the rain eventually drained into this. As in all Arab craft, there was no real attempt to make the deck watertight. Indeed, it had holes left in it for the express purpose of allowing water to drain into the hold. All the water that came aboard, even on the forecastle head, went into the hold.

Seeing the ship settle so perilously close to the border line of safety in that shower of rain, I began to wonder whether she really would be sea-worthy enough to make the voyage back to Arabia. We might get rain enough, in the southwest season, before we were away from the Afri-can coast. She was very deeply laden. What would be the position, I won-dered, if she shipped a few seas? It would take very few to finish her, for you cannot bail out the sea. Her rails, though they were built up with washboards and matting, were very close to the level of the water. The mangrove poles were a heavy, dead cargo. They were not even secured, for it was not the Arab style to secure anything. The ship was full of poles and there they lay, and it seemed to me that we should need some help from Allah if we were to reach Arabia. This reflection, however, did not seem to occur to any one else on board, or perhaps it was with them always. They were not worried. I asked Hamed what would happen if a sea came aboard, but his only reply was that Allah was compassionate. After some time he added that the longboat would float off, as if he had been turning the matter over. I admit, however, that not for the first time I wondered just how foolhardy it was to stay in the ship knowing the chances she really was taking and I wondered, too, how good an insurance risk I might be supposed to be. Not that that mattered, for I had no in-surance and wanted none; but I am a poor swimmer, and I did not wish to lose my photographs. At Mukalla, after the blindness; again at Shihr, when our horde of Beduin came on board; and again at Kwale, when I watched the ship settle until she almost foundered in a shower of rain,

I wondered whether I was wise in staying to see the voyage through. But I could not give up: if the Arabs stayed, I would. Perhaps Allah would give a hand to me also. As Hamed said, if the worse came to the worst, the longboat would probably float off.

We went on from Kwale in the morning, with a little better weather. My friend, Mr. Anton, was not aboard, for there were many ships to clear. We went in with the bailed-out cutter and got our papers, and sailed without further formality. Again it was raining heavily, but there were partial clearings, and we went on easily under the jib, so that she could be brought up quickly if danger showed. We passed near the upturned wreck of what looked like a bedeni, which must have gone down in a squall. The wind was light from the south'ard, and in the afternoon it cleared. We set the mainsail then. The horizon was still very black all round, but occasional brief clearings showed us the picturesque sails of our sailing companions, the other dhows. Crosseyed Abdul-razzaq was still with us, and the dignified old Bedri, as well as three sambuks from Sur and two bedeni. During the afternoon, with a little spasmodic sun, we sailed pleasantly to the north, for we were now past the worst dangers. In the evening we saw Ras Kimbiji light, and it was good to see a welcoming navigation light again after that month of mud-bound wet hell.

The next day we were back in Zanzibar. Having taken so long to load the first cargo, there could be no thought of going back to the Rufiji for a second. It was now April and the southwest wind had come. It was time to be on our way.

We came in by moonlight to the crowded dhow anchorage at Zanzibar, and I thought Hamed did a good job of taking up a berth in that congestion, though Abdulla criticized him loudly. We moored astern of Sulieman Said's big *Hope of Compassion*, which we had not seen since Haifun. As soon as we were in, and before our anchor was down, Moosa her muallim was aboard giving us the news. There had, it seemed, been a minor uprising at home in Kuwait, and there was a big fight between the Suri and the Somali in the *suq* at Zanzibar. Our sailors gathered excitedly on the poop to hear this news, and Abdulla dashed ashore to look for Nejdi.

Chapter 13

HOMEWARD BOUND

THE TROUBLE in Kuwait had apparently come to a head while we were in the Rufiji, loading our mangrove poles, during March, when the sailors gathered nightly to tell me what a beautiful and peaceful place their home port really was. Now they gathered excitedly to discuss the latest news of the riot or whatever it had been, and there were soon as many versions current on board as there were sailors. According to Hamed bin Salim, there was only one trouble with Kuwait. It was, he said, too close to Iraq, though what he meant by that remark he did not explain. According to old Yusuf, there was nothing the matter with Kuwait: but by their very nature the Arabs could not face a peaceful life, without intrigue. They had to intrigue about something, against somebody. Sometimes their intrigues got them into trouble. That, he judged, must have been the case on this occasion.

In the course of time I gradually came to understand something of what had been going on in this great dhow port which I then had never seen. Old Yusuf's version was nearest to the truth. But having disclosed his views, he never mentioned the subject again. Abdulla, Nejdi's brother, was my best informant, and certain Arab gentlemen in the *suq*. Some of these gentlemen seemed surprisingly well informed on happenings in the Persian Gulf and elsewhere in the Arabian peninsula, even so far away as Palestine, and were in touch with political events throughout the world. As far as I could gather, trouble had been simmering in Kuwait for some time. There was no Arab town, principality, sheikhdom, village, or even Beduin tent where some form of intrigue was not going on either openly or under cover, and the rumors and the gossip and the general condition of talkative unrest in the city had, apparently, bothered no one very much. But it seemed that there had been some real basis for discontent.

Some Kuwaiti, alongside the headstrong and somewhat self-satisfied new country of Iraq, decided that they had too little to do with their own government. They wanted more, and gradually acquired the habit of saying so. There was nothing wrong in this, and in the course of time, their Sheikh, His Highness Sir Ahmed ibn Jaber al-Sabah, had agreed to the appointment of an elected council. The council had been duly elected. Then it fought the Sheikh, desiring more and more control of administration and expenditure—especially of expenditure. The Sheikh, who liked things as they were and thought that Kuwait had been going on comfortably, fought back. The council tried to raise the people. The people were apathetic, on the whole, and certainly not interested in lost causes. They loved intrigue as much as the next man, but they were in no mood to be shot for it, particularly not at the bidding of businessmen whose motives seemed suspiciously in their own interests. The greater part of the best men of Kuwait were at sea.

Trouble dragged on and on. If the situation in Kuwait showed signs of settling down in the lethargy natural to any well-run Gulf town, some mysterious person in a privately controlled radio station in Baghdad hurriedly heaped coals on the fire. If there was no fire, he started one. He was indefatigable: for him there could be no peace in Kuwait. He did not want peace. Who he was and what business it was of his, I did not know nor did the Arabs; but he did much harm. Trouble which might otherwise have died down continued to simmer. Conspirators lurked in coffee shops, round merchants' courtyards, in the inner sanctums of lesser sheikhs. One day a local firebrand overstepped the mark and, with his eloquence, raised the rabble to a mild show of interest in what was going on. They began to demand their "rights." They badgered the Sheikh, more for the fun of the thing than with any real animosity. At heart they really liked their Sheikh, who was a good man; but one does not get the chance of badgering a sheikh every day. It was good to be able to bawl in the *suq*, "Oh Sheikh, how about spending some money on this and that?" It didn't matter much what the this and that was. It was nice to yell at authority.

The Sheikh had to put up with a good deal of badgering. The Sheikh was at heart a quiet and peaceful man who desired nothing better than to live at peace with his subjects. But the firebrand would not let him. In the end the firebrand became unbearable. He was arrested, beaten, and led off through the *suq* to the jail. As he was being led through the *suq* some of his friends tried to raise a riot to free him. The ringleaders were Yusuf Murzook, a shipowner, and Mohamed Kitami, a nakhoda who had been given a shore job by the elected council of state and was now showing his gratitude. The Sheikh's guards, as they took the prisoner through the *suq*, repeatedly warned Murzook and the others not to interfere, but since neither of them paid any attention, they at last opened fire. They shot Murzook in the foot but they killed Kitami. This was unintentional; they had no desire to kill him. They fired as a warning, and he jumped in front of a bullet. Shot in the abdomen, he fell mortally wounded. The mob then ran, and for a moment or two nothing could be seen but the dust of their flying feet. Afterwards a vast number of sandals, cloaks, and headcloths remained in the covered street of the *suq*—sandals, cloaks, headcloths, and the dead body of Mohamed Kitami. But the citizens had fled.

That was the story of the "riot" in Kuwait in 1939. Doubtless the intrigues continued, for many of the ringleaders had escaped to Iraq; but the citizens—the Persians, the coolies, the descendants of the Africans and the Beduin—had fled. They did not return that day to reclaim their sandals.

"It was," Hamed bin Salim said, "no place for a self-respecting seafaring man." He was glad that he had been at sea. Who wielded the power in Kuwait was, he went on, of no interest or importance to him: for his life would always be at sea, making money for the merchants. If any chose to be shot down in the dust of the Kuwait *suq*, that was their business. But he and the others were sorry that if any one had to die, it was Mohamed Kitami. For Mohamed was the brother of our friend Abdulla Kitami, and he was well known to them all.

When Nejdi came back he was full of gloom at the news, for Mohamed Kitami had been a friend. He was more gloomy at the sad fate which had overtaken Mubarak the Suri, our "pilot" for the Rufiji. Mubarak had been fined one thousand shillings by the court at Utete, and Nejdi had had to help to pay it. What sort of intrigue had gone on behind all this I was not told, but it was easy enough to guess. It seemed to me that Mubarak had been lucky to escape with a fine. He had been given his sambuk back, and was then on his way to Zanzibar from Salale, a sadder, wiser, but not a reformed man. Nejdi, in addition to this feeling of deep gloom and a great capacity for finding fault with all that had been done with the vessel, brought back from Dar-es-Salaam some washed-out, characterless photographs of himself which he exhibited to me as masterpieces of the photographer's art which I should do well to study. If the reason for his stay in Zanzibar had been to collect passengers for our return voyage to Arabia, he had wasted his time, for he had secured only three Swahili schoolteachers. These he had undertaken to carry for nothing, as a favor to the Seyyid Sulieman.

What interested me more than the politics of distant Kuwait and the fate of pole-stealing Mubarak the Suri was the dispute going on ashore in Zanzibar between two or three baggalas of Suri, and five sambuks of Somali. This at one time showed promise of being an excellent engagement: that it came to comparatively little was not the fault of the Suri, for they wanted the Somali to come outside in their sambuks and have a battle royal on the sea. For two or three exciting days it seemed that this encounter might really be staged, but in the end it petered out in a minor riot behind the fish market. It was too bad. I should have liked to see a clean fight on the sea.

This dispute with the Somali had begun over a slight misunderstanding about money. In this case, Italian money, a parcel of paper lire, which the Suri had collected in Haifun but could not smuggle out because they were too closely watched. For a consideration, the Somali in a near-by sambuk had undertaken to do the smuggling. The Suri showed them how to go about it. They had to put the wads of notes in hollow pieces of bamboo, then put the cane into ghee jars, and fill the jars with ghee. No customs officer would ever detect a wad of lire in a jar of rancid ghee. The Suri delivered the notes to the Somali, together with the bamboo and the ghee jars, and then sailed away in their baggala. After some time, they met the Somali in Zanzibar. The Somali were very rich. They explained, with apologies, that they were unable to hand over the lire because the bamboo which the Suri had given them had disintegrated in the ghee. So, apparently, had the lire. It was an accident profoundly deplored.

Perhaps it was, but the Somali had more reason to deplore having thought of it, for the Suri fell upon them in the crowded Zanzibar *suq*, and beat them up in the most thorough fashion. They would have made an end of them had not the Swahili constables foolishly intervened. The constables, however, were in duty bound to intervene, for it looked as though a major riot might rapidly develop if they did not. The rival factions of Somali and Suri were led to their longboats by the waterfront, and told that if they came ashore again to continue their brawling they would be imprisoned. This did not deter the Suri, who thought highly of the Zanzibar jail; and it did not bother the Somali. What did bother them was the reflection that there were a great many more Suri than there were Somali in Zanzibar, and if they came ashore again there might be a massacre. So they retired to the outer edge of the native anchorage, in their mean sambuk, and waited until the rest of the Somali fleet were loaded and ready to join them.

That was the state of hostilities when our *Triumph* had come back from Salale. There were the Somali, glowering in a corner of the anchorage. And there were the Suri sambuks and baggalas massing round them, imploring them to come outside and fight where no constabulary could interfere. I watched with interest for several days to see if the Somali would accept this sporting challenge, while the whole anchorage looked on and a police launch patrolled to see that war did not break out in the harbor. Six Somali sambuks were at length assembled, their tall, lean sailors as noisy, impetuous, and impertinent as ever. They had very large crews but their crews included many boys. So did the Suri. They were fairly evenly matched. Day after day the Suri baggalas, loaded and ready for the voyage home to Sur, moved through the fleet and fetched up to their sailing moorings alongside the Somali. There were five of them—five Suri, six Somali. It should have been a fair contest. Morning, noon, and night the anchorage resounded to the threats and imprecations of the warlike Suri imploring the Somali to come outside and fight. Day after day the Somali stayed, and would not go. Days passed. A week passed. Still the Somali stayed grimly at their anchors. Ship after ship of the Arab, Persian, and Indian homeward-bound fleets had been obliged to sail with the issue still undecided, giving up their chance of seeing the fun. Two of the Suri baggalas sailed at length, on the tenth morning, to see if the lessened numbers would tempt the Somali out. But the Somali knew that those Suri were probably only waiting outside, somewhere in the narrow waters of the Zanzibar channel. They stayed at their anchors.

Meanwhile the southwest season settled in with more and more determination. Sometimes strong winds and rain drove across the native anchorage. It became obvious that neither the Arabs nor the Somali could wait much longer. The Suri outside must have been driven away by that time, in the fresh squalls, if they were not lurking in Pemba, and the authorities would have something to say if they tried that. At last the Somali made a dash for it in a squall one rainy, blowy night, running for their lives out of the harbor when the remaining Suri were too busy tending their anchors to observe their departure. In the morning there was a great wailing from the Suri and, though they immediately gave chase, they had slight chance then of bringing the Somali to action. They dared not follow them into an Italian port, and with the strong southwester blowing, they could not hope to overtake them earlier. It was too bad.

On this second visit to Zanzibar we stayed two weeks, during which very little happened. We sold some twenty score light rafters from the top of our cargo, being offered a satisfactory price for them by a local Indian, and we tried again to sell *Afra*, which, somewhat battered from her hard work in Rufiji, was beached and cleaned. But no buyers came, and eventually we had to sail and leave her on the beach, in charge of the ship's agent. Our crew were given a few shillings each and refreshed themselves in the time-honored manner, though now that most of their smuggling was done and they could raise funds in no other way, they were very careful of their shillings. Not many of them went to the local ladies. Instead, the sailors bought cheap manufactured things, most of which came from Japan, as presents for their families at home. Babies' rattles and simple toys were favorites, as well as safety razors for themselves, cheap pocket torches, and cigarette lighters. Dishes and small cups were also popular, and one of the most sought after was flavoring for sherbet.

In the Rufiji and at Zanzibar the sailors had been busy in their spare time bottling lemon juice, which they squeezed with wooden pegs out of the juicy lemons which were everywhere available, preserving the juice with a pinch of salt. We had hundreds of these bottles of lemon juice stowed everywhere it could be stowed. This was the crew's own venture, and the customs of the dhows made it necessary to find space for them. Throughout our stay in the Rufiji, ragged Swahili had brought canoe-load after canoe-load of lemons, and at Zanzibar they were plentiful and cheap. A canoe-load could be bought for a shilling or two. All hands joined in the work. Empty bottles, corks, and even packing cases had been brought from Aden. The bottles were cleaned out roughly in the river water. The sailors, now and again, sucked a lemon with some salt on it, as fruit. I tried one of these salted lemons. It tasted abominably to me and was not in the least like fruit, but the sailors enjoyed them. Lemon juice would bring three or four annas a bottle in the bazaar at Kuwait, where it would be diluted and used in the making of sherbet. It was a good business.

Zanzibar harbor during this second visit was a very busy place, with the native fleet assembling for the voyage home—Somalis bound back to Haifun and Berbera and Eritrea; Suri loading for the Mahra coast and Sur; Persians loading for anywhere; Indians coming up from Madagascar and elsewhere, putting in for water before beginning the long run to Bombay or Goa, or the Gulf of Cutch; Kuwaiti, homeward bound from the Rufiji to the Persian Gulf and the Gulf of Oman; little double-ended things from the Hadhramaut and round Seihut way, which looked as if they were barely fit for river sailing. One morning I counted seventy-two dhows of one sort and another at the anchorage, not counting Swahili and Lamu boats. At least half these seventy-two ships had waterlines less than fifty feet long, and they were all very deeply laden. However, they would probably arrive.

When we had been in Zanzibar ten days and the sailors were beginning to feel restive about the delay in setting off for home, we took on board a cargo of coconuts and stowed it among the mangrove poles. We loaded also some bags of cloves, a few boxes of soap, several drums of coconut oil, and a hundred cases of vermicelli. With all this on board and the longboat stowed on top, we sailed from Zanzibar in the early evening of Friday, April 14, bound, as far as I could gather, towards Muscat direct, for orders. Bedar's baggala *Bedri*, next to us in the anchorage, was to sail with us, and they were getting the sail on her as we came by. We carried a hurricane lamp at the flagstaff aft to show the *Bedri* where we were, and ran through the English Pass with a fair wind from the south. We had taken aboard the three Swahili schoolteachers, and the Seyyid Sulieman had kissed them good-by. He also kissed Nejdi, who appeared much affected. Abdulla had been sent in a baggala to Lamu, to make his way back to the Persian Gulf by way of Mogadishu to clear up our debts there on his way. Going out of Zanzibar we were thirty souls all told, and I hoped we should arrive in Arabia.

In the morning we were off the northern end of Pemba, with that island in sight on our starboard hand and the coast of Tanganyika to port. There was no sign of the *Bedri*, and we did not see her throughout the passage to Arabia. The breeze was fresh from the southwest, and we bowled along handsomely towards the north, in spite of our heavy cargo. The sailors spent a busy morning restowing the coconuts from Zanzibar and flaking the cables down on top of them, along the cargo on the main-deck, to keep them in position, and stowing the cases of vermicelli and other things in nooks and crannies among the poles in the space beneath the poop. Our vermicelli was an odd lot bought by Nejdi at bargain prices through a friend of the Seyyid Sulieman's, and he hoped to sell it at a good profit in Muscat or Kuwait. It was part of an overstock, laid in at Zanzibar for sale to the Swahili during Ramadhan. Our other odds and ends—the mottled soap, some cheap and highly perfumed soap, the drums of coconut oil, the lemon juice, the bags of cloves—would, I was assured, all find ready market. Indeed, we began to use one sack of the cloves at once, and from that time onwards our coffee was always flavored with cloves. I did not care for this, but the Arabs seemed to like it.

We still had our Rufiji thatching over the bench aft. It had been put on well and it served to keep off the rain so long as the southwest wind was with us. The sailors made themselves a rough shelter by night by throwing the clew of a sail across the lower mizzen yard, and there they lay between the longboat and the cutter, on top of the cables. The cables were of tough coir and could not have made satisfactory mattresses, but the men slept soundly and were content. When we set the mizzen they had no shelter, but we did not set that sail until the rainy weather had ended.

At first the wind blew fresh, and we bowled along making perhaps eight knots. Nejdi said it was ten, but I doubted that, and there was no way of measuring. Nineteen hours out of Zanzibar, we were abeam of Mombasa, which was not bad going, but I found it difficult to accept Nejdi's optimistic forecast of sixteen days to Muscat. I was surprised to notice that he made no attempt to lay off a course for the Gulf of Oman direct, and make for the place, as I should have done had I been in command of a ship on that voyage. Instead, we hugged the coast, exactly as we had done on the passage down. We had come down from Arabia with Africa on our right. Now we went back with Africa on our left: and that was the only difference in our "navigation." From Zanzibar to the Gulf of Oman direct is perhaps 2200 miles: by coasting up we should add at least 300 to that total. Nejdi said that he certainly would coast the whole way. That was the way to go, he said, as if it were a road: he knew no nonsense about going direct. He knew the way, he said. If he wandered off onto the Indian Ocean, who knew what might happen to the ship? All the Arabs coasted on that voyage. They coasted down from Arabia, and coasted back again. It was not merely a matter of navigation (for he was not able to discover his ship's position by any means other than visual): he knew the winds and the currents along the coast, he said,

On the halliards

and they were more important than saving a few hundred miles. What did these few miles matter?

I had to confess that there was something in this argument. Indeed, there might have been a great deal. By coasting up, Nejdi certainly played for safety. His big boom, with the heavy cargo she was carrying, could easily founder any time a few seas came over her rail. If she did that, it was as well to be able to pull the longboat in to the land. Nejdi said we should coast as far as Ras Asir and then run on towards the coast of South Arabia, passing inside Socotra, as we had on the way down, and then coast along the Hadhramaut, the Mahra, and the Oman coasts to Ras al-Hadd. I expressed my surprise that, after all their centuries of ocean wandering, an Arab nakhoda like Nejdi should have no knowledge of astronomical navigation, though he had spent his life making long voyages. Well, he said, he coasted to India as well as to Africa: it was all coasting. But he regretted the decline in the Arab art of navigation and confessed as much that night. He blamed it on the bad influence of the Europeans who, with their cut-throat competition, had left the Arabs only coasting trades.

We very nearly foundered the second night out from Zanzibar, and I was glad then that we were near the coast. The first night we had a touch of what might be in store for us, when the ship passed through a few rain squalls in the confused seas off Malindi. We began to roll heavily, and to slop the tops of a few seas aboard over either rail as she rolled—nothing heavy, but enough to keep the sailors busy at the well every hour. Sprays broke over the poop when a cross sea got up and smashed at the vessel, but there was no weight in them. It was a confused sea but not a dangerous one. Once in a fresh squall, a sea lifted the cutter in its falls and threatened to tear it away: it was hurriedly taken inboard and stowed on top of the cargo. With the ship's heavy rolling, the chests on the poop took charge, and careened about like a lot of unsecured guns. *"Allah karim,"* said Nejdi, smiling, but the three Zanzibar schoolteachers were plainly scared, and Hamed bin Salim looked anxious. Our bailing system was working at full pressure for three hours while the tops of seas came aboard, but the wind gradually subsided and we worked through the area of confused seas. It was a meeting place of the currents, and the sea is always bad at such places. The ship rolled and pitched violently under these conditions, and the mast worked horribly on its step—so much, indeed, that in the heavier squalls the mainyard was half lowered to ease the strain on sail and mast. But the ship behaved very well, all things considered. She was all right. Her vulnerability, then as always, was owing to her overload and the lack of elementary precautions on the part of her builders, master, and crew. The gear stood and we suffered no damage that night, beyond the wetting of several of the chests.

I wondered in the morning how the old *Bedri* had fared and, when we did not see her, feared that she might have gone down. She was even more heavily laden than we were, and she had been carrying heavy cargoes half a century before the *Triumph* was thought of. The trouble with these big dhows, as I saw it, was that they could not stand up to anything like a heavy sea, and it seemed to me that they would quickly disintegrate in anything like weather—in anything like, say, the conditions of the Roaring Forties, the North Atlantic, or the great storms of far southern seas with which European square-rigged ships had always to contend. Their one huge sail, though a glorious puller in ideal conditions of continuous trade wind without squalls, is a definite source of danger under any other conditions. It is a poor sort of ship which dares keep the seas only with an assured continuance of azure conditions.

The very next night, somewhere off Kisimayu, we ran again into the same bad conditions of a cross sea with rain and heavy squalls. Again the squalls were not really heavy for a well-found and wholly seaworthy ship. I could have carried the topgallants in the *Joseph Conrad* through all of them. They were bad-tempered squalls, with lightning and much noise, and a cross sea ran eerily throwing up soapy crests which caught queer lights from the flashes of lightning. It was worse than the previous experience. In a heavier squall than usual, about midnight, the wind shifted suddenly to the northwest with vicious rain. The thunder boomed and the lightning lit the decks, and the tops of the seas breaking over the rail—they were only sprays—threw up a greenish light. The wind had been in the southwest, working to the west'ard and freshening. We knew for once where the ship was, for we had seen the lights of Kisimayu shortly after sunset, forty-eight hours out of Zanzibar. The westerly wind brought rain, and in one of these rain squalls the wind jumped twelve points. It was a freak squall, and a really nasty one for the moment. As in all lateen-rigged craft the tack of the sail had to be to windward, and this sudden shift made it necessary to dip the yard. This was always a work of difficulty, even under good conditions. The conditions now were anything but good. To dip the yard, the great sail bent to it had to be allowed practically to get out of control, for the yard had to be brought in vertically to the mast and swung across to the other side, while the whole

of the sail took a turn in itself over the yard, the mainsheet going over
—or, more properly, right round—to the other side, at the same time as
the tack was dipped across. This was a maneuver comparable to trying to
turn over the tarpaulin of a huge haystack in a heavy gale, with rain or, if
such a thing were possible, to swinging the wings of a big monoplane
end-for-end in flight. It was like turning a very large circus tent inside
out, in a minor hurricane, with very few ropes on the canvas to control
it.

The maneuver on this occasion was further complicated by the rolling and pitching of the vessel, by the obvious danger she was in of sailing
straight under, by the absence of light other than the spasmodic and
frightening lightning flashes, and by the constant and extremely loud singing of the crew, who made so much noise, even in that predicament, that
they could hear no orders. The wind howled and the rain lashed and the
tops of sprays dashed aboard. The chests on the poop took charge again,
for their extremely temporary lashings during the previous evening's
blow off Malindi had been cast off. The longboat and the cutter rolled
precariously on top of the cargo. Loose coconuts and long mangrove
poles rolled about, and there was scarcely a secure place to work on
board. The binnacle lamps blew out, as they invariably do on such occasions (not only in Arab vessels); the sail took charge, which was under-
standable when both its sheet and tack had to be let go, and it had no
other gear. The mast creaked and groaned with its working: the canvas
thundered and roared with its wild flappings, and Nejdi roared even
louder. Through all this the scampering sailors still sang, their singing
punctuated now and again by the shrieks of some poor victim who had
been struck by a loose mangrove pole, or the curses of a mariner who had
slipped on a coconut. Yimid, my monkey, had got loose and scampered
to the top of the lateen yard, where he hung chattering madly.

To make things worse, the mainsheet carried away and the whole
area of the great mainsail now flapped round mast and yard so that, while
it roared and crashed and cannonaded and tore itself into pieces, the yard
could not be lowered or the sail got down. The ship rolled and pitched,
and the sea got up so viciously that I was sure she must be overwhelmed,
but the *Triumph* seemed to fight back at that sea as if she knew she was
in peril and was fighting for her life. As the foaming sea dashed at her on
one side she raised herself towards it to shoulder it off, so that instead of a
fatal wall of water thundering aboard nothing but spray dashed harm-
lessly over, though the spray reached halfway up the mainmast. Again,

Sambuk outward-bound

as she dug her long nose deep into a trough and another sea came up to take her on the quarter, she rose to that, avoiding it—always avoiding the worst weight of the seas like a real thoroughbred, never permitting them to overwhelm her or even to get a part of their real weight aboard. God help us if they did!

Still the rain hissed across the contorted face of the waters and the sail flapped and thundered, but that, indeed, may have been our saving. For the sail, blowing itself out, let go its fatal hold of mast and yard and we could at last get the yard lowered, right down to the top of the cargo, and the remnants of the sail unbent. With the sail lowered we did not bend another, but lay like that through the night. The sudden freak change in the wind which had put us in such danger did not last long, and it went round quickly to the west'ard, and blew more quietly. This was all right, for we could then lie and drift off the land. About four o'clock in the morning, when the sky was beginning to gray with the dawn's first light, Nejdi grew worried lest we should drift out of sight of land, and he gave her back the smallest mainsail. We set that, and sailed on, for the weight was gone from the wind then and there were no more squalls. We had gone, too, from the cross seas, and the sea ran true from west-southwest if still a little lumpy. The ship settled to a steady lilt and dip and roll, and we wandered quietly along while the sailors spread the remnants of the blown-out main across the decks to dry, and Yimid, who had remained there all night, chattered merrily at the masthead.

After that we had no more bad weather, and we never again lay hove-to without canvas. I was interested to see the ship's behavior under those conditions. It was the nearest approach to bad weather we ever had. She lay-to very well, with the helm eased down and no canvas showing. Her high poop kept her shoulder to the wind, and she behaved quite well in the sea. She no longer even wet her decks, and though she was without canvas she was not out of control. She drifted surprisingly little—perhaps five or six miles to leeward through the night. I feared that with the canvas taken from her she might just wallow in the trough, as more than one Cape Horner of my acquaintance would have done, deep-loaded as she was and in relatively the same conditions. But she kept out of the trough, head to sea, and lay very quietly, as a ship hove-to should. I thought the more of her and of her builders, after that night's experience. Though she was in effect nothing but a pile of iron-fastened teak put together on the beach at Kuwait by a group of shipwright carpenters who could not read a plan, I knew that these men could build good ships. While they can build them as well as that, I hope no one will give them plans.

Nejdi was cautious the next night, lowering the lateen main and going on through the night under only the jib, the tack of which was shifted to the heel of the stemhead. Under this light piece of canvas we rolled on quietly with the stars out and the black sea all gone down, and we yarned of ships and storms round the chests on the poop. The sunset prayer that night was made a special occasion. Nejdi summoned the sailors to the poop to stand in a line beside him, while Hamed bin Salim led the prayers in front. Beside Nejdi on the one hand stood Ismael the musician, and on the other the helmsman Ebrahim. They offered up extra prayers that evening, and Hamed remained seated on the deck facing Mecca long after all the others had done. From that time onwards, we had communal prayer on the poop night and morning, though our Swahili schoolteachers were very irregular in their attendance. This habit of praying was of great importance to the Arabs, and none of them would have thought of missing a prayer, or of coming to the prayers not properly cleaned, but they did not always rid themselves of all worldly thoughts during their numerous devotions. Sometimes some of them would crack a brief joke while Hamed intoned a melodious verse, or the serang would sneak a quick puff at the nakhoda's hookah while the gang were prostrate in one of the attitudes of prayer. These were unusual occurrences: prayer was generally solemn. It must be a difficult thing to rid one's mind of all worldly thoughts at the muezzin's call five times a day, seven days a week.

We talked that night of a host of things, as we always did, Nejdi's quick mind flitting from subject to subject and dealing deeply with none of them, except politics, in which I was not interested. Talking with Nejdi at any time was apt to degenerate into listening to a monologue punctuated by loud suckings at the hookah: on politics, and all allied topics, his talk became a sermon. His views may have been sound and, since I had none of my own, I did not dispute them. On some other subjects he was a strangely ignorant man. He denied, for instance, that the world was round, and he had little conception of geography away from the seas he knew. He had little knowledge of the Atlantic or of the Americas, though he had heard of Paris (which he called Baris) having, as a child, seen pearl-buyers from there. He knew London by name, and most of the countries of Europe, and a surprising amount about their politics. He had very little knowledge of the stars, and almost none of natural phenomena. One evening we were chatting as usual, and the subject turned on the powers and properties of lightning. Lightning, I said, in response to his question, was nothing but stored-up electricity freed from clouds in the sky. At this Nejdi laughed uproariously. Electricity! He laughed. He called it "trick," as did the sailors. That comes in torches made in Germany and Japan: the lightning is God's. Ha, ha, ha! Such a good joke as that he could not keep to himself, and my remarks on the mysteries of "trick" were bawled across the Indian Ocean to every Arab ship we spoke. And that, by the time we had been drifting off Ras Haifun for a week, was quite a number.

We lost what little we'd had of the southwest monsoon somewhere north of Warsheikh, on the Benadir coast, and after that had nothing but light airs and calms. Though Nejdi liked a favoring wind, he wanted no part of the SW monsoon when it really set in. Daily we saw anything between ten and twenty Arab craft, all bound to the northwards, and sometimes Persians and Indians. We were one of a great armada sailing homewards from Zanzibar, and often we were treated to glorious views of the big dhows. To my surprise, the *Triumph* overhauled every ship we saw, including both Indians and Persians, though some of the Indians were showing a lot of kites, and I had never before thought our boom particularly speedy. Perhaps the cleaning at Kwale had helped her, or perhaps she was at her best deep-loaded in these light airs. By that time we had every sail aloft that we could set, which was only three—the largest mainsail, set from the extended main yard; the largest mizzen; and a jib set on a boom lashed along the stemhead. One day we stepped the mast of the longboat just for'ard of the wheel—there was a step in the deck for it—and set the longboat's mainsail there, but this was more trouble than it was worth. The mast carried away, and we did not set the sail again. We saw several Persians carrying a third mast of this kind, with the longboat's sail. Hamed said it was an old custom but it did not really help much. It helped the balance of the canvas, and consequently the steering, when the ship was carrying a big jib. Many of the Indians and a few of the Persians sported flying kites of lateen tops'ls above their mainyards, but I never saw a Kuwait ship which set this sail. Nejdi preferred to put his faith in larger and larger mainsails and did not bother with kites. They

Getting the anchor

only made work, he said, annoyed the crew, and disturbed the nakhoda's rest. Give him few sails and big: not a number of sails, small. That was all very well in the Indian Ocean, running before the northeast monsoon or before the first of the southwest, before its strength has come.

At this stage of the voyage Nejdi took things more easily than he had ever done before, and kept watch only by day. Hamed the muallim kept watch at night while Nejdi slept. The bad weather was over, and most dangers were past. We had only to sail to the north in sight of the coast, keeping always to the northeast, and in the course of time we should come to Ras al-Hadd and the Gulf of Oman. Then we swung to the left, still following the coast, and a little way up-Gulf was Muscat. Visibility was good, and the weather perfect. It was neither hot nor cold, and the nights were ideal for sleeping. We took down the thatch over the bench aft and stored it for sale in Kuwait, and after that slept in the open beneath the stars. With the end of the rains our mangrove began to dry out and the ship rode lighter, and sailed better. Kaleel the carpenter, with *Afra* left in Zanzibar and the longboat repaired after its strenuous work in the Rufiji, took his ease for the first time on the voyage, and the sailors did nothing but make rope out of coir shipped at Zanzibar, and the necessary tending of the sails. Kaleel could do little round the decks when they were beneath six feet of mangrove poles, and in any case the ship was in good order. We still had some spare ribs and balks of wood for boatbuilding, left over from *Afra*, and before long the idea occurred to Nejdi that he would like a small boat for Hussein, his son. Hussein was his eldest son, eight years old. It was time he knew something of the sea. So the chests were cleared from the starboard side of the poop, and Kaleel began to build a small *shewe*, a fleet-lined, pretty cutter, about sixteen feet long out of *Afra*'s spare ribs. Hussein and Nejdi's other sons, of whom there seemed a very large number, would have the use of the small boat during the summer months, and when the boom went out again she would take it down to Lamu or Zanzibar for sale. She would take Hussein too, for it was considered time that he was getting on with his seamanship.

Kaleel went about his boatbuilding in a businesslike way, first putting down the keel on a bed of small blocks, raised slightly from the deck, and then attaching a stempost and the stern. His next move was to add two bottom planks on each side, forcing them into shape with wedges and lashings to the deck. Then he put in the ribs—half of them first and the other half when the planking was finished. But first he had to saw the planks out of a log of Indian wood. So far as I saw he made no measurements and never planned anything: he simply went ahead and built the boat by eye. His tools were an adze, which was used most, an Indian saw or two, an Indian bow-type drill, a hammer, and a primitive plane. All day long, from immediately after the dawn prayer until time for the sunset prayer, he worked on that boat, with Nejdi watching and criticizing, and a small sailor to help. All through that voyage, Kaleel worked harder than any one else on board, but I gathered that he was considered not so much one of the crew as Nejdi's personal boatbuilder. His reward included not only his share in the ship's earnings, but an agreed proportion of the proceeds of the sale of his boats. Alone among the crew, too, he kept no night watch. He rolled himself in his sleeping carpet about nine o'clock every evening, and slept there soundly until Sultan announced the dawn prayer. He turned out for important all-hands jobs, such as getting in the sail that night off Malindi and again in the blow off Kisimayu.

We wandered on pleasantly towards the north, going more slowly the more northerly we came, for it was too early for the southwest wind to have reached up there. No matter: when it came it was apt to set in blustery and to blow really hard, with bad conditions of squalls and bad visibility. Our aim was to reach the Gulf ahead of the monsoon, and so avoid bad weather. We caught a few dolphins, which were a pleasant addition to the morning meal: at sunset we always had rice and the Indian corn called dhall. Made with a stew of chilis and other things not so easily recognized, this was not bad. I was never hungry. Nejdi had bought a sack of onions in Zanzibar and we had onions with the dhall. Sometimes he got old Yusuf to make an onion soup, flavored with chilis and dhall; and the fish was roasted in the ashes of the wood fires. We fared well. With no passengers other than our three schoolteachers, there was no congestion and life was very pleasant on board. Day succeeded day in a pleasing routine of sunshine and easy labor, while I worked on a dwindling number of patients, studied Arabic out of divers books which never agreed with the spoken word, yarned with Nejdi, watched Kaleel at his work, and learned all I could while the coast of Africa slipped lazily by and our lateen-rigged armada sailed leisurely up that sunlit sea.

It was a good life, and this was the best part of the voyage. We still had several bad fever cases from the Rufiji, and these lay in their cloaks on some sacking in the shade of the longboat. I gave them quinine, and the bad ones atebrin: they recovered, in due course, probably none the more rapidly for my treatment. But they were grateful for the medicines.

There were still many, particularly among the pearl-divers, with bad ulcers and other skin wounds, and one or two with bad heads. I was busy at my amateur doctoring and, not for the first time, wished I really knew something of that art.

One morning, when we were somewhere south of Ras Haifun, meandering slowly northeastwards with a quiet air, we picked up Abdulla Kitami's small boom. It was hazy that dawn, with the Somaliland coastline perhaps ten miles away. We were one of a fleet of eight Arab ships drifting along very quietly, the bigger fellows without much way and the small ones, such as the Hadhramaut double-enders and a bedeni or two closer inshore, ghosting along very nicely. By mid-morning we were one among ten, and Nejdi declared the sail of a boom ahead to be Abdulla Kitami's, though it must have been eight miles away and nothing could be seen except the upper part of the sail. I knew Nejdi made no mistakes in his identification of Arab ships, especially from Kuwait: though how he could tell one boom from another at that distance I do not know: the differences between the vessels were extremely slight. I had to see any two booms close together before I could detect differences: Nejdi and his crew knew every boom in Kuwait five miles away. I suppose it was a matter of being reared with them, and knowing nothing else. I could do the same with square-rigged ships. So could Captain de Cloux, or any other grain-ship master, or mate. To Nejdi all other ships were confusingly alike, but he knew his dhows. The differences between one Kuwait boom and another were so slight, a slight variation in the cut of the sail, a minute difference in the angle of the stempost or the sternpost, different lashings on the lateen yards, that only an experienced Arab sailor could detect them.

But Nejdi could only recognize three kinds of steamer. They were *markobs gaz, markobs Strick*, and *fastmail*. A *markobs gaz* was an oil tanker to Nejdi, any vessel with engines aft: a *markobs Strick*, so named from the Strick Line steamers, which trade to Basra, was any cargo vessel: all passenger steamers were *fastmails*. He was familiar with oil-tankers because the road from Abadan leads past Kuwait and he had seen them all his life: *fastmails* were the Bombay-Persian Gulf traders of the British India company.

The wind came in from the east, a pleasant sailing breeze, and we began rapidly to overhaul the Kitami boom. Nejdi set a course straight for her and looked carefully to the trim of all his sails. He was a pastmaster at the trimming of sails, which is half the sailing-ship master's art. In that ancient calling, he was, in his own way, as good as de Cloux. I could give him no higher rating. De Cloux in the Cape Horners *Herzogin Cecile* or *Parma*, Nejdi in a dhow, were at the top of their respective professions. Now he watched the trim of main and mizzen and set a larger jib, and as the breeze freshened we dashed on. By noon we had Abdulla's boom close ahead and shortly afterwards were abeam. Nejdi spoke her from the poop, and the sailors from the forecastle head. He was eight days from Lamu, Abdulla Kitami said: the sailors said they were ten. Actually they were fourteen. They were bound towards Muscat for orders, as we were, and had nothing but calms and head winds. They had seen nothing of the *Bedri*, about which we felt some anxiety, fearing that those dirty nights off Malindi and Kisamyu might have finished her. That day we were only seven days from Zanzibar ourselves, so that we were certainly making a better passage than they were.

The small boom looked very well as we sailed by, plunging along in the blue sea under her two great sails, her lateen yards waving like willows in the wind and her canvas of pure white swelled out beautifully. Now and then, as she pitched into the crest of a sea, a roll of foam turned back from her low bow or swept along her wet sides, and her wake stretched away straight and smooth. We saw a dozen Suri passengers on her deck-cargo, and eight fishing lines trailed astern. We sailed on ahead, and then Nejdi eased the sheets, and put the cutter over to pull back and visit his friend. At sunset, with us close by the Kitami boom for company, he sent the cutter back asking for his photographs, of which he was inordinately proud, and the date, which no one in the other ship knew. They did not, indeed, even know the month, having a vague idea that it had lately changed. In the day's last light, after the sun had set, the crews of the two ships prayed together, each aboard their own craft, and afterward Ismael regaled them with music. Some time before midnight our boat came back with Nejdi and Abdulla Kitami, and it was announced that the two ships would sail together to Muscat. The two nakhodas yarned away most of the night, while Hamed looked after the *Triumph*, and the ex-slave Saud sailed Abdulla's boom.

In the morning we were well ahead of our sailing companion and had to take the mizzen and the jib off to give her a chance to catch up. Nejdi said disparaging things about Abdulla's boom which were returned in kind, but we still kept company. We had a big Persian boom in sight, hull-down, ahead and a Bombay kotia alee: we might have passed both these if our comrade had not delayed us. We spent a considerable part of the day dodging about the Indian Ocean with eased sheets in order not to leave his ship too far astern, much to the disgust of Hamed who said, very quietly, that Allah's good wind should not be wasted. I venture to suggest to Abdulla that his boom was somewhat slow, but he replied that she sailed very well indeed. Perhaps she was not doing her best just then because he was not aboard, and the sails were badly set.

Indeed, I said: what about the other fourteen days coming from Lamu? The sails were set and drawing very well: to suggest otherwise was a libel on poor Saud who was as good a muallim as sails from Kuwait.

Well, said Abdulla, cornered on that, and grinning, the sails were too small and he had no money to buy larger. He swore also that his boom did not leak but, unfortunately, just at that moment his sailors began to bail out water and kept at it for the next half-hour. They hauled up skin after skin all that time. Abdulla said it must be rain. It had not rained for a week. Then he said the buckets were half full. It is a good sailor who sees no fault in his own ship; and I did not blame Abdulla. He lied about the performance of his vessel cheerfully, as a good sailor should, and refused to believe that she had any faults or even that our *Triumph* was faster. At that we sailed two rings around him, though he stood on the poop and shouted to his little boom, "Come on! Come on!" Having sailed the rings round him, we took him back to his slowcoach in our cutter and left him aboard, promising to carry any letters he might like to send to Muscat. He grinned, and we parted friends. By the following morning his little boom was out of sight astern. So much for our keeping company.

Poor Abdulla Kitami! Throughout our visit, which had been a wholly pleasant interlude, there had been no mention of the shooting of his brother in the riot at Kuwait. He did not know about it and we did not tell him. He was greatly attached to his brother, and we did not wish to be bearers of bad news. He would find out, poor fellow, in good time, when he brought in his ship from the sea.

Chapter 14

THE PROPHET'S LANTHORN

FOR A WEEK we drifted about somewhere between Ras Haifun and Ras Asir, with variable winds and calms. Sometimes we lost sight of the land, but never for long: Nejdi soon put about and stood in again until we picked up the African coast. He did not like to be out of sight of land. This stage of the voyage, from the time we lost the boisterous squalls of the southwest monsoon until we reached Mutrah Bay in the Gulf of Oman fifteen days later, was the most pleasant of all. The ship wandered along upright and placid as a Balinese girl, with no motion other than her forward speed. If this was three knots or perhaps four, it worried nobody. The sea was flat and a glorious blue. The breaths of wind we had were from the east, anywhere from east-southeast to northeast, cooling the deck by day and making the nights restful. It was a good life. No voice was raised about our decks. There was no sound other than the sounds of toil—the carpenter's adze, Hamed's clink of Austrian thalers and Indian rupees as he cast up the accounts, the lilt of happy laughter from the boyish sailors forward, the creak of the rudder tackles and the slow, easy creaking of the masts. They were good days, each very like the last but none of them monotonous. Our food was good. We caught many fish, and we still had oranges and bananas from Zanzibar. We caught a shark one day, and ate that. I did not care for it, and I noticed that Yusuf Shirazi and Kaleel the carpenter, both of whom were Muslims of a different sect from the others, ate none of it. It was pig of the sea, Kaleel said, and this view I shared. Nejdi and the rest ate it cheerfully, made into a kind of mince meat with rice and smothered with hot ghee.

It was pleasant to be on board under conditions such as these, and, though I wanted to see Kuwait, I found myself not looking forward to the end of the voyage, for I did not know when I might make another one. I often turned over in my mind the project, half-born at Kwale, of saving an old baggala and sailing her over the North Atlantic to America, but after that Malindi night it seemed to me that it would be asking a lot of God to expect to accomplish such a voyage. Any one who wished to sail an Arab baggala, rigged and handled as the Arabs sailed her, over the North Atlantic or anywhere else away from her own Indian Ocean would need more help from God than any sailor has a right to expect. We sometimes talked for an hour or two in the early evenings about long voyages and the prospects of making an Atlantic voyage in a baggala, for Nejdi and all the sailors were very interested. At first inclined to be scornful, they soon became enthusiasts for the idea. Before long they were demanding that I should do it, Nejdi offering to come as pilot for Arabian waters, Hamed as salesman for a cargo of Persian carpets, Arab brassware and swords, and Kuwait carved chests he proposed to bring, and the sailors fired by the adventure and eager to try the lures of the harem material of America.

It was a good topic for a moonlight yarn, in the pole-laden boom with the quietness of the Indian Ocean all round. The moonlight seemed to give the decks an ordered and romantic beauty they lacked by the light of day, and the serang with his watch gathered round the bole of the mizzenmast, wrapped in their cloaks, assumed the grace of a noble painting. They yarned very quietly, about Kuwait, and ships, and Zanzibar nights, and they talked to me about the outside world. The helmsman sat on the steersman's chair like Buddha: the halliards and the tackled rigging gently creaked, and the peak of the great mainsail—old *Oud*, our largest —seemed very high. There was no light but the moon's, for we had no lamps: the silvered water parted before the raking bow silently as the ship sailed on, and for all her breadth of beam she trod the sea quietly and left very little wake.

As in all sailing-ships, each day could be trusted to provide its own diversion. Sometimes we went ship-visiting, whenever one of Nejdi's friends showed above the horizon. Sometimes there were minor accidents, as on the day that five of the sailors fell overboard. Falling overboard was not at all unusual, though this was the only occasion that so many went at once. There was a slight change of wind, and we could set the mizzen and make it draw. The sail was set and the five sailors were hauling the parral tackle tight, down to windward, when the tackle suddenly carried away and they fell over the side. They were standing on the chests on the poop, and there was nothing to prevent them from falling when the tackle carried away. There was no railing. So away they went—Sultan the prayer-announcer, Mohamed with the bad head, the thin Yusuf, Nasir the pearl-diver, and Jassim the cook, who had come along for exercise while his rice boiled. They had no chance: when the tackle went, they went. She was close by the wind at the time and Hassan, at the wheel, had been shaking her while they got a purchase on the tackle. This was well, for the ship in consequence had little way and did not sail on to leave our five behind. All five of them, laughing heartily, swam like fish alongside.

Down helm! Nejdi roared, and Hassan spun the wheel down until the sails were almost aback and the ship stood in her stride, while every spare end on the poop was thrown overboard. Inside half a minute the five had climbed aboard again, spluttering and laughing, none the worse for their dip. They did not trouble to change their clothes but went straight on with their work. This incident over, Nejdi went back to his bench aft and called for his "pickchure," the washed-out one taken by an Indian in Dar-es-Salaam, the contemplation of which never ceased to give him great satisfaction. Hamed bin Salim had slept through this minor accident, and the only member of the crew who showed any excitement was Yimid the monkey.

One of the ships we visited was the small boom of Mosa-Abdul-asiz, of Dabai on the Trucial coast. Mosa was a friend of Nejdi, and we had seen him in several ports. His boom was coming up from Dima, in the south of the Rufiji Delta, bound in the first instance towards Mukalla in the Hadhramaut. She was a poor, old little ship, not more than forty tons, but she made a brave show, with her great white mainsail full of the morning wind and the long lateen yards curved gracefully. She was a lofty little thing, with very sweet, fast lines, low in the water, with a keen bow, and a sheer that promised great seaworthiness, if only her hull could be trusted to remain in one piece. They spread a carpet for us above the cargo on the poop, and Mosa, welcoming us, offered refreshments of confectionery, clove-flavored coffee, sweet tea, and pieces of a Zanzibar orange, very green. We talked for half-an-hour or so, while our two ships drifted together. She had a very ancient compass in a huge binnacle which looked as though it had come from some old East Indiaman of two centuries ago. Perhaps it had. It was from a junkshop in Bombay, Mosa told me. He did not know how old it was. A hundred years? Very likely—perhaps even more than that. He had bought it with the ship, and the ship was forty years old. He had heard that it had been in at least two other

Becalmed

Kuwait ships before that. I often noticed very old pieces of maritime equipment of this kind in the poorer Arab dhows. I noticed also that the wheel, which was a handsome brass-bound piece of ship's furniture, bore the name of one of His Majesty's Indian shipbuilding establishments of long ago. Mosa had neither sextant nor charts, and this old compass was his only aid to navigation—that, an Australian insurance company's map of the world, and a well-thumbed copy of Isa Kitami's Arab directory of the Eastern seas. I was interested in this book and turned its pages: we had no copy. Nejdi said it was no use to him for all its information was available in better form on the charts, but it seemed from hurried inspection that the book contained some good descriptions of landmarks, if nothing else.

I liked Mosa, and liked his little ship. He was a plain man, and neat. He spoke very affectionately of his ship, and his crew seemed to like him, for they all squatted about very pleased while we were aboard. The little ship was spotlessly clean, and there was peace in all the lines of Mosa's open countenance. They told me afterwards he was one of the best smugglers in Dabai.

Ten days out from Zanzibar we found ourselves off Ras Asir, the eastern extremity of the African coast. The wind was light from southeast that day, which was fair, and we ran on towards Arabia. At sunset we came in sight of the picturesque islets of Abd-el-Kuri, to the west of Socotra. It was a beautiful red sunset such as only the Indian Ocean can show, and the rocks of Abd-el-Kuri were most picturesque. The moon was very bright that night, and we sailed on upright and slowly with the wind quiet, and the mizzen and jib both furled. We were bound then on our only real open-water crossing of the voyage. I was interested to watch how Nejdi laid off his course for the Arab coast: he could not very well miss it, so long as we went ahead. He took a rough bearing of Ras Asir—a thing I had not seen him do before—and transferred it, using his thumbs as parallel rules, to the chart. Then he looked at the point, said it was thirty-five miles away, and ruled off that distance, also with his thumbs. Next he looked over the side, announced, after a brief inspection, that the current was in our favor though how he knew that I don't know, and that we were making four knots. This I thought a gross overestimate. He added that we should see Abd-el-Kuri right ahead, in two and a half hours. We did: I put it down to an Act of God.

We were out of sight of land only one day. The African coast round Ras Asir is high, the islands of Socotra and Abd-el Kuri are high, and so is the coast of South Arabia. We had picked up the Hadhramaut coast, somewhere about Ras Sharma by the second evening after leaving Africa, and we remained in sight of land until we reached our destination.

We were welcomed back to Arabia by an eclipse of the moon. This simple phenomenon was predicted in my pocket diary but, imagining it to be as commonplace to the Arabs as it is to us, I had made no mention of it. It scared our sailors greatly, and during the whole of the time that the moon was obscured, they prayed, chanted, and beat on Indian drums in a state of superstitious alarm. It was the night of the full moon in May, 1939. Shortly after the sunset prayer, with the group of us assembled round the bole of the mizzenmast for the nightly yarn, Nejdi, moaning with a bad toothache, tossed on his carpet aft—it became obvious that something was wrong. Instead of the bright clear light of the moon the light on the sea was sickly, and green. A silence fell on the sailors. One after another of them stared at the heavens, watching with alarmed astonishment while the shadow of the earth fell across the moon's face. Sultan, our muezzin, noticing this, leaped up and dashed away to his high place for'ard where he began at once to call the faithful to instant prayer, very loudly. His call to prayer was the only sound then, for the night was quiet and the murmur of the ocean stilled. When Sultan called, the sailors rose and hurriedly performed their ablutions, quickly forming up in a line behind Hamed bin Salim on the poop. Nejdi, rousing himself with a groan from his carpet, hurried to join them, though the application of cold sea water to his neuralgic face must have been extremely painful.

When they were all lined up, facing Mecca, Hamed began to pray, and he prayed steadily for as long as the eclipse lasted. There was no fear about Hamed; his faith was in Allah and the shadow on the moon did not alarm him. But most of the others were exceedingly alarmed, and it was a strange experience for me, though I knew well enough what was happening and had been looking forward to seeing the eclipse all that day, to notice how the feeling of superstitious fear rapidly communicated itself to all hands. I had to fight against it myself, though I knew it was foolish. Several of the sailors, having offered up their prayers, dashed away forward and began to beat on the Indian drums. The Swahili schoolteachers, who also professed indifference to the proceedings and knew well enough the natural explanation of what was going on, prayed as fervently as the rest, though I believe that they prayed because they did not dare not to pray. They dared not be abstainers in that display of religious fervor, though they knew it to be based on fallacy. They had prayed very little on the way up the African coast, but now that we were off Arabia they

remembered they were Muslims. The nearer we came to Muscat, the more frequent and devout did their prayers become.

The eclipse lasted only a few moments, but it was a long time before the sailors settled down. A sigh of relief went up as the shadow finally moved from the face of the moon, and they offered up a new prayer in gratitude. Afterwards the watch gathered round the mizzenmast, to discuss in awed voices the phenomenon they had just seen. The moon, according to them, was the light of the Prophet, in the heavens. The shadow upon the Prophet's lamp was a threat to the Prophet, and through him to them: that was why they prayed. They asked me what I thought about it, and I told them that what they had seen was nothing but a plain eclipse of the moon, a predictable and very ordinary astronomical phenomenon to be explained by any schoolboy. But they were not impressed, though they asked for details. It was not an easy matter to explain an eclipse to those simple superstitious men, with their background of belief in *jinns* and the superstitious basis of so much of their religion. But I did my best and held forth with the textbook explanation.

They laughed uproariously at my ignorance, Nejdi with them. This was almost as good a yarn as my explanation of the "trick," which was stored in the clouds! They laughed and laughed, so much that they gradually forgot their superstitious dread. The moon, they said, was the Prophet's lamp in the heavens: every little Beduin child knew that. The shadows were caused by some enormous *jinn* attacking the Prophet's lamp: it was a sign, a test of them, to see that they observed it and answered with fervent prayer. They prayed to drive off the *jinn.* The slowly moving line of shadow across the moon's face was the advancing and retreating mouth of the *jinn:* others said it was the drying saliva where the *jinn* had vomited the lanthorn forth. The three Swahili were scornful of these curious beliefs. Yet they, too, had prayed as fervently as the rest, and had done their share of banging on the drums. The feeling of alarm which had gripped all hands was eerie and moving. I was glad when the eclipse was ended.

They never accepted my more or less scientific explanation. I should, they said, be telling them next that the moon was made of "trick," which was stored in clouds.

Day after day we slipped slowly along the coast of South Arabia, bound towards Ras al-Hadd and the Gulf of Oman. Nejdi's toothache grew worse and worse. It might have had a chance of improvement if he

Hamed bin Salim

had left his mouth alone for half an hour, but he would not. He kept poking it, like a small boy, as if he hoped that somehow he could torment it back into its normal condition. In Zanzibar a Japanese tooth-torturer had fitted him with a bridge (of sorts) of three gold teeth. The gold was not gold and the "teeth" were not teeth, but the gold looked like gold and Nejdi was happy. At least, when we left Zanzibar he was happy. But the poor workmanship of this unsatisfactory bridge soon caused an abscess beneath it; the gold teeth pressed terribly on the afflicted part and made it ten times worse. Nejdi could neither sleep, nor eat, and life must have been purgatory for the poor fellow. He scorned the simple remedies I suggested, such as hammering off those gold teeth with anything that came to hand: he poked at his mouth, filled it with hot ghee, smoked incessantly, and moaned. He did not fear any dental operation, but he could not bring himself to part with the golden teeth. They were a too greatly prized possession. Meanwhile his mouth grew worse and worse. His face was swollen, and his spirits grew lower and lower. One day he told me how he had suffered from toothache in a pearler in the Persian Gulf as a child and, after putting up with the pain for a few days, his father pulled the tooth out with a nail and a pair of pliers. Six men held his head, he said; the operation took two hours. He suggested that I should repeat it there and then, but the tooth he pointed out to me was a sound one and I was sure its removal, even if accomplished, would gain nothing. Those gold false teeth would have to be scrapped. Moreover, I had no instruments. Nejdi admitted that, after that experience as a child in the Gulf, he had had to spend two weeks in hospital with an infected jaw. I admired his courage, but I tried to impress on him the fact that an infected jaw was worse than any toothache, and we must remove the golden rubbish. No, he said; and continued to moan.

After some days more, however, he weakened. All right, he said, the gold teeth should go. But he must chisel them off himself. He did so, using the carpenter's chisel and the head of a small adze. It took two days— two days which must have caused him excruciating agony. But he got the teeth off, though he declared at once that it was a grievous error and made no difference to his state of pain. But his mouth cleared up at once, and within a day the worst of the pain had gone.

Nejdi made Yusuf stow the gold teeth carefully in his chest, and announced that he would have them put back properly in Basra or Bahrein.

By that time we were off Kuria Muria, an old signpost on the slave-ships' road from Zanzibar. The islands of Kuria Muria are beautiful in their own way. We sailed through them, passing near a mountain of rock whose worn strata were shadowed in the overhead sun so that it looked like a designed pattern, and at the sea level was half an acre of yellow sand flung at the cliff's edge, burning in the sun. Away on our port hand lay the high coast of southeast Arabia, hazy all day and defined only at sunset and sunrise. All round in the water sea life teemed, and far out to windward a Persian baggala sailed in company, homeward bound light from Hodeida in the Yemen towards Kungk.

Nejdi, recovered from his toothache, kept a particularly alert eye open while we crossed Kuria Muria Bay, for he said that the wind played dirty tricks there and the Beduin of the coast could play worse ones. He went on to tell a story of a Kuwait boom, outward bound from Basra towards Berbera, which had got into difficulties there the previous year, and had been cut out by the Bedu. They gutted her of everything and stole the dates. It was easy for a ship to get into difficulties there, and once she did so the Beduin had no mercy. They were a hungry tribe, for their coast was a poor one, and they regarded date-laden wrecks as gifts from Allah. Piracy, I gathered, is still a real risk of the sea to the Arab dhows. Nejdi, who usually did not dilate on his own adventures, told me of a narrow escape he had had himself in that neighborhood a few years earlier, when making his first African voyage. He was bringing a small boom, the predecessor of the *Triumph of Righteousness*, on the old road from Basra towards Mukalla for orders, by way of Muscat, with a cargo of 1200 packages of Iraq dates. It was early in the season, and the northeast monsoon had not set in. The only way to make a passage to the westward at that time of the year was by standing along close inshore, taking advantage of every favoring eddy of the counter-current there, and coaxing the ship along with the land airs. Outside in the open sea all the conditions were against her, for there was still more than enough southwesterly wind, and the set was strong from that direction. It was difficult to sail close inshore, for that section of the coast bristled with dangers. Moreover, the Beduin there were treacherous and unfriendly. It was necessary to anchor frequently, for it was dangerous to stand close inshore by night. A dhow anchoring in those parts often found it necessary to keep careful watch, lest her cables should be cut and she should drift ashore to become a gutted wreck. The cargoes of Basra dates were a great temptation to the Beduin.

One night, Nejdi said, he came to anchor in a small cove near Ras Sherbetat, not far from the place where the *Triumph* was then sailing. He knew that the reputation of the local tribe of Beduin was a particularly bad one, but he did not worry. He had succeeded in making friends with worse Beduin, and he had been giving dates away generously to all the Beduin camps the ship had met. Nejdi knew that news of such generosity travels swiftly in Arabia, and he thought that the good tidings sent before him would be sufficient to assure him of safe anchorage, and at least keep his cables whole. That day he had seen no Beduin. He did not land, for he was very tired and he planned to sail again before the morning. So he showed no lights, and all hands save one watchman rolled in their cloaks and slept. The watchman, as the night wore on, must have slept, too. Some time after midnight Nejdi found himself rudely awakened, to stare into the bearded faces of half a dozen hungry Beduin who had heard nothing of the young master's generosity, and obviously wanted nothing less than his ship's whole cargo. The Beduin were armed with ancient muskets and swords, and had the familiar Oman curved dagger at their waists.

"Oh Sheikh," Nejdi said (so he told me), addressing the leader of the Beduin robber band, "to what do I owe the pleasure of this midnight call?"

The dirty Beduin gave a greasy laugh.

"Dates, dates! That's what we want, young nakhoda: dates. Every package on board!"

"But I have given dates all along this coast," Nejdi said, while the elderly muallim of the dhow, who had always been against these proceedings, openly sneered. "I will give you dates. You have no need to take them. Only do no harm to my good ship."

"We want more than dates, oh nakhoda!" the greasy one replied. "Hand over the keys of your chest. Come on, now. The ship's money will also be welcome to us poor men here. You can get more."

"Are you not all Muslims?" Nejdi implored, knowing how strongly the Prophet expressed his abhorrence of theft. The Beduin were unimpressed. If they did not steal, they did not eat. That was the usual way of their lives; to them theft was allowable, and life was cheap.

The situation looked desperate. It did not take Nejdi long to realize that his crew had been rounded up and were being kept prisoners under the break of the poop. He could see the mastheads of two small sambuks alongside. There were, he thought, at least forty Beduin on board. It looked hopeless. Some of the Beduin were already passing down packages of dates from the hold into their sambuks. Muslims or not, those Beduin were not going to be content with less than everything in sight. Very probably, when they had finished with the cargo, they would burn the ship and seize the crew to be sold in the interior as slaves. Nejdi's quick mind worked desperately, trying to see some way out of this bad situation. Suddenly an idea came to him. They wanted his chest.

He began to talk again to the old Beduin, trying to amuse him, to throw him off his guard. Nejdi affected to look on the whole thing as a joke, as an expression of Allah's great compassion for the poor Beduin. He said he would open his chest. There was no money in it: it would do no harm for the Beduin to peer in and look. They were welcome to the few clothes it contained. But there was something else in that chest, something that Nejdi hoped he could find, before the Beduin did so. He joked on. His crew, hearing the conversation, looked at him amazed.

Nejdi's arms had to be free while he opened the chest, and when he treated the whole affair so light-heartedly, the old Beduin did not think of taking precautions against him. The keys of the chest, as is usually the case on board the big dhows, were fastened with a thong round Nejdi's waist. In order to open the chest, he had to kneel over it, and bring the end of the thong to the padlock. He knelt down, calling out some pleasantry to the Beduin chief and telling him to be sure to keep the best dates for himself. He knelt down, not seeming greatly interested in the proceedings. Slowly he brought the key to the lock, fumbled a little. The Beduin crowded round, gloating in anticipation of the treasures the chest contained. Nejdi turned the lock very slowly. The Beduin craned over. Some of them were so interested they had put down their arms.

Suddenly Nejdi pulled up the lid, reached in rapidly, and drew out a big Turkish revolver.

"Now, desert scum! May the Prophet burn you all in hell! Out of my ship!" he roared, suddenly leaping to his feet. "On, sailors! Drive these pigs to the sea!"

To his own great surprise and to the considerable astonishment of the crew, who were finding his behavior until then extremely difficult to understand, the horde of Beduin took to their heels and flung themselves over the side, not waiting to cut the painters of their sambuks, and throwing down their muskets as they went. The sailors set up a terrific shouting and the cove re-echoed to the noise, while the Beduin splashed out for the shore.

Nejdi picked up the muskets. They were not loaded. They were so old that it would have been extremely dangerous to fire most of them. Then he looked, very thoughtfully and thanking Allah, at his own revolver. It was not loaded, either.

Remembering these things Nejdi now gave that place a wide berth.

He said that the Beduin, too, would remember that night and they would not fail a second time. He had been lucky. Other Kuwait nakhodas had not done so well, and the bones of many of their ships littered that hard coast—their ships and themselves.

In the nights we wandered on through a queerly phosphorescent sea with the breaking crests of the black swells looking as though they were floodlit in green from below. At moonrise black clouds piled swiftly over the western sky with a little lightning and some rumble of distant thunder, while Nejdi, still weak from his toothache, ran down the sails and let the ship drift, lest there should be a sudden shift of the wind. But no wind came and towards midnight with the stars clear we sailed again.

We were now close to Ras al-Hadd, the turning point of the Arab coastline, and the Swahili schoolteachers who had been wearing trousers throughout the rest of the voyage changed to long Arab gowns. They were a strange trio. Keeping very much to themselves they lived on the port side of the officers' bench aft crowding out Hamed bin Salim. They talked together all day long in the mellow Swahili tongue as if they were engaged in a deep conspiracy. Nejdi, who understood the language, said they were discussing the politics of Zanzibar. He upbraided them for their trousers, which he thought unseemly and for their poor performance of the daily prayers which he said gave a bad example to the sailors. But the schoolteachers took little notice of Nejdi's upbraidings: they continued their earnest talks in the strange Swahili tongue.

When I saw them for the first time I thought they were three Negroes, for they were more Negroid in appearance than any of the sailors. But they said they were two Baluchi, brothers, and one Arab, a distant relation to a prince of Zanzibar. They all spoke English well. They had been boy scouts and were proud of it. Now they were setting out to see the world. The Baluchi were the progeny of an ivory-trading Baluchi and a woman from the Congo and had been born somewhere in the interior of Africa. The Arab, who was a quarter Negro, was born at Zanzibar. They were fine, upstanding youths, aged between eighteen and twenty. What was behind their sudden desertion of Zanzibar I do not know, but they had left without proper passports. According to their own story they were rebels against parental authority and against the traditional upbringing of Muslim youth. They had been educated, and the old ideas would not do, they said. The life at Zanzibar was too cramping: besides, there were too many Indians there and the Indians had too much to say. They wished to see the world and, as a beginning, the Seyyid Sulieman had arranged their passage to Muscat with Nejdi. Nejdi, after the first flush of enthusiasm, did not seem very keen about them, and, apart from his daily criticisms of their trousers and their backwardness in prayer, left them alone. He was not being paid for carrying them and he seemed to regret the thoughtless generosity which had caused him to promise the Seyyid Sulieman to see them safely to Muscat.

I talked to them sometimes in English, which was a pleasant change from the constant grappling with Arabic. They liked the life at Zanzibar, they said, but it was too narrow. They wanted to see the world and they felt that the time for that was when they were young. They would have been glad to enlist in the British Navy at Zanzibar, if there had been any way of doing so, but now there was not. So they were going to the Gulf in the hope of finding a steamer somewhere there in which they could sign on. They had relatives in Muscat.

"Our parents, sir," they told me, "do not approve of this."

Apparently their parents wanted them to marry and settle down, but they had other ideas. I wished them luck. They were cheerful lads and very likable.

We rounded Ras al-Hadd three weeks from Zanzibar, in company with five sambuks bound to Sur, for the Suri never pass their home port homeward bound. The cargo they have not sold then they put on the beach and wait until it is time to go up the gulf for the Basra dates. Homeward bound with mangroves from the Rufiji or Lamu, they sell them along the coast of the Hadhramaut if they can, or in their own Sur. If they cannot sell them they discharge them, store them, and, after the summer's lay-up, reload them and hawk them up the Gulf of Oman and the Persian Gulf to Bahrein, Qatar, Kuwait, Basra, and the ports along the Persian side. This, I believe, was largely our reason for not returning to the Hadhramaut. We left that market to the Suri, knowing we could beat them to the better one in the more populous ports of the Persian Gulf.

We saw nothing of Sur but the mountains behind it. I was sorry not to go into that picturesque place, the home of Majid and Said the smuggler, Abdulla the Mysterious, Mubarak our delta pilot, those colorful characters. But we could sell nothing there and so sailed by, though Nejdi said he might go in the longboat if it was calm. He had old debts there, he said, and he would like to collect them. He might as well forget them, Hamed said; to go in after debts in Sur would be only to delay the ship.

So we went on with a quiet southerly wind and stood on up the Gulf of Oman, while our three Swahili-Baluchi-Arabs, or whatever they were, changed to gowns and began to take interest in their prayers, and the sailors at the evening yarn spoke more and more of Kuwait. Kuwait, Kuwait, Kuwait—that was all I heard: the place, according to them, was a paradise on earth. We should, they said, go into Muscat only to pick up mail. Nejdi's father would write to him there telling him where to take our cargo for prompt and profitable sale. After that, we should romp home to Kuwait. They seemed to take it for granted that this would be the best place to sell the cargo.

But past Sur it was calm again and we lay silent and still in the Gulf of Oman with the ship upright and mirrored in the blue sea as if she were standing there to behold her own reflection, and, liking the sight, would not sail over it. Away to port, all along our beam, stood the high burned hills of Oman, brown and sterile. Ahead we could see the white buildings of Muscat, seeming from there to be perched on cliffs. We seized the opportunity of the calm to send the sailors overside, stripped naked, to scrape the sea growth from the ship's bottom. Though I knew them to be pearl-divers, I was amazed at the length of time those sailors could stay under water. They swam slowly beneath the keel, from side to side, scraping as they went, and paid no attention to two large sharks which swam lazily astern. On his bench aft, Nejdi crooned to himself in the morning sun, his toothache gone and himself very happy, and Mohamed the serang warmed the drums at Jassim's fire, and Bizz's new kittens, on deck for the first time, rolled and played.

We drummed her in to Mutrah Bay that afternoon, twenty-three days from Zanzibar, with our Kuwait flags fore and aft, a new airplane model at the stemhead, and the decks full of drums and song. It was a stirring entry and we came to anchor among a fleet of Kuwaiti up from Zanzibar and India with their flags out to welcome us. A group of Persians, Omani, and Indians filled the inner waters of the small bay. Abdul-wahhab Kalifa, who had sailed his big boom from the Rufiji two weeks before us, was aboard: there was no word of the *Bedri* and Abdulla Kitami was not expected for some days. We had the best passage up thus far in the season and, though hasty reports from the other nakhodas did not indicate much chance of selling the cargo there or in Muscat, Nejdi was all smiles. Everything was quiet again in Kuwait, and a letter from his father had announced the birth to his favorite wife of another strapping son.

Chapter 15

MUTRAH FOR ORDERS

AS WE CAME into Mutrah Bay from Zanzibar, I wondered again about Nejdi's navigation. When I had first heard that we should coast home, after having coasted the whole way down the African coast, I was inclined to feel some contempt for Arab navigation. Now I knew I was wrong. As Nejdi said, he had come by the right road. He had often said that he was not a navigator: he knew the way. I had to admit that he did and that he had made a good passage. If I had been bringing a ship on that passage I should have tried to lay a course direct, and I could not doubt, looking back with the *Triumph*'s passage safely accomplished, that mine would have been a worse way. We had always had some wind, other than a few brief and not unpleasant intervals of calm: the wind we had was nearly always usable and helped us on our way. Nejdi had done very well. I had often been a little envious of the storehouse of maritime knowledge that must repose in his head: now I admired him. It might be true that he had no use for anything he did not know, but it was equally true that his knowledge was his own, complete and personal to him, and he did not need to look up things in books. If, as he said himself, he could make a long passage like this with comparative ease, why all this fuss about navigation? Yet I knew he would like to master that art, if he had the chance. Old Abdul-wahhab Kalifa was always after me to instruct him in the mysteries of sextant, chronometer, and tables, and often expressed his regret that there was not a school of navigation in Kuwait. He thought that the ancient art should be preserved even if there were not much need of it on the ordinary African voyage. The Arabs, he said, ought to preserve the art of navigation as well as the art of sailing, for their day would surely come again.

I liked the way all these nakhodas were friends. In Mutrah Bay, as in all the other ports we had visited, groups of them assembled on our officers' bench aft as soon as we came in, and there they sat all night and talked and talked, while the bubbling pipe went round continually. They stopped talking only for prayers and the evening meal. In the evening prayer they joined our sailors, the nakhodas with Nejdi in the center of the line behind the leader Hamed, and our sailors and their own on either flank from end to end of the vessel, all facing Mecca and intoning the mellow prayers while the light died. The boat songs of the Persians, as they ferried logs from their baggalas, were stilled then, and peace came to the anchorage. By night they slept with us, and later there were feasts, with Ismael, though he was still weak from the Rufiji fever, playing his guitar. The friendship of these nakhodas from the same home port was a very real thing and they formed a united band. They were prepared at any time to assist another's vessel in any circumstances, to perform risky feats of salvage without payment, to lend one another a carpenter, a dozen seamen, a cook, or a bale of carpets, or anything else that might be needed. In case of distress, they were prepared to carry another crew for thousands of miles. They carried one another's junior officers, sent here and there to collect long-due debts: and for none of these things did they accept payment. No Arab nakhoda looked on his brother shipmasters as a possible prey. Theirs was a real brotherhood of the sea and I respected and liked them for it. Maritime accidents were far from unknown to them, for they sailed on dangerous coasts; but they rarely lost a sailor's life. Sometimes their ships opened up and foundered under them, and it was not unknown for one to sail down in a shower of rain, coming up too deeply laden from Africa or the Malabar coast; but the crews rarely went missing. They were a good lot, those Kuwait nakhodas. I had learned to know them well in the long months with Nejdi's boom. Those who sat round our transom in Mutrah Bay were all old friends.

We learned from them now that things were not good in Muscat or in Mutrah Bay and, though the merchants wanted our poles, they had, they said, no rupees to pay for them. In these circumstances we did not delay. We landed our three Swahilis, sold a few coconuts, took in fresh water from a mosque well, sold half the vermicelli to a boom from Dabai into which it was transshipped by night, bought some of the famous Muscat sweetmeats, and departed. We were in Mutrah Bay three days, the shortest stay we had ever made anywhere. Perhaps Nejdi was eager to see his new son.

I saw what I could of Mutrah and Muscat during this short stay, but I did not care greatly for either place. Mutrah was the dirtiest place we were ever in and the stench of the beach was frightful. Mutrah is on a small bay, a mile or two to the north of Muscat, set in brown mountains, on two of which stand Portuguese forts now falling into decay. Along the beach in front of the little town are the homes of the merchants and brokers of the better class with, here and there, the minaret of a mosque. At one end of the beach is a junk yard of old ships, and here two derelict *dhangis* lay half submerged in the water. The customs landing is at the other end. The beach itself is used as road, park, junk yard, market, fish-shed, landing stage, dog house and public lavatory by all Oman and half Baluchistan. The place is full of scabby dogs, more dead than alive. Dogs, Baluchi, fish, goats, and human filth fill the Mutrah beach so that one hesitates to walk along it. Armed Omani Beduin strut in brown shirts, barefoot in spite of all the beach's putrid filth; with belts of brassbound cartridges about their waists and silver-handled daggers slung conveniently. Many carry fearsome guns, elaborately worked with silver filigree, or bound with brass and silver bands. Not all the guns are ancient: most of them look fit for use.

Once Muscat and Mutrah Bay were centers of the arms trade for the Middle East, and from here many a cargo was run across the Gulf to Afghanistan, or up to Hasa, Persia, Iraq, Kuwait. There was, perhaps, some smuggling to Iran, but now the arms trade is regulated and there are no fortunes to be made in it, not in Oman, at least. Dabai and Sharjah are more conveniently placed for smuggling into Persia. With the loss of the arms business, Muscat's importance has declined, and now it is among the lesser ports of Arabia, used by the Arabs chiefly for orders. Life is still cheap there: it is not proper, even now, for a man of self-respect to be seen unarmed. In the bazaar are many arms shops offering the Beduins' guns and the townsman's sword. The well-dressed Omani does not walk, even on Mutrah beach, without his dagger at his waist.

Along the beach lie all kinds of fish from hammerhead shark to giant ray: the nearer waters of the Gulf of Oman teem with fish and much is shipped from here to Europe as fertilizer. Occasionally, an ancient motorcar, shaken by the pot-holed Muscat road, wandered along the beach among the children and dogs. Behind the front of better houses was the labyrinth of the *suq*, a place of narrow winding streets sheltered by rough overhead matting and crowded with tiny shops offering the trash of Japan. Yet Mutrah was picturesque and it really did not smell as badly as it might have done.

The Kuwait nakhodas patronized a favorite coffee shop facing the beach near the fish market, where their longboats landed. Here I used to sit with them, when I was ashore, drinking from time to time—with intervals as frequent and as long as possible—tiny cups of clove and cardamom-flavored coffee, or tiny glasses of sweet boiled tea. From this coffee shop one could look along the beach, or watch what was going on in the harbor. It was a good coffee shop for shipmasters. The beach was always crowded with people, Baluchi—thousands of them—Omani, Arabs, Persians, Indians and Kuwaiti from the ships, Beduin armed to the teeth; women in trousers and horrid masks, who shrieked shrilly at their dreadful children, stoning dogs: children with faces painted with mascara till they looked like little clowns in their tinseled fezes and purple coats; Baluchi in voluminous trousers which had enough material in a leg to make a small tent; little girls in trousers, little boys in nothing, annoying the mangy pariah dogs. Over all, the high fortresses frowned from their burned hills and the road to Muscat wound round the rocks away to the south.

In the nakhodas' coffee shop Nejdi called loudly for a boy to relight his pipe, and Abdul-wahhab bin Kalifa al-Ganim, sipping a tiny cup of cardamom coffee, kept an eye on the mangrove poles being landed from his longboat in the surf. Two Indians were arriving at the anchorage, kotias from Bombay by the look of them, flying big silken flags with red-and-white horizontal stripes. Hamed bin Salim came in, bound to the money-changers with a sack of Austrian thalers to be changed to rupees. They were dated 1786, but had been coined at the Royal Mint in London the previous year: Hamed brought them from Zanzibar. The Omani Beduin still love the large round coins with the fat face of Maria Theresa, and they bring a good price in Mutrah *suq*. We could buy them in Zanzibar for eighty rupees a hundred and sell them for ninety at Mutrah.

Yusuf came in on a buying excursion to get sweetmeats for Nejdi's harem; he sought instructions as to the best kinds. Mates, quartermasters, nakhodas' younger brothers, from all the ships in the bay drifted into this thatched coffee shop where business is always brisk: but only the nakhodas sat on the benches—the nakhodas and the agents and brokers whose business was with ships and merchants who worked to buy from the ships' cargoes. These coffee shops are like exchanges and clubs and most of the sea business is done in them. The nakhodas never pay for what they have as it is ordered. They are known to the proprietor and pay generously when they leave. A deep-sea nakhoda of Arab dhows sets considerable store by his reputation in these coffee shops and runs accounts in them from Jiddah to Zanzibar, Ashar to Berbera, Mogadishu to Mutrah Bay.

As a change from the coffee shop a few of us sometimes wandered through the congested *suq*. It is a big *suq*, though according to our mariners nothing compared with that of Kuwait. They seemed glad enough to buy lengths of red-and-yellow cloth in it, for they told me that these were good, and they all bought small baskets of sweetmeats as presents for their homes. The sweetmeat shops of Muscat and Mutrah are famous for the quality of their wares, but they would wait a long time for custom if they were dependent on me. The sickly-sweet taste of those cloying confections remained too much for me, after six months of trying it. The *suq*, however, was interesting to walk in for a while, with its teeming life— men shaving, men writing, men turning tiny sandstones grinding knives, men and boys beating out iron in a wayside foundry; shops full of tinsel, calicoes, camel's-hair cloth; arms shops, money-changers, hardware shops with a selection of small padlocks—for the Arab locks everything he can —and simple, cheap tools. The streets of the *suq* are of hard-trodden sand, and if it ever rained the place would be a quagmire.

Compared with the teeming life of Mutrah, Muscat itself was not so interesting, for it was a quiet place when we were there, apparently much run down. I did not go there often and the sailors did not go at all. It was reached by car ride in an ancient taxicab over a well-made pass. It looked picturesque as one came over the pass, and there were some good buildings—the Sultan's palace—the ruling Sultan was a young man, whose father, a descendant of the great Seyyid Said, had abdicated and lived in Japan—the British Residency and the homes of a few leading merchants. Across the bay on the southern side was the remains of a large Portuguese fort, now used as a jail.

The prison was in the charge of a venerable Baluchi, who showed his prisoners with the air of a proprietor. There were perhaps a score of them, all leg-ironed. One was there for stealing a camel: he had been in a year, he said, and did not know how much longer he might stay there. There were four ancient sheikhs, from somewhere in Batina, in for the suspected burning of a garden in some local feud. They were dressed in long gowns and turbans and grinned expressively when asked for an account of their sins. To judge from their grins, they did not object overmuch to their incarceration. In the course of time, no doubt, Allah would be generous and they would be free again. In the meantime they were fed. More interesting than the prisoners were the drawings of square-rigged ships scratched on the walls of the entrance chamber of this curious jail. I wondered that such vessels should be depicted there in that ancient stronghold of the dhow. Nejdi said he had seen no such ships. They were good drawings, technically correct. They showed frigates and other men-o'-war of the previous century.

Lying in the sand by the side of the British Residency was a topmast from one of these frigates which had been maintained by Seyyid Said in the great days of Muscat and Oman, when Zanzibar and half the east coast of Africa were under the dominion of the Sultan. Seyyid Said had bought old frigates from the English and from India, for the better maintenance of his power and for his periodic visits to his African dominions. The Seyyid, apparently, had had a partiality for old frigates and ships of the line. He had, indeed, once sent one, a sloop named the *Sultana*, on a mission to America, but the churlish New Englanders of Salem had pulled the Arabs' beards and laughed at them and the mission came to naught.

The tradition of old British sailing men-o'-war is still strong in the Persian Gulf, and I noticed later in Kuwait that a shipmasters' directory of the Eastern Seas given me by Kalifa al-Ganim, father of the nakhoda Abdul-wahhab, was illustrated with drawings of frigates and not of dhows. It was, he said, a Muscat production and had been brought to Kuwait when the Kuwaiti were first starting as deep-water sailors. I thought I detected, too, a resemblance between some of the terms used by the Arab sailors and those in use in the old Navy—*jalboot*, for instance, from the naval jolly boat; *bowrah* for anchor, from the English bower; *kittah* for cutter; *lanch* for the naval launch.

The guns in the Portuguese fort faced the Sultan's palace. There was a mixed battery of ancient muzzle-loaders which included iron guns from India and from Yorkshire, and two beautifully carved old Portuguese guns. Their carriages were rotten and the platform on which they stood looked hardly strong enough to walk on.

Muscat had fallen on evil days: there was no shipbuilding and not much trade beyond a mean local trade from Mutrah across the Gulf to Baluchistan, or coastwise to Sur and Batina. Very few deep-sea dhows are now owned there, most of the long voyage carrying of Oman being in the hands of the Suri and the ancient ships from Batina and the Trucial coast. Beggars abound in the Mutrah *suq* and there seem more Baluchi there than Omani. The only big ship sailing out of Mutrah at the time of our visit was a former Persian boom transferred there for the greater freedom of the Oman flag, the boom of Mohamed Kunji, whom we had met in Zanzibar at the mysterious establishment of the Seyyid Sulieman bin Said.

Abdulla Kitami came in two days after our arrival. It was now considered time to tell him of the death of his brother and, as soon as he had moored, all the Kuwait nakhodas in the harbor, seven of them, went aboard very solemnly and told him the news. They told it as gently as they could, but it went hard with Abdulla. Afterwards they left, very quietly, when they had expressed their sympathy and their willingness to help the young nakhoda: only Nejdi stayed. Nejdi stayed with his friend until we sailed, for Abdulla had had much fever after parting company with us and this news was a great blow. Mohamed had been a favorite brother. Abdulla had not heard of the riot: the death of his brother was a profound and terrible shock, for such tragedies are rare in Kuwait. A man of the sea does not often give his life for political foolishness, which is more properly the domain of shore-dwellers and Abdulla found the tragedy difficult to believe. The death of his brother, he was convinced, must have been an accident. In a *suq* riot any one who has the misfortune to be near may suffer. He wished that his brother had not stayed ashore.

On the day of Abdulla Kitami's arrival the anchorage was full of Persians. Five of their booms arrived, having come up from Africa in company. The bay resounded to their haunting boat songs as their longboats pulled for the beach, with the nakhodas standing and waving as they passed their countrymen's ships. After sunset, the creak of their great halliards getting the sails aloft ready for sea again came very clearly in the intervals of dancing and the tramp of hard bare feet. Mutrah Bay that night was very beautiful under the bright stars. There was no moon, but the stars gave light as the Persians made ready for sea. One of them was an enormous baggala with a capacity of 5000 packages of dates, a lovely thing with a coppered underbody. She was the last baggala of Quishm, they said, and seventy years old. She had come in from the Malabar coast, laden with teak logs and a cargo of roping stuffs and coils of coir, with thirty dugout canoes stowed on deck and Indian furniture hanging round the poop rail. A Kuwait baggala came in the same night, nineteen days from Lamu. The wind came from the northwest before midnight, gusty, burning with the heat of all the surrounding stone and the desert beyond, hot so that it scorched the face like a furnace blast, and even aboard ship out in the bay it was impossible to sleep.

I lay awake and was thankful that I did so when, in the early hours of the morning, the great *el-Dhow* of the Abdul-wahhab al-Kitami came ramping into a berth like a great black ghost, her blocks creaking as the yard came down and her sailors calling quietly in order not to disturb the rest of the anchorage. It was stirring to see that heavy-laden great boom take up her moorings in the blackness of the night, for she came in in a gust and it was tricky work. It would have been tricky by day, when Abdul-wahhab could see the ships all round him. None of them showed anchor lights, and I do not know how he threaded a way through them at speed in that great ship and came to anchor beside the small boom of his nephew Abdulla Kitami. It would have been fine seamanship by day: by night, it was little short of miraculous. To judge distance the way Abdul-wahhab did that night, and come into a berth in an unlit and crowded anchorage with grace and style, shows the consummate seaman. These booms have always to be brought to anchorage without sail, which makes the judgment of the nakhoda all-important. If he makes a mistake at such a time he cannot rectify it either by setting sail, or backing it. He must come in with way or his vessel will not steer. The smallest error of judgment, and he must collide with probably two or three vessels at least. Yet this skilful ship-handling of a great vessel like the *Dhow* was taken as a matter of course.

Old Yusuf Shirazi, looking at the *Dhow* later in the dawn, murmured that she was back where she belonged: she had taken many a cargo of arms from that bay and he had sailed with her. He sailed with her once when the British intercepted her and took her into their naval base near Ormuz. The *Dhow* was a vessel with a history.

We sailed the following morning, going out as one of a fleet of eight which included Abdulla Kitami's small boom, now under the command of Saud the freed slave. Abdulla Kitami, broken up and sick with fever, had gone to his uncle Abdul-wahhab in the *Dhow*. Also sailing with us that sunny morning were the big boom *Samhan*, commanded by the well-known Kuwait nakhoda Yusuf bin Isa, the big baggala from Quishm, an old Kuwait boom homeward bound with fish oil from the Mahra coast, and three Persians from Africa. It was a beautiful morning and the ships going out in company were glorious to see with their great white sails above the small hulls set in the blue sea, against the background of bold mountain. We had very light airs all day, barely enough to give us way, but if we dallied nobody cared. The conditions were ideal and we enjoyed lovely views of the other vessels. We dropped most of them quickly, but we could not sail by the big *Samhan*. The two of us sailed in company through the day not a stone's throw apart, and her sailors sat in the shadow of their sail and watched ours, who sat in the shadow of our sail and watched them. She was from Lamu, with 1200 score mangrove poles. She was a very big ship, larger even than *el-Dhow* (now that the *Dhow* had been cut down), but she sailed beautifully through the water with a straight clean wake and she kept steerageway, with only the flap of her sails. At sunset I looked back at the Arab-Persian fleet, sailing up the Gulf of Oman, strung out astern of us with their gilded sails against the blue-gray of the evening sky. It was a peaceful and very pleasant sight, in this world of wars. By day and night we sailed in company and the big *Samhan* under the stars was very lovely.

We wandered pleasantly up the Gulf of Oman towards Ras Musandam and the Persian Gulf for the next five days. The wind was quiet and we could sail only slowly. Nejdi, eager to see his new son, showed a little impatience and the sailors looked forward to their homecoming. Where we were next bound I did not know, nor did any one else on board, for it would depend largely upon conditions. It was scarcely likely that she would take a full cargo of building materials direct to Kuwait without first trying to sell some of it elsewhere. We had left Zanzibar officially cleared for Kuwait by way of Muscat, Bahrein and a place called Jubail in Saudi-Arabia. Now Nejdi talked of Basra and even of the Persian side: he never mentioned Jubail. I should not have known we were supposedly bound there, if he had not given me the ship's papers. They were in English and he could not understand them: he wanted the manifest for Jubail. Jubail is a small pearling place on the Hasa coast roughly a hundred miles south of Kuwait Bay. I don't know why we had papers for it, for we certainly never went there and, so far as I could discover, never had any intention of doing so. Perhaps in certain circumstances a spare set of papers might have been desirable and Nejdi liked to be prepared.

We drifted and dribbled along, now with a catspaw and now with none, now for a few hours with a good sailing breeze, and now becalmed. Allah would bring us to Kuwait in his own good time and meanwhile it was good that he did not send the north wind. Nobody wanted the north wind, which would be right in our teeth and could blow hard for forty days. I shared the general hope that Allah would hold back this wind until we were well up the Gulf; but Nejdi, worried, said it always followed calm. In the meantime we had many visits with Yusuf bin Isa, who pulled across in his small cutter. He was a big, bluff, hearty man, six feet tall and built in proportion, who always laughed uproariously at his own jokes. He came in his long white gown and well-blued headcloth, with a Japanese umbrella to keep off the sun. He would visit us one day and yarn the afternoon away with Nejdi and Hamed bin Salim, and we would return his visit the next day. I liked Yusuf bin Isa and it was a pleasure to visit his big clean boom. He had a little cabin in the poop with electric light and radio, neither of which worked. When we went to his boom his sailors came to the poop and greeted Nejdi. When Yusuf came to us our sailors who had been with him came up and greeted him, shaking him warmly by the hand. The discipline in the Kuwait booms was excellent and they were well run: yet the sailors and the officers still knew how to behave properly towards one another without hypocrisy, without obsequiousness, and without familiarity. An officer was an officer among the Arabs, because he deserved to be. He was a natural leader and was given the respect such a man deserves.

In the afternoon Hamed and Hassan the helmsman worked at the accounts, Hamed for the ship and Hassan as the crew's representative, for with our homecoming there would be the payoff and the casting up of shares. This was an intricate and involved business and the two of them worked steadily, while Yusuf bin Isa shook his merry sides on Nejdi's carpet at his own mysterious jokes and kept his eye on his vessel, and Nejdi looked out with those keen eyes of his, dreading the north wind. There was little work at this stage of the voyage, beyond the necessary sailing of the vessel. Kaleel and his helpers continued to work on the new boat and, in the mornings, Mohamed the serang led the sailors in the laying of a new cable. We now had four sailors ill with fever, and Ismael, who had played his guitar merrily in Mutrah Bay, complained of rheumatism and piles.

Nejdi, when not entertaining Yusuf or aboard Yusuf's boom, sat on a carpet on the bench aft singing verses from the Quaran, nursing a bare brown leg while he watched the sails, the sea, and the other ships, and perhaps mused about his newest son, and his brother's luck with the ship's debts at Mogadishu. Now and again he would begin a dissertation upon politics, or ask me for the hundredth time how any conception of Christian ethics could be converted into a basis for sane living, and when I was going to say my prayers.

We were many days reaching Ras Musandam, coming slowly along the Batina coast almost under the mountains, or standing towards the Persian side. The Batina mountains looked very old, very hot and very bad-tempered, as if they were tired of having to stand for ever under the burning rays of the hot sun. Dun and sterile, their abrupt faces pock-marked, fluted, scarred, they add no welcoming note to the Omani seascape: they stand solid at the sea's edge unassailable and sheer, a frowning bar to the mariner going by, fit coastline for Arabia the backward and the land of the robber barons. As I looked at them day after day I thought of the Portuguese who had sailed this way, and of all the ancient vessels which had sailed this road—caravels, galleons, frigates, East Indiamen, junks from China bringing silks and precious goods to the great market places of the Persian Gulf. Now came our old boom, last of that great line of Eastern mariners, wandering northwards with a cargo of mangrove poles cut from a jungle in Africa. The wealth of the Indies had flowed here: here slaves, pirates, admirals had sailed and fought, and discoverers and pioneers ventured. Now an oil tanker from Abadan hurried by us, pushing half the gulf before her stodgy bow and pulling the other half behind as she hurried on with petrol for motorcars in Chelsea and Golders Green. Nejdi, looking at the steamship, murmured, "They come: they go. So it has been always, here." He looked after the smoke of the departing steamer a long time: and then washed himself and prayed.

In the sunset we had a little breeze and the mountains stood softened, dark and grand against the long line of the dying light of the sun. Away to the east the coast of Persia was a long blue haze: the mountains of Batina in that light were very beautiful. I said so to Nejdi, but he did not share my enthusiasm.

"What is beautiful about those hills?" Nejdi said: "they grow nothing. They give no life."

I answered that they are of the kingdom of Allah and He has made them beautiful. He was silent then, but he was not impressed. The idea that mountains can be beautiful did not appeal to him. If I wished to see beauty, he said, I should wait until we reached Kuwait.

Though we were in the neighborhood of Ras Musandam, where the Gulf of Oman enters the Persian Gulf and all the tankships from Abadan and Bahrein converge, and the date tramps from Basra and Bushire come and go, we showed no lights. I asked Nejdi if he did not think it wise to show at least a hurricane light on such occasions, but he answered that the camel knew its way without lights on the land. Why then, he asked, should an Arab ship go lit at sea? A camel, I ventured to suggest, could avoid collision more easily than a ship at sea and the other camels also could see. He was not interested. Our lights stayed down below. Nejdi with his ship again becalmed retired to his sleeping mat after the night prayer, and I wandered along to yarn the first night watch away with the sailors of the serang's watch in the stern-sheets of the longboat, on top of our cargo. The yarns that night were of Kuwait, as they nearly always were then. Above us the great mainsail made wonderful patterns as it rolled gently under the stars: aft the snores of Nejdi smote the peaceful air and Hamed bin Salim wrapped in his cloak and gown kept drowsy watch. Ebrahim the helmsman was silhouetted in the binnacle's glow, seated at the wheel. The water gurgled lazily along the smooth sides and at the low bow and the blocks aloft creaked as she slowly rolled.

When we entered the Persian Gulf there was a sudden end to these conditions. The calms disappeared at once and the north wind came instead, quietly at first but soon freshening. Nejdi was worried, but we bent our smallest mainsail and beat on. Before the day was out the wind howled in the rigging and the sea got up, so that we made little progress. Afterwards day after day remained the same and we beat and beat. Now we stood along the Persian coast, hoping for a windshift there: and now in desperation made a board across towards the Trucial coast, down towards Sharjah and Dabai. One after another we had slowly passed the ports which sent their fleets down to Africa—Muscat, the Batina places, Sharjah and Dabai, Kung, Lingeh, Quishm. Still we beat, day after day, for our home port was at the head of the gulf and we had a long way to go. We stood close in along many Persian beaches and passed within hail of several ports and towns. We passed close by Hanjam, which had been a British naval post and now seemed deserted. Here a Persian in a small boat boarded us, wanting to buy coconut oil, piece goods, sugar, tea and tobacco from Muscat. We passed Ruvvan, Charak and Chiru. We beat three days between Charak and the island of Kais and another day between Chiru and Hindarabi.

The wind was quiet for a while in the Kais passage and we dawdled through with time to look at that interesting island. There were a number of small pearling boats at work on banks inshore, but Nejdi said that they were poor and that the pearls on the Persian side were not good. The good pearls, he said, were on the Arabian side of the Gulf. The best of all were on the banks off Bahrein. We saw, too, the three towns of Kais, which seemed to be largely in ruins though there were substantial buildings in them. It seemed to me that the island had fallen on evil days. Hassan the helmsman, who had maintained until then that he was a Kuwaiti, now disclosed that he came from Kais, and he confirmed that things were not good there. He had, he said, left Kais ten years earlier, with his family, and gone to Kuwait. It used to be a good place, rich in pearling: now it was neither good nor rich. He would say no more about the place and seemed to regret that he had been born there.

We saw several more half-abandoned towns as we stood along the Persian coast close beneath the colored hills, some of which looked like great dumps of colored slag and seemed as if they had been put there by man. Near a town known to Nejdi and the Persians as Kalat, we saw a large castlelike fort on the crest of a hill. A sambuk lay at anchor off the town, which appeared a large one, but we saw no sign of life although we passed close by, very slowly. The people of Kalat, Hassan said, had gone, migrating in a body to a town on the Batina coast which he called Khor Fakkan. If he had had little to say about the island of Kais, Hassan was communicative about this place Kalat. It appeared that he had gone there first from Kais, and had finally reached Kuwait in a most round-about way. He told me a long story of how it all happened. First, life at Kais had become impossible, principally, according to Hassan, because of the tyranny of the local sheikh, who was a sort of local robber baron, so far as I could make out. Then, Hassan and his family—he was a boy at the time—had gone up the coast a little way to this place Kalat. At that time, Kalat was prosperous and life was good there. But there was an under-current of trouble, largely on account of the innovations of the new Shah, who, apparently, had taken a violent dislike to things as they were and was in a great hurry to change them. Rumors and reports began to trickle in to Kalat of the most astounding things going on in the kingdom of Persia. According to some, the Shah was making a monstrous attack on the precepts of Islam; according to others, he was ruining the country. It was said that he had demanded elsewhere that the old customs should be dropped. Women must no longer go veiled or be enclosed in the harem. Men must no longer wear the flowing cloak and graceful turban: instead they must free their women and wear hats.

This was sacrilege. Even then, Hassan seemed to have difficulty in believing that any Persian would put forward such proposals. But the Shah had done so. More than that, he began to see that they were carried out. The corner of Persia where Kais and Kalat are situated was remote from authority and reforms reached there slowly. But one day the dreadful edicts arrived. An emissary came from the court of the Shah to tell the people of Kalat that they must no longer carry on in the ways of their fathers. They must abandon ancient ideas, emancipate their women and themselves, as the Turks had done. Much else he said, chiefly about new taxes and the collection of customs duties, not to mention the suppression of the ancient business of smuggling. The citizens of Kalat, Hassan said, listened to the emissary in astonished silence. Then he went away. When he had gone, they paid no attention to the new decrees, for they were violently opposed to such sudden changes. They liked things as they were, and it would take more than a distant Shah with big ideas to change them.

In the course of time the Shah heard of this disobedience. He sent, then, soldiers to Kalat to enforce his decrees. The soldiers were the best equipped the people of Kalat had seen and they were most impressive. But doubtless they liked their arrack and anything else alcoholic as well as other military men. The townsmen of Kalat gave them a feast, to welcome them and cement the bonds which united them with the rest of new Persia. They plied them heartily with arrack and other drink. They had had, they explained, to offer this excellent entertainment in the town jail, for there was no other building large enough. They had decorated the jail very handsomely. However, there was more in this design than at first appeared, for, no sooner were the soldiers thoroughly intoxicated and helpless, than the citizens, who had drunk water instead of the potent arrack, locked them all in the jail and departed. Hassan said it was a great joke. He helped to lock the soldiers up himself. That done, the towns-people knew they could not remain in Kalat, for sooner or later a greater force would be sent to punish them. But they had made their plans. They could not stay in a Persia where the women would walk the streets unveiled and the men wear hats. So, man, woman, and child, they went down to the harbor, and sailed away in the soldiers' ships. It was the first time Hassan had been at sea, apart from the brief crossing from Kais, and, though he was seasick, it was a grand adventure. They took everything they could carry and sailed away, and none of them ever returned. From that day to this Kalat has been a deserted town.

Hassan said his family went to a place called Khor Fakkan, in Oman, first, and later he migrated to Kuwait by way of Bahrein. Whether Hassan's account was correct or not, Kalat was dead when we passed by. The town might have been dead, but it was not so dead that Nejdi dared anchor there, though the conditions were against us and we should have done well to anchor. He had a great dread of the modern Persians and all their works. The Persians are suspicious of the Kuwait booms, and accuse them of being inveterate smugglers. Nejdi scoffed at this and said big deep-water dhows did not smuggle: that was work for small fry. Any fool, he said, ought to know that small ships from Sharjah, Dabai, Bahrein, and Khor Fakkan, ran cargoes into Persia now. It was sense to use small ships which could run small cargoes by night, instead of large ones which took longer to unload and ran greater risks. Small craft could slip in any-where, and be beached and burned if danger threatened: large craft were at a disadvantage. Smuggle? Not he! But, he added in a whispered aside, did I not know any spot of earth where a poor Arab shipmaster might run in cargoes?

From all I could gather, a considerable amount of smuggling goes on along that Persian coast, and I doubt very much whether the Kuwaiti are entirely innocent of it. Smuggling in the big dhows running down to Af-rica is mostly a minor business carried on by a few wandering Sinbads and the crews; but the profit from running a cargo of tea or soft goods in to a Persian beach was a different proposition. Yarning in the longboat by night after we had seen a camel caravan going down in the sunset to a low point off which a small Dabai boom was anchored, old Yusuf spoke of smuggling voyages from the Trucial coast over to Kalat and elsewhere in those parts. Often, he said, they took back deckloads of Persians to lonely beaches on Bahrein, where they landed them by night and left them to seek work as coolies on the oil fields. What the Bahrein govern-ment would have had to say about this I do not know and Yusuf did not care, but it would not have been pleased, for indigent Persians have long been a problem in that island.

Yusuf also told a story about a ship he was in which was caught once landing a cargo to a camel team by night. Three Persian soldiers were put aboard to take the ship to Bushire, but on the way the crew overpowered them and carried them off, later throwing them ashore somewhere on the Hasa coast across the Gulf. What became of them then? I asked. Yusuf said he did not know, and shrugged his shoulders. This smuggling business along the Gulf must be a thorn in the side of the Shah of Persia, with his trade declining and his more independent subjects, rebellious at his strange ideas of sex equality and the emancipation of women, disappear-ing into Oman. I was told that there were large numbers of Persian ex-iles in Bahrein and Kuwait, as well as in the ports of the Trucial coast.

At this time we had five of the crew sick—Ismael, Abdul-latif the singer, Jassim the cook, Nasir the pearl-diver, and Ebrahim the helmsman. Nejdi said one look at Kuwait would make them all well again, but I doubted it. Nasir the pearl-diver, who had been diving since he was thirteen, looked far gone in tuberculosis, and his days were numbered: he was twenty-five. The constant hardships of the sea life, with its wholly inadequate food, its broken rest, often in wet and always insuffi- cient clothes, its exposures to fevers and all sorts of tropical ills— these things must take their toll. Every sailor in that ship except one sixteen-year-old boy, was gray; most of them iron-gray. Many looked old, but there were no old men. Salim the toothless, who looked sixty, was not yet forty, Yusuf Shirazi, who looked seventy sometimes, was at least five years on the right side of fifty. He had three nails torn out by the roots from hands and feet: this sort of mishap was too commonplace to receive attention. According to Nejdi, who scorned all remedies save the burn- ing iron and the bandage of good Quran texts, none of his sailors was really ill. In Arabia, he said, the weak died young: anybody old enough to be a sailor was strong. One look at Kuwait, he repeated, and they would all recover. I hoped so.

In the meantime we drew no nearer to this place of beauty, which could heal the sick and in which all joy abounded, for the wind was still ahead. It was still from the north, blowing at times with force, and we began to split our sails. In the short steep sea of the almost entirely en- closed Persian Gulf, the *Triumph* jumped and tossed and made little prog- ress. Her motion was violent and continuous, and Nejdi began to grow pessimistic. "None of my wives wants me," he moaned after the eleventh day of steadily adverse conditions, and admitted for the first time that perhaps a new mainmast might be an improvement to his vessel. He had always maintained that the *Triumph* was the height of perfection, in spite of the obvious flaws in her mainmast which worked violently with every roll. What really depressed him was that the big *Samhan* had sailed out of sight. He grew more pessimistic at the thought of trying to sell our mangroves with that great dump of 1200 score from the *Samhan* sold ahead. They would flood the market.

"None of my wives loves me: the *Samhan* will spoil the market: we have only the north wind," he moaned, believing none of these things except the obviously true last, but worried by them all.

"Why not go into Bahrein?" I suggested.

I had been looking at my charts. It seemed a good idea to have a look at the market for mangrove poles in Bahrein, and surely it would not de- lay us any more than the north wind was already doing. Also, it would be much more comfortable. Then, too, we were far enough up the Gulf, by that time, almost to reach Bahrein by going about and standing across the Gulf on the other tack.

Nejdi looked at me. For once in his life, he agreed, though he did not want to go to Bahrein. There was only one place he wanted to go to, and that was Kuwait.

"As Allah wills," he said. "If we cannot go elsewhere, we shall go to Bahrein."

What really appealed to him, I think, was the possibility of stealing a march on the big *Samhan*. While she beat on up the Gulf to the markets of Kuwait and Basra, he would slip into Bahrein and, possibly, sell his cargo without competition there. The more he thought of the idea, the better he liked it, for his father had said there was much building in Bahrein as a result of the oil company's rapid expansion and the government's increased revenues.

Towards midnight, with the wind howling from the north and the *Triumph* pitching and rolling in a confused sea somewhere off Ras Naband, we went about with the usual yelling and splitting of seams. Once safely round, we stood on a long board towards Bahrein. We went about at midnight so that the ships in company, if there were any, would not see us go: it was important to go alone and to find an unimpeded market in Bahrein, or our visit there might be in vain.

Chapter 16

IBN SAUD BUYS A CARGO

TWO DAYS LATER we anchored in the shallow harbor of Manama Roads, at the island of Bahrein, and the first thing we saw was Yusuf bin Isa's *Samhan* with her Kuwait flag flying to welcome us. Inshore was Hamed Yusuf's Persian boom from Dima, and out to sea, astern of us, the morning sun showed the big boom of Abdul-wahhab Kalifa, also full of mangrove poles, coming in. During the next few days half the homeward-bound Kuwait fleet arrived, both from Africa and India, including Abdul-wahhab bin Abdul-asiz with the big *el-Dhow*, Sulieman Radhwan with his baggala, Nasir bin Isa with his baggala *Cat*—which was not known to him by that name—and his brother Hamoud with a cargo of teak and roping stuffs from Malabar, and three or four Persians besides.

Nejdi looked gloomy when we came in to find the anchorage so crowded, and immediately announced his intention of going about and standing to sea again to beat on up the Gulf and race them to Basra. The north wind had brought them in, as it had brought us. But, as things turned out, we were in luck for once, for we had sold our full cargo within a few hours of our arrival. All the ships in harbor found their cargoes easy to dispose of, for Abdul-asiz Ibn Saud, King of Saudi-Arabia, had recently been in town and left orders with an agent to buy the next twenty cargoes of building timber that arrived. The great king, enriched by oil royalties from the American fields on the mainland, was beginning a building program in Ryadh and other towns of his kingdom. Bahrein was the logical place to buy supplies. We were in luck. Allah with His north wind had been kind. Ibn Saud's price was a good one—better than we should have got elsewhere—for the Saudi king has always been generous. We sold our whole cargo through a Persian intermediary at twenty rupees the score. The highest price for the heaviest poles in the Rufiji was less than ten rupees, so we had a good freight, after all, and the voyage which, until then, had not promised well, turned out much better than had been expected.

It was not easy to reach Bahrein, and we had to beat to get there. The set down the Gulf as we stood across forced us off our course, and instead of fetching Bahrein we found ourselves instead off Qatar, a low peninsula of sand jutting into the southwest corner of the Persian Gulf, round which the sea is a shallow green and reefs abound. These were dangerous waters: we saw the sand glare of the desert behind before we picked up the low land, and some pearlers scudding for safety behind a reef. It was a day of fresh wind, with the sea running white caps, short and steep and breaking. These were conditions unsuited to our short, beamy ship, and she pitched and jumped and flung her masts about without making much way. We were close enough on Qatar to make out a ruined town before we went about. Nejdi named it as Zubara, and said it had been an important place once: many Kuwaiti came from there, and so had many of the people now in Bahrein. It did not look much of a place, and I was glad when we went about and stood away from Qatar. There was much trouble there, Nejdi said. He put the blame for the trouble on bad sheikhs. There must, at some time or other, have been many bad sheikhs round the Persian Gulf.

When we went about and stood once more towards the Persian side, we sighted two booms, hull-down ahead. Nejdi immediately recognized one as a vessel which had sailed from Zanzibar a month before we did, which pleased him. The other was from Batina, bound north with firewood. We overhauled them steadily, with the wind hot like a blast from a furnace, hazy, and full of desert sand, and the sea short and steep and angry. We rolled and pitched violently and the sailors bailed out frequently. Spray clouds drove over us, wetting Yimid the monkey, who had come out to watch the sailors doing something and was drenched by the sea for his pains. He looked round bitterly to see who had done that to him, and chattered at the sea excitedly, as if he were telling it something. After that he crept, very wet, inside the lee of the firebox, looking malevolently aft. Bizz the cat, with more sense than Yimid, had long removed herself and her offspring to a place of safety.

In the last light of that day, still with the same tumultuous sea, we passed close by the two other booms. They were both standing along under their smallest mainsails, making good weather in spite of the sea. The pair made an unforgettable sight as they slogged along in the first of the windy night, showing the handsome lines of the Kuwait boom at its best as they alternately lifted low bow and high stern and rolled to the rounds of their bilges, lurching to windward down the side of a sea. We hailed them, and wished them good night. They looked brave little ships. It struck me then as it had before—on Kwale beach, looking at the old *Bedri;* the night off Malindi, and again off Kisimayu—what a pity it is that the Kuwaiti, building such good ships, do not build them a little better, just that little which would make them seaworthy at all times; and rig them a little more sturdily, in the Indian style. Better attention to fastenings, better selection of wood, properly watertight decks and seamanlike precautions for the shedding of water—it would take little to bring these improvements to the Kuwait ships. With them, they could go anywhere. Personally I should prefer to rig one as a ketch, if I had to take her anywhere away from the Indian Ocean.

The wind hauled fair towards midnight, and we wore round again to stand towards Bahrein. This time we made it. We came in with the daybreak on our eleventh day from Mutrah Bay, having sailed through the night. This was a creditable feat on Nejdi's part, spoiled only by his frequent assertions that no other nakhoda would do it, for Bahrein stands in a reef-filled corner of the Persian Gulf which mariners rightly dread. Its waters are shallow and the pearl banks bite perilously close at the surface here and there, ready to bite holes in any ships which try to pass over them. Most of the other nakhodas would only have dared sail in towards Bahrein with daylight, which was prudent. It was a memorable sight to see Nejdi, very pleased, unconcernedly singing behind the helmsman through the night as his ship came in. The night was moonless but bright with stars; our wake was a milky stream shot through by the phosphorescence of the indrawn lead as the sailors took soundings from time to time, the sails swollen black shapes against the stars, the helmsman hunched over the spokes of his wheel, and the sailors off duty stretched asleep on the chests.

We came bowling in at the rate of knots. It was well done and Nejdi was very pleased with himself, but his pleasure left him when the rising sun disclosed the other big dhows in the harbor. Even the fact that the best of them had cleared from the Rufiji or from Lamu at least two weeks before we left Zanzibar did not cheer him. Within five minutes of our arrival Yusuf bin Isa was aboard, laughing as merrily as usual and recounting the news of Ibn Saud's generous buying. Sure enough, our next visitor was the King's agent, out to buy the cargo. This he did on the spot and after the most cursory examination, for Ibn Saud is not a man to quibble about his bargains. The agent was a Bahrein Persian in white mushla and pale silk pantaloons beneath a cotton gown, an optimistic and energetic man who had the whole of our cargo bought within five minutes. For this his commission was the half of one per cent. We sold him 300 score, though down in the Rufiji we had paid for less than 150. How, in spite of all the difficulties and the supervision, we had succeeded in loading twice the official cargo I did not know, but I could guess who had managed it. It was Mubarak our "pilot," who had been carried off to the Utete jail.

It was deadly hot in Bahrein, which seemed even less an Arab port than Aden is. Manama was a busy and animated place, but it was not Arabic. It was full of Indians, Persians and Americans, with Arabs pearl-diving and Persians doing the labor. Manama was too hot and too humid a place for any undue display of energy in unravelling its story: it seemed to me mainly a market place for the distribution of inferior goods to Hasa, nearer Nejd, and Persia, without undue interference from the customs authorities of those places, and for the accumulation of any stray wealth the infidels of oil might have to scatter. This, in spite of American efficiency, appeared from Arab accounts to be considerable. Sleek automobiles prowl and purr through the Manama *suq*, not all owned by the oil men, and the sailors, padding barefoot, nowadays find most of the prices beyond them.

When our cargo was sold so readily Nejdi announced that we should be at Manama only three days: he was anxious to be home. The sailors shared his eagerness to be gone, but it was three days before we began to discharge our cargo. When once a start had been made, it was landed rapidly. It was ferried ashore by the sailors, using the longboat and some boats hired from the shore, and flung on the waterfront road. Before we had been in a week the waterfront road was almost covered with Rufiji and Lamu poles bought for Ibn Saud; and Nejdi, who at first had been very pleased at the rapid sale of his cargo, fretted that he had come to Bahrein, for it delayed his homecoming. He seemed almost to regret the speed and ease with which our cargo was disposed of, for this is not the Arab way of doing things: I believe he took a delight in haggling over sales for days. There we had come in, the agent had come aboard, and the cargo was sold. There was no thrill in it at all—no finesse. Nejdi loved some finesse in his business ventures: it was half the fun of living.

Nevertheless it seemed to me that he allowed himself to have a tolerable time in Manama. I went ashore with him several times, and visited other ships. The nearer they came to home the better the life these nakhodas of the big ship lived. We used to go in the longboat in the cool of the morning—to walk about in Manama after 10 A.M. was a sweat-bathed purgatory—and land at the head of a long quay of coral stones. The quay was being extended, and the fleet of harbor boats skimming across the water with their high lateen sails and their little hulls full of stone looked like a regatta. All round the inner waters of the harbor men stood in the sea, naked, breaking up coral and hauling up the broken pieces to be loaded into these boats, which carried them to the quay. On our way in we always pulled close by the other Kuwait ships and brought in any nakhodas who wished to come, which was usually all of them, though sometimes the longboat of a big ship would be waiting by its gangway for us to come by, when they would leave and we would race. How we raced! Crews singing, great paddles splashing, nakhodas exhorting their own crews and reviling the others, serangs shouting, quartermasters lively at the helm, and all the harbor looking on. We always made a great race of it with el-Dhow's people. Their longboat was a lovely thing, thirty-seven feet long, rowed by forty great men with Abdul-wahhab himself at the helm. The evening races were the best. All the longboats would be at the quay waiting for their nakhodas, to take them off to their ships for the evening prayer. The nakhodas, seven or eight of them, always came down together, strolling along from the coffee shop swinging their beads. At the pierhead they were into their boats like a shot and we would be away. How those sailors pulled, and how the harbor resounded to their songs. It was about half a mile out to where the bigger vessels were anchored—a long pull in that climate. But the sailors made a joke of it and, day after day, night after night, we raced. Honors were about even between our men and el-Dhow's. They had a lovely longboat, long and powerful and sleek. Nejdi vowed he would have a better the next voyage.

The intervals between these morning and evening races were given up to strolling in the suq, dawdling in the coffee shops, dining in the homes of merchants and sleeping on their carpets in the comparative cool of a shaded room. The suq itself, spacious and covered, had all sorts of desirable things for sale, from handsome Arab cloaks to American un-

derwear, and from Paris perfumes to evening dress ties. One could buy
almost anything in Manama and the prosperity of the place was obvious.
It was a very recent prosperity, due mainly to oil, for in the past few
years Bahrein has moved from nothing to the twelfth largest oil field of the
world. Formerly pearling had been the island's greatest industry, but that
had long been in decline, largely owing to world depression and the competition of the Japanese cultured pearl. Agriculture, once also important,
was now generally neglected. The wealth of the place was in its oil: I
found myself wondering, as Nejdi and I wandered in the *suq* past the
well-stocked shops, whether this temporary influx of wealth was altogether good for a place. I did not, however, meet any one who objected
to it.

"Kuwait," Nejdi said, "will be like this soon."

"God forbid!" I said. "Is it not a town of the Arabs?"

He looked at me. "But there is oil," he said, and then, after a while,
added: "Perhaps you are right. This is not Arab." Then he said no more.

Wandering about the *suq* with Nejdi was an interesting experience,
watching him greet relatives, merchants, friends, We called on a leading
merchant, who was a distant relative. He was a tight-lipped gentleman of
haughty demeanor dressed in sumptuous clothes. When we called on
him in his office in the *suq* he was very busy telling a number of Banyan
moneychangers, in few and not at all gentle words, exactly why their
business propositions did not appeal to him. Here, as everywhere, we were
regaled with sweetmeats, sherbet and the too bitter coffee, too sweet tea.
The merchant asked us to his home for a meal, but we did not go.

"Merchants," Nejdi said, "are tough. To them all is money."

"And nakhodas?" I asked.

"Nakhodas have the sea," he said. "To them money is only for their
ships."

We delayed a little at that merchant's place, but passed along the narrow alleys of the back part of the *suq*, where the porters' asses hurried by
laden with bales of goods and the porters ran along behind them shouting
"Make way! Make way!" We dropped into other offices, not so imposing,
where grave dignified Arabs sat at their desks doing nothing and long
lines of their hangers-on stared at them from seats on the benches, also
doing nothing. They were bare places, those offices, and what business
was supposed to be conducted in them I did not discover. They were
brokers, Nejdi said. It seems, in Arabia, that every merchant who is nothing else can always be a broker.

In the offices, where we apparently called merely as a matter of courtesy, the talk was always of merchandise, and Nejdi took no part in it.
Out in the *suq* and along the waterfront, however, we frequently ran into
groups of the other nakhodas. With them the talk was of ships and Nejdi
had always much to say. He cut a small figure in the big merchant's place,
but he was a man when there was talk of ships—or action in ships. I had
never noticed how small he was until I saw him hunched up meekly in
the merchant's chair and even the fact that he had on his best silk gown
and his most elaborately embroidered cloak could not give him his proper
self-confidence. He was always dressed in his best on these shore excur-
sions, in silks and gold-embroidered gown with headcloth of white and
gold held in position by a headrope of black Persian wool, with his hand-
sewn sandals decorated in green and red and his best amber beads in
his hand.

When we met the nakhodas it was never long before we adjourned to
a coffee shop, always the same one. It was a big one in the Hilal building
by the waterfront, where a large black sheep wandered in and out as a
pet and queer pictures lined the walls, and the hookah and yarns of the
sea were the order of the day. The pictures on the walls were of sheikhs
and voluptuous Egyptian beauties with brazen eyes, interspersed with
advertisements showing girls smoking American cigarettes and comic sections cut from some Chicago Sunday newspaper. The central picture was
a horrible colored print showing a group of non-Aryans mutilating the
prophet Isa. Above this was a lurid lithograph of the Shah of Persia, beneath which a group of indigent Persians lounged in the corner complain-
ing about the government. In another corner a gramophone brayed and
Arabs reclined on the benches sipping tea and smoking. Nejdi kicked off
his sandals and got down to the business in hand—some yarn about the
voyage—in earnest. Here we whiled away the hours, for time in coffee
shops meant nothing to customers or proprietor. You may sleep if you
wish, or spend all day playing a curious game of draughts.

Later we used to eat at an Arab place across the road, where they
served good meals of meat and fish and vegetables washed down with curdled milk. After that, it was usual to return to the coffee shop for a final
smoke, before pulling off to the big *el-Dhow* for a sleep. There we slept
the hot hours away and in midafternoon a breeze crept pleasantly to the
anchorage to awaken us to tea and prayer. Again the talk was of ships
and adventures at sea, with much swinging of the amber beads and bubbling at the water-pipe and gesturing of graceful hands. Nejdi, no longer

quiet or in any way subdued, held forth to his cronies upon the performances of his boom and the happenings of the voyage and narrated great
maritime events which never happened at all. Sometimes we yarned and
slept aboard this vessel, sometimes that. It made no difference. The nakhodas took it in turns to entertain the group. It was all very cheerful, very
pleasant, and completely unaffected. Once having got aboard a boom,
we never knew when we should leave it again: it might not be until the
following morning, or even the day after that.

I must admit that this abundant and acceptable hospitality can be
readily offered by the Arab mariner, for he has no bed to make up for
his guests and no extra chairs to draw up to the table. For a bed there is
the deck, and for covering the stars. You have your cloak and your forearm for a pillow. As for eating, there are no utensils to be provided: there
are rice and meat enough on the big dish and room for half a dozen extra hands. Yet I could not help thinking sometimes that these good men
could show us something of real hospitality: I could not help comparing
their ways with our own, and the comparison was not to our advantage.

The end of May found us still moored off Manama, our cargo discharged and the boom empty, but there were no signs of leaving. No one
was upset by that. Each day to us was good of itself and the morrow
would bring its own blessings. Some were anxious to be gone, for several
of the sailors proposed to buy themselves brides in Kuwait, and the quartermaster, Kalifa, met a man ashore who spoke to him of his new baby,
a bright little lad now six months old, whom Kalifa had never seen. He
smiled at the prospect of seeing this new baby and went about his work
with double energy, but day succeeded day and still we lay at anchor.
There was plenty of news of Kuwait in the *suq*. According to all accounts
things were quiet there now and business was good. The hotheads behind the riot languished in the Sheikh's dungeons, from which there was
slight chance of their emerging. The oil business, though still in its early
stages, promised well. Ibn Saud had lifted the old ban on his Beduin and
now allowed them to trade freely in and with Kuwait. Most of the Arab
news was word of mouth, but it was surprising how quickly it travelled,
and often, too, how accurate it was.

If Nejdi ever worried about the possible fate of his friend Bedar in
the baggala *Bedri*, of whom nothing had been heard since Zanzibar, he
gave no sign of it. That day—the last of May—I went off early to find him
aboard the boom of Hamoud bin Abdul-latif, lately come from India,

where he was seated on a carpet aft puffing at the hookah with a dish of sweetmeats before him, and a Negro sailor seated on the capstan entertaining him with the guitar. Hamoud's boom was laden with ropes, teak and timber in general, bamboos, chests, and chairs, with half a dozen small dugout canoes on top of the lot. She had been fifty-two days from Malabar to Muscat, which is far from fast, but as she was twenty days from Muscat to Manama I concluded that either she sails very poorly or was sailed badly, for these are poor passages. With Nejdi and Hamoud was Hamoud's brother Nasir, master of the baggala *Cat*. Nasir was a little man with a big moustache who laughed uproariously at his own jokes and everybody else's, even more than big Yusuf did. He was a merry little tub of a man, not five feet high, fit master for his little *Cat*. Not that she was little to him, or catlike either. It was supposed to be a great joke to call his baggala the *Cat*, though I could see nothing funny in it and it was the one joke Nasir himself could never see. According to him, the name of his craft was *Lord of the Waters*, or something equally flowery: she was no cat. However, *Cat* she was to all the other nakhodas and all the crews. The *Cat*, otherwise *Lord of the Waters*, was a lovely little baggala with a capacity of about 1800 packages of Basra dates. She had a beautifully carved stern and, though over fifty years old, seemed sound and staunch. She was the best of the three surviving Kuwait baggalas and I looked at her with interest. I still toyed with the idea of perhaps saving a baggala by a transatlantic voyage: the *Cat* looked ideal for the purpose. But I said nothing about it: there would be time enough to examine her thoroughly in Kuwait, for she would be on the beach there with us three months.

Sometimes instead of pulling back to some ship for the midday rest, we slept in the apartment of the young Kuwait merchant Bedar al-Saar, in the Hilal building. His apartment looked over the waterfront and a section of the *suq*, and it was always interesting up there. Five minutes after we were in, the group of nakhodas—the two Abdul-wahhabs, Nejdi, Hamoud, Nasir, Abdulla Kitami and a sixty-six-year-old Persian just arrived with an enormous boom from Lamu—would be stretched on the carpets asleep, each with his head covered with his headcloth and resting on his hairy arm, and their snores shook the room. The hot afternoons passed pleasantly while we slept. With the worst heat gone from the sun, life came to the waterfront and *suq* again. Flocks of fat Kuwait sheep were driven along the quay from a small boom, to be converted into Bahrein's meat; little asses with jingling bells hurried along laden with bales of skins, bags of rice, or packages of dates. A noisy group of Persians in trousers and dreadful Russian caps argued at the customs gate about the admission of a number of bundles of indifferent carpets; and all the gramophones in the *suq* started up. So life came again to Manama, with the afternoon regatta of the pretty harbor boats skimming over the nearer waters carrying coral to extend the quay, and, in the distance, the pearlers coming in from the sea and the sambuks and jalboots from Hasa.

In the streets the cosmopolitan Eastern crowd assembled—Persians, many dressed in their country's idea of European clothes, others in gowns and carefully wrapped turbans, Banyans, Punjabi, Baluchi (not many of these), Arabs from Oman, the Trucial coast, Hasa, Nejd, Kuwait, Qatar; Negroid sailors of Kuwait, stalwart and sturdy, swinging their rosaries and rolling along like men, long-haired Beduin from the desert, prisoners marching shackled down the road with a guard behind them, a Somali or two, long and lean and vociferously independent, as usual. One of these, claiming to be a poet, called on me, at Bedar's place, and read some of his poetry, which was listened to with interest. Apparently it was about the stand of the Ethiopians against the Italians in Abyssinia, and there were many throaty *taiyibs* from the assembly. Unfortunately the poetry was beyond me: the complications of Arabic prose and the spoken word were difficult enough. It may have been good poetry for all I know, but the poet did not look to me much like a good Somali. However, with some bakhshish he went on his way, in his golden waistcoat and mantle of calico, and we strolled across the square to the Persian baths behind the house, by the fruit garden. These baths were big enough to swim in, and we all plunged in and swam for an hour. Old Abdul-wahhab bin Kalifa, who was stout and large, swam like a seal, though I expected him to flounder about like a whale. The pool was often full of nakhodas, splashing about and playing like boys. It was a good place, with the scent from the flowers and the fruit blossoms blowing over it and the cooling breeze from the sea. Outside it was humid, and even to stand still was to find oneself bathed stickily in a heavy sweat. Our deep-water shipmasters managed to have, all in all, a pretty fair time.

With these pleasant interludes the time at Manama passed happily and I by no means looked forward to the approaching end of the voyage. Bahrein was our last stop. After this came Kuwait, and though the north wind called *shemaal* still blew with strength, its forty days must soon be over. Sometimes, Nejdi said, it blew only for twenty: then it stopped for ten and came again stronger than ever for forty days. He wanted to slip out and run up to Kuwait some day when the *shemaal* was off duty, because, he said, two days of good sailing would bring us home if we went direct, over the reefs. Though he spent his days pleasantly in idleness there, he watched the weather like a hawk and was ready to sail at five minutes' notice. But we could not sail too hurriedly, wind or no wind, for we had not yet been paid for our poles.

However, there was no reason to worry about that: we should get our silver in good time. There was not a better payer in all Arabia.

We went once to the dhow yard, a small place at the end of the town where the shipwrights and their apprentices were making more money by building models for sale to the oil men from America than by building booms for Arab mariners. They had once made these small models very well, but the influx of indiscriminate buyers and the rush of orders were having their inevitable effect. The models I saw were poor things, though the little booms unfinished on the stocks were sweet. Some of them had lain there unfinished for four or five years, for things were not good with the seafarers. The distributing trade to Hasa and smuggling to Persia might be all very well, but pearling, the real backbone of the place, had been cut by more than half. For other diversion we visited the Portuguese ruins. We dined sumptuously with a Persian in Muharraq, eating a great meal of meat and chicken and fish and fruit spread on carpets on his roof top, under the moon. We watched the water booms piping up fresh water from the springs under the sea. We gave feasts and attended them: we yarned and listened to yarns: we wandered in the *suq* and looked at the life of Bahrein. While our sailors worked we had, indeed, a very good time.

We went to the oil fields, a piece of Texas set in the middle of Bahrein with the climate of hell, and though the Americans had air-conditioned their bungalow homes no one could cool the works. To walk into a bungalow there was to come from desert to Chicago by the mere process of opening a door, and the sudden, unexpected transition was almost frightening. The oil field was a huge place, very well run, but to us from the sea it was a frightening array of tremendous retorts and great cauldrons and all sorts of weird pipes, presided over by men who, for all they had in common with the Arabs round them, might have come from Mars. We saw everything but oil, though there was enough of that—scores of thousands of barrels a day, they told us. We saw no barrels either, for that matter; but we saw the oil tankers carting the stuff away. The oil field belonged geographically to Bahrein and its royalties enriched the island, but really it might have been in Mexico or Venezuela. It was barbwired off from the rest of the island, but it stood sufficiently alone without barricade.

From the heights on a clear evening one could see the oil field of Saudi-Arabia on the mainland perhaps twenty miles away, where another air-conditioned town was springing up and the oilmen from Texas and Southern California were pumping liquid gold from the earth. King Ibn Saud himself had recently visited this field on the occasion of the first bulk shipment of a cargo of oil from his new port of Ras Tanurah. He had come across to Bahrein at the invitation of the Sheikh, His Highness Sir Hamad bin Isa al-Kalifa. This had happened a few days before we arrived. I was sorry we had missed the Saudi King, who was held in veneration by the Kuwaiti and all the Arabs. He had, they told me, come with 300 motortrucks and 2000 Beduin troops, who had almost eaten the Americans out of house and home. It was said that each Bedu had eaten half a dozen sheep and drunk two cases of pineapple juice.

When we were at Bahrein the oil was bringing nearly five million rupees a year to the island, of which a third went to the ruling family. We saw the sons of the Sheikh roaring round the place in the latest model American cars, with police sirens which wailed continually. Whether this marked the limit of their cultural advancement I do not know. There were those who said it did. Nejdi scowled at the young sheikhs rushing about in siren-wailing motorcars.

"Noise, noise!" he said. "It is not good, for the emptiest drum sounds the loudest." Bahrein, he went on, had changed out of all recognition in the past ten years, though he admitted that many of the changes had been for the better. But the oil field, the great towers of the wells, the rushing motorcars bewildered and worried him, and he complained that he had not seen a man in the *suq* who did not wear at least one article of European clothing. Even the women wore stockings and shoes. What was wrong with the Arabs? Did they want to ape Europeans? The women would soon be going unveiled and the men forgetting their prayers. I feared that Nejdi would begin a theological diatribe at any moment and dropped behind with old Abdul-wahhab, who took things as they came, looked at them quietly with his old eyes, and made no comment.

On a hot day in the first week of June Hamed and our agent came out with a sack of six thousand rupees—payment for the poles. We sailed the same evening, for the *shemaal* was quiet and there was no time to lose.

Our ballast was some coral rock from the floor of the harbor, broken out by the sailors and ferried in our longboat. While the nakhodas had taken their ease in Manama there had been plenty of work for the sailors. We still had a few coconuts and five bags of cloves. Everything else had been sold.

Nejdi came out with a group of the nakhodas in the cool of the evening and we sailed at once, with infinite work and too little preparation, the sailors alternately bathed in their sweat and wet with the sea as they plunged overboard to work the anchor out of the coral or to clean the cable, and then climbed aboard again to hoist the sail. We took up our boats as we sailed and the men of *el-Dhow* helped us at the halliards. Then they left in their longboat and they and the other Kuwait ships cheered us as we passed. The wind was fair but very light, and we gathered way slowly. Two other booms sailed with us, Hamoud's and the Persian Mansur's, and Nasir's little baggala *Cat*.

We headed out slowly across the shoals bound the direct way to Kuwait, for Nejdi was anxious to be home. The way from Bahrein to Kuwait direct is littered with shoals and reefs and dangerous banks, and in the ordinary way, I suppose, we should have given these danger-spots a good berth. But now Nejdi had heard that his favorite wife was very ill, from some trouble after childbirth, and he was desperately anxious to drive his ship home.

The evening breeze freshened. We stood on and all our tired sailors smiled. After many months we were now bound for home. We had six thousand silver rupees in the nakhoda's chest and the wind was fair.

Chapter 17

NEJDI'S RACE HOME

O U R   D A S H homewards across the reefs from Bahrein to Kuwait was the most dramatic episode of the voyage. Daylight the morning after sailing showed that the other vessels were out of sight and we sailed over a shallow sea through a fleet of pearlers—tiny vessels full of men who, as we sailed by, were squatting round their decks opening oysters. These were the fleet of al-Qatif and Darien, Nejdi said, and they were greatly thinned out by the depression. We hailed a few of them, asking what luck they were having, but they replied only that Allah was compassionate. Nejdi asked them also if they had seen any other Kuwait deep-water men, but they said they had not. Three or four had sailed several days before we did, but Nejdi said none of these would dare to try this dash across the reefs. The western side of the Persian Gulf from Bahrein almost to Kuwait is littered with destruction, for coral reefs and banks and shifting sands abound for 200 miles. Most of the area, being of no interest to steamships, has never been properly charted, but Nejdi had been pearling there since he was a child.

Every man in the ship knew those waters: there was none among them who had not been sailing there at least ten years. Nejdi knew every bank, every overflow, every low-sanded point. We sounded frequently as we ran on, always with the lead armed, though it had never been armed before. Some camel-fat was poked into a rough hole in the bottom of the lead, and Nejdi poked into a rough hole in the bottom of the lead, and Nejdi examined with care the grit and shells and sand brought up on this. He seemed able to follow our way in this manner, as though he were reading signs on a city street. Sometimes we weaved about leaving a wake behind us like the twistings of a snake, though I could see no safe passage nor distinguish the places where there were two fathoms of water from those where there was only one.

We saw little of the land, for the Hasa coast is low, but Nejdi seemed to know every inch of the water, every tiny craft we saw, every minute variation of the gulf-bed. This was native pilotage at its best and I watched him with envious interest. I could not have done this, not after ten years of pearling and sailing there, not with all the sextants and tables and chronometers and slide rules in the world. This was pilotage by eye and personal knowledge, almost by instinct. To navigate in this way a man must never clutter his mind with book learning: perhaps Nejdi was right, after all, in his scorn of our methods. Nejdi said that in this kind of work he was helped even by the color of the sky, for he professed to detect a change in it over the shallowest places. What I found most amazing, however, was his apparent ability always to detect which way the sets were running and the tides, and to predict them. He had no tables and he did not even know the date. The moon, he said, was enough; the moon, the stars, and the behavior of the sea.

We ran on that morning with the wind light and Nejdi impatient; for the first time in the voyage he was excited and craved speed. We had gone out with the second mainsail, not wishing to spread great Oud with the ship so lightly ballasted. A capful of wind in Oud could capsize her, with less than thirty tons of coral in the hold. But with our speed dropped to five knots Nejdi gave the order to lower the *sifdera*, as the second mainsail was called, and bend old Oud instead. This the sailors did with a will and Oud was aloft again faster than he had ever been before. No sooner was the great sail set than the wind freshened and we bowled along at ten knots in a welter of foam with the lee rail not far from the water. Let her go! Nejdi, crouching anxiously aft, watched her like an old sea eagle, and though she lurched now and again till it seemed that she must blow over, there was no sea and she ran on. She lay with a heavy list and the sea skimming past the lee side within inches of the rail, and the sailors laughed. Let her go! We gave her the mizzen and added the biggest jib, set on a spar lashed along the raked stemhead, and the breeze hummed in the rigging. The spray drove away before the bows and her wake ran behind for miles. The sea birds welcomed us, and the pearling fleet from Jubail looked up in astonishment as we raced by.

We ran on through tide rips and across reefs where the bottom rose up alarmingly to bite at us; but Nejdi said there was water enough. We avoided the worst places. The quartermasters not on wheel duty sounded

The Persian Gulf and the Gulf of Oman

continually with a handlead on each side, and their chanting of the depths sounded sweetly in the wind.

We saw nothing of the land but the gulf bottom and of that we saw enough. Once we saw the low spit of the point of Abu Ali, which was nothing but sand. All the Hasa coast beyond this brief glimpse of yellow sand was hidden in haze. All day we foamed and raced along and in the evening still kept all sail, though we were then in one of the most dangerous quarters of the whole Gulf. During the day the sailors had scrubbed the maindeck and the poop and cleaned their chests and all the brasswork. We raced onwards beneath the moon, a spotless ship with her white sails bathed in beauty and moonlit decks cleaner than they had ever been before. The sailors gathered round the bole of the mizzenmast wrapped in their cloaks and grinned happily and talked about Kuwait. Kuwait, Kuwait! That was all I heard. Kuwait, Kuwait! At last this paradise on earth was just below the horizon's rim and on the morrow would arise. Kuwait, Kuwait, where every ship was a sturdy clipper and every girl was beautiful, where the houses of the Sheikh and the merchants were mansions full of the wealth of the Indies, where the water was sweet and the fruit glorious and the melons lying upon the earth were flavored with myrrh and honey. What a place this Kuwait must be—more fruitful than Zanzibar, more blessed than Beirut, more healthy than the Indian hills.

So the sailors raved, and Nejdi, squatting on his bench watching the driving ship, for once said nothing. Well, I should soon see. The patriotism of the Kuwaiti was not to be questioned, but I wondered what sort of town it could really be, from which so many men had to sail out in great ships most of the year, wresting a poor living from the sea. Though I wondered, I said nothing, for the enthusiasm of the group was infectious. Gone were all ills, even Ebrahim's fever, and little Jassim the cook hopped and skipped while Ismael, who a few days before had been suffering agonies of rheumatism, played merrily on his guitar. Sultan and the dying pearl-diver Nasir spoke cheerfully of the girls they would marry the day after we came in, and Kalifa the helmsman smiled about his new baby. He had the best girl in all Kuwait, Sultan boasted. No, *he* had, said Zaid: and Saoud the little surly seaman said neither of them could have, for he had already married them all. Hassan the helmsman, coming forward after his trick at the wheel, spoke of his two wives waiting for him, both with child, one aged about twenty and the other, new last year, aged sixteen. He found he needed two, he said, in his brief summer at home after nine months at sea: one was not enough. Now he was looking forward to acquiring a third, for the two he had got along splendidly and were a delight in his life. With three it would be paradise. Two wives, he said—apart from the initial expense—cost no more than one: three would cost little more. The two he had were the best of friends and kept his little home spotless and pleasant always. He slept with one in the noon siesta, the other at night, in strict rotation, he said: there was no jealousy.

"If you will listen to an old man," Yusuf said when Hassan had ended, "you will consider long before you take this third wife. If you are so doubly blessed as to have found two women who will get along together and keep peace in your home, leave well alone, my son. For there are no three women on earth who can share one man; and the third may be a virago."

"Oh moaner, thy wife is thirty!" Hassan rejoined and they all laughed at this joke. To say that a man has a wife aged thirty was to condemn him to the society of the ancient. But old Yusuf, though his wife might have been thirty, looked forward to seeing her and his home again no less than the others. Poor old fellow, his feet were in a dreadful state from the constant hardships of the voyage, lacerated on the jagged knots of the Rufiji poles, torn on the coral of Manama roads, bruised and battered by the heavy work. His feet, like those of all the sailors, were tough and tremendously hard: their soles were of calloused skin a quarter of an inch thick. Yet the coral and the pronged wood had broken through even this armor, and now his feet bled whenever he ran. I looked at them for him, though he did not ask. There was little I could do except bathe them in boracic lotion and wrap them in adhesive tape, but my adhesive tape was all gone. No matter, Yusuf said, his wife would fix them up when he reached home. She understood how very well: she always fixed him up between voyages. I had a vision of old Yusuf in his little home in some back street of Kuwait, his little home with his three children, his herd of goats with their kids, and his chickens (for he had told me of these things), and being made ready for another voyage by the tender ministrations of his wife bathing his feet and anointing his eyes. Only the strength of his body could keep that little home going, and the pace in the Kuwait ships is hard: no man receives favors. No man, that is, unless he is a musician of the standing of Ismael, who could bargain with nakhodas anxious to exhibit his talents down the African coast.

The pace in the Kuwait ships is dreadfully hard and the style killing. It must be especially hard on a man who has previously been pearl-diving. All jobs are rushed at, all orders obeyed on the run day and night,

all sailors live on the sufferance of the nakhoda who, if he be impatient and overbearing, must still be put up with. Consideration for others is not a noticeable quality in the nakhoda class: life goes hard, I fear, with the old sailors. One who cannot stand the life drops out of it, I suppose: but usually he drops out in harness. There comes a day when he dies. The pace in the Kuwait ships is hard, foolishly hard, for there is no need for all this rush.

"It is our manner," Nejdi said, not excusing or explaining it, but surprised that I should ask. The sailors themselves take pride in this rushing at all jobs, though some of them are often knocked down in the rush. It is a matter of pride to be first, to be the highest aloft, to pull the longest oar, to stow the heaviest poles. The Suri did not do it, or the Yemenites, or the Hadhrami, or the sailors from the Trucial coast and from Batina, or the Indians, or the Persians. It is the style of the Kuwait ships alone—smart, efficient and very impressive; but, I fear, also sometimes killing. I wondered how long old Yusuf would stand up to the rigors of his life, and what would become of his little home when he was ended. He spoke to me of a younger brother who had died in a boom at Karachi the previous year; it seemed to me that he would need the three-month rest in Kuwait between voyages. Not many sailors died ashore. Old Yusuf said it was the pearling that killed them, mostly, and he thanked God that he had to do that no more. His own small debt had been worked off, for it was five years since he had been diving, and in all that time he had paid twenty rupees a year from his deep-sea earnings. With his debt gone, he was free. Compared with pearling, he said, even a month in the Rufiji loading mangrove poles was a holiday.

Next morning we still foamed on, for Nejdi had driven his ship without sleep or food through the night, squatting on his bench abaft the helmsman watching, watching, examining, in the binnacle's light, the sand and the shingle brought to him from the arming of the lead, sniffing at the wind. Sometimes we would fall off and change our course, this way or that, though I could see no reason. Nejdi said there were reefs, many of them. I knew that: it was how he knew where they were and how he found a channel between them, that baffled me. But he did. By midmorning of the next day, storming past headland after headland, we were abeam of Ras Zor which marks the southern border of the city-state of Kuwait. The breeze freshened and Nejdi pointed to the land, murmuring "Kuwait, Kuwait!" as if he could hardly believe that at last, after all these months, his homeland was again in sight. He called to me.

Jassim, the cook

"Kuwait, Kuwait!" he said, pointing. "There, there is a land of beauty for you to see! Do you not see that that is beautiful?"

"What, that piece of sand?" I asked, pretending to be unimpressed.

Nejdi looked horrified, though the coastline of Arabia in the neighborhood of Ras Zor is in fact far from impressive, and none but the Kuwaiti would see much beauty in it.

"Sand! Piece of sand!" Nejdi almost shouted. "Look at it, Nazarene! Here are no rough mountains, but the soft, low land, gentle as the swelling of a virgin's breasts. Are you not ashamed that you said the mountains of Oman were beautiful, those useless hills? Look now at this Kuwait!" And he looked himself, very long, and kept on looking, no longer caring whether I was impressed or not.

It looked very much like any other piece of sand and about as impressive as the Benadir coast south of Ras Haifun. But I did not say so, for I could see the emotion on Nejdi's dark face and the tears in his tired eyes. He had said during the night why he so drove his ship, with her lee rail skimming the sea and the seams of great Oud splitting in the fresh south wind. He had heard at Manama that his favorite wife was in danger and might die.

Now we foamed by the islet of al-Kubbar, where the birds rose in cloudlike flocks as we ran by, with the ship making perhaps twelve knots. We overhauled and sailed by the slow mail British India steamer which had left Bahrein when we did, carrying Nejdi's letter announcing his homecoming. We foamed by, and Nejdi showed the flag of Kuwait while the sailors laughed. The drums were warming at Jassim's fire, for the distance from al-Kubbar to Kuwait is less than twenty miles and we might be there in two hours. The sailors, in great excitement, rushed about getting out their best gowns and their most heavily blued headcloths, trimming their moustaches, cleaning their teeth. Some of them were too excited to do anything. Nejdi, with all dangers safely passed and only Kuwait before him (for al-Kubbar marked the end of the worst waters), made Hassan shave him and scrub him down, bathing him with water from the sea. After that, Yusuf perfumed him, and rubbed some Paris scent into his forehead and behind his ears, and searched through his chest to put the gold ornaments for his wives on top, handy for landing. Even the monkey, Yimid, joined in the excitement, hopping about and looking at the shoreline of Kuwait, while Bizz the Somali cat led her offspring Fahad, Farid, and Fatima in a raid on the fire-box—when Jassim was not looking. The sea was very green there, and there was a white sand-glare over the land (abeam and ahead), for we were close to the head of the Persian Gulf.

But when the wind dropped, steadily, and we sailed on slowly, taking the whole afternoon to make the twenty miles between al-Kubbar and Ras al-Ardh, the slow mail steamer passed us again, and this time we did not look. We picked up the low island of Failachah to the west'ard of Kuwait Bay. It was the last landfall. The voyage was done. It remained only to turn the corner, and anchor in Kuwait Bay. We saw the houses of Failachah and some sambuks on the beach, the water booms and the firewood booms, and the little belems coming down from Basra between Failachah and the mainland. We saw the tiny date-frond boats of the fishermen fishing in the sea off Ras al-Ardh, the fishermen sitting more in the water than out of it, for their boats are but bundles of water-logged reeds afloat, not watertight or meant to be. We rounded the triangular beacon on Ras al-Ardh and saw the light there flashing, as we stood in for Kuwait Bay—slowly, now, very slowly, with the breeze dying away and the tide against us.

With the last of the light we came in sight of the town of Kuwait, with all our drums going and the decks full of song. We came on slowly past the Sheikh's house. The night shut off the view of the town as we came to it, and we came to our anchor in darkness while the drum-banging and the singing went on and on. We were forty-eight hours from Bahrein—fast mail time, Nejdi said (though the slow mail beat us), and, though he had driven his ship so splendidly home and brought his long and difficult voyage to a successful conclusion, he was consumed with disappointment because we arrived by night, and he was robbed of his triumph. If we came by day the town would see us, and boats full of his friends would come out to cheer and welcome, and all the waterfront would know that Nejdi was back again, up from Africa by way of Bahrein with a "fast mail" passage—Nejdi, the driver of ships and men, Nejdi with the *Triumph of Righteousness*, triumphant over the seas again. It was a blow to him to have no welcome, for we were unexpected and his letter announcing our coming would not be delivered until the morning.

The sailors still drummed and sang, but the sense of achievement was ended, temporarily, for Nejdi. The sails were lowered and unbent for the last time this voyage, the sailors singing all the time, singing praises to Allah and praise of Nejdi—singing, singing, first as we came in under the shade of old Oud with his fifty-nine cloths, and then at the anchorage under the stars.

Hassan at the wheel

We hailed some big Persian booms anchored near by, and learned from them that ships which were known to have sailed from Bahrein several days before us had not arrived. At this news Nejdi was pleased, but he continued to sit lethargic on his bench, very tired, with half the spirit gone from him now that the day was ended and the voyage done. He advised the Persians to return to Bahrein and sell their cargoes there. This was a good tip, and they set to work at once to get under way, for the best price of mangroves in Kuwait was eight or nine rupees a score. His voice as he answered "Boom Nejdi" to the Persians' hail of "What ship?" had a ring of pride in it; but he was bitterly disappointed that it was not day. But the voyage was done. It remained only to go ashore; and yet, after driving the ship and himself so hard to reach her, he seemed to dread landing to meet his wife.

With the sailors' songs of praise still echoing over the harbor, the long-boat was swung out, and everybody went ashore—Nejdi, and Hamed, the serang, the quartermasters, Yusuf, everybody—leaving only three of us aboard: Ismael, who was an orphan and had neither wife nor home, old Salim from the desert, and myself. All the others had gone, making the longboat fly across the water, still singing their songs. I heard the echoes of their song until they landed; and there the boom was, anchored in Kuwait Bay, with her cargoes all discharged and her voyage ended. I sat alone on the transom to think about the voyage, while Ismael and old Salim slept.

What a voyage it had been! Ten thousand miles, and nine months of hard life and hard sailing, from mid-August of one year to mid-June of the next—to Basra first, after the summer's lay-up at Kuwait, to load a cargo of dates for Mukalla for orders: then down the Persian Gulf and the Gulf of Oman, standing out into the Arabian Sea before the last of the southwest monsoon had gone, with a call at Muscat for water on the way. Water may well be needed for the long beat along the South Arabian coast from Ras al-Hadd, where the Beduin still may turn pirates and pilotage is difficult, where conditions are adverse, and the coast harborless and dangerous along much of its length. Then Mukalla, and orders

The mate takes a shave

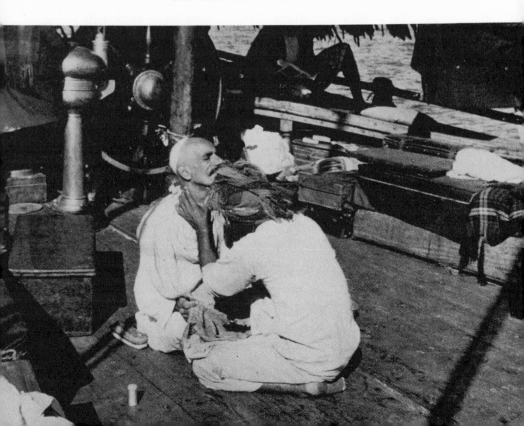

for Berbera across the Gulf of Aden: to Berbera, and the dates discharged for sale there, in Somaliland and Abyssinia, the sailors working painfully in the heat landing the heavy packages through the surf, and afterwards beaching the ship. Then Aden, the traditional turn-round port for African voyages, a hot oven with the cheapness of the trash in the bazaar its only attraction. From Aden beating again, eastbound towards Mukalla and the ports of the Hadhramaut, to complete the cargo and load Beduin for Africa. Then away for Africa with Haifun, that hellish dump of salt and sand; Mogadishu, where business was impossible and Abdulla was still trying to collect debts; Lamu, the first pleasant port of the voyage, but not much better for business than Mogadishu had been, for we had found Lamu depressed. Then Mombasa, the sunny island, where our passengers were landed and the decks could be cleaned; and so to Zanzibar, isle of delight. Then the Rufiji, after the call at Kwale—the terrible swamp of the Rufiji where all hands grew thin and half of them caught fever while they worked under conditions almost intolerable. From the Rufiji to Zanzibar again, where the soft arms of the houris and the caresses of the local bints drive away dull care: and then the long haul from Zanzibar along East Africa and up the Arab coast to the Gulf of Oman again, homeward bound. Muscat, the beat up the Gulf, Bahrein; and now the last run home.

What a round it had been! Ten thousand miles, down with one monsoon and back with the other, and not by any means so easy as that might indicate, for there were many adverse conditions, and many perilous places to be negotiated. Yet it had been done, and well done, without accident and without fuss; done as one of a fleet of a hundred Arab ships making much the same voyage; done by a group of skirted mariners illiterate and fanatic, but seamen to the backbone—men who knew no fancy knots or tricks of the sea, many of whom did not even know the points of the compass, men who spend most of their sea lives without storms, without even seeing rain. Yet they could do a day's work alongside any man, and they suffered hardships enough. They could handle sails and masts and yards cumbrous and awkward often far beyond the danger point.

I thought of the life these men lived, and of Nejdi and his muallim, Hamed bin Salim, who led them. Nejdi had his faults, and I have not spared them. Headstrong, often inconsiderate, no ascetic when a pretty bint was in sight, satisfied with his own knowledge, and secure in his expectation of a paradise where God speaks only Arabic, he was a sailor of outstanding qualities, an able leader, a pilot and ship-handler of supreme merit, and a shrewd man, able to stand up to merchants and brokers ashore. Nejdi was a man and I liked him. All our crew swore by him, and the sailors in the other ships respected him, though they did not always respect other nakhodas. Even the sailors of the big *el-Dhow*, swaggering through the Zanzibar bazaars, looked round when Nejdi passed. For three years in succession he had paid his sailors higher shares than any other nakhoda on the African voyage from Kuwait, and that was a fine reputation. He had sailed his *Triumph* well all that time, though he had only recently come from the Indian trade. He had always kept her free from accidents. And he had always been a good friend to me, a friend from whom I learned much.

Hamed bin Salim, who took command when Nejdi was not there, was a real man, too. Aboard that ship Nejdi was God and Hamed never more than a very minor prophet. Nejdi commanded and Hamed never really took his place. He did no more than deputize temporarily in his absence. But what he did, he did well. Quiet, intensely reserved, profoundly religious, he was at first hard to know. But I liked him, too, from the first, and he improved on acquaintance. Hamed had stayed with the ship throughout the hard nine months of the long voyage and had never had a rest. Hamed was always there, awake when Nejdi was asleep, in charge of the ship in the Rufiji, solving the awkward problems which followed Mubarak's arrest. Hamed was more considerate of the sailors than was Nejdi, because he had been a sailor himself. That Nejdi had never been: he had always belonged to the nakhoda class, and Hamed had only married into it. I hoped that by the next season he would have a ship of his own. He hoped so, too; but he did not permit himself to hope for it too fervently. Certainly he deserved one.

The crew were good fellows, without pretence and without any nonsense. They knew their work, and did it well, and no sort of hardship deterred them. They lived a life of toil and extreme hardship. They had not even six feet of the deck to call their own. They were paid no wages apart from a share in the earnings of the ship. They ate nothing for which they did not pay, for in the computation of the ship's earnings the cost of the sailors' food was always first deducted. They knew nothing of workmen's compensation, and insurance was against the rules of their religion. They had neither adequate clothing, nor a bed to lie upon. They seldom had a night of unbroken rest, and life in ports was no less trying than life at sea. Yet they extracted a great deal of joy from their daily life, and there was none among them who did not feel a strong affection for the ship and the sea. They were true seamen, a true band of brothers. There may be port officials and customs officers in half the ports of the East who would like nothing better than to see them under lock and key, for they are inveterate smugglers: there may be irate tanker captains who would wish all unlit dhows driven from the sea, for they are a menace to powered navigation: there may be harassed port officials in Mogadishu, Mombasa, Zanzibar, and the ports of western India who pray every night, while the northeast blows, that they may never see an Arab or his dhow again. Yet these mariners of ours were fine men, and if Kuwait, of which I had heard so much, could produce ship after ship of them, it must be a good place.

I looked at the stars, and at the darkness which was Kuwait. There was nothing to see, for it was midnight. I thought of Yusuf whose wife was then, perhaps, bathing his feet, of Kalifa with his little son, of Hassan with his two good wives and of Nejdi. I hoped they had found things well at home, all of them; for they were good men and deserved a good homecoming.

I fell asleep: and slept late into the morning, for there was no prayer call, and no one to bake the morning *khubz* or boil the tea. But the longboat was out early, with the serang and all the sailors and Hamed bin Salim. They at once set about the work of rigging down the masts and getting the ship ready for beaching. She was to be rigged down and all her gear taken ashore, and then she would be floated in at high tide to a safe berth behind the small breakwaters of coral which stood along the waterfront. Here, covered with a roof of date fronds and mats to protect her from the too strong rays of the sun, and with more mats hung round to protect the undersides, she would wait until the new season's dates were ready along the Basra River.

The sailors fell upon this work with a will. Arrival in the home port, though it might mean the end of the voyage, did not mean the end of the work, for the sailors had not finished until the ship was shored up in her safe berth and all her gear was landed. They showed me Nejdi's house, on the waterfront road, in front of which they said the boom would rest through the summer. I thought it a good arrangement that a nakhoda should have his ship berthed opposite his front door. All along the waterfront I could see these shored-up booms, and the nakhodas' houses beyond them.

It was three days' work, Yusuf said, to get the ship ready and beach

her. After that, they would have to oil her inside and out. Then they
would have finished and could consider themselves free. They would not
be paid until Abdulla returned, for the outstanding debts in Mogadishu
had to be collected before the shares were computed. It might be a month
or two. In the meantime, he said, they could get any money they needed
in advance from Nejdi. What with advances at the setting-out and the
payments in Aden and Zanzibar, some of the crew had very little coming
to them. No matter, Yusuf said: they could draw against the next voyage
enough to see them through the summer, if they wished. I gathered that
they usually wished. A sailor's life in Kuwait seemed to be financed almost exclusively by this sytem of advances, so that most of them were always in debt, and they were considered bound to the nakhodas to whom
they were indebted.

Nejdi was out before noon, with four of his sons who stood and stared
wide-eyed at everything. His wife, he said, was not so ill as he had feared,
and he had much to be thankful for. But he still regretted missing the
triumph of a daylight entry after that great run from Bahrein. We were
the first of the African traders home to lie up. The ships already beached
were back from voyages to India, or pearlers waiting for their season, due
to start almost any day.

With Nejdi came merchants, brokers, other nakhodas, among whom
was a pearling nakhoda looking for his crew. Our sailors were nearly all
pearlers of one sort or another, divers or tenders. Once a pearler always a
pearler, and those who owed money to nakhodas still in the trade had to
go out to the banks with them. If the nakhodas went, they must go. They
must do one thing or the other—go pearling, or repay the advances.
For a few years, the depression had saved them, but now, apparently, the
nakhodas were going to try their luck again. I saw melancholy looks on
the faces of many of the sailors, for pearling had been so depressed for
years that many nakhodas had not gone, and debts had been in abeyance.
It was no use going when they could not hope to make money. This year,
however, more than a hundred ships were fitting out, and pearl divers
were needed. I saw the terrible disappointment on Sultan's face when
a merchant approached him, for Sultan had saved his poor share to get
himself a bride. Now the merchant was requiring that he should either
pay or go pearling. *Allah karim!* Sultan said, though the sentiment seemed
inappropriate. Perhaps it was a prayer. The small Mohamed, who had
saved his share to make the pilgrimage to Mecca was also cornered. *Allah
karim!* Seven or eight others were in the same position.

Poor fellows, here they were back from their long voyage, with one foot on the beach, and they were being impressed for pearling. They had no alternative. If they had once accepted a pearl nakhoda's advance, they were done for: somehow or other these advances never seemed to be earned. There was no crying, not even grumbling, when the first shock had passed. It was the custom of the port. They had known of it from their infancy. There was always a chance. Fortunes had been made at pearling, too. It was not all hardship and poverty. The sailors, like most of their kind, were inveterate gamblers. Before long, those who had been impressed had recovered their spirits and were joking with the others about the huge pearls they were going to find in the coming season, and the wealth that would be theirs. That day, however, there was little mirth in their joking.

I was glad no nakhoda had impressed old Yusuf, for he needed rest. It was several years, he had told me, since he had been pearling. He ought to be safe now. He had worked out his debts and would be careful to contract no new ones. He had had enough pearling to last him a lifetime. I looked along the decks to see my old friend, always a leader in the heaviest work. There he was, singing and working.

But what was this? A pearl merchant approaching him, taking him by the sleeve, beginning a long harangue? He could have no business with old Yusuf, for Yusuf's debts were paid.

I was wrong. Business with old Yusuf he had, though he was not Yusuf's own nakhoda. He was, I learned afterwards, nakhoda of the belem in which Yusuf's brother had served. Yusuf had succeeded to his dead brother's debts, and he must go pearling again. This was a hard blow. It seemed that the Islamic law, as interpreted by pearl merchants, required a man to work out a dead brother's debts. It was the practice of the port, old Yusuf said. Debts must be paid. If his dead brother's nakhoda wanted him, he must go. He must give up the idea of spending the summer at home. The brother had owed 400 rupees, marked up against him over twenty years of pearling. It was not a large sum: there were divers who "owed" thousands. But it was a sum far beyond the capacity of Yusuf ever to repay. It was doubtful if his whole earnings in any year, from long voyages and from short, ever exceeded 200 rupees, and he had a home to support. The cost of living even for an Arab sailor in Kuwait, with a tiny home, is the best part of a rupee a day—twelve annas, at least, if his family is not to starve.

It seemed to me iniquitous that poor Yusuf, just in from the sea, should be compelled to go out again and to be a pearl-diver, hardest of all sea professions. Even he, accustomed to a life of hardship as he was, admitted that pearling was nothing but continuous heavy toil under conditions of severe discomfort, and the prospects of coming through a season without becoming more in the nakhoda's debt were slight. God is compassionate, said old Yusuf, and even smiled as he bent to his work with redoubled effort, raising his voice in the praise of Allah.

I decided that if old Yusuf was to go pearling, I would go with him. They would not go for a week or two, he said. In the meantime I could look round Kuwait, which seemed to become more interesting. Far from being the heavenly paradise it was reported to be, it produced no fruits and little but fish and sheep, and in summer it had no good drinking water. This had to be brought from inside the Basra River at the head of the Gulf, in small booms, which came and went throughout the day. The beautiful sand which so delighted Nejdi that it appeared to him soft and warm as a woman's breast, blew about the harbor and got in my eyes. It was gritty and thoroughly uncomfortable, and the glare from it became quite trying. There was old Yusuf, singing, and four sons of Nejdi staring about them wide-eyed. The pearl merchants, after claiming their divers, clambered down into their small boats and departed.

Chapter 18

EL KUWAIT—PORT
OF BOOMS

THE WALLED CITY of Kuwait does not look its best seen from the anchorage, but it has one of the most interesting waterfronts in the world —more than two miles of it. In 1939 the place was one great shipyard of Arab dhows. All along the waterfront running east and west by the shore of the shallow bay, from the British Residency in the east to the American hospital in the west, almost from wall to wall of the town, the big ships and the little ships jostle one another. On the beach, on the tidal flats, and in the sea they lie cheek by jowl. Long lines of them stand behind stone breakwaters facing the sea, six or eight in a row, square on their long keels with their bows pointing to the sea, their rudders unshipped, their sides skirted and their decks protected with mats. The big ships stand on the tidal flats and the small ships high and dry on the beach.

Though it was only mid-June when we came in and many booms had still to return from their long voyages, there were already a hundred deepwatermen snugged down at their summer berths, their hulls propped up with Lamu or Rufiji poles and the trunks of Indian trees, and all their gear ashore. Other ships were being floated in, or rigged down at the anchorage in readiness for grounding with the next tide. Longboats full of singing sailors were towing in their booms, carrying out lines to the breakwaters and to anchors embedded in the sand, to bring them to their berths. Big booms, small booms, old booms, new booms, there they were, and their sailors hurried along the busy waterfront in a ceaseless stream. Sailors staggered up the beach bearing the long rolls of canvas which were the mainsails, the jibs and the mizzens of their ships. Sailors danced and sang as they hauled up longboats and tucked them away in their summer coverings of frond mats; sailors sweated at capstans, heaving in their ships; sailors chanted and danced as they floated in heavy masts and long slender spars, and made neatly lashed parcels of them fore-and-aft on the beach among the litter of capstans, longboats, cutters, gigs, Malabar teak, anchors, rudders, washboards, water-tanks, fire-boxes and all kinds of other maritime paraphernalia with which the whole length of the place was littered.

Persians passed in the dusty street carrying the burdens of the town. Persians seemed to do the porterage, the water deliveries, and most of the coolie work of the port, as well as the labor in the dockyards. There were thousands of them. They were sawing planks out of huge Malabar logs, frightful work in that hot climate; they were unloading the water booms, driving their asses into the sea to take their dripping loads of waterskins: they carried the firewood, the bags of rice, the packages of dates, and everything else which was being taken to the warehouses of the merchants. Persians and pack horses were doing the work of the town: the Kuwaiti were doing the work of the sea. I stopped with Nejdi to watch some Persians getting a boom ready for launching from a shipyard where five partially completed dhows stood in a row behind a mud and coral wall. The coolies were knocking down the wall in front of a completed boom, and carrying out a large bower anchor into the shallow water. It would take only an hour or two to build the wall up again, Nejdi said: they would heave the ship out and haul her on to the flats at low tide, and the next flood would float her off.

"But why bother to build up the wall again," I asked, "if it has to be knocked down every time a new boom is launched?" There were at least a dozen of these graceful vessels being built in such enclosures, and half a dozen more on the open beach where they towered over the other vessels.

"It is good that the boom should be protected while it is being built," he said.

"But why?" I asked again.

"The wall keeps out *jinns*."

"But what of the booms in the open, along the beach?" I asked then. "Aren't they just as subject to *jinns*?"

"Well," he admitted, "some owners and some nakhodas don't bother much about *jinns* nowadays: but there is one thing they always watch most carefully. That is to see that no woman jumps across the freshly laid keel of a new boom."

"Whatever for?" I asked. "Why should a woman want to jump over the keel of a boom? And if she does, why shouldn't she?"

Nejdi looked at me with amusement as if I ought, having sailed with him for more than six months and with Ahmed the Yemenite before that, to know something of these things. "Anybody," he said, "knows that a barren woman will conceive, if she can only jump over the keel of a new boom."

This was news to me, but it was a serious thing for a wife to be barren in Kuwait, where the principal business of women seemed to be the bearing of children. I had not heard of this strange custom of leaping over the keel of a boom in course of construction, but, I asked, if to be barren was so much dreaded, and sons were so welcome, why not encourage the girls to jump over the keels of all the booms?

"Ah, my friend," said Nejdi—"a life for a life, do you not know that? It is so, with the *jinns*. If a woman leaps across the keel of a boom and afterwards conceives and bears a child, the life of the nakhoda of that new boom is forfeit. A life for a life: do you not know that? If not the nakhoda, then one of the carpenters will die before the boom is launched. It is very bad."

We walked along, and I imagined that I saw crowds of the barren women, beating their laundry on the hard rocks by the beach, looking enviously at the keels of the booms. Nejdi went on to tell me that, day and night, twenty men watched the keel of his *Triumph* when she was under construction, for he had no intention that his life should pay for the satisfaction of any child-desiring woman. I noticed, too, that the shipwrights, when the keel was laid, worked furiously until they had built up planks enough on either side to prevent a woman from jumping. If she wished to jump over the keel she would have to be quick, and come down on the first day of the keel's laying.

The women we saw along the waterfront that morning were mostly Negroes and Persians, all swathed in black. The women washing clothes in the sea had their faces covered with heavy black veils, though they were often immersed in the water, and every curve of their bodies showed against the clinging calico of their gowns. Most of them were old and haggish, but there were some who were not. Nejdi did not look at them, for it is not fitting that a man should notice the activities of these women washing in the sea. They were mostly the wives of coolies, and I saw very few who needed to leap over the keel of a new boom: the great majority had large numbers of pretty children with them, pretty little bright-eyed girls and boys who romped in the sea while their mothers worked.

I trudged on in silence beside Nejdi while he greeted the many long benches of nakhodas sitting in the shade of the walls before their homes. The walker, he said to me—for it was time I learned something of the etiquette of the nakhodas' home life—must always salute the sitter; and the rider the walker. The returned shipmaster and the stranger arriving in the city must greet all the sheikhs. As half the nakhodas in the place were sitting down, and the town seemed well populated with sheikhs, it seemed to me that we were in for a busy time. But we ourselves often sat and sipped sherbet or coffee, or both, with groups of the nakhodas and merchants. Then all the sailors and the townsmen passing by saluted us. "Peace be upon you," ran their mellow greetings. "And upon you peace," we would answer: and then "God grant you good-morning" from them, and a similar response from us. Often nakhodas kissed Nejdi, and he kissed relatives and friends, on both cheeks. Those who did not kiss grasped his right hand and right forearm, looked affectionately into his eyes and asked repeatedly after his health.

Apparently it was the custom in Kuwait to ask after the man's health, at this first greeting, all the time he was within earshot. People asked so frequently and with such insistence that it seemed to me they never heard the reply. Not that a reply was given or needed, for they all were obviously in excellent health.

We were going along the shore road towards the palace of the Sheikh of Kuwait, His Highness Sir Ahmed ibn Jaber al-Sabah, to pay our respects, for the nakhoda newly come in from the sea and the stranger in town must do that. When we were halfway to the Sheikh's palace we met him, coming round a bend in the road in an American car which was preceded and followed by large trucks of armed Beduin troops. After the troubles His Highness deemed it unwise to go through the town without a guard. The car stopped, and we salaamed. I took an instant liking to the Sheikh of Kuwait. He was a handsome man, stoutly built, with a black moustache and beard, and large, flashing eyes. He was dressed in the picturesque robes of an Arab sheikh, a long white gown covered with a cloak of camel's hair embroidered with gold wire, like Nejdi's but much more elaborate. On his head was a flowered headcloth through the fine material of which could be seen his crocheted skullcap in floral designs.

His aghal was of gold wire, solid, with the ropes arranged so that they lay upon the headcloth more squarely than round, in the manner of an Arab chieftain's. His complexion was dark olive, and his countenance was very open. Here was nothing of the tyrant, obviously, and I began to wonder more about the riot when Mohamed Kitami died.

We made our salaams, and His Highness welcomed me to Kuwait, asking me to be his guest in his town palace, which was a large house built round a courtyard along the east wall of the town. I thanked him for his courtesy, but said that if he did not mind, I should like to stay with my friends, at any rate for the time being. I had only one purpose in coming to Kuwait and that was to learn all I could about its ships. I feared I should not learn much in a sheikh's palace. His Highness said he hoped I would make Kuwait my second home, and drove on with a smile. Later in the day we had coffee with His Highness at his waterside palace, the one in the heart of the city where his grandfather, the Lion Mubarak, had decorated the bedrooms with ceilings filled with the lithographs of actresses and queens. This palace was now unused, except for the daily court, which any citizen might attend, and no one is doomed to toss upon a sleepless bed gazing at the hard eyes of painted actresses and queens. In a room of this strange palace, I noticed a photograph of Lord Kitchener on horseback, autographed by the great soldier.

We also paid our respects to Sheikh Ali Kalifa, the right-hand man of the Sheikh of Kuwait. We found him smoking in the shade of the portico of his stockade, looking out over the large square at the southern side of the town, not far from the main gates. The square was almost empty when we came, for it was mid-morning and the day's life died down as the sun waxed. In a large space by the sandy roadway leading to the gates, a herd of camels rested knee-haltered in their desert harness, while their Beduin owners shopped and gossiped in the town, their arms left at the guardhouse by the gate and their bright eyes wide open at the marvels in the *suq*. Kuwait's *suq* is famed among the Beduin of all North Arabia as far as the borders of Syria and Transjordan. A shepherd came in slowly with a flock of black sheep, strolling behind them in the robes of an apostle but with a cheap Japanese umbrella held up to shield him from the sun. Camels moved with dignified tread from the gate towards the square. Some Persian women veiled in black but with their long trousers showing frills at their bare ankles came from a merchant's house, though it was late for women to be buying in the *suq*.

Sheikh Ali Kalifa, a bearded handsome man in his early fifties, was

Sheikh of Kuwait with political agent

surrounded by a wild-looking gathering of Beduin troops armed with modern and very businesslike rifles. He rose as we came, and coffee and sherbet were brought. I liked Sheikh Ali Kalifa. Besides being an able and far-famed generalissimo he was something of a humorist. As I had chosen to come to Kuwait in a dhow, he said, when the time came to leave I must go on a camel. I said I should be happy enough to leave in a dhow.

We greeted many sheikhs that day: Sheikh Abdulla bin Jaber, who presided over the pearling court—we found him ordering a ragged Beduin to go at once to sea with his nakhoda; Abdulla bin Salim, who was president of the town's *Majlis* or council; Fahad, nephew of Sheikh Ali Kalifa, who had been to Beirut University and talked a great deal; Sheikh Sabah, who was admiral of the pearling fleet—we found him in the pearlers' coffee shop, opposite the mosque of the *suq*—old sons and relatives of the Sheikh who were managing police posts, armories, and offices. There seemed to be dozens of them. We found the Sheikh Abdulla bin Salim holding court above the dungeons where the political prisoners languished in irons after the recent trouble, with a group of long-gowned dignitaries seated round. He was a large florid man, with mouldering thoughtful eyes. Most of the sheikhs, except Sabah, who was pearling admiral, deemed it wise to have slaves and Beduin guarding them, though how much of this was for show and how much really necessary I did not know. The Sheikh of Kuwait himself—Sheikh Ahmed Jabah, as his subjects invariably called him—never moved without a considerable bodyguard, some of whom were armed with submachine guns.

From the houses and the stockades of the sheikhs we returned to the waterfront to Nejdi's house, with its blind wall facing the sea and his harem windows latticed against the prying onlooker. Nejdi's house was a large one, not far from the old British Residency, near the basins where the smaller pearlers were docked. It was two-storeyed, built of coral laced with a rough cement of sun-dried mud, like most of the other 8000 houses in that city of 70,000 inhabitants.* The walls were irregular and the building squat, but it was not without beauty. The carvings on the teak gateway were well done. From the roof top a large number of long spouts extended over the roadway. These were a feature of all the Kuwait streets, and it struck me as odd that, in a place where water was so scarce, such thorough arrangements should be made for wasting any little rain that

---

* These figures were supplied to me through the Kuwait Town Council. The houses in the town had then been numbered, but no vital statistics were kept.

might fall. Nejdi said that in winter there might often be a heavy shower, and the flat roofs of the coral-and-mud houses could not stand a heavy rain. So they were fitted with spouts, most of which were the halves of hollowed date palms, to carry off the water. In a heavy rain a year or two before, he said, 2000 houses in Kuwait had collapsed. He went on to explain that the circumstances of that shower were peculiar and such a heavy house mortality was not usual. There had been a soft penetrating rain first, for two days or so, which wore down the houses. After that a sudden heavy shower had mown down the weaker houses, for all their lacing mud had been washed away by the earlier rain. The noise of collapsing houses was like that of a battle, he said, and several people lost their lives. Thousands were homeless for months. So far as I could see this disaster had not brought about any improvement in the style of building. Houses were still without foundations, still only walls of coral stones. Here and there I saw new houses laced with Japanese cement, and some of these looked a little better. The habit of using cement was on the increase, he said: but he doubted its value, for the local builders put too much sand in the cement.

In the street near his home we passed a little boy, naked and freshly circumcised, crying against a wall. He was about six years old. The street barber had been round that morning, Nejdi told me. A little farther on we passed two more, also bawling. They would get over it, Nejdi said, and shouted to them to desist from their unmanly noise. They paid no attention, but went on bawling. A merchant passed us leading his son, also freshly operated upon, with his gown tucked above his waist and a daub of black ointment on him. He was walking as though he were lame, but he was not crying. "There goes a man," Nejdi said.

We entered his home, where a group of relatives and other nakhodas, and some merchants and pearl-buyers had assembled for the mid-morning meal. We ate in silence in the shadow of the verandah before the main living room, facing the courtyard. The verandah was supported by carved posts from Malabar, and the roofing was Iraq date mats on lattices of bamboo resting on Lamu mangrove poles placed closely together, the mats being covered with mud and rubble. Beneath this roof two large Persian carpets had been spread, and upon these was the food, on white cloths. There were two sheep, roasted with stuffing of dried fruits and herbs and hard-boiled eggs; chickens, roasted so that they shredded easily at the touch of the hand; large dishes of the delectable fat flounders for which Kuwait Bay is famous, and other fish; mounds and mounds of rice, boiled

with raisins and other things I could not recognize, and smothered with
ghee; and tremendous dishes of watermelons from the plantations along
the Shatt-el-Arab in Iraq. It was a good spread and, after washing our
hands, we fell to without ado. There was no idle chatter until all present
—there were about forty men there—had had their fill. Nejdi's father was
there, eating heartily, though he was over seventy years old. He was a
little man with an enormous paunch and bright, piercing eyes. He was
much fairer than most of the others, though many of the guests could
have passed for Spaniards or Portuguese if they had worn European
clothes. Some had blue eyes. Other were almost pure Negro, though I
was told they were all Arab. The Negroes were the sons of merchants
or big nakhodas and their slave concubines.

Though I was a stranger to most of these people their natural good
manners forbade them to display any curiosity about me. I liked these
feasts ashore. There was elbow room, for one thing, which there rarely
was aboard the dhows. The food was excellent, and the idea of spreading everything out at once and tucking in was a good one. So was the
absence of chatter. It is bad to talk at meals, Nejdi said: it upsets the nerves
of the stomach. So we ate. And how we ate! The sheep were especially good, and so were the chickens. Each man had a chicken or two as
an appetizer, then a few pounds of rice shovelled down in handfuls; and
then anything from three to seven pounds of lamb, with a few fish. I sat
between Nejdi's father and a leading merchant, who was at work on a
trough of rice and sheep like a steam shovel. From time to time one or
other of them would tear off a few pounds of steaming mutton, or skilfully split away the starboard half of a fowl, and fling the delicacy to me.
I was expert at doing my own rending by this time, but in the matter of
capacity I lagged far behind. It was not fitting to pick at one's food on
such occasions: the proper enjoyment of a proper quantity—anything up
to half a sheep, and five or six chickens—was required by the rules of
courtesy. I was hungry, being just in from the sea: but the south wind
blew that day and it was hot and humid. I never have liked rice.

Though I ate what I should have considered supplies for a month even
in a Cape Horn ship, I was rebuked for my sparrow's appetite as we all
fell away from the carpet, washed our hands again, belched, drank the
clove-flavored coffee, and sat heavily about on the carpet in the verandah's shade.

I looked across at the long pearling sweeps piled in a corner of the
yard and the masts of the booms outside, and Nejdi's father began to ques-

tion me, this being the proper moment when we were all well filled with food. How many sons had I? Where was my harem? Had his son treated me well? What happened at Zanzibar? Big Myouf al-Bedra whispered to me that the Seyyid Sulieman, who had kissed Nejdi a fond farewell, had written to his father reporting his son's scandalous behavior in the African island. I knew nothing of Zanzibar. I had no sons, I was sorry to admit: no sons, no harem. What, no harem? No, no harem: I preferred ships. What, ships to women? This raised a laugh as if it were a great joke. I should have no sons from ships, the old man said seriously. In the Europe I knew, I wanted no sons, I said. Ah, there I had spoken wisely, said the old man. But why not stay there with them? In Kuwait there were many desirable maidens. It would be easy to settle there.

This suggestion seemed to appeal to the assembled merchants and and mariners, and there were many murmurs of approval. Perhaps there was something to be said for it. Indeed, the life of these Kuwait nakhodas seemed from many points of view one to be envied. I liked their homes along the Kuwait shore road, and the endless panorama of the busy ships before them. I liked these fleet stately vessels which they sailed to Zanzibar and the Malabar coast, to Somaliland and the Yemen: I liked their generosity, their fine open-handed hospitality, their utter lack of cant, and hypocrisy. I had a momentary vision of useful work, there along the Kuwait waterfront, learning what I could of Arab maritime history, doing what I could to improve the breed of ships—a little better building, a little care of waterways and shedding the sea, a little better method of stepping the masts, sewing the sails, and perhaps a navigation school too. There were requests enough for it. The older men did not like the way that knowledge of real navigation was slipping from the young ones, for there were few among them who really knew the way on the sea. They were content with the way along the coasts. Nejdi's father had a grand idea. If some delectable dark-eyed damsels might serve me in that sea paradise, it could be paradise indeed.

But these pleasant illusions were pipe dreams—pipe dreams, without the pipe. The idea was good: but in these days we do not find escape from ourselves, or from the mess we have created, so easily as that.

With our bellies full, we slept, and a cooling air stole under the verandah's shade from the punkahs agitated by the slaves. This was the life. What, Nejdi asked, had America and England to offer that was better than this? What indeed? Why then should I trouble to go back? It was only my first day in Kuwait. We should see.

We awoke to tea and little cakes from the Persian bakery round the corner: then the guests trooped off to prayer, and the family prayed on the verandah. It was early in the afternoon, and again the sounds of toil and dance and song began to echo along the waterfront as the sailors returned to their work. We walked slowly past the grounded pearlers, many of which had not been to sea for years, towards the abandoned palace of the Sheikh of Muhammerah, and the wall in the east end of the town. The palace of the Sheikh of Muhammerah, with the base of his harem near by, is a prominent landmark between the British Residency and the Sheikh of Kuwait's town house. They are large buildings standing alone in an open space, looking rather as if they were sorry for themselves in all the long years they have waited for the return of their master. In one of them, the more dilapidated, there still lives one of the Sheikh's widows, the youngest one, a girl-bride he married on his last visit to Kuwait. He fell ill and died before the marriage could be consummated. There she still lives, no longer young, this strange virgin widow: I never saw her, or indeed any sign that either palace was now lived in. But her wedding-chest, a great Arab chest of teak with beaten brass designs, stands in the drawing-room of the British Agency at Kuwait, and the Political Agent assured me that a widow still lives in the palace.

Down by the waterfront were the fish traps, and some of the Sheikh's Beduin troops shooting birds. We passed a large house which was abandoned and growing derelict. Nejdi said it had been a pearl merchant's. The pearl merchant, he said, still had sacks of pearls, but there was no market. He had bought the pearls before the slump and could never sell them: he had held them and held them, and still held them, though he had lost his home, his ships, his business, everything. He had only the pearls, and they were not now worth a fraction of the money he had invested in them. He could not bring himself to part with his beloved jewels at so low a price, and now they were all that remained to him.

Out in the harbor two large booms were coming in, light after discharging their Indian cargoes. They came swooping in like great swans under their clouds of white canvas, and the crews filling their decks sent the music of song and the rhythm of their beating drums across the bay. Nejdi looked at them enviously. "We should have come in like that," he said, "but we had to come by night." He still felt it keenly.

We strolled back, past the maze of windowless side streets running from the shore road with mud walls and long spouts from the roof tops, and here and there a group of sailors or of nakhodas sitting in the shade. Once we joined a group discussing a bad passage back from the Malabar coast, and a bearded nakhoda was tracing his route with a Zanzibar stick in the sand. Here was India, here Arabia, here the Persian Gulf. He showed how he left Calicut, together with two other ships, bound towards Muscat for orders. The northeast wind came very light down the Arabian Sea and the set was towards the southwest. The wind, he said, never gave them a chance: the three ships drifted slowly across the Indian Ocean headed towards Socotra, and made painfully slow progress. They tried to regain the Indian side, but the current was against them and they could not. So they stood on. Weeks passed. The conditions grew no better. They saw no ships, no land. They sailed alone. They did not know where they were, for there were only two among them who understood the sextant well enough to get a noon sight and work up the latitude. These two were in the same ship, but the three sailed in company. They kept together. Two months passed. One ship was short of water. The others gave her some. Seventy days passed. Two ships were short of water, and the third was running very low. Still there was no rain, no improvement in the sailing conditions. They were far from the steamer lanes. On the seventy-fifth day they had no water among the three of them. They all came together in a calm and prayed fervently to Allah to send them rain. And there was rain! A great black squall rose within the hour, with the wind fair for the first time that voyage, and the life-giving rain! Truly Allah was compassionate, the nakhoda said.

Truly it was a piece of excellent good luck, I thought, and asked how it had been possible to take so many days on a comparatively short passage. Nejdi said that in midsummer there was often little wind, and the ships made long passages between the Malabar coast and Muscat. If they were driven or drifted out of their course they could not get back again: they had water for seventy days. It was very unusual to be longer. He himself had had to go in to Socotra for water on such a voyage. It was the way of the sea, under the will of Allah. So be it. *Allah karim.* I said this might be a comforting philosophy, but a better knowledge of navigation would surely be an advantage. Yes, it was so, said Nejdi: but what could they do? There was no school in the town, no school in Arabia. And no knowedge of navigation would have any effect on the wind. It was Allah's will, and seamen must bow to it.

It was Allah's will too, I suppose, which caused the loss of the big boom *Light of the Oceans,* of which I heard many conflicting stories that day.

There seemed no general agreement even about the vessel's name, though I talked with her nakhoda and several men who had sailed on her fatal voyage. Some said she was the *Light of the Sea*, others the *Light of the Sea and the Land*, others again *Inspiration of the Oceans*. She was a famous boom of some 500 tons built by the Kuwaiti on the Malabar coast some twenty years ago—there was vagueness about this too—and lost on her first voyage. She was built on the Malabar coast to save the freight on the timber to Kuwait. Instead of bringing the timber, the Kuwait shipwrights went where the timber was. This was not the good idea it may have appeared, for the quality of the local labor was indifferent and the ship took six months to build, costing 120,000 rupees. The Bahreini merchant Abdul-rehman Za-ahni financed it: the nakhoda was a Kuwaiti; the supervising shipwrights were the famous Kuwait builders Salim bin Rashid and Mohamed Thwaini. The crew for the maiden voyage were thirty-seven Kuwaiti, forty men of Calicut experienced in the ways of the sea, and three boys. The boom had a capacity of 7500 packages of Basra dates; her main halliards were of 19-stranded coir; a man could climb through the sheaves at her mainmast-head, according to the tailor Saoud, who had sailed in her. She loaded, said the legend, all the cargo in Calicut, went out to sea to the banging of drums and songs and with flags all over her, sailed cheerfully all day, struck a squall of rain in the night, filled in the rain, and foundered. Her coir swelled and she burst and just sailed on down. Saoud said he swam a night and a day to reach the shore: he still had scars from the exploding timbers.

I met the nakhoda that same day. He was then an old man with a gray beard, still taking booms to sea. When I met him, with Nejdi, he was walking cheerfully in the *suq*. The loss of the big boom was an act of God, he said. It was Allah's will. I still thought it strange that a great ship which could not survive a shower of rain had more than a little ungodly wrong with her: why had he not protected the cargo? This, he said, was not done. He did not expect rain. Allah sent it. It was clearly Allah's will that the great ship should not make her voyage. Since then the Kuwait shipwrights had built their ships at home and there had been no more expensive ventures to the Malabar coast.

So we wandered in this amazing place Kuwait which never ceased to interest me. I was there four months, not all that time in the city, for I made a pearling voyage and wandered here and there—down the Hasa coast, to Iraq, and to the Gulf islands. But all that time was tremendously

The covered suq, *Kuwait*

interesting. Every day, every walk along the waterfront, taught me something new, yet in the end I left knowing how much I still had to learn. I lived at first with my friends the al-Hamads at their country place at Dimner, outside Kuwait, in a walled house by the beach of Kuwait Bay. Here we lived the life of the well-to-do Arab, and lunched on succulent fish and dined on sheep day after day. We bathed in the dawns and the sunsets, and slept through the hot noon hours. Sometimes nakhodas came to visit us, and we yarned of the sea. At other times pearl merchants came, and wanderers from so far away as Syria, Singapore, Harar, and Zanzibar. The al-Hamads were among the leading merchants of Kuwait. They were shipowners, plantation owners, and business men, with establishments in Kuwait, Basra, and Aden, and branches up and down the Red Sea. They were five brothers, the sons of the venerable Abdul-latif al-Hamad, who had then been dead some years. The brothers were Khalid, Ahmed, Yusuf, Ali, and Abdulla. Khalid ran the Aden establishment, Ahmed the house in Basra, Yusuf the business in Kuwait. Ali was resting and Abdulla travelled to India. He had recently returned from Berbera to help in the date season, before going to Calcutta or wherever else his brothers might decide to send him. Abdulla was prepared to go anywhere at five minutes' notice, and rather hoped to be sent to America.

With the three younger brothers and their families, I lived at Dimner. We slept in a sand lot protected by a low cement wall to keep out the snakes: the sand lot was outside the house, beyond the walls. It was near the sea and we slept nightly with the murmur of the quiet surf in our ears, and the stars overhead for covering, and awoke in the dawns to bathe. It was a good life. Here the men gathered before sleep and the talk was of ships and ship's business. Many of the nakhodas who visited us carried the al-Hamad's cargoes, and they were all good friends of the family. When their ships came in, they all wandered out to Dimner. One of the most interesting of these nakhodas—and they were all good—was the sturdy Myouf al-Bedar, son of one of the Bedar merchants and an Abyssian woman. Myouf sailed the boom *Fat-el-rehman* for the al-Hamads, and had taken Basra dates that season to Gizan, returning with a load of soap from Aden to Basra. Myouf was a famous nakhoda, a wiry, handsome,

A Beduin family

virile man, who usually arrived in the early mornings shortly after the dawn prayer. He had walked from Kuwait, and began the day by eating all the children's butter from the breakfast mat. He ate all the butter he saw whenever he saw it. I liked Myouf. He was a downright, forceful man. He knew what he wanted and took it if he could. He padded about in his sandals with his cloak over his head to protect him from the sun, and the gold tassels hanging down. Myouf's yarns of the sea were amazing and possibly sometimes truthful. It was unusual for a Kuwait ship to go so far into the Red Sea as Gizan; Hodeida in the Yemen usually marked the limit of their voyages up that coast, and not many passed Aden. Myouf was proud that he had sailed his big ship along the reef-filled way to Gizan, but not so proud of having taken sixty-five days to beat back again, empty, from Gizan to Aden.

Myouf, Saoud the maker of cloaks, Abdulla the youngest of the al-Hamads, Nejdi, Ali Abdul-latif—these were my friends, and the days at Dimner and Kuwait slipped by very pleasantly in their company. It was dreadfully hot but life was organized for that. The north winds brought stinging sand across the bay, and the south winds and the calms caused humidity. It was always better at Dimner than in Kuwait itself, because we had the cooling air of the sea, and the worst of the desert sand did not blow there. We used to go into the *suq* in Kuwait each morning—no Arab would spend a whole day out of the *suq* if he could avoid it—arriving there about 6:30, and then spend the morning visiting and being visited, drinking coffee, chatting, calling on this merchant and that, greeting sheikhs and wise men, sitting on carpets outside shops or inside shops, looking on at the teeming life all round. So passed our mornings until about eleven, when we returned to Dimner for the morning meal. That eaten, we slept; then rose and bathed, drank tea, yarned, and went off to the waterfront and the *suq* again in the cool of the afternoon for more salaams, more visiting and being visited, more sitting in the coffee shops listening to good yarns and bad gramophones. In this manner the merchants passed their days, while their businesses prospered and the nakhodas grew fat from good feeding and indolent from the enjoyment of their women.

"Pray, eat, and enjoy our women. That's all we do at home," Myouf said one day. "It is good: but it is also good to return to the sea."

If the merchants and nakhodas had this good life the sailors had not, and after a few days the familiar countenances of the *Triumph's* mariners disappeared from the *suq*. Many of them had gone pearling. The pearlers begin their season when the big ships come in, and end it when it is time for the big ships to go out again. To a considerable extent the same sailors work both, and life is hard for them. For a few days the sailors in from the long-voyage booms swagger in the *suq*, dressed in their best clothes, swinging their canes and their rosaries, sitting in the coffee shops, drinking from the hookahs, visiting and exchanging stories. Some have no homes, but this is no inconvenience, for they may sleep on the beach or in the streets. By night the beach along the waterfront in the summer months resounds with their snores, where they lie asleep wrapped in their cloaks beneath the stars. A sailor, if he is young and single, needs little to keep him going: his food may be bought for a few annas a day. Without money he will not starve. There is always an eating-mat he may join. His clothing is made up of gown and cloak, headcloth and aghal: all he owns he can carry and he has no bed. His chest is left for the laying-up season in his nakhoda's shed. If he goes pearling he will not need a chest. It is for the carrying of his trade goods, not his clothes. No sailor could fill a chest with his own clothes. If he could he would sell them. The youthful unmarried men sleep on the beach in the shadow of the ships they serve so faithfully, careless, happy men, superbly fit and in good condition. When the pearling is over it is different. Pearling is hard.

Days passed. Weeks passed. Old Yusuf had gone pearling, to dive in his dead brother's place. Abdulla Kitami had come in, and his boom rested now on the beach before the Kitami house, by the waterfront. The two Abdul-wahhabs, Radhwan with his baggala, Ganim bin Othman's big boom, Yusuf bin Isa, Nasir with his little *Cat*, Mahmoud with the *Glory of the Morning*, Mosa, Isa, Hamoud, Ismael, Saqr, Mohamed, Said bin Ali —all these were in, and the nakhodas swelled the crowd sitting in the shade by the waterfront or wandering in the *suq*. Still there was no news of Bedar's *Bedri*.

When we had been back a month, however, she turned up at Muscat, after a long passage from Zanzibar, and went to some place in Qatar to discharge. She had had a bad time that night off Malindi, and again off Kisimayu: Abdulla, Nejdi's brother, was not yet back but there was news of him. He was coming up slowly from Mogadishu with the Suri, changing from ship to ship as he came along the South Arabian coast. He ought to be home within a month. The crew of the *Triumph* had not yet been paid and the shares had not been cast up, but Nejdi gave them money as they needed it. Indeed, many of them would have very little coming when the shares were cast up, for the system of advances and debts more

than swallowed up their earnings. It was hard for a sailor not to be in
debt, and so far as I could see none of them tried very much not to be.
Debt was an accepted thing, and to spend a lifetime owing money was apparently usual. The sailors owed money to the nakhodas, the nakhodas to
the merchants, the merchants to other merchants or the Sheikh. Working without any banking system, with insurance, usury, and even interest
forbidden—at any rate in theory—by the Islamic law, the economic side
of the port of Kuwait was a dark maze. It was obvious enough however
that the whole industry rested on a structure of debt. It was equally obvious that the nakhodas, though they imagined themselves to be the
owners of their booms, were not the real owners at all. The merchants
owned them. It suited the merchants, apparently, to finance the nakhodas
rather than to run the ships themselves, and for this there were many excellent reasons. The nakhodas, perhaps, paid more for the financing they
received than the ships could lawfully be expected to earn. In other words,
money advanced to nakhodas to run ships for themselves, brought larger
dividends than the same money would have done if the merchants had
invested it directly in the ships and then paid the nakhodas to run them.
The merchants did very well out of it, and the nakhodas made a good
living too. But it appeared to me that, by this system, the merchants really
owned the nakhodas as well as the ships, for the nakhodas could scarcely
expect ever to be free of debt. Indeed, so far as I could see, they made little active effort in that direction. They were satisfied. They led good
lives. If a man bestirred himself and had a chance to start level, he could
rise to be a merchant himself. Very few of the merchants, however, had
ever been nakhodas.

In their turn the nakhodas owned the sailors, for the sailors were considered bound to any nakhoda to whom they owed advances. Most of
them owed the balance of some advance. The nakhodas were tied to the
merchants, and the sailors to the nakhodas, though they were not slaves.
There was little slavery in Kuwait. There was little need of it. Slavery
had become uneconomic. It was better to own a man's work than to own
and support the man himself. To own his work you had not to support
him.

I should have gone pearling with old Yusuf, as I had intended, but for
one thing. I could not find room in his ship. He went off in a little sambuk about two weeks after the *Triumph* came in, and though the sambuk was only forty-six feet long she carried a crew of more than sixty

men. I could not understand how they could all sleep on board, unless they slept in tiers. But they went off with song, old Yusuf singing as lustily as any of them and lending a hand at the sweeps. It was a hot, breathless morning when the pearlers went. Fifty-seven of them went out that day, all gaily decorated with flags and with their sailors singing and banging drums. The admiral's sambuk—the pretty sambuk of Sheikh Sabah—led the procession, and they looked like a fleet of galleys going out from Tyre two thousand years ago, as their sweeps flashed in the sun and their freshly oiled hulls gleamed on the bay. It was a stirring sight, but I was sorry for poor Yusuf. He was to be gone a hundred days, he said, while the sea was warm. He would be back, probably, just in time to join the *Triumph* for her new voyage. He looked thoughtful and I saw that his feet were far from healed. Along the waterfront road, I saw a tiny figure wrapped in black waving to him as his sambuk sailed, and the tiny figure looked after that fleet of departing ships a long, long time.

Chapter 19

THE GULF PEARLERS

IF I COULD not go with Yusuf, I was determined to get to the pearl-ing banks somehow. It was easy to see something of the industry from Kuwait. During my four-month stay small pearling vessels were coming and going from the nearer banks for water and food. Many of the small vessels did not go more than thirty or forty miles from the bay, and fleets of them were accustomed to anchor each evening under the shelter of near-by places such as Shi'aiba, villages along the coast of Kuwait which were connected with the city by bus service. From time to time buyers went to these anchorages to meet the nakhodas on the beach or to be pres-ent at a dawn opening of the oysters and see how things were going. This was helpful to them in gauging the probable "take" for the season, and the consequent state of the new market. The smaller ships, many of which were boats less than thirty feet long, opened the season earlier than the larger ones. As the big booms came in from their long voyages, many of them sent out their longboats, rigged up and temporarily decked, to try their luck at pearling, manned by a quartermaster of a younger brother of the nakhoda, with some of the sailors as his crew.

In 1939, one hundred and fifty craft of all kinds went pearling from Kuwait. Forty years ago the number would have been six hundred at least. The fleet which went out the summer I was in Kuwait was the largest since the slump. Many of the merchants who had been most badly hit by the slump had gone out of the business entirely, leaving new ones to come and try their luck. In the meantime the competition of the Japanese cul-tured pearl had come to mean less and less. The cultured pearl, when it was comparatively rare, was a worse competitor, I was told, than it is to-day, when it is commonplace. When it first came on the market it sold at something like one third of the price of a real pearl: now it brings more like a thirtieth, and it competes more with the better-made artificial pearls than with the real. This may be so, but the effect has been to cheapen all pearls whether real, cultured, or the product of laboratories. The better-cultured pearls defy detection even by the Arab expert, and there was not one merchant in Kuwait who, in spite of a lifetime in the business, could distinguish a cultured pearl from a real pearl without the most exhaustive examination, and often destructive tests. By the time he knew whether the pearl was real or cultured it was spoiled. If the expert could be so inconvenienced, the laymen had no chance. The result had been a general falling-off in the demand for real pearls, for milady scorns to wear gems which will be regarded as cheap. Pearls have been cheapened.

Since men buy pearls to please women, and women are not pleased when men give them something which cannot immediately be recognized as both genuine and expensive, it follows that the pearl market has suffered a very severe decline. Real pearls do not bring a tenth of what they did in Kuwait or Bahrein even fifteen years ago.

In such circumstances, it has hardly been worth while to dive for them, and the Kuwait beach is littered to this day with the hulls of hundreds of pearlers which have lain neglected so long they are fit for nothing but firewood. This in spite of the fact that many of the larger vessels, and nearly all the booms and sambuks, have been bought by Persians, by the people of Batina and the Trucial coast and Mahra, and converted for use as passenger-carrying cargo vessels. Hundreds of ships have left Kuwait registry in the last ten years, but many still remain. There is a basin, not far from the American hospital, where the pearlers lie almost as thick as the discarded shells of empty oysters on a pearling beach—big ships and little ships, jalboots, sambuks, belems, shewes. The shapely timbers of the little craft throw long shadows under the moon and beautify the beach, but they are warped and rotted now and they can sail the seas no more.

Kuwait has long been a pearling port of great importance, second only to Bahrein in the whole Persian Gulf. This position it still holds, but the decline of the industry has been steep and probably also permanent. From some points of view I should hardly say that it is to be regretted. The pearl season—known locally as the *ghaus*—must have been dreaded by the divers, for it was accompanied by hardships almost intolerable, by risk to health and life and limb, and its rewards were scanty, often distributed most unfairly, and sometimes withheld from their rightful earners altogether.

All through history, the Persian Gulf has been famous for its pearls, and pearl-diving there is an industry of great antiquity. The pearl oyster has always thrived on the great banks which cover so much of the Arabian side of the Gulf. The formation of the Gulf, its shallowness, the intense heat of the summer sun—the pearl oyster seems to like warm water—together, probably, with the proximity to the great and wealthy market of India, which to this day buys most of its pearls, made the waters of the Gulf the most famous and prolific pearling ground of the world. At the turn of the century there were probably between seventy and eighty thousand men engaged in Persian Gulf pearling. Shortly after the end of the European war, in 1919, the number was not much less. It is doubtful now if there are many more than ten thousand, pearling from Bahrein, el Qatif, the Trucial ports, and Kuwait. Compared with the five thousand craft forty years ago, perhaps there are now a thousand. Bahrein, for instance, sent out six hundred ships and more even as recently as ten years ago. When we were there in the *Triumph of Righteousness*, less than half this number had been licensed for the current season. If oil had not been found it is probable that Bahrein would have been close to bankruptcy, for the island had no other industry. If Kuwait could not so readily have changed to the deep-sea carrying trade it, too, would have suffered badly.

As it is, the worst effects of the decline of the pearl market have now passed. As the merchants of Kuwait were saying when we came in, that season they might as well try their luck again, for the market could not very well get any worse. If they could afford to fit out a few ships on the expectation of prices no worse, and no better, than those then prevailing, it was probable that in the course of time the industry might get back some of its old importance, on a much sounder footing. It was always something of a gamble. The meanest ship might take the most valuable pearls. Mere size did not mean anything. To this day, the ways of the pearl oyster and the success of the season remain unpredictable. In some seasons, pearls are numerous but not of high quality. In other seasons, they are both plentiful and valuable. This was the case in 1939, but the outbreak of war in Europe ruined any market there might have been. At other times, the pearls are neither plentiful nor valuable. Sometimes one bank will give good pearls, and all others in the Gulf give nothing but indifferent ones. The best banks have always been recognized as those closest to Bahrein, north and east of the island, but there are others near Kuwait. Sometimes for several years in succession a bank will yield scarcely anything, and then, for no apparent reason, it suddenly begins to produce oysters loaded with rare pearls. There is no rhyme or reason in it. Each nakhoda on the banks has only his own knowledge and his luck to guide him. The banks are not charted: there is nothing scientific about it. The ancient methods are still used, without variation. Diving is without costume, without gear. All the banks are free, though usually those nearer inshore are left to the fleets from the nearest port: out in the Gulf, the larger vessels fish together. I have seen more than a hundred on one bank, most of them from Kuwait.

Though the banks are free, there is a homicidal prejudice against the introduction of new methods. The Persian Gulf, the home of pearl-diving, is no place for divers, and the only diving gear in the Gulf belongs to the lighthouse tender *Nearchus* and the Royal Navy. The Arabs dive with a peg on the nose, and no other gear. Most of the diving is on banks with from five to twelve fathoms of water. Big ships stay in the open waters of the Gulf, but smaller ones usually run in to neighboring anchorages by night. There are two seasons, first a sort of free-for-all, not closely organized, in which the smaller craft go out and test the nearer banks and more accessible places as soon as the summer sun has made the water warm enough for shallow diving. About a month later the main season begins, when all the ships go out, and this season lasts so long as the summer sun warms the water. That is usually about four months—most of June, July, August, September, and a little of October. During these months the climate of the Persian Gulf is more like that of an inferno than of a habitable region, but the intense and continuous heat is necessary to warm the water so that the naked divers can bear the almost constant immersion. They lie in the water beside their boats or grope on the sea bed half the day, and dive to sixty and seventy feet of water. For any human being to stand this—even the tough, magnificent Arab or the huge muscular slave —over a period of months with little food, the water must be warm. Immediately the water begins to cool, the diving must stop, and the boats return to port. The principal duty of the admiral of the fleet is to fix and announce this quitting day, before which it is not considered proper for a large ship to return. What the small craft do is largely their own business, for they never have sufficient pearls to affect the market.

When pearling was at its height and as many as twenty thousand men took part in the season from Kuwait, Beduin, Persians, slaves, and any one else who could be induced or compelled to go, went with the fleet to the banks. There were many more pearlers than sailors. Now there are more sailors than pearlers. Sailing on long voyages was formerly a change from pearling: now pearling is a change from sailing in the cargo-ships. When I was in Kuwait, probably about three thousand men were engaged in the pearling industry. While many were deep-water sailors, others were not, particularly the divers. I saw many among these who were obviously Beduin, with long hair; but I never saw a long-haired Kuwait or Saudi-Arabian Beduin in a deep-water Kuwait ship. The explanation was that these Beduin had inherited the obligation to dive. They were young men who had inherited their parents' debts. This passing on of debts from father to son has been stopped now, in Kuwait, and has been abandoned in Bahrein for the past ten years. But if a man went diving to pay off his father's debt and then incurred a debt of his own, as he invariably did, he must go out to pay off his own debt, even after the inherited debt had been annulled.

The whole economic structure of the industry, even more than in ship-owning, was based on debt. Everybody was in debt—the diver to the nakhoda, the nakhoda to the merchant who financed him, the merchant to some other merchant bigger than himself, the bigger merchant to the sheikh. Even the broker who came out to buy the pearls was probably heavily in debt to some money lender who financed him. The whole business was based on debts, debts which were rarely paid because the paying of them was impossible. If money in Islam could not earn interest in banks, and there was no banking system, it certainly found a way of more than making up for the disability. The man who advanced money usually saw that there was a big return, though it was never called interest. The return was disguised in all sorts of ways, but it was always there. The divers paid interest on their advances by open and barefaced robbery and chicanery of every kind. They were an optimistic, gambling, irresponsible class who often died young. The nakhodas paid their interest by all sorts of subterfuges in the selling of the pearls. I heard of one financier who had a rule that all ships financed by him should give him their pearls at four-fifths of their value, a barefaced rate of interest of 20 per cent over four months. This would not be the only profit. Having got the pearls at four-fifths of their Kuwait value, he would pocket the difference and sell them in Bombay for anything up to five or six times the sum he had invested in them. Moreover, if the ship's earnings, as calculated by himself, did not come to the amount he had advanced, the difference remained owing, and until it had been repaid that nakhoda must go out and pearl for him, under the same conditions. The nakhodas were tied no less than their men, and the merchants were tied no less securely to larger merchants. Though large profits could be made, losses could be incurred. There was a considerable element of gambling all through the industry, and many of the leading Kuwait merchants would have nothing to do with it, not even as a personal favor to their own nakhodas. Pearling, in their opinion, was a business best left alone. The more I learned of it the more I shared this view.

In Bahrein the worst abuses have long disappeared, though it was difficult to bring about reforms. In Kuwait, things are much better than they were. The Bahrein government, which appears to have received little thanks for its pains, has effected far-reaching and permanent reforms, which cannot but make themselves felt throughout the Gulf. Formerly no accounts were kept—the divers keep none now, in the Kuwait ships— but the Bahrein government insists that all divers shall be given clearly made-out account books, properly kept, and sends round inspectors to see that this is done. Not only are the divers' interests looked after, but the nakhodas also are protected. Formerly there was much trouble and a great deal of sharp practice over the amounts of the advances to be made to the divers and the tenders at the beginning of each season. It was realized that unless advances were controlled, the debt system could never be. The government now calls a meeting of the merchants and other interested parties before the season begins, and the amount of the advances is agreed upon and proclaimed. So much and no less—and no more—may be paid. This innovation met with organized opposition, especially from the divers themselves, for they were misled by cunning propaganda into imagining the restriction of advances to be a curb upon them. It was difficult to convince an ignorant and improvident man, told that he could have an advance of thirty rupees instead of sixty, that the cut was in his own interest, since, if he earned sixty rupees, the government would see that he got them and, if he did not, the difference would not be added to his debt. The divers only knew they had less money in their pockets. They did not mind increasing their debts, for that was a condition to which they were well accustomed. There were riots, which grew serious enough to involve shootings and loss of life. But the innovations stood.

At the same time Bahrein abolished the practice of hereditary debts: a diver's debts died with him. The pearl merchants' court was abolished, and merchants and nakhodas were no longer allowed to compel divers to work for them in their gardens in the off season. The pearl merchants' court in former days settled all questions of law between divers and nakhodas, but, since only the nakhodas and the merchants were represented, its decisions could hardly be expected to be fair. There is still a pearlers' court in Kuwait, but it is fairer there. There are keen-sighted enthusiasts to keep an eye on it, to see that its decisions are not too grossly unfair, but at the same time it is recognized that changes in an industry so loosely knit and so ancient ought to come gradually if their effect is to be permanent. Kuwait is already a long way along the road first opened by Bahrein.

Along the Hasa coast also pearling has suffered a severe decline, and the ports of al-Qatif, Darien, and Jubail send few ships to the *ghaus*. Many of the divers now work instead for the Standard Oil Company of California, which has the valuable oil concessions there. They pay a proportion of their wages to the nakhodas to whom they are in debt, and the nakhodas, since they can sit back and enjoy these sums regularly, have not much desire to go pearling. The market is bad, and the life is hard. It is better to sit on the beach at al-Qatif and enjoy the fruits of the oil men. The pearlers of al-Khobar and al-Qatif now stand rotting on their beaches. At al-Khobar I saw the last of the famous *betils*, those curiously decorated craft which once were the galleys of the pearling admirals of the Gulf. The admiral of al-Khobar now works for the oil company, though his task is not arduous and his income from his debtors is probably much greater than his earnings.

From all this it may be seen that pearling, as it is practiced on the banks of the Persian Gulf, is an arduous, difficult, and complicated business. I looked forward to finding out what I could about it and, though the prospect of spending the season in a sambuk really alarmed me, I was determined to go out some way or other. Having survived six months in Nejdi's boom I thought I could stand anything. However, I had imagined wrongly. I thought, too, that I had graduated in hardship and crowding aboard Arab dhows but when I saw the pearlers, I knew I was looking at really overcrowded vessels for the first time. The maindeck of a Kuwait pearler going to sea was like a platform of the subway at Times Square in New York at the rush hour with no trains coming in. Compared with the pearlers the *Triumph* had been an ocean liner. If she stowed human beings like cattle for the run from the Hadhramaut to Africa, with frequent calls at ports, the pearlers packed them in like sardines in a double-layer tin and called at no ports at all. If life in the *Triumph* had sometimes been hard, existence in the pearlers must always be a nightmare. I quailed at the thought of going in them. I had to confess that the degree of hardship involved in a real pearling voyage over the Persian Gulf banks, working with the crew for a hundred days in that frightful climate and under the dreadful conditions prevailing, was more than I could hope to stand. I could not, by myself, alleviate the conditions. I suppose I could, had I so wished, have financed my own ship; but in that way I should have learned little of the real conditions and probably only succeeded in deluding myself. No, if I went at all it must be properly. So I compromised, having first looked over the banks on a trip with the Political Agent in his comfortable launch, by arranging to ship for a buying voyage with Sheikh Mohamed Abdul-razzaq. Mohamed Abdul-razzaq was a buyer of good pearls for the Bombay market, where his father sold them. He had a jalboot, a large retinue, a bundle of mysterious equipment tied up in a large red rag, a clerk, and a lifetime knowledge of the industry. Moreover, he was a good fellow and I liked him. I shipped with him for a buying voyage from Kuwait across the banks and the whole of the way down the Hasa coast to Bahrein. It would, he said, take at least a month. It took two months, and we never reached Bahrein. But it was extraordinarily interesting, and I learned a great deal.

We sailed from Kuwait one fine morning in early August, three weeks after our sailing had first been announced. Sheikh Mohamed's—he was a sheikh by courtesy—jalboot was about thirty-six feet long, a beamy little thing with one high mast. She was loaded to the waterline with seven sheep, half a ton of rice, fresh water in drums, camel-thorn fuel, a firepot, four dozen bottles of sherbet, six trunks and three chests, several hundred-weight of sheep feed (grass from the Shatt-el-Arab), two hookahs, a large quantity of sweetmeats, sugar and other stores for two months, twelve human beings and a chest of rupees in a dark space underneath the poop. We had our sleeping mats with us, a small carpet each and a cloak, and there were leaning pillows round the poop. We could, the Sheikh said, go into some quiet cove along the beach and sleep on the sand each night. It seemed to me that we should have to, for there was not room to sleep on board. We would eat the sheep, change the rupees for pearls as opportunity offered, and go where the wind took us.

It appeared to promise a good program. So we set off, out of Kuwait Bay, hours after the hour announced, twenty days later than the announced day. We saw very little either of pearlers or pearls the first day, and fetched up for the evening at a walled place called Shi'aiba. Here we ate a sheep and then stretched ourselves to sleep on the sand. It was a good place, but there were no pearlers there: the fleet had gone on to the south.

We sailed again in the morning after the dawn prayer; and for a month after that, we dodged about the nearer waters of the northern Gulf, now coming in to some lonely beach to sleep, now anchored for days in the rolling sea behind a reef with the fleet of pearlers jostling round us, now spending a day or two with the Beduin of the Sheikh's acquaintance, living on camel's milk and the flesh of sheep. We went where the pearlers were and sometimes spent a week round one reef, while Sheikh Sabah's big sambuk led the Kuwait fleet combing the bank. It was often stirring to watch these fleets of pearlers on the banks with their sweeps out and the divers near-naked in the sea, their crews chanting and dancing while they shifted the sambuk to a new berth. Sometimes we were one of a fleet of sixty Kuwait pearlers; at others, one of six. The big fellows kept the sea and only the smaller craft came in by night to the beaches. At dawn they opened the oysters taken the previous day. Then we hovered about, listening for news, waiting for the cheers that would greet the finding of a really good pearl.

I soon discovered that Sheikh Mohamed was not after good pearls cheap, but first-rate pearls for next to nothing. That is, if he could get them. Very often he could not, for the nakhodas were alert and not anxious to sell to brokers visiting the fleet in launches, so long as they had hope of a rising market in Bombay or Bahrein. Some of them had to sell, to buy more dates or rice, or water.

What the buyer really loved to see was a big pearl whose value was unrecognized by nakhoda and crew. Such pearls were rare, but they did exist. The Sheikh told me that a pearl of seemingly little value, if operated on properly by an expert, could sometimes be made into a gem of rare beauty. He excelled at this art and was constantly on the lookout for gems on which to practice. We did not find many. Blister pearls, which he could skilfully remove from the shell, large discolored pearls which he would carefully peel, misshapen pearls which he would whittle down in the hope that only the outer skin was blemished and out of shape—these we purchased. They were cheap. He usually paid about five rupees for them, and the "operations" took days. As a rule, after he had "operated" on them, they were not worth even one rupee. The blister pearls proved to be excrescences covered with a thin layer of pearl tissue, the misshapen ones remained misshapen, the discolored ones retained their unprofitable idiosyncrasies through all their skins. No matter: it was a gamble. The whole business was a gamble. *Allah karim!* One day would come the pearl bought for five rupees, worth five hundred—even five thousand. It was a risk worth taking: performing the "operations" was interesting, and it served to pass the time. We had a great deal of spare time.

I do not mean that the Sheikh Mohamed ever doctored a pearl. That was impossible. He simply tried to detach blisters from their shells in the hope that there might be a good pearl inside, or peeled a skin from a big coarse pearl in the hope that there might be a perfect gem under it. Such were his "operations." He did not adulterate anything: he loved his pearls too much for that. Every one in the Persian Gulf pearling business knew that the only way he could retain a market was by the strictest and most thorough honesty. It would, apparently, be easy to introduce a parcel of Japanese cultured pearls into a group of real gems, since their detection is so difficult. But in fact it would be almost impossible to do this: the supervision of the catch is too strict. Any one found doing such a thing would run the risk of instant execution. Justice in Arabia is summary, and often final. Even the importing of cultured pearls to any of the Arab market places is a most serious offense, punished by penal servitude. Penal servitude there means languishing indefinitely in a dungeon.

For diversion, we sometimes went hunting with falcons with a Beduin sheikh on Ras Zor. The smaller pearlers came to the beach to rest their crews one day in every ten, and when they came we came with them to visit their ships and see what sort of catch they had. Usually they had very few pearls, and only of a poor quality, and we did not often buy from them. But we had some good visits with the Beduin who wandered along the coast with their flocks, coming in to the waterholes for summer and going to the desert again for winter and spring. They all kept falcons, which are favorite hunters in Kuwait. The falcons were better fed than some of the children. They also had large numbers of hungry dogs which came running to the tents every time they heard the smacking of lips. When we were not engaged in falconry or watching the flocks we lolled against the camel saddles in the tents, a partition of coarse matting separating us from the harem. It was a free, untrammelled life: I wondered why any of the Bedu trouble to go pearling. Our friends of Ras Zor certainly had no intention of doing so.

Though the intervals ashore were pleasant, I liked best to be out on the banks with the pearling fleets, learning the methods of working, getting some knowledge of the secrets of the trade. Being with the Sheikh Mohamed was an ideal way to study pearling, for in that way I could watch everything—the dive, the maneuvering, life in all kinds of vessels, buying, selling, "operating." I learned how the brokers competed with one another, each always anxious to hear of a great pearl before any of the others knew of it, so that he might dash off and buy it before competing bids forced up the price, and before the nakhoda discovered its real value. We distributed largesse right and left to make friends amongst the nakhodas in order to hear these tips—a sheep here, a tin of sweetmeats there, a piece of camel meat to one friend, a pound of tobacco to another. All news was by word of mouth and most of it was unreliable. Several times we dashed after reported great pearls, but we never found any. The brokers, I noticed, brought nothing but bad news. Our visits to the pearlers were always introduced by sad accounts of the dullness of the market— true enough, unfortunately—designed to decrease the nakhodas' expectations for his pearls. Then, after some time—we were never in a hurry once we had got aboard a vessel—the nakhoda, after discussing every other subject on earth, would dive into a mysterious recess beneath his tiny poop and drag out a chest. It was often a dilapidated chest tied up with string, but usually it was locked in some way or other, and the keys were tied to a short thong around the nakhoda's waist, beneath his gown. The divers always watched as the pearls were brought out. The chest would be opened slowly, as became the receptacle of so many hopes, and as we watched, various small bundles tied up in scraps of red bunting or bits of black cloth would be extracted. Often in the smaller vessels each bundle was identified, usually by the manner of tying its knots, as the property of such and such a diver: in the larger vessels the take was pooled, but there was always a division of the pearls. They were not graded, for no nakhoda on the bank bothered to grade or to value his pearls until the season was over. They were kept in separate parcels according to the banks on which they were taken. Most of the pearls were useless. The red bunting contained mostly tiny seed pearls, and discolored or misshapen lumps. But there always were some perfect gems.

Usually the nakhoda would uncover one small parcel and hand it round to us for examination. No one watched the individual pearls, though all hands, except those actually diving and tending, watched the performance. There was obviously scrupulous honesty on board. If there was sharp practice in the industry, it was not between the men and their nakhoda on the banks. No man kept his own pearls. The nakhoda had them all. Often, when a parcel was produced for our examination, Sheikh Mohamed, pretending to despise it, would give it only a cursory glance before tying it up and throwing it back. He often did that with ten or a dozen little parcels before we got down to business in earnest, and it was sometimes hours before his clerk, his brother Mosa, produced the sieves and the scales and all the rest of the buying apparatus.

We used to board these ships by small boat from our jalboot, and our cargo was invariably the same, a sack of jingling silver rupees, Sheikh Mohamed's red bundle, some sweetmeats and some Arab cigarettes as gifts. The Sheikh's red bundle contained magnifying glasses, a small neat balance to be held in the hand, two sets of agate weights and some tiny weights of very light metal, a book in Hindustani on the grading and value of pearls, another book with the Sheikh's secret information of the prices ruling in the markets at Bombay and Bahrein, a set of small brass sieves with carefully graduated holes for grading pearls, and a piece of red cloth to keep the wind from the scales. The scales were held by hand and hardly accurate but the Sheikh was very skilful at getting an idea of the weight of a take with them. I noticed that he never overweighed them. He piled all the small pearls together, and deducted 10 per cent for stray bits of oyster adhering to the pearls. (We often weighed them and examined them almost fresh from the fish.) When the pearls had been thoroughly examined, despite the appearance of casualness, there would be another interval of pious discourse. Then at last would come the query, how much? The nakhodas were generally most reluctant to name a price, and the Sheikh was always reluctant to pay anything. The nakhodas had a good idea of the value of their pearls. The dialogue might go something like this:

The nakhoda, reluctantly, after a long pause, fingering the red bundle: "Four hundred rupees."

Sheikh Mohamed bursts into ironical laughter. He gets up to leave. He comes back again. He bundles up his apparatus.

The nakhoda: "Four hundred rupees is little enough."

Sheikh Mohamed: "There is no market for pearls. You know that! Anything I spend now I may lose. If you can get four hundred rupees for that I will give six hundred."

The nakhoda: "Four hundred."

Sheikh Mohamed: "I offer two hundred and fifty. And that's final. There is no market for pearls. There is not a good pearl in the bundle. It is only our old friendship which prompts me to make this generous offer. Hold them, if you wish: see if you are offered any more than I offer now. By the grace of Allah, I am generous."

The nakhoda: "Four hundred. See how many poor men must share in this. We have dived for these gems two months—two hard months. They are worth four hundred rupees."

Sheikh Mohamed: "*Allah karim!* I cannot help the bad market. I will give their worth. You know me. But I cannot give more than their worth. It is bad. All the markets are bad. Bad, bad, bad." And then follow many pious exclamations, which impress the crew.

The nakhoda, also exclaiming piously and now sadder than ever: "Four hundred rupees."

An hour later, the pious exclamations rambling on and on and the red cloth having been opened and tied up again three or four times, while the gaunt divers warming themselves at the tiny firebox stand and look on, Sheikh Mohamed suddenly seizes his brother's hand, takes it by the fingers, and slips a red cloth over them so that the onlookers may not see what is being done. This is his way of finding out what his brother thinks the pearls are worth. He will not ask him straight out. This is a brokers' consultation. I see the fingers working: he touches a nail of this finger, takes hold of the third joint of that, shifts rapidly to the second joint of a third. His brother responds just as rapidly. The mathematics of this finger-juggling, time-honored method of pearl-buying in the Gulf are simple to grasp: but the practice itself takes years to learn. Each finger, each joint in every finger, each degree of pressure, has an exact mathematical value.

I was told, by the sailors, that brokers and merchants communicating in this way could even fix the amount of bakhshish to be divided between them, and the practice could be used dishonestly. With Sheikh Mohamed, it was always merely a part of the proceedings: it was not the whole. The price was agreed upon orally and not by this covered touch system. He used that only to communicate with his brother during the driving of bargains, for his brother also was a shrewd judge of pearls, and had better eyes.

After a long time, we buy the parcel at two hundred and sixty rupees. Then the sack of silver coins is opened, the agreed price counted out (every coin being rung), the pearls transferred to the Sheikh's pocket, and after a round of coffee we return in the small boat to our launch. It was amazing after a day's buying had been done, to see how the value of the pearls increased once we had bought them. Sheik Mohamed would bring them out, gloat over them, weigh, grade, and value them properly, instead of just haphazardly as he did when buying, and tie them all up in a large parcel with the others he had bought. He did not keep them separately, or try to grade them until his buying was finished. On the banks we kept all the pearls in one big piece of bunting, locked in a chest. He had them out of that chest ten and twenty times a day, when buying was not in progress, and he and his brother gloated over them. The transfer of a parcel of pearls from the nakhoda's piece of bunting to their own seemed to double the pearls' value. Probably it trebled it.

While we were anchored off the beach at a place called Ras Misha'ab, a small pearler came in to bury one of her divers who had died. He looked to me as if he had died of scurvy, which was not at all surprising, for the diet on the banks was very poor. All there was to eat was rice and fish. The rice itself might have been nutritious and with a liberal covering of real Arab ghee might have sufficed to keep scurvy at bay for a few months. But, recently, the nakhodas had taken to the purchase of artificial ghee, made in Europe and imported by the merchants to Bahrein and Kuwait. It looked all right, and it was cheap. It was nothing but a low-grade cooking oil, and it had practically no value as nutriment. So the divers were getting scurvy again and the nakhodas were surprised.

The burial of the poor diver was a simple ceremony. It was over in a few minutes. They carried him up the beach and put him in the sand. The poor, worn-out old body seemed pitifully easy to carry. I looked to see that it was not my old friend Yusuf, for I feared it could easily have been. It was not: it was a man from Hasa. I had seen this artificial ghee aboard the ships, in tins; and I asked Sheikh Mohamed if he could not induce the nakhodas to stop purchasing such stuff. But he could not, he said: it was cheap, and they were ignorant men. They used it liberally, not knowing it was useless. The real ghee of Kuwait was expensive, he said: the nakhodas were poor men.

So they were burying the diver in the sand. How many divers died like that? I asked. Death was rare, the Sheikh said. Some drowned. Some just died. But I noticed we were never aboard a ship on all those banks which had not at least one sick diver lying wrapped in his desert cloak on the bare boards aft. Most of them looked like scurvy cases.

Some miles south of Ras Misha'ab we came upon the main Kuwait fleet, sixty ships on one large bank, and others grouped about lesser banks. There were more than a hundred craft in sight altogether, but most of them were small vessels. The sight was a stirring one—the burned brown hulls of the pearling ships with their long sweeps out looking like ancient galleys, the flags flying from the admiral's sambuk, the beating of drums and the chant of lusty voices as here and there a jalboot or a big belem moved with slow grace towards a new berth with melodic swing and splash of the great sweeps, the deep chest grunting of her two-score sailors as a large pearler took up her berth and the oarsmen bent together for the final burst of sound. Occasionally, a small vessel would set a great genoa jib and skim over the water for a mile or so. All the vessels used these maneuvering sails on the banks and rarely set their big lateens except for leaving and making the anchorages night and morning. Usually they were shifted during the day only by their sweeps.

A fleet of vessels would take up positions on a bank, each anchoring on the outer edge in such a way that by veering out cable they would drift across the bank, and then slowly work their way across with divers out on each side, veering out cable until the farther edge of the bank was reached. Then they would weigh and stand back to the other side, under the sweeps, with song and chanting. Everything was done with a set style. They would anchor again a little farther from their old position, and once more slowly scour a section of the bank with divers out on either side.

This method of cleaning up a bank was thorough, and after a day or so the bank would have been dealt with almost as efficiently as a ploughed field. The different craft crossing and recrossing the beds of oysters with their divers out on either side of them were like harrowers going across a field: they missed very little. Each time the vessel lay to her anchor the divers scoured the bottom until they could not see an oyster left. Then the ship slacked away again until a new place was reached. Each ship had her own track, her own section of the bank, and it was not considered proper for others to anchor anywhere in her path. Occasionally, some of the smaller vessels, apparently despairing of getting their due share of oysters from a bank so thoroughly combed, would weigh anchor, set their big jibs, and be off somewhere to a bank of their own.

The skill of the nakhodas was in their knowledge of the banks and their efficiency in cleaning them, for, with fifty or sixty vessels on the one bank, it was a shrewd and determined man who knew always how to keep his vessel anchored in virgin water and his divers bringing up oysters by the basketful. Sometimes we would board a vessel where the divers, try as they would, never brought up more than two or three oysters apiece, yet near them the divers of another sambuk might be bringing up baskets filled with big shells. It was not luck. It was intuitive skill: you had it or you didn't have it. Sheikh Mohamed used to point out to me the nakhodas who did have it, and usually, though not always, these had the larger ships. One of them was blind. He was quite blind, but according to my merchant friend he kept his skill. We saw many nakhodas who dived themselves, though they did not stand their regular turns. They made the first dives to test the beds.

In the evenings, while we were with the main fleet, we anchored behind a reef far out in the Gulf, out of sight of land. It was about midway between Kuwait and Bahrein, in that part of the Gulf which is most dangerous to ocean vessels. It was not dangerous to us for all these nakhodas knew the banks as if they were garden beds. The small craft used to come hurrying in of an evening like a crowd of yachts returning from a regatta, though the odor that came from them was not that of a regatta, and the lithe brown sailors pulling at the sweeps chanted haunting songs. Aft the divers were always huddled, seeming only half-alive, bent and shivering.

The big ships and the main fleet had been working downgulf like that for two months: they worked down until they met the Bahrein fleet working up, and afterwards smaller ships came behind them to take the leavings. Little pearlers worked close inshore, using different methods. Sometimes we saw these with all their crews swimming about looking very queer with their heads in boxes, pushing the boxes along. The box had a piece of glass in its underside, in the water, and through this glass the swimmers could see the bottom clearly. When they saw oysters they let go the box and dived down for them. They swam about for hour after hour and seemed never to tire or to suffer any inconvenience.

In this way the banks of the Gulf, at least the shallower of them, must be scoured of their oysters efficiently, in spite of the persistence of ancient methods and the sharp decline in the number of ships and men in the business.

We stayed in this reef-anchorage while the fleet was on the adjacent bank, and Sheikh Mohamed bought many parcels of good pearls. In the evenings, in the brief interval between light and darkness, we ate our meal, and then visited the other ships or were visited, yarned with nakhodas and other merchants, admired their pearls, and gloated over our own. With the setting of the sun came the muezzin's call, and then the evening prayer. After that a drum might beat aboard a Beduin craft from the Kuwait coast, or there might be a brief flare of camel-thorn as a late comer warmed some coffee. After that, silence, for the night is given to sleep. The little ships rolled and pitched at their anchorage and jostled and bumped together, but the pearlmen, packed like sardines, slept the heavy sleep of the exhausted until daybreak. Then they were up again, opening their oysters: the previous day's catch always stood in its sacks overnight for the oysters to die. They were more easily opened when they were dead. While they were being opened the sun gained strength to light the

The pearl-divers

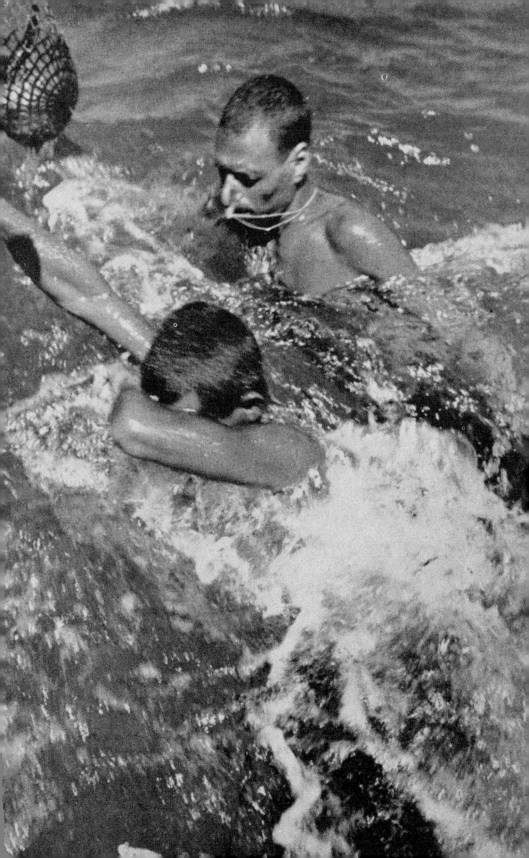

divers at their undersea work. It was no use to dive before the sun was strong. It was no use to dive, either, on days when the fierce north wind filled the Gulf with stinging sand, and visibility was so impaired that the divers could not see one fathom down; or when the sea ran white-capped and the little ships plunged and bucked so much that diving was dangerous. There were many of these off days, but for the most part the weather during the diving season was settled.

One of these days at the reef anchorage we found old Yusuf. It was evening when he came—a very beautiful, calm evening with the sunset colors soft and grand, and the songs of the pearlers coming in by sail and sweeps giving the scene a romantic atmosphere which was far from real. The lovely lateen sails were mirrored in the deep blue. He came in with his sambuk, which had moved to the bank that day from some mysterious bank in midgulf which apparently was that nakhoda's own. I was horrified at the change in his appearance. His face was strained and gaunt, his gray hair was grayer and more scanty than ever, his cheeks were sunken until they seemed only skin stretched over shrunken bone; his feet and hands were lacerated, though he had leather tips on his nails to protect them from the jagged rocks and coral spikes. His stomach was hollow, as though there were nothing in it and had been nothing for weeks. He could not stand upright: his body had bent over his empty stomach. His legs were thin, worn almost to the bone. His feet and hands were water-worn, and shrivelled. The skin on his thin legs was covered with a rash of what appeared to be small pimples, many of which had come to a head and broken.

Many of the divers in his sambuk—and in the others—had this disease on their legs, and some also on the arms. It must have been very painful. I had noticed it before in the *Triumph*: it never responded to any treatment, though if the sailors could be kept out of salt water for a time it appeared to show some improvement. Poor Yusuf was a sorry sight. He had aged twenty years, and he seemed more dead than alive. He greeted me cheerfully, however: there was nothing wrong with his spirit. If he accepted his fate with resignation there was nothing stolid or apathetic about him. It was a courageous kind of resignation.

He told us their take of pearls was bad. They had found many, but none of the first quality and very few of the second. It was amazing to notice how rare first-quality pearls were. In the two months I was on the banks, seeing pearls by the bagful every day, I don't think I saw more than a dozen which were really large, flawless gems. Sheikh Mohamed said the Gulf fisheries yielded no more than two first-rate necklaces in any year.

In the morning I went out with Yusuf's craft to spend the day on board and watch the diving. The old man would accept nothing from me except a few cigarettes and a handful of dates. The divers, he said, could not eat. It was better not to eat. A few dates in the morning and some coffee, a bite at night when the day's work was through—that was all. They could not dive on full stomachs, or they would die. He had only another six or seven weeks to go. He could stand it: he had stood it for twenty years before. At first it had been hard, after having, by the grace of Allah, been away from the banks five years; but now he was used to the hardships. Only six more weeks. It would have seemed an eternity to me.

We were out on the banks when the sun had been an hour risen, and the water was limpid and clear. The seven sacks of oysters from the previous day, opened at dawn immediately the prayer was ended, had yielded only a teaspoonful of pearls, none of them of the best quality. Truly the luck was bad, for other craft at the anchorage had taken good pearls and the admiral's sambuk had 10,000 rupees' worth already. *Allah karim!* The Lord was merciful. Their luck would change. I hoped so, as I watched old Yusuf make ready for the dive.

The sambuk was an old one which had been on the beach four years, but it was larger than most, and in good order. It had eight sweeps a side. It was decked, and without bulwarks, like all the pearlers. When the sambuk was anchored the sweeps lay athwart the ship, lashed to the tholepins and standing out over the sea at right angles to the ship. The sweeps were always left like that out on the banks, for they were of importance to the diving. To each sweep there were two divers, and one tender. The divers' lines passed over their sweeps to prevent any possibility of becoming entangled. Over each sweep—and they were worn by the constant passing and repassing of the lines—hung a piece of coir line about fifteen fathoms long, to which a stone was attached. The divers went down with this stone, which was hauled up again as soon as they had reached the bottom. They took down with them another line to which was fastened a light basket made of roping stuff on a neck of twisted cane. This they held, and it was their lifeline as well as oyster basket. If they lost hold of this, they were done. They dived in tiny black shorts, and wore no other garments.

Yusuf had a piece of string round his neck, with a nose-clip attached

Pearling sambuk, Persian Gulf

to it. His nose-clip was made from a piece of ram's horn, but some of the other divers' were of wood. Before each dive he carfully adjusted this clip: it was all the protection he had. I asked him why all the divers wore something black, and he said that the big fish, the sharks, did not like black. So long as they wore black they were safe. This was a comforting belief, but I wondered how well-founded it was. If there were giant rays about, he said, they would also wear a wisp of white. There were no rays that day, and they all wore only these black shorts. Each diver seemed to possess two pairs of black shorts and one sarong. As they came up shivering after their turn of ten dives and were hauled on board again, they changed their shorts, hung the wet ones to dry, and stood round the camel-thorn fire until it was time to go down again.

There were two shifts of divers, one to a sweep on each side, each doing ten dives and then resting ten. Yusuf said he dived about 120 times a day, more in shallow water. Each dive averaged about a minute: anything from forty seconds to ninety seemed the rule. Thus he spent two hours a day on the bottom of the Gulf, without air. Two hours a day!

It seemed a great deal to me. But there were spells, he said: they rested one day in ten, though sometimes if they were on a good bank in diving weather, they worked eighteen days and rested two. They went in to a beach for rest, because the ship needed fresh water and fuel. The sailors, who did the tending of the divers, went in search of fuel and water while the divers had a meal and slept.

Now old Yusuf, hanging to his rope, was in the water by the aftermost sweep on the starboard side. That was his place. It was the place of the head diver, who was always expected to bring up the most oysters. He hung there a moment, treading water and adjusting his nose-clip. The tally of ten bones rove on a date frond on a stanchion aft showed that no dives had yet been made. As a dive was made the aftermost hauler moved one bone along the frond: when all ten were moved he shouted, and the divers came back aboard to be relieved by their mates. There were thirty-two divers, twenty tenders, a nakhoda, a clerk, a cook and five boys. As far as I could see, all the boys did was to keep the hookahs filled, to fetch water to wash the sailors' hands at meal times, and to stand in a group about the nakhoda every time the anchorage was shifted, ready to pass on his orders with a shrill yelling that could be heard above the din of song from the sixty men. One of the boys was Yusuf's son, aged six.

"I see him, when he is here," the old man said. "But I will see he incurs no debts."

Yusuf was ready to dive. He took his basket, holding it by the rim. He took a twist of one leg about the rope with the stone, with his foot on the stone. He looked up at his tender. The tender let go: down he went, down, down. I could watch him drop three, four fathoms. I saw the tide take him and sweep him astern, a brown blur in the blue water. Then he was gone. A few seconds and, feeling it loose as it took the ground, his tender hauled up the stone, caught it with a slippery hitch about the sweep, and then took Yusuf's basket-line and carefully tended that, slacking out and feeling for the slight tug which would indicate that Yusuf's lungs could stand no more and his dive was done. How long he was down! It seemed a long time waiting there. I did not count the seconds, at first. They seemed like minutes. All the divers were down now. There was silence aboard as the tenders, erect and alert, held the lines. Still the divers were down. The lines were taut, all leading aft, each separated from the others by the round arm of the sweeps. It was obvious that there must be a considerable set running there: Yusuf, the aftermost diver, must have been thirty yards astern of the ship. Still he was down. A minute had passed. It seemed like five minutes to me. Now! A slight tug, barely perceptible, and the tender was hauling in fast, hand over hand, long pulls and strong. He hauled and hauled, but it was a long time before I saw any sign of Yusuf. Now I could see a faint brown smudge deep below, at an angle of forty-five degrees from the vessel. Quickly the smudge grew: it became the blurred outline of a man: it was the head and shoulders of a man, the close-cropped gray head of a man. It was old Yusuf. Here he came, breaking water at last. His oyster basket first, well filled with oysters, then his old head with an arm thrown up to shield his water-tired eyes from the glare of the sun, and his shoulders streaming water like a seal. He blew once, like a whale, slipped off his clip, drew in the air, trod water at his sweep by the ship's side. The tender hauled the coir basket aboard.

Now all the divers had come to the surface: Yusuf was the last. The tenders took their baskets. Some were half-filled, some were quarter-filled, some had as few as two or three oysters in them. Each tender held his basket aloft, turning inboard. Then, "*Allah karim!*" was the shout, followed by a deep-toned "*Y'Allah!*" as the contents of the baskets were thrown on the deck, making a clatter as they fell. "God is merciful!" "Oh, God!"

By this time the divers were sufficiently rested. They dived one minute, rested two; then took their baskets again and their stones, adjusted their nose-clips, and were down. Again the long, almost alarming pause before the gray heads broke surface again, and the muddy oysters came up in their bags. Again the shout "*Allah karim! Y'Allah!*" again the clatter of oysters on the wet deck, the shifting of the tally bone, the blowing of the divers.

Ten times they dived, while their reliefs sat aft, dispassionate, stolid, seemingly disinterested. Ten times they dived, and then were hauled in again: their mates slipped into the water to take up the work, while Yusuf and his shift shivered and shook round the cook's poor fire, where nothing was cooking. A scrap of sail had been spread there to give them a shelter: the day was young and they felt the cold. To me the day was almost unbearably hot, for the early morning shade temperature was over a hundred. Yet the divers, bent and haggard, stood and shivered in their sarongs.

As the strength of the sun increased, awnings of cheap Japanese material were spread fore-and-aft, for the sun beat down all day on the hard-working tenders. If the divers ate nothing they also went without food:

if the divers could not eat, no meal was cooked. There was no midday meal on the banks. Many of the divers were Beduin, many of the tenders Persian, and others Negroes, ex-slaves. By this time, twenty dives had been made in the one place and all the oysters had been scoured from there. The cable was veered and the ship dropped back thirty yards, in the tide. Again Yusuf slipped to the side and into the sea; again came the ten dives, the number of oysters in his basket decreasing each time. I asked him how he worked—how he managed to stay down, without weights. It was an eight-fathom bank. He said he crawled along the bottom with his eyes open: he had to fight his way, clutching coral spikes and rocks. When he saw oysters, he forced them from the rock and put them in his basket. He had to be quick. He went as far from the ship as he could. Each man kept to his own part of the bottom, going back with the set from his sweep, and immediately his stone was on the bottom, setting off as directly at right angles to the ship as he could. In this way they covered the bottom thoroughly, missing little.

Again ten dives, ten rests: ten dives, ten rests; more cable veered. Half a sackful of oysters had been taken. The oysters were kept in sacks by

Resting divers

the bole of the mizzenmast. The decks were wet and the whole ship was nothing but a wet, congested working platform. The tenders sweated and the divers shivered: the tenders were fat and the divers painfully lean: the tenders knew no rest and the divers no warmth. Gaunt, hollow-cheeked men, they squatted by the fire until it was their turn to dive. The tenders wore red-and-blue sarongs, the nakhoda a white shirt, the divers only their black. The wet and crowded decks had only space for the men: by the fire were some bundles of camel-thorn, and empty waterskins. The fresh water was in wooden tanks in the hold. Aft lay the inevitable sick diver—there were two in this sambuk. Forward were some fish-traps made of coir weighted with oystershells: underneath the poop, by the nakhoda's bench, was the chest of pearls. There was only one chest on the poop, the nakhoda's: there was only one rough sleeping place. Above the poop and all round were tied the little bundles of the crew's possessions, each in his own small bag—a rag of clothing, prayer beads, a leaf or two of coarse Persian tobacco, a toothstick. Nothing else, no bedding, no medicine, no comforts.

Still they dived, broke surface, blew, and rested. The cable veered; the boys piped their loud "Belay!" The decks were a mess of sea slime and crawling things from the newly caught oysters. The sun climbed high, and its heat shimmered over the broiling sea. It was a day of dead calm. Away from us, away on either beam across the banks were the other ships, scores of them, now with the splash of sweeps glinting in the sun and the chant of the toiling crew, now silent for the dive, the farther ones miraged so that they seemed immense, and the genoa jib of a Beduin shewe looking like a flaccid balloon. As the day advanced, the heat grew until, though I thought myself acclimatized, it was nearly unbearable. Still the work continued. These were ideal conditions for diving.

With the cable veered to the end it was hauled in again, the divers huddled by the fire not sharing in this work unless they wished to stamp some circulation back into their bones, the sailors dancing and chanting. The sailors did the tending and the ship's work: the divers only dived. They were too weak to work: every ounce of energy they had went into the dive.

Now the sailors dance along the deck in two endless lines, round and round, clapping their great hands and singing as the taut cable comes in, fathom after fathom of it, dripping wet. Now the anchor—it is a piece of stone with a spike in it—is up-and-down: it is broken out: "Man the

sweeps!" Two men to a sweep and three at the stroke, the sailors dip
lustily into the sea and strain at the huge sweeps. Each of the sweeps is
eighteen feet long. I begin to understand what life in the old galleys must
have been like, and to see, too, why big craft can never be moved at speed
with only one tier of sweeps. It is slow, heavy, painful work, all done with
chant and rhythm. I think I see now, how much of the Kuwait deepwater
style has come from these banks. They are the same songs, the same
chants, the same hand clappings, the same deep grunting, the same powerful deck stampings, the same steps in the brief intervals of dancing.

The long sweeps flash through the air with perfect rhythm, bite
deep into the sea: the straining sailors, wet with sweat, walk their inboard
ends along the deck, their muscles bulging, their throats vibrant with
song. The nakhoda, hawk-eyed old man, watches. He must know these
waters better than most of their own fish, though how he gains such
knowledge is a mystery. How he tells one bank from another, I do not
know, for they are out of sight of land here. Yet he knows: he knows exactly where his ship is to go, and sees that she goes there. His clerk is at
the tiller: he nods to him to steer this way or that. The boys stand ready
by the mizzenmast to echo his orders. The drums are beating forward to
mark the rhythm of the sweeps. Now and again comes a burst of labored
breathing from a sailor at the sweeps, but always they sing—praises to
Allah, prayers for great pearls. The sambuk crawls across the burnished
sea in a din of song. Now, now it is enough! A nod from the nakhoda, a
shrill shriek from the boys—belay, belay! Way enough! The stone anchor
goes down: the sweeps are secured outboard: the stones and the basket-
lines are thrown across them.

Before the dive starts at this new place, the sailors gather round the
mainmast. Hands over their ears or on their jawbones, their bodies bent,
they give out that great chesty growl of Kuwait, that long-drawn noise
of rumbling that comes only from the extraordinary vocal cords of the
Gulf sailors. It sounds like a pack of subdued lions hungry for a meal, like
a pit of heavy bears growling for a bone, like the rumbling of a deep vol-
cano. It is an extraordinary noise, and I could never make it, try as I
would. The amazing growls continue a long time. Why? I ask old Yusuf.
Is it to scare off sharks, stingrays, *jinns?* But he does not know. Nobody
knows. It is the Gulf style. Perhaps it is the survival of an ancient ritual
for scaring off bad *jinns,* calling up good ones, or intimidating the oysters
far beneath the keel. There are many survivals in these Kuwait ships. Why
is there always the strange black end to the long stemheads, themselves

perhaps survivals from phallic worship? Why the sacrifice of the kid at launchings? This is done to this day at Ma'alla, and elsewhere. Why now this curious noise-making on the pearling banks?

Now there has been grunting enough. Suddenly at a nod from the nakhoda the boys shrill forth again. The noise stops. The divers shuffle to the side: the dive begins again. Ten dives down, ten rests: basket after basket of slimy oysters flung down on deck: *"Allah karim! Y'Allah!"* the cable veered: ten dives again, ten rests: the gray heads breaking the blue water, the tired arms flung across weary eyes, great chests bursting into a sob of breath as the nose-clips are removed. Ten dives again, ten rests— and the cable veered. Ten dives again, and ten rests: and the cable veered. The sun is high now, the heat dreadful. The weak shade of the awnings serves only to darken the decks and not to shade them. Still the haggard divers shiver and crowd by the brushwood fire. Some pray. It is the mid-day prayer. There is no siesta on the banks. Ten dives again: ten rests. And the cable veered. No food. The air is breathless and deadly hot. A boy hauls in a fish trap forward: no catch. Ten dives again, ten rests. Poor Yusuf! This life must be the death of many good men.

I know that hardship recorded from a writer's notes may often be more harrowing than the actual experiences. The stories of some Cape Horn roundings are painful. But the capacity of the human frame to endure punishment can be well-nigh unbelievable. Yet, judged by any standard I know, compared with any form of maritime hardship I have experienced, or seen, or read about, pearling in the Persian Gulf can be terrible indeed. I came away from Kuwait favorably impressed by most aspects of its life, keenly enthusiastic about its ships, and an admirer of its seamen. But the infernal *ghaus*, the hellish diving, is another matter. If there must be pearls, let them be dredged.

I left poor Yusuf there, making his ten dives, shivering through his ten rests, as fervent a believer in the mercy of Allah as any of them. God has been merciful to him if only in the granting of that comforting belief, a belief without which his life would be unbearable.

A month later I was back in Kuwait. The smallest ship I had seen was a little thing fourteen feet long with a crew of one old man and four boys, aged between twelve and seventeen. The largest was the sambuk of the admiral, Sheikh Sabah. I had seen quite enough of pearling and found nothing to admire in that romantic industry, except the courage and the fortitude of the crews.

Chapter 20

THE OTHER WIFE

BACK in Kuwait all was activity. It was not yet the end of August, but many of the ships were being got ready for their new voyages, and the two miles of the waterfront hummed with the activities of the fitting out. During the latter part of August and throughout September, ship after ship was floated out of her laying-up berth and taken into the Bay to be rigged and ballasted for the passage to Basra, where the dates had ripened and the export of the new season's crop was in progress.

At each high tide from ten to twenty of the larger ships were floated off, and the smaller ones were towed out with every flood. The basins along the length of the town resounded all day long with the chanting of the sailors, and the shore road was full of hurrying nakhodas and seamen joining their ships. Wherever there was an open space, sailors squatted, sewing sails. Carpenters worked feverishly to complete the new booms in time for the season. Here one was being hauled out on the mud at low water; there another was being pushed broadside into the Bay at the top of springs, for it had been built in a restricted place on high ground and could only be launched broadside. It went in with a splash, rolled once or twice, with its flags flying, and then steadied, its sea career begun. The sailors who had helped to launch it leaped at once into the water and swam out to the new ship, in their clothes, to begin the work of rigging. The booms are launched as stripped-down hulls and rigged out in the Bay. It does not take long. A few days suffice to see the masts stepped and the lateen yards rigged up, the wheel shipped, and the compass placed in its binnacle.

Ships, ships, ships, all along the sea. Sailors, quartermasters, carpenters, nakhodas, all along the shore road—what a place this Kuwait was. The ring of caulking irons, the throaty songs of sailors stepping the masts, the thump of Indian drums and the clapping of great hands as the undersides of the deepwatermen were paid with tallow and lime, the clankclank of ancient capstans warping in a pearler to the beach, the shouts of the sailors hauling out her yards to a newly floated boom, the ring of the marine blacksmith's irons as he beat out ironwork for the ships, the ripping of the Persian saws through the logs of Malabar teak high on the cutting stage, the thud of drums and the burst of joyful song from a pearling sambuk coming in from the *ghaus*—these were the sounds of the waterfront all day and every day, with respite only for prayer.

The weather was milder as September passed and sometimes there were tolerable days, for the worst of the dreadful heat of the sun was gone and the Beduin were moving out of town. As the big ships went out the Beduin went, and the pearlers came in. The Beduin went out to the desert, the sailors to the sea. If activity had increased along the waterfront, so it had also in the bazaar, for the Beduin made haste to complete their purchases, and the businessmen and the money-changers had their hands full. Sailors were buying their scanty needs, and a venture or two to take with them: the coffee shops were crowded nightly, and the pearling coffee shop was busy all day with the pearl men come in from the sea to sell their pearls. The deepsea nakhodas cast critical eyes at the Persian carpets dragged in the dust, seeking bargains to take to Mogadishu and Zanzibar. The nakhodas' coffee shop was deserted in the daylight hours and the crowds came only in the evenings, for the nakhodas were busy buying for their ships and fixing freights, collecting advances on their freights, and giving advances to their crews. From merchants' office to merchants' coffee shop the nakhodas hurried, fat after the summer at home but not so fat that they could not hurry when there was business to be done.

This year there was much business, for during the long summer evenings on the waterfront there had been much discussion and many decisions had been made. The nakhodas of the deepsea ships demanded that every vessel on a long voyage should carry a muallim as well as a nakhoda, for it is not right that one man only should know the way. They demanded, too, that the merchants should pay demurrage when they fixed the freights from the Shatt-el-Arab and then kept the booms waiting for weeks before the dates were delivered—an old grievance this, and one difficult to avoid. One thing more they wanted, an end to the practice of holding a nakhoda always responsible for his ship's debts, and all advances of freight and so forth, even after his ship is lost. This is another old practice, and not a very honest one, for the nakhodas though they nominally own their ships are rarely the real owners. It is unfair, the nakhodas argued, that if they lose a ship which never really belonged to them, they should still be responsible for its debts. In other words, the existing system of nominal ownership was not good enough: by permitting the nakhodas to finance the ships themselves the merchants transferred what rightly should be their own risk to the nakhodas. If a ship were lost, the nakhodas argued, that should be loss enough: the loss of the freight should fall on the merchant. But the merchants argued that they lost the dates and that was loss enough. The ships belonged to the nakhodas and the debts to the merchants. Debts must be paid. I heard a great deal of argument about all this and it seemed to me that right was on the nakhodas' side, but the merchants granted only that a muallim should be carried. If the nakhodas could make new rules, they said, so could they, and they were in a better position to enforce them than the nakhodas were. The nakhodas had decided to stand together, but they did not. Here and there one went over to a better merchant. Soon their points were lost, and they went out again without demurrage, still responsible for finance as well as freights, still as heavily indebted to the merchants.

It did not pay the merchants to own and run ships themselves, for the liking of the Arab for private trade and bargain-driving was too ingrained. If the nakhodas ran the merchants' ships, they were too prone to run them only for their own benefit. It was better then that the merchants should finance the nakhodas to run the ships and use them only for such freights as they needed. The advances were well secured. There was no insurance to pay: the unfortunate nakhodas, it seemed to me, were the insurance. When they lost their ships they lost their livelihood and the merchants' money besides, but they had to repay the merchants' money. Interest was not charged. It was forbidden by the Prophet. But they were often required to pay back more than they had borrowed.

The nakhodas' worries however were the nakhodas' own, and not the sailors': the sailors held no meetings and drew up no rules. They went out again in the ships to which they were bound.

Days passed and ship after ship moved out to the north, many of them going lightly rigged, for the passage up to the Shatt-el-Arab is very short. The muallims, many of them newly appointed, often took the ships to the Shatt-el-Arab to wait for the dates, while the nakhodas adjusted financial matters in Kuwait or stayed as long as possible to enjoy the delights of their harems. The scene along the waterfront remained busy and most interesting. By the al-Kalifa mosque a gang of sailmakers worked in the shade, sewing a mainsail a hundred and sixty feet long. Wooden watertanks were being fish-oiled, anchors freshly tarred carried out to their vessels, parrals of the lateen yards adjusted, sails carried along rolled up like circus tents, longboats taken from their summer coverings of matting and floated into the sea. Small boys played about with model booms which they sailed and scampered after in the shallow water, singing the sailors' songs as they played. Nakhodas interviewed muallims, generally their own relatives, along the shady stone benches on the west side of their homes. Ships were being built, paid, caulked, repaired, launched, floated off, rigged, danced to, and sung about. The little reed huts of the *khubz* makers and the wayside stands of the sherbet sellers did a good business.

In one of the basins near the middle of the town, Nasir's little *Cat* stood silent, the last deepwaterman left behind her nigger, and little Nasir himself sat on his bench waiting for the pearlers to return. Nasir was a poor man and the *Cat* was old. He could not afford big advances and his little *Cat* could not earn much. Nasir, then, must take such seamen as he could find; and so he waited for the pearlers to return. The poor pearlers, more penniless than ever, after their dreadful season, were in a better mood to accept the little he could offer. The *Cat* could wait. There would be dates enough for her.

For the hundredth time I walked across the flats to look at the lovely lines of the ancient *Cat*, which had never seemed catlike to me. She was a sweet-lined and beautiful old vessel, but I had long noticed with regret that her hull was strained, after half a century of timber carrying. Her decks were warped and sunken by her mainmast; she wept a fastening now and then, and I picked them up, poor rusted spikes of indifferent iron, in the mud all round her. No, it would not do. It would be foolhardy to take such a ship on a long voyage in the Atlantic Ocean, without hoping for—and urgently needing—more good fortune from the weather and from God than the mariner has a right to expect. The poor *Cat* must stay in Kuwait: I could not save her. She might be bought for 5000 rupees: little Nasir, who knew my interest, always sang her praises—not that he wished to be rid of his sweet baggala, for he loved her. Yet he knew her days were done. If I took her, it was better than the Suri. He could buy a boom with the money.

But I could not take the *Cat*, much as I should have liked to: it was September now and there were more serious things afoot in Europe than the saving of the lovely *Cat*. So I left Nasir, waiting for his pearlers. He had sailed the *Cat* twenty-three years, I knew, with a year off once for the pilgrimage. I knew, too, that I am unlikely to find a sweeter old baggala in these days, or ever again, for she belonged to the days when Kuwait ships were built by craftsmen who added each plank with loving care, after the most painstaking deliberation. Her carpenter was a man who so loved the ships he built that he left instructions that his body must be buried where ships would be built over it: he wished to be near the ships he loved, even in death.

One day I met our carpenter from the *Triumph*, the youthful Kaleel. He was shipbuilding again and I found him helping with the laying of the keel of a new boom. He was working hard and all the carpenters were rushing at their work almost as hard as the sailors do at theirs. "What is the hurry?" I asked.

"We always hurry like this now," he said. "It is not good—rush, rush, rush! That is not the way to build ships. Here, you will see that we build three planks a day—three planks a day on both sides."

He went on to tell me of the days when the *Cat* was built, and the big *Samhan*, and all the best of the Kuwait ships. They were the days, he said. None but bearded carpenters touched the planks of new ships then, and the proper rate of progress was one plank a day. Work was leisurely, painstaking, and thorough. Nothing mattered but that it should be well done. Only old skilled men, shipwrights with beards, were permitted to do the actual placing of a vessel's timbers, and all others—even carpenters of ten years' experience—sawed planks and drilled holes. A plank a day was the proper rate of progress, for everything had to be first-class and no other condition was tolerated. Discipline over apprentices and laborers was strict and apprenticeship long and arduous. Every man, when a ship was launched, felt a sense of personal pride in the achievement, and the old graybeards went from ship to ship along the waterfront criticizing, commending, improving. There was time for embellishment and good carving in those days, and old carpenters asked to be buried in the shipyards, beneath the keels of ships. Those were the days! Kaleel said. He was not an old man; he was only twenty-four. He scarcely remembered the conditions he depicted. He had heard of them from his father, a carpenter before him, and regretted their passing. Now all was rush and bustle, he concluded, with as little care in the workmanship as in the selection of the timbers. A great ship instead of taking eight or nine months to build was turned out in two: and in less than fifteen years she was fit for nothing but scrap. Fifty years was a great age now for an Arab ship: it used to be a hundred.

I listened to much the same kind of talk in my evening walks around the waterfront. I always stopped at the home of Kalifa al-Ganim, head of the clan of the Abdul-wahhabs, those fine nakhodas. Kalifa al-Ganim was a man over seventy, a dignified, bearded man with a soft gentle voice and a great knowledge of the history of Kuwait and the ways of the sea. I often sat and chatted with him, sometimes in his private room in the house overlooking the waterfront, with its yard before it where his sons' booms were built: sometimes I talked with him and the other wise men in their evening meetings. For these they always sat in a long row, seated on carpets and leaning against cushions, with their aghals thrown off and their sandals on the street before them, and their backs against a wall. They were a dignified, stately line of elderly gentlemen, and I was honored to be received among them.

We used generally to talk of the early days of Kuwait and how ship-building had grown there. Kuwait, they said, was perhaps the youngest port of the whole Persian Gulf. Kalifa al-Ganim said that, as a city, it was probably not much more than two centuries old. It had always been a sea-faring place, first because the Beduin had to fish to live; secondly because Bahreini and Hasa pearlers moved up there, for it was a better base for the northern banks; and thirdly when the Persians overrunning Basra seriously affected the carrying and distributing trade of that port, much of it went to Kuwait. Kuwait was well situated geographically as a port of distribution for northern Nejd. Remaining independent, it was, moreover, an excellent port for the infiltration of goods over a wide area of Iraq and Iran. Its merchants were good merchants and its shipbuilders, brought in from Muscat and Bahrein and from the Persian ports of Qishm and Lingeh, made a name for themselves throughout the Eastern seas.

More and more settlers came, people from Zubara in Qatar, who had gone there originally from Nejd; people from Zubair on the Iraq frontier; people coming directly from Nejd; and later, many Persians. Kuwait had a tradition of good government, old Kalifa said: this tradition it has kept. Its merchants, too, had a name for fair dealing. Its nakhodas were good men and its sailors, even a hundred years ago, had a name for being the best from Arabia. A hundred years ago, Kalifa said, Kuwait could send two hundred ships to sea, not counting pearlers. Most of them were small, but he spoke of a baggala of over 400 tons which his grandfather remembered. Perhaps twenty were vessels of more than 100 tons. Their trade was to India, in the Gulf, round the coasts of Arabia, and to Red Sea ports of Africa. They did not then sail much to East Africa. That was a trade jealously guarded by the Omani. The town was prosperous enough to satisfy its hard-living inhabitants, and not rich enough to tempt the marauder—not, at any rate, when Basra was so near.

Kuwait came to the forefront of Arab ports under the great Sheikh Mubarak, who murdered his way to the sheikhdom shortly before the turn of the last century. Kalifa pointed out to me the house where the murders were done. Mubarak's usurpation was a good thing for Kuwait, he said, though the Kuwaiti did not at first approve of it. Mubarak was an ambitious and despotic man, but he governed the city-state with an able patriarchal hand, and it prospered. The decline of other ports farther down the Gulf; the slipshod methods of the easy-going Turks who succeeded the Persians in Basra; troubles in Bahrein and in Persia; the decline of Muscat after Seyyid Said—all these things helped Kuwait. Its pearling prospered; its ships continued to make good voyages. Now the port could muster upwards of a thousand ships of all shapes and sizes—150 large deep-water booms, 200 smaller Gulf traders, 200 pearlers, with 300 more on the beach, if there were trade for them, 200 fishermen.

The Kuwaiti, with their background of desert hardship and of troubles elsewhere, appreciated the comparative quietness of Kuwait, and I found in them all a great love for the city-state. Sometimes the intelligentsia, dropping in at these evening talks, were more apologetic than they needed to be, and spoke of the democracy of Iraq as an ideal to strive for. Youths coming back in silk trousers from Iraq affected a great discontent with their own Arabian Kuwait: but it seemed to me an honest, straightforward, and satisfying place, despite the backwardness which they alleged. The silk-clad youths could leave again, if they did not like it: Kuwait was for the real Arabs. I should hate to see its women suddenly unveiled and all its citizens in trousers and the curious Italian headgear affected in Iraq. I should hate to see Diesel engines put into its fine booms, the sheikh in a sun-helmet, the stalwart habitués of the coffee shops trooping into cinemas. Kuwait is all right as it is, and its citizens can effect the necessary improvements gradually—good schools, paved streets, a proper water system, hospitals, control of public health. Kuwait has had a municipal council for seven years: it has taken these things in hand. The coming of oil, still in the experimental stage when I left, will provide the revenue.

Late one afternoon I met Nejdi in front of the divers' shop in the *suq*. The divers' shop is not far from the women's market where elderly women squat in the street and try to sell junk from four o'clock onwards every afternoon. It is on a side street, among the old clothes stalls, next to one that sells old Finnish uniforms. Its wares are nose-clips, black shorts, white diving shirts (to frighten off the rays), cane rings for the oyster baskets, lengths of roughly laid coir, lead weights—I did not see these used—and black diving suits to be used, I suppose, in waters where sharks were particularly bad. Here I met Nejdi, not looking at anything in the divers' shop: he was merely passing by. He told me that Abdulla his brother had a new boom which the family had just bought and that he would be sending both Abdulla's boom and his own to Basra within a few days. Would I like to come down to the dancing when they were paid? It would be good. But I had had my fill of dancing along the waterfront every morning, for all the booms in Kuwait were being paid and the ceremony had become commonplace. He had, he told me, managed to pay off his sailors with 135 rupees a share—poor, he knew, for the previous year it had been 165. But his was the best rate paid in Kuwait that season. Radhwan had paid only 95; Abdul-wahhab, 125; big Abdul-wahhab, 120. It was a bad year.

He thought his sailors would manage, for their needs were small. They were young men. Few maintained even one household. They had their own earnings too, of course, from the goods they had traded to their own account, and each would have a bonus from the additional hard work involved in the mysterious doubling of our official cargo of mangrove poles. If they wished, they could have an advance against the next voyage. They could live in the *suq* on a few annas a day.

I had long since learned that the European idea of a harem was not for the seafarers, indeed, not for any Arab. There was no such thing as a sort of stock of desirable young women in any household, waiting on their lord's whim. The purpose of the multi-wives idea was the production of male heirs and fighting men. In a land where infant mortality could be high, women too often barren, and diseases such as smallpox very real threats, a man had to spread his risks and his seed if his line was to prosper. But the seamen had nothing to leave to their heirs except perhaps pearling debts. Under the law of Islam a man might have four wives, but he had to be able to afford them. In the better families, each could demand her own separate household, if she wished. Merchants could afford this sort of life. Indeed, they had to, if they were to have families at all, for they often had to leave Kuwait and live for years in distant trading centers. It was usual to set up another family even if they were moved only as far as Basra.

There were plenty of eager bints available on a casual basis, of course, but these might serve for dalliance but not as mothers of a respectable

Abdulla al-Hamad

man's sons. It was astonishing how much intrigue could go on behind blank walls and veiled faces. There were certain young bucks in Kuwait who were well known for their prowess. When I walked the quieter streets away from the *suq* with one of these, it was astonishing what could happen. My friend would keep a bold eye on the flat roofs. If a pretty girl showed up there, my young merchant friend Abdulla told me, she was ready for adventure. Fair hands emerged from latticed windows and perfumed notes fluttered down. Old Swahili women, household slaves, would run after him, and pass a message hurriedly as they slipped by. Little boys, younger brothers, would carry his notes back for him. A meeting could be arranged. In all these amorous adventures Abdulla had one rule, and that was never to touch a virgin, for the Prophet had forbidden men to tamper with these. A non-virgin could not marry: if she did, she would be driven from the deceived bridegroom's house in public disgrace on the wedding night.

But this restriction did not bother my friend, for inexperienced virgins were young and closely watched, and they did not send notes fluttering down from their windows. A marriage would be arranged for them as early as possible. How could such a young girl marry when she meets no man? I asked. Easy, said Abdulla. It was arranged by close relatives. The girl had nothing to do with it. She would not see her prospective husband, nor would he see her until the wedding night. But she would be described carefully to him by his sister, perhaps, and he to her by her sister, though she could see him distantly in the street if this were arranged.

Abdulla explained his specifications for a suitable bride. She must be pretty with good features that would last: she must not be too well educated but skilled in the things of the home and the management thereof: she must be of a family noted for strong sons: she must be of gentle nature with never a hint of the incipient virago. As for beauty, on no account could she have a large mouth. She must have color in her cheeks (I supposed to assure him that she was not anemic), strong thighs and legs, large breasts and soft, a long neck, and be firm and warm to the caress always. This last she could learn: but she must not be flabby nor an incipient heavyweight.

All this amounted to something of an order, but Abdulla assured me that the supply of desirable young maidens meeting such requirements was ample, not only in Kuwait. He was quite prepared to marry on his family's and his favorite sister's say-so, and never see his intended bride. Indeed, he was contemplating just such an act in the very near future, and had instructed his family to report upon a young and lovely girl living in Zubair. Why Zubair? I asked. It was about a hundred miles north of Kuwait on the road to Basra, very conveniently placed for both, he said. He could set up a small home there and reach it easily. Though in Iraq, the place was a desert town and unspoiled.

The report was favorable, and I was invited to the wedding. We arrived at Zubair, a romantic and truly Arab township, by night, and went to the courtyard behind the wall of the maiden's house, just as if we had dropped in for the usual evening salaams, chat, and coffee. The bride's father and an uncle were there, some of Abdulla's male relatives, and I. No women were in sight. We solemnly drank the three ceremonial cups of strong coffee proper on such occasions. While drinking this, an elderly imam arrived from the mosque. He wasted no time, but took Abdulla's hand in his own right and the bride's father's in his left. He said a few words which sounded mellifluous enough, and looked very solemn. That, apparently, was his part of the wedding ceremony over. More coffee was passed round, with a little *halwa* and a whiff of incense smoke which we wafted inside our head-cloths in the proper manner. Then we left, and slept in the courtyard of Abdulla's relatives.

It was the third hour after sunset of the following evening before Abdulla came to his bride. We walked down the narrow street of Zubair again to the place where the bride's family lived, Abdulla in his best gown and cloak and rich head-cloth, his bright eyes shining with anticipation. By the doorway stood a group of Zubair women, swathed from head to feet in black. We strode past them quickly. For some reason my friend did not want this wedding publicized (probably to keep knowledge of it from his wives in Kuwait). But one of the women began to shout. "What kind of wedding is this? You come up the dark street without lights or music! Who is the groom?" And so forth. But the courtyard gate swung open and Abdulla sprang inside. He whispered that his other weddings had been done better than this. Six hundred men walked with him to the home of his other brides. It was the first time I had been a stand-in for 599 men.

This time we entered the house, where an additional room had been built on part of the flat roof and made gay with tinsel and bright candles. In it were a table, a big sofa, a harem chest, and a double bed. The floor was covered with beautiful carpets. We filed in. The bride's father was there. We salaamed, sat a while, drank sweet tea and coffee with cardamoms, and ate sweetmeats and little cakes. Abdulla could scarcely contain himself: I had not known an Arab to be so excited. Now, he whispered, I shall soon see her!

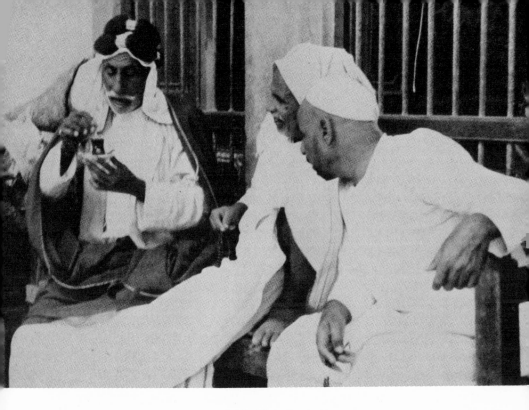

In the coffee shop

We sat for about ten minutes. Then, taking our leave, and congratulating Abdulla and wishing him well, we solemnly filed out and down the stairs again. We passed quickly through the considerable crowd of women now waiting there. We had not gone very far before we heard a strange shout, half lamentation and half joy, from the women at the courtyard.

"Aha, the bride is taken! All is well! Allah is merciful," said Abdulla's brother. For this, I gathered, was the accepted signal from the wedding bed, the acclamation of the good news.

I never saw the new wife, nor any other. But when I next saw Abdulla he smacked his lips and said that he had done very well.

There was a noticeable lessening now in the numbers at the sailors' coffee shops and even in the nakhodas'. By night along the waterfront the voices of the old men were raised again. The young men were gone, and the graybeards came into their own again as the booms departed. Most of the pearlers were in, for it was the end of September, and the gaunt Beduin went off to their flocks when the sailors, thin and worn, returned to their ships. There was war in Europe, and the pearl market, which had been bad before, was almost nonexistent. They were bad days, bewildering days, to the Arabs, who asked me what it was all about. But I was as bewildered as they were: and I had to go.

It was time to leave Kuwait and my friends the Arab sailors. I paid my final respects to His Highness the Sheikh, and went the round of the other dignitaries. His Highness was seated at his morning court on the upper verandah of Mubarak's palace, and I looked for the last time at the faded beauties adorning the rooms there, all with ornaments of large pearls, and out across the Bay, where some of the great ships were making ready at anchor. Mubarak had been gone for many years: but the beauties still looked down on those unused rooms, and Mubarak's grandson held his court on the verandah overlooking the sea. I thanked His Highness for the pleasure of my stay in Kuwait, drank coffee with him, and chatted a little. A Beduin with a Bren gun stood behind His Highness, and other Beduin squatted about with loaded rifles in their hands, but this martial appearance was belied by the orderly peacefulness of the proceedings. He hoped, His Highness said, that Kuwait had been my home and that it

The cloak-makers

would be so again. It had, indeed: and I wish I could have shared his hope for the future.

I went then to Sheikh Ali Kalifa's, at his stockade. Two pearl thieves from Hasa hung on the cross in front of it. Where was my camel? asked old Ali Kalifa. There was war, I said, I had to hurry. "You will haste enough to this war on a camel," the good sheikh said. I salaamed and went away. They were taking the thieves down from the cross to lead them, disgraced, through the *suq* to the jail. I paid my respects to the admiral of the pearling fleet, Sheikh Sabah; to the president of the pearling court, Sheikh Abdulla bin Jaber; to Sheikh Abdulla bin Salim, the president of the Council of State; to my friends the old nakhodas, the wise men, the merchants. It took me some time to make my last round, for it had been easy to make good friends in Kuwait. It was in the heat of the noonday sun that I left at last, going out through the south gate with a Beduin wedding party dancing their way out arm-in-arm, and a flock of sheep and camels coming in. Asses ambled in water-laden from the wells beyond the walls, and the Beduin were striking their tents.

So I went from Kuwait, bound across the desert road to Basra and Europe, and I was sad at leaving the good city behind me. Troubles it has had, though less than most Arab towns of comparable size: difficulties it must surmount, too. But it has overcome its difficulties and solved its problems until now, and there is no reason why it should not continue to do so. Its ships and sailors are favorably known throughout the Eastern seas, the luster of its pearls is famous in Paris and New York, its merchants are respected from Syria to Singapore, from Cairo to Calicut. It is a pleasant place where the citizens live at peace, where the rich merchants—as is required of them by the Islamic law—take care of the poor, and the Sheikh is father to them all.

As I left in the sunshine, with the camel-trains coming in laden with brushwood and camel-thorn from the desert and a crowd of donkey-boys hurried, singing on their tiny asses bound to the city's wells for garden water, I felt that I should have liked to stay there, to buy a baggala, to sit with the wise men another season, and learn more of the ways of the Eastern seas. The sun shone brightly in a clear sky, but it was not hot. It was mild and pleasant and peaceful and I thought that the red ensign of Kuwait, flying from the stockade and all the ships in the bay, was a standard I should like to sail and live under once again. Adieu, Kuwait! You build good ships, and your sailors can sail them.

Epilogue

IN THE shimmering waves of sticky heat that hung low over the Basra River the hulls and masts of a hundred dhows were miraged strangely, so that the nearer vessels seemed to dance and tremble like leaves in a passing wind, and the dhows farthest away were separated from the water by a clearly defined but nonexistent band of intervening air. It was October, but the port of Fao at the entrance to the Basra River was still insufferably hot. The day was windless, sultry, and humid almost beyond bearing. The green palms along the Iraq side stood with their roots in water and their moplike heads in hell, and the ripe yellow dates clustered thick among the fronds. Away to the north, the smoke-wrack of Abadan, that mighty port of Persian oil, smeared ten miles of the inoffensive sky. The yellow waters of the wide river flowed swiftly out to sea, bearing laden dhows outward bound with dates. Dhows sailed and dhows came in. All kinds of dhows lay off Fao, or moved slowly on the water—sweet-lined great booms from near-by Kuwait, shapely baggalas and sturdy sambuks from Sur, kotias from Bombay and the Gulf of Cutch, Persians, Omani, Hadhrami, dhows from the Mahra coast and the Trucial coast, and from Batina. Dates brought them all: they were the forerunners of the season's date fleet, to distribute the produce of Iraq over the Eastern seas.

It was an animated and interesting scene, and might have been a pleasant one had the day been not quite so hot and Fao not so excessively humid. At the small landing-stage in the heart of the port, longboats were coming and going, bringing in nakhodas, muallims, and quartermasters from the dhows. Stately Persians in white gowns and carefully rolled turbans, bearded and hennaed Suri in brown shirts and embroidered waistcoats, lithe Kuwaiti in gowns and headcloths of well-blued white, Hadhrami in knee-long sarongs and wisps of black worn below the knee,

Indians in folds of flapping, diaphanous cotton stuffs and silk shirts worn as coats—these came and went along the landing place, bound on errands for their dhows. Far outside, beyond the bar at the river's mouth, the lovely triangles of lateen sails blurred upon the hot horizon showed where a trio of the date dhows had sailed that morning, and now fretted in the calm outside waiting for wind. As I watched, the big *el-Dhow* came slowly in from Kuwait, bound upstream to take her cargo from the landing stage of a riverside plantation. Her skirted sailors hung round her rails feasting their green-hungry eyes upon the gardens as their ship sailed by. This green and this fresh water made up the Kuwaiti's Paradise. This was Hamed bin Salim's Paradise—this land where the water flowed and all things grew, and all a good Arab need do was to sleep and take his ease while the dates ripened and the fruits of the earth came to his table.

Yet for Hamid bin Salim and all his kind, their eyes gave them their only share of this favored spot: for Hamed bin Salim and all the muallims and nakhodas were outward bound again to sea. Amongst those hundred dhows were Nejdi's boom and his brother Abdulla's newly acquired dhow, and Hamed bin Salim, having faithfully brought the *Triumph* to the river and loaded her with dates, was to go out as muallim of Abdulla's dhow. The two dhows were ready: only Nejdi was not there. I had come down with the merchants who had provided the freights, and had come now to clear the dhows out to sea. To them nothing mattered but the prompt dispatch of their laden dhows, for there was war again in Europe and, with steamship traffic dislocated, for the first time in years there was a real urgency in sending off the new dates to market. If the steamers took no dates to Aden, the dhows must race to the market, and the first in would earn good profits.

So the merchants had come down to see that their dhows made all haste to sea, and I came with them to see the dhows go. Nejdi was coming that day: he had been summoned from home, and told his dhow was ready. While we waited I saw an old bus come down the Fao Road. It passed us, and we saw Nejdi. The bus stopped. Out of it, climbing down slowly like stiff and travel-weary men, came Nejdi, followed by Ismael the musician, and Yusuf Shirazi.

"Peace be upon you," Nejdi said.

"And upon you peace," the merchants returned. Then almost at once, "Sail! Sail! There will be wind tonight and your dhows are laden. Sail, sail! Hasten to Aden. May Allah send you good winds!"

Nejdi stood barefoot in the Fao Road with his gown stained from his long ride and a fold of his headcloth about his jaw to keep some of the desert from his mouth. He was dusty and tired, and sad at leaving his Kuwait home. He plucked at his close moustache and gently murmured "*Taiyib, taiyib.*" "Sail, sail!" the merchants said, for that was all they knew. Sail, sail! Make haste to the sea!

I thought of that hawk-eyed man standing there and of the long, hard voyage before him—out again along the nine-month, ten-thousand-mile road that leads from the Basra River round half Arabia, and along the Hadhramaut and past the east coast of Africa, down to Zanzibar, and Tanganyika. Sail, sail! That was all the merchants could say. And Nejdi gently murmured "*Taiyib.*"

Only Ismael, fat from four months of guitar-playing in the *suq* at Kuwait, seemed the better for his stay on shore, but he too was sad, and he turned tired eyes towards the river. Poor Yusuf Shirazi stood silent, a gray gaunt wraith of a man shrivelled in his long white gown. He had just come from the pearling banks, his only reward for the summer's pearling a new debt of his own to add to the inheritance of his dead brother's. Poor Yusuf! Off again now for nine months of hardship and work which, in spite even of the grim Rufiji, would be a holiday after the *ghaus*. Yusuf smiled as the three men turned and padded barefoot down the Fao Road, bound for the sea.

APPENDIX

INDEX

Appendix

I

The following is a list of the various types of Arab dhows as I saw and knew them; together with the distinguishing features of each. The differences are in nearly all cases hull differences only. The Arab differentiates between types by variations in the shape of the hull, and the rigging in all is essentially the same.

Here is the list.

BAGGALA   The baggala is the traditional deep-sea dhow of the Persian Gulf and the Gulf of Oman. Its distinguishing features are the five-windowed stern, which is often elaborately carved in the manner of an ancient Portuguese caravel. Baggalas have quarter-galleries, and their curved stems are surmounted by a horned figurehead. Baggalas are built now only at the port of Sur, in Oman, and are practically extinct at Kuwait. There are probably less than fifty in existence.

BEDENI   The common craft of the smaller ports of the Oman and Mahra coasts. Their distinguishing features are their straight lines, their flat, sheerless hulls, their upright masts, and the curious ancient method of steering by means of an intricate system of ropes and beams. The sternpost is carried up very high, and when anchored, or in port, the rudder is usually partly unshipped and secured to either quarter. Bedeni are usually small craft and often have one mast only, though two-masters are common in the trade to East Africa.

BELEM   Usually small craft trading from the Basra River in the nearer waters of the Persian Gulf. They have often only one mast, and are pretty little

Note: The Indian kotia is very like the Arab baggala, as also is the other common Indian type known as the ghunja or ganja. Today the Arabs rarely buy Indian vessels. Suri and Persians often buy from Kuwait; but Sur and most of the other ports usually build their own vessels.

There are minor variations in type in the smaller Red Sea and Hadhramaut ports, but these craft are very small. The deep-sea dhows are usually booms, baggalas, or sambuks, with ɀ sprinkling of jalboots and bedeni.

double-ended craft with curved bows, lacking the projecting stempost of the boom and the built-up horn of the sambuk and baggala. Belems are much used in the Kuwait pearling fleet.

BETIL   Now practically extinct. I saw only one, laid up on the al-Khobar beach, not far from Bahrein. Betils were double-enders and were marked by their elaborately decorated bows and sterns, both the stempost and stern-post being carried up in a series of distinctive designs. Betils were formerly much used in Persian Gulf pearling and were favored by the pearling admirals. Their embellishments, though picturesque, served no useful pur-pose, and they have now been discarded.

BOOM   The boom has taken the place of the baggala as the general sea-going Arab dhow, particularly from the Persian Gulf. Booms are double-ended, have their straight stemposts built out into a sort of planked bow-sprit, and are further distinguished by their yoke steering. The port of Kuwait uses booms almost exclusively for its deep-sea trade, and the Persians also prefer this type of vessel.

JALBOOT   Distinguished by its bolt-upright bow and transom stern, reminis-cent of the old English naval jolly boat from which its name is probably derived. Used considerably on the Gulf pearling banks, particularly from Kuwait and Bahrein, and also by the Suri and Omani in general in their deep-sea trades. Jalboots never approach the size of the larger booms and baggalas, and are generally from 20 to 50 tons.

MASHUA   A general term for a longboat, usually propelled by oars but also rigged on occasion. Longboats may have either straight or curved stems and usually have transom sterns.

SAMBUK   Perhaps the most common of all Arab types. Indeed it is so com-mon that the term sambuk is often used as applying to all vessels, as the European uses the term dhow. Sambuks proper have low, curved stems and high, built-up sterns, which are square and often decorated but with-out quarter-galleries or the traditional stern windows. The stern is often pierced—usually in four places—to ventilate the space below the poop, but there is an entire absence of the beautiful carved embellishments which so distinguish the baggala. Sambuks are common in the Red Sea, along the southern coast of Arabia, and in Sur, where they are replacing the baggala as that ancient port's most favored type. The lines of the sambuk are usually very beautiful. Like all dhows, it is a smart sailer. The big sambuks from Sur are decked, but the smaller Red Sea craft are usually undecked.

SHEWE   Small boats common in Kuwait. They are very like sambuks except that they are much smaller (rarely exceeding 15 tons), and there is a slight difference in the manner in which the timbers of the stempost are carried up into a pillar above the bow. Shewes are much used as pearlers from Kuwait.

ZAROOK   A sort of double-ended sambuk, small and very fast, commonly used from the Yemenite ports of the Red Sea. They are undecked, and rarely exceed 50 tons. The ordinary zarook has much the lines of a first-class English lifeboat, but not the strength.

II. Economics of a Deep-Sea Dhow

The average cost of constructing a large boom at the port of Kuwait, in normal times—my figures are all gathered from the years 1937 to 1939—works out at from six to seven rupees* per package of Basra dates. Since the capacities and the tonnage of the ships are reckoned always in terms of stowage of these 180-lb. packages of Basra dates, it is reasonable to keep that unit for arriving at the costs. A boom of 1000 package capacity could be built for 6000 rupees. The *Triumph of Righteousness*, which could carry some 2300 packages, cost, as nearly as I could discover, between 12,000 and 13,000 rupees, though the reason for this comparatively low cost was partly due to her nakhoda-owner's great care in buying her timbers and equipment, and partly because he contented himself with comparatively indifferent masts. She was worth 14,000 rupees—about £1050. A pure sailing ship, ketch or schooner-rigged, of the same dimensions, would cost at least twice that sum, built of softwood in Finland or Estonia, two and a half times as much built of oak and elm in Denmark or South Sweden, and probably three times as much built of good Tasmanian hardwoods in the shipyards of Tasmania, but any of these vessels would be far more seaworthy and, with the possible exception of the softwood craft, much longer-lived than the Kuwait dhow.

A nakhoda intending to build himself a new boom often brings his own timber from the Malabar coast, selecting it with an eye chiefly to its cheapness. As a result, the timbers used for planking are frequently indifferent. The ribs and knees are natural-grown timbers, imported from Persia, Iraq, and India. The masts—an expensive item—are Malabar teak trunks. If the nakhoda is in a hurry and has not imported his own timber, he buys from the timberyards in Kuwait. Having bought the timber, he contracts with a master-shipwright for the finished hull. The shipwright, in his turn, engages the necessary carpenters, apprentices, and coolies. Carpenters may be paid two and a half rupees a day, working from dawn to dusk, and the coolies are doing well if they receive one rupee. An exceptionally good carpenter may receive three rupees a day. Their meals must be provided for them.

In the case of the *Triumph of Righteousness*, the cost of wood imported for her from Malabar was some 6000 rupees. A contract was made for her building with a master-carpenter, for 2800 rupees, for the bare hull and rudder. Masts were bought separately for another 1000 rupees. A suit of sails cost 2000 rupees. The work was done by the sailors, who were not paid for it, this counting as part of the necessary fitting-out of the vessel and the labor going

* Indian rupees, worth normally about one shilling and sixpence each, or 33 American cents.

into the general effort necessary in the earning of their shares. If the sailors wanted jobs in the new ship, they must sew her sails. They were given small advances, in the usual Arab style, in order to keep their homes going during the fitting-out. The rule is that when a sailor has once accepted a nakhoda's advance he is bound to that nakhoda's ship.

The sailors also rig the ship, so that this operation (which would be quite expensive in Tasmania, or Denmark, or on the New England coast) also costs nothing. The sailors sew the sails, rig the ship, pay her bottom, and float her away from the dockyard. The carpenters are responsible only for the building of the hull, and caulking. The sailors ship the rudder, the wheel, the binnacle, the capstan, and any other fittings that may be carried. Usually these, in addition to the items listed, are limited to a longboat, a gig for the nakhoda (which may be an old dugout canoe), a firebox, some old anchors, and a couple of wooden watertanks. The nakhoda buys all these things as cheaply as he can, and also the caulking and paying stuffs, the fish oil, the fastenings, the deadeyes, and the few blocks with which the vessel may be fitted. He also buys roping stuff, and his sailors, when they have been engaged and in the intervals when they are not sewing sails or rigging the ship or otherwise helping to fit her out, lay her cables and all the ropes for her halliards, tacks, sheets, falls, and such adjustable standing-rigging as it is proposed to provide. The cost of the rigging is reduced to the cost of this roping stuff, which, since it is cheap coconut fiber from India, is very little. The cost of the sails is reduced to the cost of the cotton stuff necessary to put into them, which, being a product of India or cheap mill-ends from Japan, is comparatively inexpensive. Roping is of coir, stitches are indifferent, seams are round and very rough. Refinements such as a little Stockholm tar to add life to the yarn are unknown. The cost of the masts is reduced to the bare purchase price of the wood. Anchors, wheels, compasses, binnacles, are usually extremely second-hand, having, perhaps, been originally acquired from a junk yard in Bombay many years before and used in at least two other vessels. Longboats are built on the beach under a shade of mats while the boom is building. A large longboat is expensive at 8 rupees a foot. The average cost of a longboat thirty feet long is between 200 and 300 rupees, but one may be had much more cheaply. This cost includes her mast and one sail, as well as a small anchor.

The building costs of the boom *Triumph of Righteousness*, then, may roughly be set out in this manner:

	Rupees
Cost of the timber	6,000
Carpenters' contract price for labor	2,800
Sails	2,000
Masts	1,000
Longboat	200

Rupees

Gear, including capstan, compass, binnacle, watertanks, firebox, four anchors, and necessary roping stuffs and blocks	340
Caulking and paying stuffs, including fish oil for outside and inside coats	100
Gig	60
Total	12,500

The proper number of sails with which a new boom is provided would be seven, including three mainsails (in varying sizes, the largest of all—known as *Oud*—having nearly twice the size of the smallest, which is meant for use only in strong winds), two mizzens, and two jibs or headsails. Often, however, a boom is sent out on her first voyage with by no means this full complement.

A baggala of similar capacity would cost at least 2000 rupees more, because of the considerably larger amount of timber she would need with her square, built-up stern, and because of the extra labor involved. The carving alone, if well done, would cost at least a thousand rupees. No baggala has been built at Kuwait for over a quarter of a century, and the baggalas now built at Sur are often without much decoration.

Fastenings are always of poor iron, beaten out by hand at a waterfront forge. The iron is not treated in any way before being driven into the ship.

Finance is always provided by a merchant—usually a merchant with an interest in date plantations on the Basra River or some sort of interest in the date business of Iraq, who wishes to use the new vessel for carrying his dates but does not want the bother of owning her. Therefore nakhodas are financed and permitted to be the nominal owners. No nakhoda ever has sufficient ready cash to finance the building of a ship himself; if he had, he would be a merchant.

There is no insurance: the method of financing makes the merchant's investment really the nakhoda's responsibility. If the ship is lost, the nakhoda is still held responsible for the debt. Depreciation on a well-built ship is practically nonexistent for the first five years. Indeed, such a ship as the *Triumph of Righteousness*, which was built by a first-class carpenter at an exceptionally low cost, actually appreciates considerably in value during this period, when her reputation as a fast sailer and a first-class seaboat is established. After the first five years, average depreciation on a large ship of this tonnage is about 1000 rupees a year, from the fifth year to the tenth. Thereafter, until the fifteenth year, her value should remain fairly constant. After the fifteenth year it may show a sharp decline, particularly if the vessel has been allowed to run down.

Stores are bought as cheaply as possible. Kuwait is a free port. Roping stuffs, sailcloth, lime and tallow for paying, cotton for caulking, anchors and other marine paraphernalia, dugout canoes from the Malabar coast, paddles made of Lamu and Rufiji rafters with a square or circular blade lashed to one end— all of these are cheap. The ship's longboat is her tug, invariably; her crew are her stevedores and dock workers: her carpenter is her shipwright; her nakhoda is her surveyor, the designer of her sails, her pilot on all occasions. Charts and other aids to navigation are kept at a minimum, and though if she be intended for the Indian trade she must carry sidelights, these are trimmed but never lit and are a source of no expense beyond their original purchase price. There are no life belts or life buoys, or flares or rockets, or anything of that kind.

As for the earnings of an average voyage in such a ship as this, perhaps some sort of approximate balance-sheet—which I fear is all I can offer, for these details are jealously kept and guarded—may give some idea of the manner in which the ordinary trading voyage of a deep-sea Arab dhow is carried on. Consider then, the business side of the *Triumph of Righteousness* during her 1938-39 voyage. First, she carried dates from the Basra River to Mukalla for orders, and then discharged them at Berbera, in British Somaliland. From Berbera—except for a sack or two of frankincense carried over to Aden as a favor for a Kuwait merchant—she earned nothing for the run to Aden. At Aden, using the money earned as freight for the dates, she bought salt, rice, sugar, canned milk, Indian corn, and a few other odds and ends, all these goods being intended for sale in the ports of Italian Somaliland, Kenya, and Zanzibar. In the ports of Mukalla and Shihr, in the Hadhramaut, she loaded a little tobacco and Hadhramaut honey (which is much relished by the Arabs on the African coast and is supposed to have strong invigorating qualities), ghee, and Arab cooking stones. She also embarked 130 passengers, of whom the men paid eight rupees for the passage to Africa, and the women twelve. At Haifun, finding normal trade impossible because of Italian restrictions on the export of currency, the ship had to content herself with exchanging some rice and sugar for the local dried fish, and more salt. Here an old boat was sold for 100 rupees. At Mogadishu, normal trade was again impossible, but a few passengers were picked up for Mombasa and Zanzibar, and ways were found to dispose of most of the ghee and the cooking stones, as well as various other goods. At Lamu, the ship earned nothing, but a few passengers were shipped for Mombasa and Zanzibar. At Mombasa, some ghee was sold, as well as a little of the rice, and more passengers were shipped, this time for Zanzibar only. At Zanzibar, the whole of the outward cargo was cleared, and all the remaining passengers landed. With some of the money earned in this way, the ship went on to the Rufiji delta, and there bought and otherwise secured a full cargo of mangrove poles. Returning to Zanzibar, she sold a few of the lighter poles, took on board cloves, coconuts, vermicelli, and some odd lots of soap—all of which were intended for sale in Muscat and the Persian Gulf ports —and returned to Arabia.

The proceeds from the sale of these goods, as well as the income from passengers and the total selling price of the mangrove poles, were all regarded as profit, and the business side of the voyage worked out something like this:

Item	Rupees Earned	
Freight on 2300 pkgs. dates, Basra River to Berbera, at 1½ rupees a package	3450 Rs.	
Purchase price of salt, rice, sugar, canned milk, etc., at Aden. *Balance*	3000 Rs.	450
Mukalla and Shihr: embarked passengers, fares collected for 103 men at 8 rupees per head, 15 women at 12 rupees per head		1000
Haifun: sold a boat		100
Also exchanged rice, etc., for dried fish and salt. Profit on this transaction when fish and salt sold later at Zanzibar		500
Mogadishu: fares of various passengers for Lamu; including odd earnings (sale of ghee, stones, etc.)		250
Lamu: fares for odd passengers to Mombasa and Zanzibar		100
Mombasa: fares for odd passengers to Zanzibar		100
Zanzibar: gross profit on sale of cargo (not including result of Haifun barter)		800
Rufiji Delta: total cost of mangrove cargo (including various unofficial fees, etc.)	1700	
Selling price of same, Bahrein	6000	
Profit on poles. *Balance*		4300
Homeward voyage: profit on soap, cloves, vermicelli, coconuts, etc. (Approx.)		1000
Earnings, source and manner not recorded but crew entitled to share. (Approx.)		1000
Total Gross Earnings		Rs. 9600

From this total of 9600 rupees, which was 3000 rupees less than the ship had earned the previous voyage, the cost of the food was deducted when the balance sheet was finally made up at Kuwait two months after the end of the voyage. All hands shared in the cost of the food, which in accordance with tradition is always deducted from the gross earnings. The cost of the food, at the rate of 3 annas a day for thirty men over a period of two hundred and seventy days, was some 1500 rupees. This when deducted from the gross of 9600 rupees leaves 8100. By the Kuwait method of arriving at the shares this sum was then halved. Of it, 4050 rupees went to the ship, and 4050 were divided among the crew. Out of the ship's share, the boom had to be kept up and the regular voyage expenses met. As far as I could gather, the actual sharing of the sum of 4050 rupees was worked out practically on a basis of equal shares, except that sailors who had responsibility received extra half or quarter shares. The system of dividing the shares in the *Triumph of Righteousness* was as follows:

	Shares
Nakhoda	5
Muallim	3
Quartermasters: 3, at 1½ shares each	4½
Serang	1½
Serang's mate	1¼
Cook	1½
Storekeeper-Steward (Yusuf Shirazi)	1¼
Sailors, 18 at one share each	18
Total	36

Of these, the nakhoda's four and the muallim's two extra shares come from the ship's half, not from the crew's, so that the crew's 4050 rupees are divided equally into thirty shares, making 135 rupees a share. Of these shares, the sailors take one each, and the others—the petty officers—take their single shares, and fractions. The carpenter is paid by the nakhoda, personally, and does not share in the crew's proceeds. His income comes from the sale of the boats he has built during the voyage, whether sold or unsold.

In addition to the extra portions accruing to the petty officers, such men as the solo singer, our Abdul-latif, Ismael the ship's musician, and the sailor whose duty it was to serve coffee to the officers, are invariably given bakhshish by the nakhoda, either from his own share as nakhoda or from the ship's half of the gross earnings. The general principle of this bakhshish is to keep everybody happy. Sailors who have worked particularly well, or who have done extra work of any kind, or who distinguish themselves by especial alacrity or unusual capabilities, also receive bakhshish. In addition to his shares, such a man as Yusuf Shirazi would receive some bakhshish to recompense him for his extra work in attending to the nakhoda.

In addition to their share of the ship's legitimate earnings, nearly every one on board has some other source of income, whether from minor smuggling or by the lawful sale of trade goods. Each sailor may bring one chest and one chest only, and by tradition he can fill it with such goods as he thinks he can best sell. The nakhoda, too, has his private ventures, which often include half the great cabin full of Persian carpets, and a few old carved chests. Money-changing, the carriage of messages and small parcels, the importation and sale of texts from the Quran and sacred amulets, talismans, and such things—all these bring such grist to the mill as may be ground from them. But it is improbable that the average earnings of the ordinary sailor from his ventures and the sale of his goods, both outwards and homewards, exceeds fifteen or twenty rupees over the whole voyage. A nakhoda, however, may make a thousand, if conditions are good and he restrains his profligacy. A muallim may easily make several hundred rupees. The musician often does very well—so well that he can afford to buy off his pearling debts. He may make so much from his music that his pearling nakhoda prefers a share of the income from this source rather than the doubtful proceeds of the musician's enforced work on board his vessel. Our Ismael was usually given bakhshish by leading merchants and other prominent men who were entertained at our feasts. He was provided with his instrument by the nakhoda, who also gave him suitable bakhshish at the end of the voyage. He was an important man, for his music helped to make a success of the nakhoda's feasts and, by increasing his prestige, made business the easier. The solo singer received his bakhshish because his efforts helped to make the ship happy, and to lighten the work. He would receive perhaps fifteen rupees for the voyage.

When boys are carried, they are not paid regular shares, but receive bakhshish from the nakhoda and crew.

Here is a list of food consumed during the nine-month voyage of the *Triumph*, as nearly as I was able to compute it. It should be borne in mind that the collection of statistics from Arabs is no easy matter, and only the most dogged persistence and a thorough examination of every item of expense as it was incurred (as far as this was possible) gained me any knowledge at all. Nothing ever seemed to be done in a thoroughly straightforward manner. The figures are not presented as completely accurate, but may serve as a reasonably correct guide.

Our consumption, as closely as I could discover or estimate it, was, then, as follows:

	Rupees
Dates, at 3 Rs. per package: 40 packages	120
Rice, at 8 to 10 Rs. per bag: 53 bags	500
Flour, at 6 Rs. per bag: 12 bags	72
Sugar, at 12 Rs. per bag: 7 bags	84
Dried fish (only bought when fresh not available: price varying, but never high)	40
Dhall (Indian corn), at 15 to 16 Rs. per bag: 6 bags	90
Salt, at 2 Rs. per bag: 3 bags	6
Tea (a great deal consumed, but very poor quality). Say	50
Coffee (a great deal consumed, but very poor quality). Say	30
Ghee (some first-class, from Kuwait, at 20 Rs. a tin: other inferior)	120
Saleet (oil). Total	50
Pickled stuffs (very mysterious: for use in stews, at feasts, etc.)	50

	Rupees
Chilis (a great favorite: always bought fresh)	10
Onions (used in stews and feasts)	50
Potatoes (very little used)	30
Cloves (for the coffee)	5
Ginger (for the coffee—an abominable habit)	5
Tomato essence (used very sparingly, for flavoring goat-entrail stews, etc., at the feasts. This was bought at Aden in very small tins: half a case for the voyage)	15
Canned milk (also used very sparingly)	20
Sesame seeds (for the unleavened bread: used rarely, as a treat)	5
Ladies' fingers and peppers (almost as popular as chilis, bought fresh in the *suqs*)	5
White radishes (at Aden)	5
Lemons	5
Other fresh vegetables (bought sparingly)	15
10 live sheep, bought at Berbera at 4 Rs. per head	40
15 live sheep and goats, over rest of voyage, at 5 to 6 Rs. per head	80
Total	Rs. 1502

I believe this is a generous estimate, for a well-run and well-found ship. Sometimes a few fresh chickens are bought for a feast, but if this is done the nakhoda usually pays for them. In ports merchants sometimes send on board gifts of a goat, a sheep, or a few chickens, or some fruit. Fish are caught plentifully almost throughout the voyage.

The average cost of feeding a sailor in a Kuwait ship works out at about three annas a day—something less than threepence halfpenny, or seven American cents. In making this average, the cost of feeding the first-class passengers, and the Swahili pole-cutters in the Rufiji, is included, as well as most of the cost of the ship's feasts, of which there was at least one in every port, except Salale.

I was informed, but could not verify, that sailors in the Sur ships are fed at an average cost of two annas a day, and are fortunate if their round-voyage earnings bring them sixty rupees.

III

The following is a brief list of Arabic words used in the text, together with their English equivalents:

Abba	Arab cloak
Abu	Father
Aghal	Headrope to hold headcloth in position

Allah	God
Allah karim	God is merciful
Baggala	Ship (see list of ship types, Appendix I)
Bakhshish	Tip, graft
Bebe	Girl
Beduin	Nomad: Arab
Bin (also *Ibn*)	Son of
Bint	Girl
Ghaus	Pearling
Ghee	Clarified butter
Emir	A ruling chieftain
Hadhramaut	District of Southern Arabia
Hadhrami	Arab from the Hadhramaut
Hajj	The pilgrimage
Hajji	One who has made the pilgrimage
Halwa	Sweetmeat
Hookah	Water-pipe
Inshallah	If God pleases
Khubz	Unleavened bread
Kuwaiti	Arab of Kuwait
Muallim	Mate (of a ship)
Muezzin	Prayer announcer
Nakhoda	Captain
Nejd	Interior plateau of Saudi-Arabia
Nejdi	An Arab of Nejd
Oud	Large
Omani	Arab of Oman, in Southeast Arabia
Quran (often *Koran*)	The book of the Prophet Mohammed
Ras	Cape
Serang (an Indian word)	Boatswain
Seyyid (sometimes *Sayyid*)	Descendant of the Prophet
Sheikh	A ruler: also used widely as courtesy title
Suq (sometimes spelled *Souk*)	Bazaar: market-place
Suri	Arab from the port of Sur, in Oman
Swahili	Natives of the east coast of Africa
Taiyib (sometimes *Taib*)	Good

Index